D0993709

A history and politics teacher by day, Jon Spurling is
the author of three previous books on Arsenal, including
Rebels for the Cause: the Alternative History of Arsenal. He writes
regularly for *FourFourTwo* and *When Saturday Comes*, and lives
in Kent with his wife Helen and daughter Phoebe.

HIGHBURY
THE STORY OF ARSENAL IN N.5

JON SPURLING

AN ORION PAPERBACK

First published in Great Britain in 2006
by Orion
This paperback edition published in 2014
by Orion Books Ltd,
Orion House, 5 Upper St Martin's Lane,
London WC2H 9EA

An Hachette UK company

1 3 5 7 9 10 8 6 4 2

A CIP catalogue record for this book
is available from the British Library.

ISBN 978-1-4091-5306-1

Printed in Great Britain by Clays Ltd, St Ives plc

The Orion Publishing Group's policy is to use papers
that are natural, renewable and recyclable products and
made from wood grown in sustainable forests. The logging
and manufacturing processes are expected to conform to
the environmental regulations of the country of origin.

www.orionbooks.co.uk

FOR PHOEBE

CONTENTS

N.5

FOREWORD

ALTHOUGH THE N5 postcode remains the same, much else has changed about the match-day experience following Arsenal's move to Ashburton Grove. Gone are the cramped views from the East and West lower tiers, the art deco feel, and the sense of tradition. Instead, there are unparalleled views of the pitch, and a grandiose feel to games, which was never the case at Highbury. Although some Arsenal fans have spoken gushingly of Arsenal's new ground, others have struggled to come to terms with the 400-yard hike across Islington. It doesn't always help matters that in order to reach the Emirates via Finsbury Park and Arsenal tube stations, you still have to walk past Highbury, parts of which are being dismantled and torn out.

Fans still congregate around the East Stand, possibly reflecting on old memories, or trying to get a peak through the locked gates to see what the workmen are up to. There's always the possibility of getting a piece of Highbury memorabilia on the cheap too; workmen were selling the distinctive tiles with the AFC logo on them for a fiver prior to the Sheffield United match – a snip compared with prices quoted elsewhere. 'It doesn't feel like home yet,' one Arsenal fan said of the new ground. 'It's like going to a new *house*, but there aren't the memories or the Arsenal paraphernalia to make it feel like *home* yet. It's too new.' I suspect this supporter isn't alone in thinking that. A recent *When Saturday Comes* article suggested the whole Emirates experience was rather soulless, and questioned whether the club's beating heart would remain at the site where Highbury once was. Aside from references to the 'space age feel to the place', similar feelings were expressed when Arsenal moved away from Woolwich in 1913.

Until Arsenal defeated Liverpool in November 2006, I also questioned whether or not watching Arsenal would really be the same again. Ashburton Grove doesn't have quite the same 'get-at-ability' feel that Herbert Chapman realised Highbury had, and it felt rather like visiting Cardiff's Millenium Stadium every other week. But having got off the train at Finsbury Park tube (my habitual disembarking point), strolled down St Thomas's Road (my favoured route to Highbury), popped into the Auld Triangle (my pre-match hostelry of choice in the Highbury days) and seeing Arsenal thrash one of their biggest rivals 3–0, I felt as if I'd finally moved on.

I'm still irritated by the long queues leaving the new ground, the fact that executive fans appear more interested in the half-time drinkies than watching the team, and that thousands of supporters will probably never see the end of a game again, such is their desire to avoid the queues, but it does finally feel more like home. It's impossible to avoid glancing sideways at our old home on the way to Ashburton Grove, and remembering the myriad triumphs and experiences enjoyed by fans and players inside Highbury. Let's hope that Arsenal fans and the club don't have cause to look back over the forthcoming years. At least not too much.

Enjoy the book.

Jon Spurling, November 2006

HIGHBURY

N.5

THE BEGINNING

N.5

○ INTERLOPERS ○

WITHOUT SIR HENRY NORRIS, Highbury Stadium would never have been constructed, and Arsenal Football Club would not be the world famous name they are today. Gunners fans owe him everything, and yet he remains arguably the most controversial figure in the early days of professional football in England. Although he died nearly seventy years ago, his name continues to provoke controversy. 'Googling' his full title on to the Internet throws up some useful information on him. No less than twenty Spurs-related sites cite him as the prime reason to hate Arsenal – sites which continually refer to the club as the gypsies and 'the Woolwich interlopers'. One writer even claims that Norris was solely responsible for the nagging sense of inferiority which Spurs fans feel towards their rivals from the opposite end of Seven Sisters Road.

More bizarrely, a sixteenth century diplomat of precisely the same name was also a Falstaffian rogue of the highest order. Granted unprecedented access to Henry VIII, he was later executed for 'intriguing' with the king's young wife, Anne Boleyn. Noted for his raffish charm, he revelled in his reputation as the playboy diplomat of his era. It seems apt, therefore, that his great (several times over) grandson was also such a notorious character. As it turned out, both men were destroyed by the Icarus factor: they flew too close to the sun.

The second Sir Henry Norris, after buying Woolwich Arsenal in 1910, controlled his club like a medieval fiefdom. In an era when directors and chairmen tended to sit on boards in order to heighten their exposure in the local community, Norris broke the mould. He sprung a variety of 'questionable' fiscal tricks, and used bully-boy tactics which made him powerful enemies within the game. The game's first 'Soccer Czar' has become a creature of myth.

Born in 1865, Fulham-based Sir Henry (or just plain old Henry, as he was in 1910), was a self-made man, who had accumulated his fortune through the property market. His company, Allen & Norris, was responsible for transforming Fulham from a semi-rural area into an urban jungle. In the process of constructing, renovating and selling houses, he'd built up a formidable network of contacts in the building and banking professions, many of whom owed him favours. This proved invaluable in future years, particularly when the time came to build a new football stadium. Norris loved to mingle with the hoi poloi, and his networking skills were legion. *Who's Who* from 1910 lists his interests as wine societies, dining clubs, and vintage car rallies. As a member of the Junior Carlton Club, Mayor of Fulham, leading light in the local Conservative Party, and eminent freemason, his name was well known throughout the capital. Being a God-fearing Tory, he believed it his duty to perform philanthropic acts in the local community. For several years, he worked closely with the Battersea vestry and the local orphanage. Yet, political opponents believed him to be a self-serving fraud, who'd used his position simply to befriend, among others, the Archbishop of Canterbury. Norris always refuted these allegations, but the Archbishop certainly proved to be a useful ally for Norris in 1913. Returning favours was the preserve of this particular social circle, also.

Photographs and written accounts prove that Norris was a terrifying man, bearing an uncanny resemblance to Dr Crippen, the notorious wife murderer of the day. Standing at well over six feet tall, invariably with a pipe stuffed into his mouth, he dwarfed his rivals literally, and metaphorically. Immaculately turned out in a trench coat, crisply starched white shirt and bowler hat, he would glare demonically at them through a pince-nez. The lenses of the pince-nez were so strong that his gaze was totally distorted. This proved to be useful in board meetings; he could make his directors uncomfortable by bawling at one while, apparently, looking at someone else. Norris's accent, a mixture of upper-class wannabe, with a cockney twang, betrayed his working-class roots. His parents had sent him to a minor public school, but on his own admission, 'school was not for me'. Aged just fourteen, he was articled to a solicitor's firm, and made rapid strides. A year later, he left, tempted by the cut-throat world of building. He had several chips on his shoulders, admitting that he disliked authority figures and time-wasters. Norris was a man in a hurry, and he wanted to run things his way. One of his chief gripes was that Northern sides had always dominated professional football. He firmly believed that a London team should be in command.

Norris was also a master at charming potential opponents and getting them onside with sheer enthusiasm and gusto. As a successful estate agent, he knew only too well how to smarm when appropriate. When he branched into the building trade, he honed his skills further. If it came to constructing houses in a 'tricky' area of London – Wimbledon was notorious for having a fearsome NIMBY regiment even then – he could chat to his buddies in the local community and, in a jiffy, a new housing complex would go up. One of his rivals in the building trade dared to suggest that Norris ran a protection racket in order to preserve the status of his construction company. He retracted the accusation when Norris threatened to let loose his lawyer on him. So even before he became connected with Woolwich Arsenal, Norris was well versed in sharp practice. Where better than the world of football to become a grandmaster of such chicanery?

In the early years of last century, with Norris already a director of Fulham, he decided to expand his business interests in the sport. He wanted to buy a football club, and surveyed the leading teams in Southern England: Chelsea, Spurs, Orient and Woolwich Arsenal. The first three clubs were fairly secure financially at that time. The boys from Woolwich on the other hand, remained in an awful mess. Even in Division One, Manor Ground crowds averaged at around 10,000 – four times less than those at Chelsea or Spurs. In addition, a touch of the farcical always surrounded the club. Woolwich Arsenal reached the 1905 FA Cup semi-final, but lost 1–3 to Sheffield Wednesday. The match, played on a mound-like pitch, was memorable because neither goalkeeper could see each other, and bizarrely, neither could the linesmen. As with all dictators, Norris made his move when matters were at their lowest ebb. Woolwich Arsenal's misfortunes turned out to be his gain, and in the manner of other twentieth century autocrats, he injected new life into the club, stopping at nothing to enforce his beliefs.

The board welcomed him with open arms, having heard of his political skills, when he had negotiated Fulham's frankly unbelievable rise through the Southern League up to Division Two. That this meteoric rise took place in just four years led furious directors from other clubs to suggest that substantial amounts of cash had been handed over to the Football League, but no firm evidence of back-handers was ever found. Norris was already the undisputed master of covering his tracks. On buying his majority stake in Woolwich Arsenal, he proposed a merger with Fulham, in order to create a London super-club, and a permanent move to Craven Cottage. He was blocked by the Football League (the only time they stopped him getting his way), but they couldn't prevent him staying as a director of Fulham, while also serving as Arsenal chairman. From that, you can guess that the Monopolies and Mergers Commission did not yet exist.

Foiled in his plan to merge the two clubs, Norris set about reju-venating the ailing Woolwich Arsenal. In 1912, he realised that the club had to move elsewhere after an embarrassing catalogue of disasters at the Manor Ground, which, like many of the club's old haunts, flooded regularly. A match with Spurs, which Arsenal won 3–1, was described as a 'mud revel' by *The Sportsman*. A local newspaper described the ground as: '... a perfect quagmire, as water lay in a pool along the touchline'. On that day, the weather was so appalling that factions of the crowd refused to pay the shilling entrance fee, preferring to stand on the sewer pipe and watch the game from there. At least they got wet for free. The press claimed there had been a near riot between the law abiding fans and the refuseniks. That wasn't quite true, but it was a fact that opposition team charabancs often failed to reach the ground on time, due to heavy traffic and poor accessibility. These embarrassments reflected poorly on Norris, and he wasn't one to suffer fools gladly. The club was relegated in 1913 with the worst ever record in Division One at that time: P38 W3 D12 L23. For Norris, there was only one option.

In early 1913, *Kentish Independent* readers were gobsmacked to read the following front page headline: ARSENAL TO MOVE TO THE OTHER SIDE OF LONDON. In an official statement, Norris pointed out the benefits to the club of moving to a district which had a population of around 500,000. The relocated club could tap into the huge reservoir of supporters in Finsbury, Hackney, Islington and Holborn. Through his contacts in the Church, he found that six acres of land at St John's College of Divinity at Highbury were available. Where better to move than a spot which was only ten minutes away by tube from London's West End? Norris would require all his arrogance and political skill to negotiate the minefield of red-tape, pressure groups, and NIMBYs blocking his path.

He didn't figure on the furious reaction from Woolwich Arsenal's hard core supporters. Norris mentioned the 'push' factor from Woolwich; that people from the region simply did not turn up at games in large enough numbers. Many reckoned Norris was using dirty tricks. In the relegation season, they believed he'd deliberately leaked news about the proposed move and underinvested in the team, which he knew would drive down crowds, and make the case for relocation even stronger. Letters to the local press accused him of being a heartless capitalist, and of selling the club's soul. One letter, sent to the *Kentish Gazette*, by Mr Paul Donaldson, would ring true for Wimbledon fans today. It said: 'Mr Norris has decided that financial gain is more important than protecting our local club. He is making a mistake. You cannot "franchise" a football club – Woolwich Arsenal must stay near Woolwich. Would Norris advocate moving Liverpool to Manchester? People like him have no place in Association football.'

Mr Walter Bailey's letter, published in the *Kentish Independent*, went further. He wrote: 'There is, and has been, sufficient support to run the team on a business basis . . . Many clubs in different parts of the country would be glad of such support. Woolwich has been found guilty of apathy . . . because it cannot furnish the huge gates that Tottenham and Chelsea get The most distant part of London to which they intend moving will effectively prevent those who helped to make the club, and can morally claim it as their birthright, from having anything further to do with it. Is this right?'

The local press ran a series of cartoons, one of which, in the *Woolwich Gazette*, claimed Norris was kidnapping Kent's 'only son'. He countered, and further fanned the flames, by claiming that he'd always regarded Woolwich as part of London anyway, not Kent, and that it was about time the club enjoyed the capital's spoils. It was alleged that he received death threats after proposing the move, yet he pressed on regardless. If the reaction from the Woolwich public was extreme, it was tame compared with the lynch mob that awaited him in London.

○ ANNOYING THE NEIGHBOURS (1) ○

REPRESENTATIVES FROM Orient, Spurs and Chelsea were quick to protest, 'in the strongest possible terms', about Norris's proposal to move Woolwich Arsenal to Highbury. They were terrified that another London club would erode their traditional fan base. The *Tottenham Herald* published a cartoon which portrayed Norris as being the equivalent of the Hound of the Baskervilles, prowling around farmyards, in an enormous spiked collar, ready to rip apart the Tottenham cockerel, and steal its food. An FA inquiry was set up to investigate the whole affair. Norris successfully packed the committee with his buddies and furnished them with some useful facts. Birmingham, with its population of 400,000, and Sheffield boasting 250,000 housed two top flight teams each. Why couldn't an ever-expanding London – population two million – house four? Unsurprisingly, the committee ruled that the opposition had 'no right to interfere'. The *Tottenham Herald* placed an advertisement begging its fans: ' . . . not to go and support Norris's Woolwich interlopers. They have no right to be here'.

The next hurdles to be overcome were the formidable Highbury residents, quivering with righteous indignation about 'undesirable elements of professional football' and 'a vulgar project' on their doorstep. The Islington Borough Council minutes recorded Highbury Park resident Mr Coventon's comments: 'I ask whether it is open to the Borough Council to protect the district from what, in my opinion, will be its utter ruin.' Mr A. Bailey of Avenell Road wrote: 'There will be considerable annoyance and inconvenience suffered by the residents in Avenell Road as a result of the erection of lofty stands by the Woolwich Arsenal Football Club. Can the council please help us on this matter.' *Islington Gazette* journalist Henry Waller – writing in February 1913 – went further, suggesting: 'It will be a sad day for the district if these interlopers set up stall around here. A respectable, decent neighbourhood will be transformed into a rabble-infested den of noise, and, I fear, drinking. I believe it is time that the people of Highbury rose up and gave notice of their intentions to fight this proposed move. I have no objections to Woolwich Arsenal playing in their rightful home, Kent, but simply speaking, they do not belong here.'

Norris knew only too well the power of the NIMBY brigade, being so well versed in local politics. He launched a charm offensive on opposition groups, assuring them that they'd barely notice a football club in their midst, and in any case, that 30,000 plus fans in the district every other Saturday would be excellent for local business. This was enough to convince several members of the opposition, many of whom stood to gain from the construction process. Those who continued to moan, were effectively silenced by Norris's contacts in the local press. Highbury residents discovered that their vocal anti-Woolwich Arsenal meetings had never taken place, and that local protest groups simply didn't exist, in the Orwellian sense of the word. With censorship skills worthy of Nazi propaganda chief Goebbels, Norris's buddies starved protesters of the oxygen of publicity, and their efforts to prevent the move failed.

Leslie Anderson's father – Donald – was one of the locals who opposed Woolwich Arsenal moving to Highbury. I interviewed Leslie Anderson in the early 1990s, and he clearly recalled Norris's irresistible will-power: 'My dad knew him [Norris] from the building trade. Dad was a strictly no nonsense man, who'd fought in the Great War and survived the trenches for four years. But I'll tell you this. He was terrified of Norris. After his meetings with him, he'd come home shaking and down a double whisky. Basically, there were many people around at that time like Norris, who because of their social position could do whatever they damn well liked. Dad was furious at the way he talked down to the protesters. But it did Dad no good, and they were totally ignored. A group of them used to go to Highbury and protest when Arsenal first started to play there. They used to have huge banners saying: GO BACK TO WOOLWICH, but they had to stop doing that because Norris moved the police in on them. He was good friends with the Chief Constable and they were both Freemasons. Arsenal were there to stay.'

The final group that Norris needed to deal with, and one which certainly could not be silenced, was the Catholic Church. Many on the ecclesiastical committee believed football to be 'ungodly'. Local residents believed that the thought of the Church of England agreeing to a football club buying the land was inconceivable. But Norris's contacts went right to the top. After waving a £20,000 cheque under their noses, the church committee virtually bit his hand off, and his old buddy, the Archbishop of Canterbury, personally signed the deed. Of course, Norris agreed that no games would be played at Highbury on holy days, and that no 'intoxicating liquor' would be sold at the stadium. Yet within a year, in the manner of most dictators, he had quickly reneged on his promise. In the early twentieth century, football began to replace organised religion as the main passion among the working classes. How apt, therefore, that the devilishly cunning chairman of the nation's least saintly club should begin constructing Highbury Stadium on land where would-be priests once played bowls and tennis.

It would be easy to gain the impression that Woolwich Arsenal's move to Highbury was opposed by the vast majority of locals, despite Norris's attempts to gag them. Pat Standen's family lived in St Thomas's Road at the time the club was sorting out the move, and he remembered things rather differently. Speaking in the early 1990s, he recalled: 'The vast majority of us were very excited about the arrival of a football club in our area. I was only a little lad at the time, but all the talk was of Woolwich Arsenal's stature, and their potential. There were some fairly big arguments between those who favoured the move, and those who didn't. "Bloody church fanatics," Dad always used to say about those who didn't want Arsenal to come. I think that a lot of people feared the amount of drinking and blasphemy that would go on. That was a big issue in those days.

'At that time, Highbury was a bit of a backwater. Nowadays, people around the world know of it because of the Arsenal. But in those days, there wasn't really much to do. This was the era before cinema, and Mum and Dad certainly didn't have the money to go living it up in the West End. Even going drinking in the local boozers meant that Dad had to scrimp a bit. As a carpenter, he wasn't paid anywhere near enough to go squandering it on booze.

'But even in those days, the talk was that ordinary working people had more disposable cash to spend than they once had, and crowds at Highbury were always healthy right from the off. Right from the start, Dad made it clear to Mum that he would be "off to follow the new boys" on Saturdays. Mum knew better than to argue! A football team on our doorstep gave us pride and stature. Many of us kids made banners which we planned to hold up at the first game. I remember making one from an old sheet, and writing: WELCOME AND GOOD WISHES TO THE TEAM, using an old tin of red paint. It all sounds a bit naïve now, but the local pubs were full of talk about this new football club. My dad always said that Henry Norris was very clever. In those days, players and fans would mix far more freely than they do today. Some of the Woolwich Arsenal players – George Jobey and Jock Rutherford were two – used to drink in local pubs, and attend local functions and that sort of thing. I think that was the club's way of gently putting out the feelers. You used to see posters up on walls, and bits and pieces in the local papers, advertising the fact that such and such a player would be here and there on certain days. For blokes like Dad, who'd never mixed with footballers, it offered a bit of escapism, and there was a certain curiosity towards the players. So as the first game at Highbury approached, us locals already thought of the "interlopers" – which those who opposed the move called them – as part of the community. Norris really knew what he was doing.'

By 1913, Norris's Arsenal (the Woolwich was now dropped – permanently) had indeed completed the move to their home. Emotions continued to run high both in the Highbury district, and back at the former haunt. In a bitter parting shot, a fan from Kent, who decided not to make the regular one hour trip to Highbury, wrote in the *Kentish Independent*: 'Henry Norris has gambled away the club's soul. He is a Mammon worshipper. We've not heard the last of this bounder, you may be sure of that'. He had no idea.

○ SETTLING IN ○

ACCORDING TO THE *Daily Gazette*, Woolwich Arsenal secured 'the area south of the London College of Divinity bounded by Avenell Road, Highbury Hill and Gillespie Road' on 20 February 1913. The *Athletic News*, on the other hand, reckoned it happened at some point in March. The month's difference is largely irrelevant. The facts were that Norris had roughly six months to galvanise assorted local tradesmen, and commission an architect, in order that the new stadium would be ready for the opening game of the 1913–14 season. The *Daily Gazette* of 27 February noted smugly that 'Norris has already been rejected by several notable London architects'. The tone of the piece is understandable, given that arch Arsenal hater Henry Waller, who'd recently been vocal in opposing the move, penned the piece. Once again, Norris opted to take the scheme to the very top. *Who's Who* of 1912 notes that one of his many interests included 'architectural design'. As an estate agent, and a wealthy politician, he networked tirelessly early in 1913.

In the early part of last century, Archibald Leitch, an engineer and architect, moved his practice from Glasgow to Liverpool. Leitch had been behind the construction of Manchester United's Old Trafford ground, one of the few stadia constructed inside a symmetrical perimeter wall. In true Norris fashion, he just happened to be close friends with Manchester's mayor James Whiting. They were Freemasons and Whiting happened to be pally with Leitch, and contact was made. It seems likely that as early as January, Leitch was commissioned to design Woolwich Arsenal's new stadium. Until now, Arsenal historians have relied solely on A.G. Kearney's account as evidence of the chaotic six-month construction period of the new stadium.

Kearney was drafted in as Leitch's second assistant, and in the official programme for the Leicester City match in 1963, he described graphically Norris's numerous dodges. Kearney alluded to the unrelenting opposition of Henry Waller, who'd continued to harp on in the *Daily Gazette* about the move being a 'vulgar project'. Waller made one final, last ditch approach to block the move. Kearney confirms that,

'Mr Norris pulled a few strings and I was able to get on'. Curiously, Waller's contributions to the local newspaper dried up shortly afterwards. Norris also suggested to Kearney that he ignore the out-of-date Parish Council office in Holloway Road, when trouble was brewing over the construction of 'the high brick retaining wall at the College End of the ground'. Kearney confirms that the old boys in the office didn't know the difference between a 'retaining wall and a retaining fee'. Further evidence that a degree of cunning in the early part of the twentieth century would enable the likes of Norris to bypass outdated Victorian practices. Norris also gave Kearney permission to purchase two houses and demolish them, in order that an entrance be constructed at the Gillespie Road end, opposite the tube station. Leitch's assistant confessed that 'everyone but myself became more pessimistic and depressed, wondering whether the ground could be got ready'.

The club placed an advert in assorted local newspapers, inviting locals to write in, and suggest names for the new stadium. Presumably this is the first recorded instance of the club seeking a 'constructive dialogue' with their supporters. Mr W. Dykes of Camden Town thought that Avesbury Park – a combination of Avenell Road and Highbury – would be a suitable choice. Mr H.W. Cooper of Islington believed The Gunners in 'The Fortress' would be ideal. Another writer, who chose to remain anonymous, reckoned 'The Gun Park' would be apt. In time honoured tradition, the club decided to ignore the advice of their fans and simply named the ground 'Highbury Stadium'.

Ninety-three years later, fresh insight can finally be provided on this frantic construction period. In 1990, I was introduced to David Yates, after placing an advert in the *Islington Gazette* requesting anyone with recollections of football grounds under construction to come forward. With the assistance of his son Daniel, David Yates proved that even though his hearing and sight may have been failing, his memories remained as sharp as ever. He recalled: 'In the months leading up to Arsenal's first game, an entire range of craftsmen and tradesmen converged on Highbury to try and get the ground ready on time. To Mr Norris's credit, he could have contracted the work out elsewhere, but he tried to get locals as involved as possible. He thought that if lots of us actually built the place, we'd have more pride in the team. As a young fella who'd just left school, it was my role to be a general labourer. The first problem we had to solve was that the land was covered in bushes and trees and craters, and it needed to be flattened.

'We couldn't bring in mechanical diggers in those days, so it all had to be done with picks and shovels and barrows. I seem to recall that one end was higher than the other (the College End was six feet higher than Gillespie Road), and so the difficult part was to build the embankment at the other end to level it all out. There really was a huge sense of camaraderie among all of us. It felt like we were all in it together, and we'd often sing songs to help us carry on working. The hours were long, and you could tell that our foremen were under a lot of pressure to get things finished. But when we arrived every morning, porridge and hot tea was always there waiting for us. For lunch, soup and bread was laid on, on top of what we brought with us. So the working conditions were actually quite good – better than most labouring jobs of that time. At break times, we'd chat about stuff in the world – like the threat of war; and those women who wanted the vote – the suffragettes. Young blokes like me couldn't get our heads around what their problem was!

'Some of the players also helped out. I recall that [Jock] Rutherford and one of his mates helped out on the carpentry side of things. Some of the others helped to build up the terraces. How times have changed! The carpenters built the turnstiles and exit gates, and got stuck into making the rails and passages needed to get up on to the Spion Kop. The closer that first game got, the more carts and trucks rolled up with raw materials. When we'd finished flattening out the pitch, there was the Spion Kop to work on. That was where the West Stand is now. In those days, it wasn't covered in concrete or anything like that. It was mostly just like flattened down clay, mixed in with earth dug from the new Piccadilly tube station. Hundreds of us had to compact it down by stamping on it. When we'd finished work on the ground early in the morning of the first game, there was still no running water inside the stadium for the players, or for drinks; no refreshments or anything of that sort. The dressing rooms were incomplete. All the workers were going around saying "This is a proper Fred Karno." He was a guy who was in the Charlie Chaplin mould, and we were just laughing about how last minute and farcical everything was. And Norris knew that the game had to kick-off that afternoon. How it did, I'll never know.'

A few days before, Leitch obviously felt that his company had failed to complete the new ground on time, and he disappeared for a week in order to escape Norris's wrath. Kearney was left to take the flak, but as a reward for the team's Herculean efforts in those final days, Norris treated him to a superb Italian lunch, near the stadium, two hours before kick-off. Local printers were also hard at work, attempting to run off 10,000 programmes on time. In the first official programme, the editor described the partially completed stadium as 'the most get-at-able ground in Greater London'. Lying only fifteen minutes from the West End, and an hour's journey for those diehard fans from Woolwich who were willing to make the pilgrimage, this was no idle boast. But could the team live up to the sense of occasion in their Division Two clash with Leicester Fosse, on the opening day of the 1913–14 season?

○ THE FIRST MATCH ○

THE MATCH against Leicester Fosse kicked off at 2.30 p.m. on 6 September 1913. Due to the novelty factor of 'the interlopers' finally completing the move from Woolwich to London, a crowd of 20,000 turned up. On the eve of the game, a local resident commented in the *Islington Gazette*: 'Several of my pals have only ever seen Tottenham play, and I feel it will be fascinating to see just what these new boys from Woolwich are capable of.' Correspondence over the next few weeks in the local press confirms that those early crowds consisted of enthusiastic locals, and Woolwich diehards. The vast majority walked to the ground, but, as the programme for the Leicester Fosse game mentioned, the 'get-at-ability' of Highbury meant it was easy to get to the ground from Drayton Park, Gillespie Road, and Finsbury Park.

Railway companies, realising the benefits of capturing thousands of potential new rail users, laid on dozens of extra trains that day.

The whole event nearly ended in disaster. A.G. Kearney recalled that workmen had left the exit gates open, and it would have been easy for hundreds of people to have stampeded into the ground, aware that they could have got in for free. 'Hundreds of people were lining up at the entrance four or five deep in Avenell Road . . . it says much for the sportsmanlike spirit of those days that they didn't just walk in.' As a reward for having worked so hard in the construction process, David Yates was given a complimentary ticket for that opening game. His testimony is the only one which has survived: 'That afternoon, it was like Highbury was the centre of the universe. Everyone seemed to be headed for the stadium. Although most people walked in, lots also appeared to have come by bike. It says a lot for people at that time that even though they may have opposed the move, they were still happy to leave open the gates at the sides of their houses for people to leave them there. A lot also came via open top bus – it was quite a sunny day – but as I said, most walked it. It was clearly a very well advertised event. You had people from all over London come and see the new boys – from the East End, Chelsea, wherever. There were no Fosse fans though. I don't think long distance travel was really available at that time.

'In those early games, Arsenal charged a sixpence for fans to get in. It cost more for those who wanted to pay a bit extra to sit. The old East Stand was covered, up to a point. There were huge tarpaulins at the back of the stand to provide some shelter for those in the East Stand, but the rest of the ground was totally open. Not all of the terraces had been finished, and some people just sat on flat wooden boards watching the game. There was a real feeling of expectation from the crowd. This was something totally new, and it's always exciting to be there at the start of things, because you never know how they'll turn out. It was a chance to mingle with other people, and it was pretty clear that a lot of the crowd had come all the way from Woolwich to see their team. I think that slowly died away after a while. There was no real chanting or singing, there were no scarves or whatever. It was just really orderly; but there was a lot of clapping and cheering when Arsenal scored. People were a lot more reserved in those days. Some threw their hats off into the air when the team scored, and others would say things like, "Well, steady on old chap!" It's not quite like that now.

'There was quite a lot of drinking on the terraces. No one checked you as you walked in, so it was easy for men to smuggle in beer and spirits. It got passed around a lot – it added to the community spirit. My dad, who later joined me for some Arsenal matches, reckoned it was medicinal, and that you needed it for some of those winter games. At half-time, vendors would come around selling peanuts and roast chestnuts – no crisps or sweets in those days. Another thing that struck me at that first game was that the opposition lobby still wouldn't give up easily. There were still banners against the club, and a few locals stood tut-tutting at their gates. I think that Arsenal won the game 2–1, and George Jobey scored the first ever goal at Highbury. Apart from the fact that the match made history, it was pretty uneventful.'

David Yates was right. The following extracts appeared in the *Athletic News* match report on the following Monday: ' . . . there was something in the winning of this game which cannot afford a full measure of satisfaction to those who have the well-being of Woolwich Arsenal at heart. An infinitely better impression was formed of the Fosse attack than that of Woolwich Arsenal. In the absence of a centre forward of proven ability, the London club had to call upon George Jobey, who made his name with Newcastle United as a half back to lead the line . . . in the second half he met with an accident which may mean his absence from the field for many weeks . . . earlier Jobey neatly deflected with his head and Brebner in the Fosse goal had no chance . . . later Devine drove the ball past Brebner and secured full points for the home club. The Arsenal vanguard was not convincing.' It was hardly the most auspicious of beginnings, and the full picture of Highbury's fledgling team lay behind the scenes.

The facilities at the new stadium were so incomplete that after George Jobey was stretchered off the pitch, Arsenal trainer George Hardy was forced to commandeer a milk float from 'Lewis the milk', to take Jobey back to his own lodgings, and treat the player there. Letters to the *Daily Gazette* also complained of 'the singular lack of refreshment facilities in the new stadium'. Things would gradually improve. Yet the club faced bigger problems than complaints about a lack of catering stalls at the new ground. The Assessment Committee of the Islington Borough Council charged a huge rental fee for the ground. Although the precise figure was never disclosed, it was believed to be twice the amount which Tottenham paid for White Hart Lane, and nearly three times as much as Chelsea paid for Stamford Bridge. Little wonder that Arsenal faced huge financial problems from the moment they kicked a ball at the new ground. Letters to the local newspapers reported seeing hundreds of boys sneaking in, without paying, via the Gillespie Road entry. The gates were left open by tradesmen, who continued bringing cartfuls of raw materials to Highbury.

Norris ensured that the club worked a charm offensive, thanking fans through the medium of the official programme for braving the 'unknown discomforts of an incomplete ground'. Also, he personally wrote letters of apology to locals complaining of disruption on matchday. But Second Division Arsenal's future remained uncertain. By April 1915, the team still showed little sign of awakening from its slumber, and despite the more glamorous location, it was nigh on impossible to attract more glamorous players. Percy Sands and Jock Rutherford – though popular enough among the hard-core support – were hardly world beaters. The board's advertisements in the local press smacked of sheer desperation. Would-be season-ticket holders were informed that, 'A season ticket is at your disposal in exchange for 21 shillings, entitling you to admission to the ground. The Secretary's name is GEORGE MORRELL. His address is 32, Pemberton Road, Harringay. He wants to sell you a ticket. Do not let him be disappointed.'

The notoriously tight-fisted George Morrell had hastened Charlie Buchan's departure from the club back in 1910, when he refused to reimburse the youngster's tram expenses, which amounted to the then equivalent of 55p. It later cost the club over 5,000 times that amount to buy Buchan back. It was unheard of for a club to publish the home address of the Manager Secretary – as they were called in those days. The story went that Norris had been unable to pay for a permanent secretary who would handle season ticket requests. The financial situation became desperate as the team laboured at their new ground. For Norris and Arsenal, things would get worse before they got better.

○ THE TOTTS ○

TWO YEARS after the first game at Highbury, Arsenal appeared no closer to regaining their Division-One status. In March 1915, promotion seemed to be within reach, but a dreadful series of results in April and May saw the team finish back in fifth place. The Gunners' tepid performances saw crowds fall away, and a hard-core 15,000 attended those desperate end of season clashes. Just 10,000 turned up to see Arsenal crush Nottingham Forest 7–0 on 24 April in the final match of the 1914–15 season. In the First Division, Arsenal's London neighbours, Spurs and Chelsea, occupied the bottom two places, and seemed set to join them in the Second Division. Although the diehards could never have predicted it, they had just witnessed a piece of history. This was to be Arsenal's last ever match outside English football's top flight.

As the First World War dragged on, Norris's hopes appeared to have destroyed Arsenal's chances of becoming a major force. Between 1915 and 1918, he had to fork out a further £50,000 to keep the ground up to scratch, without any significant gate receipts coming in to offset the expenditure. David Yates regularly went to Combination games during the war years, after the normal league programme was suspended at the end of the 1914–15 season. He recalls: 'It's hard to say if you were watching a football match, or a propaganda exercise designed to get blokes to join up. Posters around the perimeter of the ground were very bold about it, asking "Why don't you and your football pals go to Highbury or Haringey recruitment centre and join up?" Lots of people my family knew did just that. You could visit either centre on any day and sign on the dotted line. Rumour had it that Kitchener himself visited Highbury once to shake up the supporters to get them to enlist. You can see why: where else in our area would you get such a huge number of blokes together in one place?

'Then again, if you didn't feel like joining up, you could always go to the Scala Theatre in Tottenham Court Road, and watch the Brits and Germans fighting in one of those Kinema colour shows. It's amazing, but there were posters all around the ground at that time advertising it, and the Arsenal programme sometimes mentioned it too. It was one of those films which suggested that all Germans were mad sadists, and the English Tommies were sweetness and light. Really – watching the football at that time was secondary. What was also interesting was that, as the fighting in France grew, there was quite a lot of criticism of clubs and the Football League for continuing to stage matches at a time of national crisis. But by the later stages of the conflict, it was pretty evident that attending games did have a big impact on raising morale among blokes in the country.'

When League football resumed four years later, Arsenal found themselves back in the top flight, after Norris was implicated in the 'dodgiest ever scam' in English football. It was widely believed that the two extra places in the First Division would be occupied by Spurs and Chelsea, who would most likely receive a reprieve from relegation. After 'corresponding with a few financiers here and there' (in manager Leslie Knighton's words), he successfully convinced League President John McKenna to promote Arsenal to the newly expanded Division One ahead of Wolves and Barnsley, who'd finished fourth and third respectively. At the same time, a bewildered Tottenham were relegated to Division Two. Norris had successfully got to work on his contacts within the committee, and convinced fellow directors that weekend jaunts to Highbury, with its proximity to the West End, were a far more appealing prospect than excursions to Wolverhampton and Barnsley. Norris had also ensured he got friendly with Chelsea's chairman, and assured him that Chelsea would receive a reprieve, as long as Arsenal benefited. When the vote was taken, Chelsea received their reprieve, and Arsenal – unbelievably – were promoted, by eighteen votes to Spurs' eight. Tottenham's parrot, presented to the club on its 1908 South American tour, promptly dropped dead at the news, giving rise to the cliché, 'Sick as a parrot'.

Pulling such a stunt meant that relations with North London neighbours Tottenham plunged to an all-time low. Unhappy with Woolwich Arsenal's arrival, Spurs had spent a good deal of time and effort trying to persuade locals against making the trip to Highbury. As late as 1915, the *Tottenham Herald* still ran adverts pleading with locals 'not to go and support the interlopers'. To the surprise of even their most fanatical supporters, Spurs bounced back immediately from their relegation, and during the early 1920s, vented their fury on Arsenal. In a filthy match at White Hart Lane in September 1922, the game turned into a brawl. Reg Boreham's brace of goals pinched the points for Arsenal, but the reporter from the *Sunday Evening Telegraph* noted 'the most disgusting scenes I have witnessed . . . '. The League Commission found Spurs' Bert Smith guilty of 'filthy language' and Arsenal's Alec Graham guilty of retaliation. The bad feeling between both clubs was reflected in events off the pitch. Even the normally ultra reserved Bob Wall – later Arsenal's general manager – commented: 'The roads and pubs outside Highbury and White Hart Lane could be dangerous places back then. Often the knives were out – quite literally – between fans before and after the match.'

An interview I conducted with eighty-year-old Philip Jones, back in 1990, casts new light on the (mythical) view that football fans visiting Highbury in those days were impeccably behaved. Jones recalled: 'Back in them days, there was often real bad feeling between Arsenal and the Spurs. I think that things had changed a bit after the war. Blokes came back and the innocence had gone. I mean, they'd seen things that no blokes should have to see. And there was lots of unemployment as men who'd been demobbed from the army couldn't find work, or couldn't fit back in with normal living. Some of them was really bitter. They seemed bored and restless. And even though I was only a nipper, I suppose I caught on with the mood. Young blokes always like to rebel and put on the angry front, don't they?

'You noticed it a lot at the football. The Arsenal had increased the size of Highbury and now they pulled in big, big crowds. Forty or fifty thousand when it came to playing Spurs or Chelsea. But there was always more trouble against the Spurs, 'cos we was so close geographically. And there was no segregation between fans back then either. Sometimes, the Manchester lot brought a few fans down, but for us, it was always the Spurs who we looked out for. Over the years, you got to realise that if you wanted a dust up, you stood on the Laundry End. Some games, you saw the steam rise from where the Laundry used to be at the back of the North Bank. It was never organised trouble at first, but our little gang was big on "digging people". Like gawping at them and saying "What are you looking at

John?" type of thing. And the Spurs lot did the same back – it was a code of honour that you never looked away. We also used to swear a lot, like blaspheming. People in the crowd – which was mainly made up of working-class blokes – used the "F" word all the time, but it was still a big thing to say things like "Damn" and "God".

'Often, you'd play a game where you'd see who could snatch a cap and throw it away – or stamp on it. Some of us even wore red scarves back then and their mob would wear white. It was at the time when Lenin's lot was beating the whites in Russia, and we quite liked that comparison. Fans wearing colours was really rare in them days, and it was another way of saying you was different. And sometimes you'd give the Spurs lot a clout and blokes around you in the crowd would call you a daft bugger and tell you to stop, or they'd egg you on and it became a bit of a free-for-all. The cops weren't really in the crowds then. But if they caught you, they'd clip you round the ear, or give you a whack in the guts. The crowds were so dense, it was hard to get through for them anyway. Sometimes, you'd get behind the Spurs without them noticing, unzip your trousers and take a leak so you flooded their feet. All stupid pranks really.

'But we was just pups. There was a gang which ran along Seven Sisters Road which clashed with the Spurs lot all the time. And everyone knew they used knives and fists. They were blokes in their twenties, but the police really didn't have a bloody clue what was going on. There was a few stabbings, but it never came out that it was about football. There was more to it than that. As I said, a lot was bad behaviour come out from surviving the war. The war had made a lot of people a lot more violent, and sent a few people nuts I reckon. Going to football brought the aggression out quite a lot.'

The battle wasn't simply confined to groups of fans. After Arsenal's unexpected promotion, the 'lucky' and 'boring' tags began to be affixed to Arsenal at regular intervals, labels which had their origins in the *Tottenham Herald*. As ever, Norris rarely lost an opportunity to spit poison at Spurs. Bizarrely, a piece in the *Tottenham Herald* had mocked Arsenal for never having staged a match in front of a 60,000 plus crowd. 'Can we deduce from this that there simply isn't the interest in Arsenal to pull in a crowd of this size?' the *Herald* asked. On 22 January

1920, Arsenal played Spurs in front of a heaving 60,500 crowd, their largest Highbury attendance to date. The *Daily Gazette*'s match report – usually rather downbeat – had an air of triumphalism about it, and mentioned no less than three times the size of the crowd. It was almost as if Norris himself had placed his guiding hand on the piece – something he was rumoured to do on occasions, whenever something about his team was written. Yet cracks were beginning to appear in his armour plated exterior.

As Philip Jones admits, 'The Spurs were a far better side than the Arsenal in the early 1920s.' With the club now £80,000 in debt – a crushing amount in those days – Norris's investment appeared to have been a complete waste of time. Crowds once more crashed to around the 10,000 mark. A letter to the *Gazette* from Fred Wright of Blackstock Road said: 'I am totally fed up with watching these fellows' displays. I will not be renewing my season ticket for the start of the 1925–26 season, as after a full twelve years at Highbury, the "star" talents which Mr Norris promised have failed to materialise.' A year later, Mr Wright wrote another letter to the *Gazette* admitting he 'deeply regretted my decision'.

Highbury's slumbering giant was about to stir.

○ ARSENAL'S FIRST SUPERSTAR ○

SATURDAY, 29 August 1925. Bank Holiday weekend in Britain, but the residents of Islington were hardly in a relaxed mood, judging from the letters page of the *Daily Gazette*. One local resident complained that 'newfangled washing machines' would never be as effective as good old-fashioned hand washes. A concerned mother voiced her disgust that her fifteen-year-old son's school was to pilot a project to deliver sex education to its pupils. It was, she reckoned, a 'sure-fire way to send him to eternal damnation'. Mr Richards, of Blackstock Road, who'd recently 'endured' Charlie Chaplin's silent movie *Gold Rush* at the Finsbury Park Picture Palace, predicted that the cinema would 'never usurp the popularity of the music hall'. And an anonymous writer, proudly proclaiming himself to be a 'British Fascist', insisted that his party was 'a tolerant organisation which in no way interfered with freedom of speech'. On the surface, this remained yesterday's world.

Yet other events in the capital proved that times were changing. Roaring London was stirring. At the Locarno Club and the Palais Dance Hall, the 'bright young things' with their Eton Crops gleefully accepted the invitation to 'dance 'til you drop'. *The Times* claimed that women's 'scandalous fashions were utterly incompatible with a female's dignity'. London's tube network grew at an alarming pace, and the government had recently been forced to rescind its ban on traffic in the Piccadilly area. A crisis was brewing over house prices in the capital. The MP for Islington commented that £500 for an average semi in the area was 'far beyond the reach of an average worker'. After all, three quarters of the capital's labour force survived on an average of £2 a week or less in the mid-1920s. The 'light industries such as plastics, rubber, chemicals and electrics were beginning to flourish in the South East, and the North–South divide became more pronounced.

They couldn't have known it at the time, but those 50,000 Arsenal fans who streamed into Highbury on the opening day of the 1925–26 season to watch the North London derby were about to witness the early stages of a football revolution. Leslie Anderson sat in the old East Stand for the match. He recalls: 'The old stand stood until the early 1930s when Herbert Chapman decided it needed to be demolished. It was a really rickety wooden thing, and when the crowd got excited, they'd rap their feet, and make a rare old noise. It was hardly the safest construction in the world. Most of the crowd seemed to smoke back then, and they'd throw their smouldering dog-ends on the floor, and push them with their toes between the cracks in the floorboards. There was so much paper rubbish underneath, that it's a miracle we didn't have a major fire disaster on our hands. Highbury was a sprawling bowl, really. By the time Herbert Chapman arrived, it held 50,000 but it was always half empty, because the team was a bit of a let-down, really. We'd ask each other, "When will these fellows ever win anything?" It says a lot for the club at that time that the most famous thing about them was the chairman!

'Then it all changed in 1925. I can remember the great Charlie Buchan making his debut for Arsenal like it was yesterday. He had genuine star quality. And he was signed by our new manager, the great Mr Chapman. You can't overestimate the impact that their arrivals had on the club. We were a nothing team, really, and then suddenly, we have Huddersfield's treble championship winning boss as our manager. Incredible. But it's players' arrivals which excite. And Buchan was a massive signing. There was the whole thing about his transfer, too. Sunderland got an extra £100 each time Charlie scored for us. "There goes another £100" we'd laugh, each time he bagged one. That was a lot of money back then. He was the first Arsenal player to make people think that it was worthwhile getting out of their chair to go and watch them play at Highbury. When he led the team on to the pitch in his first game, there was a genuine buzz, whereas before you would just politely applaud the team as they ran on. Right through the twenties and thirties, Chapman's purchases of star players boosted Highbury crowds to massive levels, and Buchan was the start. Here was a guy who'd scored goals by the dozen for Sunderland, and played for England. You could tell just from his aura that he was a true great. And he was a twenties style hero, who'd travel to games on the tube with the fans. And he was really modest about things, too. There was a story that early in his Highbury career, when he was struggling for form, he was sat next to two chaps on the tube, who were criticising his form, and he never said a word in response. But that Spurs game when he made his debut, there was a real feeling that with Chapman as the manager, and with Buchan on board, this was the start of things. And it was, but as I recall, the team made a slow start to the season.'

The Gunners – as they were now universally known – lost 1–0 under the scorching sun to a goal by Tottenham's Jimmy Dimmock, after Arsenal defenders Andy Kennedy and Billy Milne indulged in a spot of 'after you please', according to the *Daily Gazette*. Arsenal regulars slipped away disappointed, but were aware of Herbert Chapman's advice to 'not expect too much in too little time'. Even *The Times* was mightily impressed by the club's new star striker, commenting: 'Some of his touches reveal the master mind of a great thinker.' The vibe surrounding Buchan was sensational. Seen as something of a maverick within the game, he was very much a product of his generation. After taking exception to Arsenal manager George Morrell's comment about his travel expenses back in 1910: 'How can an amateur footballer run up such an extortionate bill?' he admitted to 'never ducking an argument with an official again'. Aside from his scoring feats with Sunderland, his ten-year spell in the North East was littered with run-ins with authority. There was another bust up with officials over the issue of expenses incurred while playing for England. Buchan decided that, rather than walk five miles back to his house after getting to Sunderland train station, he'd catch a cab home. Buchan never saw his reimbursement. His subsequent arguments saw him dropped from the England team for seven years.

Acutely aware of his worth as a professional footballer, he opted to parade his skills wherever he chose. During a summer holiday to Canada, he earned the equivalent of two weeks' wages after turning out for a friendly match in Montreal. A zealous English football fan snapped Buchan in action, and decided to mail the photos back to FA headquarters. The FA insisted that he hand his earnings to them. Despising the view that footballers should be treated like ignorant serfs, his business interest – a prosperous sports outfitters in Sunderland – made him arguably the wealthiest player of his generation. Envious of his earnings, Buchan once received a letter from the FA checking that ' . . . your business life does not interfere with your chosen profession – playing football'. Ignoring the thinly veiled threat, Buchan continued to show that, with endeavour, it was easy to bypass the maximum wage which was in place for footballers at that time.

Buchan's rebellious streak made him 'an instant hero to Arsenal fans', comments Leslie Anderson. Like many of the fans who watched him each week, Buchan had witnessed the horrors of the Western Front ten years earlier. Drafted to serve with the Grenadier Guards, he'd fought in the battles of the Somme and Paaschendale. After the war, he was unsure whether to pursue his football career, or become a teacher. As a physical education instructor, he later recalled 'thrashing insolent boys with the cane', and suffering badly due to his rotten teeth. Throughout his playing career, he also smoked like a chimney.

Once a thirty a day man, he began pipe smoking because he had been informed 'it's good for your lungs'. Although much of this detail was unknown to the Arsenal fans of the 1920s, the snippets of information they'd heard via football's grapevine were enough to convince Leslie Anderson that: 'Here at last was a man with whom we could identify. Buchan quickly assumed almost supernatural powers. Nowadays, he'd be labelled a talisman. He quickly became one of us.'

As Buchan's good friend George Male admitted, Charlie the hero also possessed a flashy temper, and a stubborn streak. After Arsenal slipped and slithered in the early months of the season, and the new boy failed to score in the opening four games, Buchan endured some criticism from the Highbury crowd. On the tube, he overheard fans verbally savaging him, and after a horrendous 0–7 reverse against Newcastle in October, he vowed to quit Arsenal. Yet Chapman realised that in Buchan, he had an experienced player who could help mould team tactics. In a heated team meeting after the defeat at St James's Park, Buchan and Chapman pushed through the tactics that would alter the entire course of Arsenal's history. From now on, Arsenal would employ a 'stopper' at centre half, and a midfield link man. Such tactics, coupled with an influx of big-name signings, would turn Arsenal into the team of the thirties.

As Arsenal's fortunes gradually improved, controversy continued to dog the team – and Buchan in particular. With just four games remaining in the 1927–28 season, the bottom ten clubs – including Liverpool and Manchester United – were locked in a blanket finish to avoid relegation. Pompey travelled to Arsenal, languishing just above halfway, and needed an away win to stand any chance of staying up. London bookies noticed a flurry of bets on an unlikely away win, and the crowd figure – 15,416 – was by far the lowest of the season at Highbury. Something was wrong, and suspicion grew when Arsenal players barely seemed to be trying. Philip Jones recalls: 'It was evident that Arsenal weren't interested in trying to pull back the goals they needed, and the crowd got on to the players. Even Buchan didn't seem especially bothered.' After Portsmouth raced into a 2–0 lead, both sides appeared content to play keep ball for the rest of the match.

Tottenham, who were relegated later that week, were furious, especially as an Arsenal draw would have ensured their survival, on goal average. Philip Jones recalls: 'Once again, there were rumours that we'd done for Tottenham. Twice in a decade? And all on Norris's doing. It's lucky that Spurs didn't return for a few years to Division One, otherwise we'd have had a bloodbath.' A year later, an FA panel suspended Norris from football indefinitely, and quizzed him about the Portsmouth game. 'Did you instruct your players to give less than full commitment?' he was asked. 'Sir Henry is deeply distressed by such insinuations,' argued his QC. It remains part of 1920s' football folklore that each member of the Arsenal team was delighted to receive – in Charles Buchan's words – 'one of these newfangled refrigerator things' as a gift from Norris two weeks after the Pompey match. 'We'd tease Charlie a lot about all the gadgets he had in his house,' laughed former Arsenal defender George Male. 'A lot of people in the game reckoned he'd bought all of these things on the back of the alleged bung he got from Norris to come south. That was rubbish – he worked hard on his writing and his business. He just knew how to earn money.'

1930s

N.5

WHAT CHAPMAN DID FOR HIGHBURY

IN ORDER to appreciate the extent of Herbert Chapman's Highbury vision, it's important to consider the profile which football had in the early 1930s. The media saturation of the sport, so prevalent in the modern era, simply wasn't present back then. Neither did football have a stranglehold over working men. In those far off days, speedway was a major contender, and big meetings could regularly pull in crowds of 30,000 or above. Chapman didn't care for speedway, describing it as a 'noisy and uncomfortable experience' in his *Express* column. Yet with only an estimated ten per cent of the nation in ownership of a car or motorbike at that time, speed and engines had a genuine fascination for large segments of the population. So did greyhound racing, and at the White City, crowds of over 50,000 gathered. Chapman continued to argue that in the long term, football would outstrip its sporting rivals, but in the meantime, he realised that the product needed to be sufficiently attractive to pull in the punters. After the FA decided to ban Norris from football for good, Chapman was free to build his 'dream team' without Sir Henry's tiresome influence.

Norris had found himself the subject of an FA inquiry after the *Daily Mail* ran a series of articles alleging that he was guilty of making illegal payments to Charlie Buchan in order to entice him south. Both Buchan and Norris strenuously denied the claims. What *was* undeniable was that the proceeds from the sale of the team bus (£125) had found their way into Norris's wife's bank account, and that he'd decided to pay for the cost of his chauffeur through an Arsenal Football Club expense account. Norris challenged the *Mail*'s allegations about the illegal payments in court two years later, but after narrowly failing to implicate Chapman in the scandal, he was forced to relinquish control of the club. Chapman proceeded to break all traditional managerial moulds. Fortunate that Samuel Hill-Wood was now the main mover and shaker on the board, Chapman agreed with Hill-Wood's motto:

'Why interfere when you've got experts to do the job?' No manager in the game wielded as much power as Chapman, and he oversaw player sales, administration, and controlled training procedures. A benevolent new dictator was in place.

Chapman realised that disposable cash among many supporters was short, and apart from capturing the signature of a host of stars, good facilities at Highbury were needed to keep attendances high. 'We can't take our fans for granted you know,' George Male recalled Chapman saying in the late 1920s. 'Herbert knew that he needed to give them something extra. Arsenal had a hard core of about 20,000 fans, who would generally turn up whatever. The rest needed something more. Chapman realised that the club needed to excel not just on the pitch – but also in crowd comforts.' The biggest problem with Highbury in the early 1930s was that three sides remained uncovered. Arsenal fan Brian Kilbride recalled: 'Rain was the biggest thing to affect crowds in the thirties. People generally don't mind freezing to death, but getting soaked was another matter. Crowds could veer between 70,000 to 20,000, and you'll find that they often fell if it was raining.'

Via Chapman's guiding hand, Highbury quickly became the most talked about – and modern – stadium in Europe. At a cost of £45,000, the West Stand (complete with 4,100 seats) was opened in December 1932. Brian Kilbride comments: 'That stand being built made all the difference, because it replaced the huge, open terrace on the west side, which left you open to the elements. It also ensured that more of the crowd noise stayed *inside* Highbury. Beforehand, a lot of it would disappear upwards.' The phenomenon provoked controversy in the Highbury district – and beyond. Islington resident Nigel Franks wrote to the *Gazette* and questioned '. . . whether such an outrageous fee can be totally justified. It seems virtually immoral at a time of national crisis that such a sum could be lavished on a football stadium.' George Male commented: 'Chapman's response to the doubters was to point out that Arsenal's crowds bankrolled the expenditure. Critics seemed to think that taxpayers' money went into the building of the stands. It came from turnstile receipts and generous directors.'

Chapman didn't simply advocate the construction of larger stands.

Aware that the West Stand had taken away standing space, the club decided that the Laundry End should be 'banked up', by asking local tradesmen to dump rubbish into holes at the back to extend it further. Brian Kilbride recalled '. . . all sorts of carts darting to and from the back of the stand. It was reminiscent of 1913 again, when Highbury was first being built.' The legend of the Highbury horse has now passed into folklore. The story went that a horse backed so close to the North Bank that both the animal and the cart toppled in. Dan Brennan – in his *Official Arsenal Miscellany* – points out that no such archaeological evidence was found when the old North Bank was demolished in 1992. Brian Kilbride cast further evidence on this urban myth: 'The story went around the area for some days about the fact that some chap had lost his cart and his horse. It later emerged that a grocer from Finchley had put this story around. He was known to be a teller of tall stories. But that's all it was. Pure pub talk. It would be nice to think it was a true story, but it wasn't!'

It was the completion of the luxurious East Stand ('a building of wonder and unparalleled in football' in the words of the official Arsenal programme), which made Highbury the most famous ground in the world. Its art-deco frontage simply set the ground apart from others. Travelling supporters and visiting players were in awe of setting foot near Highbury.

Middlesbrough striker Wilf Mannion played regularly at Highbury in the 1930s: 'You'd see the front of the stadium, and straightaway you'd feel a bit inferior. It was such a difference with Ayresome Park, which always seemed to be falling down from the minute it was built! Highbury was swish and awesome. You'd walk into the East Stand and the commissionaire would doff his cap at you – not something which usually happened to players of my era. The dressing rooms in the East Stand were beautiful – the marble baths, the undertile heating. It was pure luxury. You have to remember that this was in an era when a lot of clubs would deliberately leave the heating off in winter or turn it up high in the summer to unsettle you. It said so much for the Arsenal that they provided for your every need. I'll always remember the white towels laid out for us after games, and even the beer and sandwiches afterwards were of the highest quality. Arsenal had the class to treat all opponents as equals.'

Huddersfield fan Tommy Williams also made the pilgrimage to Highbury whenever his team played Arsenal: 'To a lad who worked in a factory in a smoggy old town like Huddersfield, visiting Highbury in the thirties was the equivalent of going to see the Pyramids, or the Taj Mahal. My pal Eddie and me used to stand in front of the East Stand and gaze in wonder. It was gleaming white. Brand spanking new. Beautiful. Then, we'd wait for the Arsenal team to arrive. They'd stroll through the crowds, and even though all footballers supposedly earned the same at the time, you could tell they were a different breed from our lot. I recall that Eddie Hapgood always seemed to have a permanent suntan and he radiated health. Then he'd disappear into this heaven where the commissionaire almost bowed at the players. It was almost unreal. You could have written a soap opera about it. It was like *Dallas* or *Dynasty* – a different world. My team Huddersfield had dominated the previous decade, so I suppose I should have been annoyed that Arsenal now took their place. But the Highbury of the 1930s was a fantasy world. It was *the* setting for a team like that.'

Matters also improved for those standing on the Laundry End in 1935. Chapman saw to it that a roof was erected to shelter them from the elements. Brian Kilbride recalled the banter between the Laundry End's 'innies' and 'outies' in the thirties. 'We used to call those fans who stood under the roof softies. We were the hard lads who stood in the wet weather whatever the opposition. Looking back, I suppose that we were the stupid ones. But putting the roof on the Laundry End often meant there was a rush to get to games early. You'd have people under the roof from midday some days if rain was in the air – laughing at those who didn't get some shelter in time.'

Not content with introducing the latest architectural designs, Chapman attempted to add a few mod cons. In 1932, he advocated the use of a giant 45-minute clock, so the crowd could see precisely how much time was left in each half. 'Chapman knew that football was an event, and he wanted fans to be part of the game. He believed that a clock would add to the tension of the game, with countdowns adding to the atmosphere,' explained George Male. The FA didn't buy into Chapman's way of thinking, and banned the mechanism, claiming it would place referees under pressure. They did finally allow the famous clock on the South Bank. 'So the fans could count down anyway,' Male added sarcastically.

Some locals remained adamant that turning Highbury into a football mecca was unjustified. George Male recalled: 'Some of us received letters from angry locals. I'm sure that Chapman did too, but he never told us. The gist was that times were hard in London, and it was distasteful that Arsenal were spending so much on a fancy stadium, when the working man was going through the Depression. They had a point, but the projects were hardly vulgar, and were paid for by success on the field. Speculating to accumulate. That's good business in anybody's language.' Chapman's big money purchases always seemed to coincide with another piece of bad news for Britain. In the week that David Jack arrived from Bolton Wanderers for a record £10,000, the press announced an alarming downturn in the fortunes of the building trade. As he swooped for Cliff Bastin, Britain's unemployment level reached an all-time high. The newly nicknamed 'Bank Of England' club needed to pull in 40,000 punters to every home game in order to break even. It was a tall order as the Depression started to bite London. Yet his gamble would pay off.

There was always a contradiction lying at the heart of Chapman. As Huddersfield manager, he frequently reiterated the fact that spending large sums of money on players or stadiums was 'a regrettable part of football'. He also believed that the status of footballers as professionals should preferably be avoided. Yet no other manager spent so much (comparatively) on players or ground improvements until the Premiership era dawned. George Male claimed: 'Above all, Chapman was a showman. Everything – spending money included – came second to his team putting on a fantastic show.' As Gunners fans from the era testify, there was no finer performance in London in the thirties than watching Arsenal play at Highbury.

○ CONFESSIONS
THE BUILDERS ○

CLIVE BAKER, BUILDER

'During the early 1930s, times were pretty hard for chaps like me who were in the building trade. It's always the first industry to suffer at a time of economic recession. So when W.J. Cearns – the company I worked for – was hired to work on Highbury, it was fantastic news for all of us. Especially when we learned that Arsenal wanted the new stands in the art-deco style. It would be something completely new. At that time, Archie Leitch's ideas were seen as the way to go in terms of designing stadiums, and we saw Arsenal's move as being a daring one for the time. But my main concern was that I put some food on the table for my family. I was just twenty-one, and already had a couple of kids to support.

'It seemed incredible to me that Arsenal were prepared to splash out so much money on the West Stand. Then again, Claude Ferrier and William Binnie – who were the designers behind developing the stadium – were very practical about things. Ferrier in particular realised that the whole of the stadium needed to be opened up in order to cram more fans inside the ground. It was estimated that if the plans to expand and develop all sides of the ground went ahead, the club could cram in an extra 20,000 a game, and pull in £5,000 in gate receipts every time. That was a phenomenal amount of money, but the club needed the extra revenue to invest in players. So it all made good economic sense.

'I'd like to say that I had fond memories of working at Highbury in the early thirties, but it was a pressured time. Herbert Chapman regularly talked to us about our work. We all liked him a great deal. He had the air of a man who was restless to build Arsenal into more than just any old club, and he often talked to my foreman about his dreams for Highbury. He wanted it eventually to be a large sprawling bowl, preferably with a cycle track around the outside, because believe it or not, cycling was a major crowd draw at that time. Like all ambitious people, he also got out of his depth on occasion. I heard that he drew up plans to buy all the houses on Highbury Hill, and basically shift Highbury in the direction of St John's College. That showed he was a bit naïve when it came to planning permission. It also showed that as far back as the thirties, Arsenal were struggling because of the lack of space around the ground.

The chain of command cracked the whip very hard. I'm convinced the pressure stemmed from Chapman himself, and that he told the board that the longer the building work dragged on, the less they could invest in the team. So the board pressured Binnie and Ferrier, and they in turn hassled W.J. Cearns. My foreman used to give us grief all day, it seemed. We had a little catchphrase among us all which was "Get a bloody move on", because that was all the foreman seemed to say to us. The first thing we had to do was to build up the North Bank (or Laundry End as we called it). It wasn't easy. Its foundations were originally made from clay, and this needed to be scooped out and replaced by harder stuff, which included local traders' rubbish. We also had to build up the College End, and what I remember most from that time was a constant stream of tradesmen coming in to dump their stuff.

The problems arose because the company believed it could do the job with too few men. We got a bit upset when we were accused of being lazy and shoddy. We were supposed to have all the terracing banked up and extended by early 1932, but by Christmas we were still way off target. Binnie and Ferrier came to the site on a couple of occasions with faces like thunder, because the work just wasn't being done quickly enough. We were worried, as it became clear that until the work was done, Cearns Ltd wouldn't get paid. And where would that leave us? Ferrier was a hard-nosed sod, in the end. Because we were late finishing the work on expanding the terracing, he cut the amount of money Cearns got by thirty per cent, and even then Arsenal dragged their feet in paying him. We never got our full pay for ages. The whole episode was absolute bloody chaos, with large parts of the terraces shut off while we finished working on them. But the problems could have been averted if Cearns had employed a few more blokes in the first place.'

ROBERT HUME, BUILDER

'Bloody, bloody arguments all the time. Especially over the speed of time it took us to do the work on the West Stand. When we arrived at Highbury, the west side was a huge open terrace. It was a real pain for fans to get to, because the houses behind meant that fans had to get on to the terrace either from the Gillespie Road or Avenell Road entrance. There were regular terrace surges when things got a bit tight, and people were trying to get through. The only solution – if Ferrier wanted to build the West Stand – was to buy some of the houses at the back to create an entrance to it. There was a lot of hassle over it, but eventually, he bought a couple of houses which opened up the whole scheme, and allowed us to get our building materials in through that side of the stadium. As the stand began to go up, you got some sort of indication of what an incredible structure it would be. There's a famous picture of Alex James on the pitch being dwarfed by the gigantic structure going up behind him. It was all about comfort for the fans, and I suppose, sheer grandeur.

The upper deck had space for 4,100 seats, and the bottom section, which was still a terrace, was supposed to be covered by what was above. It didn't quite work like that, because if the rain drove in the other way, you'd get soaked anyway. I worked on the executive entrance gate at the back of the stand. The whole thing cost about £50,000, a phenomenal sum in those days. Obviously the West Stand is now very old, but for its time, and particularly the entrance to it from Highbury Hill, the art-deco aspect of it is still very impressive. Many of the lads who worked on the project went to the official opening in late 1932, and there was huge excitement because the future King Edward VIII opened it. There were flags and cheering crowds all along the route he took through Highbury. He didn't know Wallis Simpson in those days! The boozers were granted special opening hours. The whole thing was a carnival occasion. It was a massive event for the whole district.'

STEVEN LOWRY

'I first saw the East Stand in 1936, shortly before it was opened. I went to the stadium to do a safety check on some of the wiring, but one of the club officials asked me if I also wanted a tour of the stand. He mentioned to me that William Binnie had done most of the work on it, after Claude Ferrier was killed in an accident. On the surface, it looks like a mirror image of the West Stand, and is still art-deco. But inside, it was very impressive. There were covered toilets, which was very rare for football grounds at that time. There were heated dressing rooms, the Horseshoe bar, beautiful tearooms, lovely offices for club employees in which to work . . . and the front of the East Stand took your breath away. So did the Marble Halls. All that marble and mahogany, and Herbert Chapman's bust. It was designed by Jacob Epstein, and at that time, you just didn't expect such a world renowned figure to get involved with a football club. Everything was beautifully clean and elegant. You realised that the stand was a message to the rest of the football world that Arsenal was a number one for style.

'The chap who showed me around also pointed out the new directors' box, and the place where in future, TV broadcasts could be made from Highbury. At *that point, I stopped listening to him. It all sounded a bit too far-fetched, and I couldn't really see TV taking much of an interest in football. Then, when he told me that the East Stand cost £130,000, I was flabbergasted. I reckoned that Arsenal needed their brains testing. That was far too much to spend on a football stand.'*

○ THE TAJ MAHAL ○

SO WHAT WAS life like for Arsenal fans at the 'Taj Mahal' that was Highbury in the 1930s? Several of the fans that I spoke to in the early 1990s confessed that the rose-tinted specs syndrome may have kicked in. Two recalled the fights outside the ground when Portsmouth came to town. Clive Williams recalled: 'Pompey brought a huge following, and as many of their fans were sailors, they had a fearsome reputation. Unlike most other clubs, they would bring a good few hundred, who broke into pockets around the ground.' Others recall sporadic outbreaks of trouble when Tottenham visited Highbury.

The vast majority of supporters concurred on several issues. In the days before segregation, it was possible to banter with away supporters, and at half-time, to swap ends, if you could push through the swathes of supporters on the terraces. Above all else, nothing could beat the intoxicating feeling of being an integral part of the heaving mass of supporters on a terrace in the era when 70,000 plus crowds were commonplace at Highbury. In March 1935, with Arsenal poised to complete a hat-trick of championship victories, a record crowd of 73,295 crammed in to watch the Gunners take on Sunderland. The gates were locked fully one hour before kick-off. As the following chapters prove, there was a less palatable side to the thirties' terrace experience, but for George Stephens and Richard Maud, Arsenal fans really had never had it so good.

'As a nipper, my Mum and Dad's friend Pete used to come and collect me from our pub,' recalled George. 'We'd have a spot of lunch first, and then hop on the open top double decker down at Blackstock Road. You'd have to arrive about an hour early if teams like Chelsea or Tottenham were there, otherwise you'd be stuck out on the road. For a little lad like me – I'm still only five foot seven – I used to get pushed about quite a lot. Pete took a flask of coffee with some whisky in it, and at half-time, he'd say, "Oh have some, go on, your mum and dad won't mind." A lot of the chaps used to have booze they'd pass about. It was more communal then. There was a rule that if you were small and got stuck in the middle, where you couldn't see, they'd pass you down to the front over the heads of people. My lasting image is of knocking against all those bowler hats. That's all you could see at that height – a sea of bowler hats and clouds of cigarette smoke. I got right to the front for many games, and then met Pete at the end. Once I got so close to the pitch that I touched Alex James's shirt. I don't think I washed my hands for the rest of the week!

'I think everyone wore suits to games in those days. It was what the working man did. Either that, or blokes would come straight from work in their overalls or boiler suits, and grab a pint in the pub beforehand if they could afford it, because most people worked five-and-a-half-day weeks back then – or more – because in times of Depression you couldn't turn any work down. It was never especially colourful inside the ground, more like a sea of grey and brown. A few wore scarves, but it wasn't really the done thing back then. One of the few gimmicks was the red and white rattles. That's about the extent of club mer- chandising at that time!

'Sometimes, I'd be allowed into games for free. Pete would push me up against the turnstile clicker, look at the fella in the booth and say, "Oh go on, he's only a nipper." And sometimes the fella would wink at you and say, "In you go then." You'd see other kids being let in like that, so the crowds in that era were probably even bigger than officially recorded. Before the game, blokes would walk around the perimeter track and hold up wooden boards with the players' names on them. They'd do the same with half-time and full time scores, and by word of mouth the results would gradually filter up the terraces. I remember in those days we listened out for Villa and

Wednesday scores. And the Spurs score, of course.

'And finally, and most importantly, the team. Those pure red and white shirts – all pristine and clean. We got locked out a couple of times and couldn't get into the England v Italy match in 1934, because so many Arsenal players were in the team. Sometimes, when it was hot in August or May, they would shut the gates early so people wouldn't overheat. You'd have blokes who would fry in the sun, rather than take off their jackets. Nowadays, I see some chaps go bare chested if it's too warm. How times change!'

Richard Maud proudly attended the majority of big games in the 1930s, and agreed to talk to me in 1991. He recalled: "It was *our* game back then – the working man's game. It cost me a shilling to get into Highbury to stand, in the 1930s. I mean, even allowing for inflation, the price of watching football has risen massively since then. It costs my son seven pounds to stand and watch Arsenal now. That's ridiculous – they'll be charging a tenner next.' (Author's note: 14 years later, it cost £44.50 to sit where Richard Maud's son stood – more than a six fold increase again.)

'We used to have a drink and a smoke in the pub at Holloway, get the tube – which was all smoking in those days – and get out from Arsenal tube near the ground. You had a bit of a sing-song. You'd normally chant the players' names. That was it really. We just didn't have pop songs which fans base their chants around these days. The teams would run out in those heavy old cotton shirts, and it was like a real theatre in the 1930s. You should have seen the players that came here. Dixie Dean was one. He was a great player, but he never seemed to have much luck against Copping or Roberts. But there was no malice towards him if the move didn't come off. You respected him, and you paid your money to see *him* perform – as well as your own players. You cheered *your* side – you didn't sneer at the others.

'We used to enjoy seeing Pongo Waring come here with the Villa, and a young Stan Matthews with Blackpool. And again, you wanted to see those chaps play well. It's like if you went to a show, you wouldn't cheer if the leading man had a stinker or whatever. There was a group of about thirty players in the division whom everybody respected.

Maybe we were more innocent back then. And if the opposition scored, you'd applaud – as long as it was a well constructed goal.

'Where we used to stand, there was one chap who would bring a live duck to home games. I've got absolutely no idea why. Mad as a hatter he was. Once, the duck escaped, and a steward chased it around, but fell over as he tried to grab it. The steward didn't find it very funny – but the whole crowd near me were doubled up with laughter. The crowds were huge. Sometimes, it got uncomfortable – but there was little thought given to crowd safety back then You just put up with it – that was football. I went to the Sunderland match where it was Arsenal's record turnout. It was mad – everyone swaying around, pushing and shoving. It wasn't something you considered at the time, but with Hillsborough a few years' back, it's amazing how something similar didn't happen at Highbury on that day. Lots of my pals had their coats and shoes pulled off, you were that closely packed. Then, if anyone bore down on goal, you'd go scurrying down the terraces. As I said, it was just what happened. There was swearing too, though not as bad as today. A chap would swear, and often he'd be told to be quiet by someone nearby. "There's ladies present," someone would say, and that would be the end of it. I get quite embarrassed with some of the things crowds sing these days. I'm from a different generation!'

George Male acknowledged the crowds in those days: 'We'd run out to these gargantuan crowds which reached back as far as the eye could see. Money was tight, and some of these people had saved all week just to come and watch us. It was something Herbert Chapman never tired of reminding us. "Go and entertain them," he'd urge. And that was his thing. A packed stadium, and a great team. Sometimes, the whole drama of it all just took your breath away. Every time I ran out at Highbury to those crowds, I thought I was the luckiest man alive.'

○ 'WEE ALEC' ○

IF CHARLIE BUCHAN was Arsenal's first true superstar, then Alex James was Highbury's first true icon. Even seventy years after his playing career ended, he remains arguably the most influential player Arsenal ever had. Gunners fan George Frey recalled: 'There was a saying which did the rounds back then. You'd go to the cinema to watch Garbo or Chaplin; the ballet to see Nureyev; and football to watch Alex James. He was the first footballer to be compared with people in the arts world. That was how influential he was.' Even before he arrived at Highbury in 1929, the Scot had star quality. He'd found fame as a member of Scotland's Wembley Wizards side in 1928, and earned rave reviews as the fulcrum of Preston's excellent side in the mid-1920s. Chapman lured him south in order to fulfil his insatiable desire to have superstars parade their stuff at Highbury.

His Arsenal team-mate Ted Drake recalled: 'He was the one who made Arsenal tick in those days. And that was saying something, considering the great players Arsenal had. But with a mazy dribble, or a clever flick, he could literally control the outcome of matches. How would I describe him? He was the first true midfield general in British football. It's a term which is bandied about far too much these days, but Alex really had the ability to boss any side.' George Frey commented: 'I bloody loved Alex James. People talk about Ian Wright or Charlie George as being legends. But James played in Arsenal sides which either won, or threatened to win, the league every year. And he was the first stellar talent the club had ever had. I can't imagine a more unlikely looking guy to be a great player though. He looked about fifty when he was twenty-five. He was short, a little tubby, and everyone knew that away from the pitch, he liked a cigarette and a beer or two. He'd run on to the pitch and look knackered straightaway, with his sleeves pulled right down, and those baggy shorts down to his knees. He was the footballing equivalent of old man Steptoe – a right scruffy so-and-so. He was also a genius – the best I ever saw.'

Alex James was a man of total opposites. The 'scruffy so-and-so' described by George Frey actually enjoyed wearing tailor-made suits, and even had a penchant for wearing sandals when other footballers wore polished shoes. For all his cheerful exterior, he could be extremely moody. Chapman allowed him far more leeway than other Arsenal players. Early on in his Gunners career, as he struggled for form and fitness, Chapman ordered him to bed to rest up and relax. A few days later, on the morning of a crucial FA Cup-tie against Birmingham, the boss paid James a visit, telling him to get out of bed, as the team needed him for the Highbury clash.

George Male recalled: 'At times, it could be very annoying for the rest of us when Alex was given what we saw as special privileges. Alex openly admitted in front of Chapman that he'd never chase an opponent in position. If I'd ever said that, I'd have been kicked out of the club. It took a long time for many of us to realise that Chapman got it spot on with him. You can't treat players in exactly the same way. People are different. Before that FA Cup-tie against Birmingham, there were several doubters in the dressing room as to whether Alex could cope at Highbury. And the crowd was on to him, too. But in that game, he proved to everyone inside Highbury what he could do. He proceeded to destroy Birmingham, and Arsenal went on to win the cup that year – our first major trophy. A lot of that was down to Alex James.'

Aside from his prodigious football gifts, his life away from the game made him a terrace hero. Although he was happily married with two children, James mixed in circles which other thirties stars couldn't reach. His job as a 'sports demonstrator' at Selfridges enabled him to socialise with the likes of Wimbledon champions Suzanne Lenglen and Fred Perry. He also counted transatlantic flier Amy Johnson as a friend. James was one of the first footballers to break out of the purely working-class straitjacket. His high profile saw him invited to numerous London nightspots and parties. As his iconic status grew, so did his socialising.

George Frey bumped into James at the Clippers Bar in Piccadilly: 'There he was, drinking with a large group of friends at about one a.m., and I realised it was a Friday night. In just over twelve hours, I'd be watching him play for the Arsenal. In those days, if you approached footballers, you knew that they'd talk to you as equals. So I muttered something to him about me being a huge fan of his. We were both pretty drunk, and he shook my hand and chatted to me for a bit. It was hard to understand him though, with his strong Scottish accent. When it got to about three a.m., I asked him what time he was planning on calling it a night. He fixed me with a solemn look and said: "When the sun comes up, son." Whether he was exaggerating or not, I don't know. But every weekend, you got to hear that he was seen at some party or event. He was lucky that these were the days before the newspapers took an interest in what footballers did "out of hours". Next day, Arsenal were at home to the Villa. He ran out of the tunnel, and judging from his appearance, he looked like he hadn't slept for a week. And he played a blinder. Alex bloody James.'

James spotters didn't need to venture as far as Piccadilly to catch a glimpse of their hero. Ted Drake recalled: 'After games, you'd get lots of boys wielding their autograph books outside the ground. Eddie Hapgood was a tricky one to get hold of, I was told. If anyone approached him on a Sunday, they'd be dismissed with a curt "You should be in church". But I'd say that eighty per cent were waiting for Alex. And he'd not disappear until he'd signed each book. He really was excellent with the kids.' Local resident George Ridley recalled: 'The entire Arsenal team was very approachable in the thirties. As part of their pre-match training, they'd pound the streets around Highbury, so you could catch a glimpse of them that way. Several of them used local sandwich bars for lunch, and Alex was known to use pubs after matches. People would stop and stare at him purely because of who he was. Herbert Chapman also saw to it that the club did a lot in the local community. They'd attend schools for special events, and Christmas carol concerts, and things like that. So what I'm saying is that Alex might have been a legend in many people's eyes, but he was unbelievably accessible, too. Not like it is today!'

At the end of James's first full season at Arsenal, he scored one of the goals in the FA Cup final against Huddersfield, which delivered Arsenal's first piece of silverware. For the first time, Islington had the opportunity to celebrate as the team paraded the trophy for their fans. The ten-year-old Larry Harris recalled: 'Arsenal had to play a league game against Sunderland on the Monday after the Cup final. For the first time, I remember splashes of red and white at a game, with scarves and rosettes. The club also organised a fireworks display – red and white only – of course. It was bloody big party. The Sunderland team respectfully formed a guard of honour when the Arsenal team ran on to the pitch. At the end of the match, the whole crowd was chanting "We want Alex". He, and the rest of the players, did this lap of honour around the pitch, and he was walking about shaking hands. Grown men in front of me were almost swooning "Alex James touched my hand. I'll never wash it again." I've never seen an Arsenal player inspire the kind of awe that he did in fans, and I've seen a few good 'uns in my time.'

○ THE SADDEST MATCH ○

THE SIXTH OF January 1934. Just another normal Islington day. The pages of the *Gazette* showed that locals had their usual gripes. House prices (now averaging £4,000) were adjudged to be far too high, and the growing traffic congestion, according to Mrs Eileen Pollett, was 'shambolic'. 'It took my husband over an hour to work his way up Seven Sisters Road last Tuesday,' she complained. Criticism of Marlene Dietrich also found its way into the letters column. Mr Paul Clarke disapproved of 'her lewd hand gestures and overtly sexual movements in her latest picture'. He stayed until the end of the film anyway. The *Daily Telegraph* highlighted the fact that more telegraph instalments had taken place over the previous year, and Winston Churchill warned: 'Britain has never been so defenceless,' as Adolf Hitler began his none-too-secret rearming of Germany, in direct contravention of the Treaty of Versailles.

For Arsenal players, it was a crushingly ordinary morning. The team was perched at the top of the league, although George Male had recently commented in the *Daily Express* that the team 'was falling well below their normal standards in recent weeks, as shown by the dour goalless draw at home to Birmingham a couple of days ago'. With crowds starting to tumble beneath the 40,000 mark – required for the

club to break even each week – a home win against Sheffield
Wednesday that afternoon was imperative. The players were unaware
that Herbert Chapman had already told director George Allison in late
1933: 'The time has come to rebuild.'

But Chapman never had a chance to do so. As the players filed into
pre-match training that morning, they were stunned by the headlines
on newspaper placards which read HERBERT CHAPMAN DEAD. The
grief ran deep in the local community. Tommy Jezzard lived in
Aberdeen Road, and recalls: 'My wife was out the back pegging out
some washing, when our son walked in and said that Mr Chapman
had passed away. We were dumbfounded. We'd heard that he'd got a
nasty cold, but to be dead from pneumonia two days later? We were
all in a state of shock. He was so well respected by the locals. He used
to take strolls near the stadium with his players, and he was always so
polite. Always raised his hat and said "Good morning". My wife said,
"Well that's it. It's the end for Arsenal." And that's how it felt to all of
us – the end of the world.'

Paul Drury attended that afternoon's game against Wednesday: 'It
was a big crowd but it was also eerie, because virtually no one said a
word all game. I remember one fellow near me arrived and started
singing – he obviously hadn't heard the news about Chapman. And
when everyone told him to be quiet, and explained why, he looked so
embarrassed. I did feel sorry for him. The players were subdued as well.
They went through the motions a bit against Wednesday, a game
which they drew. The team then lost a few games in a row, as if they
couldn't really get their bearings for a while. There was a home game
against Spurs soon after, and it became known as 'the Chapman
match'. We all had to go to show how much we thought of Chapman.
We got there two hours before kick-off, and you couldn't get near the
stadium. Seventy thousand were there, and we were locked out at one
o'clock. That was awful. I was so upset, because we all wanted to be
inside to show our respects. The strange thing was that we carried on
standing near the Arsenal tube station, and you could hear "For he's a
jolly good fellow . . . " ringing out all game. There must have been
twenty thousand locked out against Spurs, but I'll swear that no one
went home. We were rooted to the spot all game. There was enough
time passed where it was appropriate to sing it as a mark of respect.

But to actually have sung it at the Wednesday game wouldn't have been appropriate.'

If fans felt a sense of loss, it was nothing compared to the devastation felt by the players. On 10 January, Herbert Chapman was buried in Hendon. The pall-bearers – Jack, Hapgood, Lambert, Bastin, and James represented a who's who of thirties football. George Male recalls the period surrounding Chapman's death: 'I played the game against Wednesday in a real trance. I think a lot of their players did as well, because Chapman was so respected throughout the whole of football, not just at Arsenal. Just before kick-off, Joe Shaw, who'd taken over from Chapman as a caretaker, urged us to go out and perform in front of the crowd as Chapman would have wanted. That was just impossible. The crowd was flat. Literally – it was a funereal atmosphere. And after that, it was hard to get ourselves going for a few weeks. We played that big game at home against Spurs. So many people were there rooting for us to win, and were chanting Chapman's name, but we couldn't raise ourselves. It remains my biggest regret in football that we couldn't win that day. And then there are your personal fears. "Will the new manager rate me as much as Chapman did?" Questions like that race around inside your head.

'It speaks volumes for fans at that time that even when we had the Spurs match, all the wreaths and flowers outside Highbury remained untouched. Imagine that, a derby day when supporters on both sides had the decency to leave all the lovely messages as they were. As players, I think many of us read most of them. It was a very moving time for all of us.'

There is a fairly decent body of evidence to suggest that Chapman's ghost haunted Highbury for years afterwards. Bob Wall and other staff swore blind that they could hear his footsteps every night at the stadium, and Wall noted in his book *Arsenal From The Heart,* that he regularly checked to ensure that Chapman wasn't pacing up and down the corridor. Chapman's successor, George Allison, also felt the weight of Chapman's millstone around his neck. But it was Chapman's bust, situated in the East Stand foyer, which provoked distinctly mixed reactions from his successors in the post. George Graham, who for a while seemed poised to eclipse the Yorkshireman's achievements, was rumoured to want his own bust carved out next to that of Chapman.

Famously, Billy Wright regularly shook his fist at the bronze edifice, fully aware that he was failing to live up to the high expectations set by Chapman thirty years earlier. It wasn't just Chapman who weighed heavily on later Arsenal players' minds. After winning the Fairs Cup in 1970, one player allegedly informed a director, 'Now you can stick your Alex James and Herbert Chapman.'

George Male took a long time to respond to my question: 'What was Chapman's greatest legacy to Arsenal?' His response surprised me: 'Renaming Gillespie Road tube to Arsenal.' Chapman used all of his political persuasion to ensure that tickets, signs, and timetables were altered to cater for the new name. This was after he'd barked at a government official: 'Gillespie Road – who ever heard of that? It's Arsenal around here.' Male explained: 'I talked to a lot of Arsenal fans at that time and they'd say, "George, we've got a wonderful stadium, and a wonderful team, but how on earth did Chapman pull the strings to get the tube station's name changed?" And I had no answer for them. Cliff Bastin always said that Chapman should have been Prime Minister. For many Arsenal fans, having the Arsenal tube station was the best of all!'

George Male explained that Chapman's one unfulfilled wish was to have a floodlit match at Highbury. 'He'd seen it done abroad, but he was told he couldn't do it back here because of fuel shortages in the Depression. It's a shame, because Highbury always looks beautiful when it's lit up. I always like to think of Chapman standing in the middle of a floodlit stadium, with a full house, and him as master of all he surveyed. He was unquestionably twenty years ahead of his time.'

○ THE BATTLE OF HIGHBURY ○

IT'S NO exaggeration to say that in the early 1930s, England football selectors weren't keen for the national side to pit their wits against continental opposition. George Male recalled a conversation he had with an FA official about why the England team had opted out of competing in the inaugural World Cup in 1930. 'We'll learn nothing from playing against spics and dagos,' came the unequivocal reply. Undeterred by the xenophobic response, Male argued that by playing the likes of Brazil and Uruguay, the English team could learn more about continental tactics. 'We can't have you playing a bunch of darkies, Male,' the official retorted. 'You'd come back from swampland eating bananas and with a dose of the clap.' The government's view on the matter of England playing foreign teams was confused. In early 1933, Foreign Office representative Neville Henderson warned the FA: 'Beware in advance contests between British and foreign teams. Most of them are seeking victory in order to boost their political regimes.' Later that year, when asked by a *Mail* journalist to clarify his position, he commented: 'There is no possible suggestion that the government dictates which countries British teams play.'

By the summer of 1934, the government was forced to alter its position, after Fascist-controlled Italy won the World Cup. Benito Mussolini went by the adage 'Good kicking is good politics', and with both the FA and the government fearful of being outshone on the national stage, a 'friendly' was set up at Highbury where England would take on the *'azzuri'*. Ted Drake – an automatic choice in the England line up at that time – recalled: 'Even though the Italians had the World Cup as proof, the FA, and British journalists, still claimed that we were "moral" world champions. It was as if by not turning up, we'd taken the moral high ground. Pure nonsense.'

The backbone of the England team comprised: Copping, Bowden, Male, Moss, Drake, Hapgood and Bastin. The *Daily Express* called it: 'This Highbury occasion', and the *Daily Mirror* claimed that an 'Arsenal Armada' was about to set sail. The game's popular title – 'The Battle of Highbury', was apt, considering Mussolini's belief that 'the only beautiful thing in life is war'. It was rumoured that he'd already heard of Wilf Copping's reputation on the international stage. The Arsenal right back's mere appearance struck fear into the hearts of opponents. He rarely shaved on matchday, believing it gave him a meaner appearance. Not that he needed it. Ted Drake described Copping's temper as '. . . volcanic. He was just what was needed against Italy'. Wilf was built like a middleweight boxer anyway. After a stormy clash with

Bill Shankly in a 1933 England v Scotland game, Shanks had said of him: '. . . Copping had done me down the front of my leg. He had burst the stocking – the shin-pad was out – and cut my leg . . . he would have kicked you in your own backyard or in your own chair.'

Before the contest began, the England players also got wind of the fabulous bonuses which were on offer to the Italians if they won the return match at Highbury. A press leak revealed that the Italians stood to win £150 a man, a brand new Alfa Romeo car, and most importantly for them, exemption from the dreaded national service. 'It gave us another gee up,' confirmed George Male. 'That was money and riches way beyond our wildest dreams.' The Italians were supposedly amateurs, and the professional England players only received a £2 appearance fee. Copping always believed that three lions on the shirt was motivation enough.

The *Daily Mirror* claimed that a 'ten goal victory must be our aim', but the 54,000 crowd, boosted by a huge Italian contingent, realised that the match would be a red-hot battle. The Italian team was snapped at Victoria Station, glamorously suited and booted, with the following message from Mussolini ringing in their ears: 'You must make use of all your energy and will-power in order to obtain supremacy in all struggles on earth.' Ted Drake recalled seeing the Italians for the first time: 'They seemed to be from a different planet. They looked wealthy, healthy, and classically Latin. They were a good-looking bunch of lads. Then there was the England team, with broken teeth and cauliflower ears. We were never going to win any beauty contests.' The game began in sensational style. With scarcely a minute on the clock, Manchester City's Eric Brook put England 1–0 up, and he added another two minutes later. After fifteen minutes, Ted Drake scored England's third. Maybe the *Mirror*'s prediction wasn't quite so ridiculous after all. But the trouble on the pitch had already erupted. Just a minute after Brook had cracked England's opener, the Italian centre half and captain Monti broke his foot in an 'accidental' clash with Wilf Copping. The legend goes that Wilf deliberately removed him from the equation, but no photos verify this claim, and the radio commentator on the game just happened to be Copping's manager, George Allison, who conveniently glossed over the incident. George Male commented: 'Nothing would have surprised me with Wilf. He was so fired up for the game. But if he did break Monti's foot, he did it fairly subtlely. I certainly didn't see the stamp go in.'

The Italians promptly went ballistic, and England captain Eddie Hapgood bore the brunt of their fury. Italy's right-half scuttled over to him, thumped him in the face and broke his nose. Hapgood carried on playing, but later wrote in his book, *Football Ambassador*: '. . . it's a bit hard to play when somebody resembling an enthusiastic member of the Mafia is scraping his studs down your leg.' True enough, though Hapgood's book is a clear reflection of European hostilities of the time. Even without Monti, Italy continued to fight, literally and metaphorically. Through Meazzi, they'd pulled it back to 2–3 by the sixtieth minute, but Wilf Copping employed Pesciesque methods to ensure that the Italians got no further.

Towards the end of the first half he'd clashed with the Italian centre forward and during the interval, Copping inquired of the doctor how he was. The doctor informed him he 'wouldn't be back'. 'Bloody good job. He'd soon be back in the dressing room anyway,' came the reply. Employing his shoulder-charge in the second half, two other Italians also ended the game limping, and he simply terrified the rest of them, his body language suggesting that it wasn't a wise move to venture near England's penalty area. England somehow clung on to win 3–2, in arguably the filthiest football match ever played. The casualty list was extensive. Eric Brook suffered a hairline fracture to his elbow, Hapgood was taken to hospital to have his nose reset, and Drake, Bastin and Bowden all needed medical attention from Tom Whittaker.

In the treatment room after the game, there is a famous picture of all the aforementioned players, plus Copping, being treated. Ted Drake recalled: 'Tom Whittaker's treatment room was a thing of wonder in the sporting world. He had heat lamps, massage equipment, sponges, everything. Boxers, jockeys, and cricketers used to come from miles around to get treatment from Tom, because he really did have healing hands. Cliff Bastin's cartilage, for instance, regularly got dislocated during games. But Tom could always somehow manipulate it back into place. I was told that when Cliff later had it removed, it got put on display, because it was so disfigured.' Copping's expression is Mona Lisa-like. It has an elusive quality, somewhere between a grimace and a smile, which summed up the situation perfectly. He'd emerged from the pitch bruised and bloodied, so he was in obvious pain, but his reputation as football's hardman was confirmed, and against the world champions too. Though team-mates, and the watching Italian ambassador, claimed he'd played 'within the rules', FA officials, disgusted by what they'd seen, threatened to ban all future internationals. In typical FA fashion, they were immediately forced into a humiliating climbdown.

The press remained in typically bullish mood. The *Mirror* reported: 'Here is irrefutable proof that the Italians are world champions by name only.' *The Times* added: 'Can Italy really claim to be the best team in the world after this defeat?' George Male said: 'Despite the fact that Italy should probably have won, no one at the time would accept it. The seeds were sown for years of underachievement by England. Having said that, the match was unforgettable – and it was great to play it at Highbury.'

○ 'TIME TO MEET THE BOYS' ○

'I WAS JUST a lad from Southampton. I'd scored a few goals for the Saints, but to supplement my wages I still did shifts as a gasfitter. Then, when I got a call saying that Arsenal were interested in signing me, I immediately jumped into a different world. It was pure fantasy. You stepped into the marble halls, and it occurred to you "Bloody hell, I've arrived now". And that was before I'd even met the team!' Ted Drake's recollections of his first day at Highbury reflect the feelings of awe which many had when entering the stadium environs for the first time.

Drake was new manager George Allison's first signing, although Herbert Chapman had been tracking him for months. He recalls: 'To be honest, I didn't stop being bowled over by Highbury from the minute I arrived. The day I came up from Southampton – I arrived by train from Waterloo – there was a cabbie waiting for me. Somehow he knew who I was "Mr Drake," he said. "I'll be driving you to the ground." It sounds so simple, but in those days, most clubs didn't tend to drive you around by cab. Being chauffeured made me feel twenty feet tall. We swept through London, and arrived at the ground. The cabbie pulled up outside Highbury, and immediately, the commissionaire opened the door. "Good morning, Mr Drake," he said. "We've been expecting you." Now as I said, at that time I was a nobody, and to call a footballer anything other than "Drake" was very rare. After a minute or so, George Allison appeared, and said, "Good morning Ted, it's good to meet you." Ted? *Ted?* My boss at Southampton would sooner have shot himself than call me by my Christian name!

'At this time, the old wooden East Stand was there. There were no marble halls or anything like that, and yet Highbury still had a majesty about it that wasn't there at other big places. The first thing George did was walk me around the stadium. Now George was always immac-ulately dressed, and spoke in these really clipped tones. I remember his shoes were always immaculately polished, and he looked more like a bank clerk, to be honest. But he knew how to work Highbury's magic on you. We walked out of the players' tunnel, and on to the pitch. I couldn't get over the sheer scale of the place. The terraces seemed to go back for ever, and the newly completed West Stand was awe inspiring for its time. I was thinking to myself, How on earth am I going to get used to all of this? Then he told me that within five years, a brand new East Stand would be built, and it would take my breath away. I had absolutely no doubts that it would. George chit-chatted with me for a while, before fixing me with that beady stare of his, and saying, "Right – time to meet the boys."'

Ted Drake was taken to the dressing room, where 'the boys' were changing after a training session. This remained every inch Chapman's team, and Drake – who came to represent the dawn of the post-Chapman era – admitted he felt 'almost like an impostor'. Most insiders have testified to the sheer togetherness of the squad, and they didn't require group hugs to reaffirm the fact – not that such huddles would have been approved of in the thirties. The difficult economic situation clearly played a role. As George Male commented: 'Deep down all of us knew that we weren't just fighting for our first-team places at Arsenal, we were also fighting for our livelihoods. Many of us were footballers born and bred, so we knew that if it wasn't for football, we'd have nothing. Some of the other chaps, like Wilf Copping, had been miners, and realised just how tough real life could be. Herbert Chapman and George Allison never mentioned it, although they occasionally hinted at the fact that if we lost our first-team places, we'd face an uncertain future. We also knew the price we'd have to pay if we misbehaved, and George and Herbert knew that we knew.'

The Arsenal mix worked. Drake recalled: 'I walked in, and the first people I met were David Jack and Jack Lambert. It was a bit frightening, because I was sort of signed to replace them. David Jack had a hawkish face. He looked like an artist, who should have been wearing a smoking jacket and reclining on a chaise longue. His hair made him look even more aristocratic. He still made me very welcome, as did Jack Lambert, who said to me: "You're only the fifth player Arsenal have signed to replace me." And he still kept his place in the team, which was testament to his ability. Alex James was great too. He punched me on the arm, and mumbled in that heavy accent of his: "We've paid £8,000 for this guy, and he can't even comb his hair properly."'

'The guy I never properly hit it off with was Cliff Bastin. He was Arsenal's boy wonder, and I felt that his nose was pushed out of joint a bit when Arsenal signed me. I was a bit annoyed when his autobiography came out, because he basically said that he didn't think I was an A-grade striker. He was also a bit stand-offish, although by then, he was having hearing problems, so maybe that accounted for what I took to be his aloofness. But as team-mates, we got on fine. You don't have to be someone's best pal to link up well with them on the pitch. And with the maximum wage in operation, there was no squabbling over who was getting paid the most, which you get at a lot of clubs now.

'It's no surprise that the team was so fit. The facilities were so far ahead of Southampton's it's untrue. At the back of the Clock End, there was a court devoted entirely to playing head tennis, which most clubs didn't do at the time. It improved your first touch no end. There was also the most up to date gym equipment, and some tensile tubes which were designed to build up your leg muscles. It was such a well drilled bunch of players. George Allison didn't know a huge amount about the game, but the players did, and he was happy for people like Alex James to talk tactics. It was devastatingly simple too. Alex was the midfield link, who'd get the ball out quickly to Cliff Bastin, or Joe Hulme, and they'd square it in the box for myself or Jack Lambert.

'No other team could cope with it, because they didn't have the players. Pure and simple. The reason Arsenal got labelled 'boring Arsenal' is because other teams tried to copy us and turned it into long ball, yawn-yawn football. You couldn't copy what we were doing, because our players were far superior to theirs. But it *was* simple, and so easy for new chaps like myself or Crayston or Copping to fit in.'

The Gunners were criticised by several visiting managers in the thirties. George Male recalled: 'Everton always seemed to have a rough time when they came to Highbury. Dixie Dean never seemed to be able to score against us, and their manager always used to complain that we were dull, and played destructive football. It was pure jealousy.' Ted Drake commented: 'Once we played Grimsby at home. And their manager reckoned they had seventy per cent of the ball, and still lost five nil. He was going nuts, accusing us of stifling tactics, and all that. But the point was that his team didn't have the strikers to do us any damage. Then Herbie Roberts would snaffle the ball back off them, knock it to Alex, who'd just give it to the attackers. A journalist calculated that in several games, we'd score within fifteen seconds of breaking out of our own box. I don't call that dull. I call it devastatingly effective.'

Herbert Chapman once said: 'You can attack for too long.' And he was absolutely right. At some clubs, style and looking good is all that counts. But I think Arsenal fans at Highbury have a far more canny attitude. They know that there has to be an end product. Yes, you are paid to entertain. But you are also paid to win. In the thirties team, we always realised there needed to be balance between style and winning trophies. Arsenal fans understand that too. That's why the club has been so successful.'

○ BOO BOYS ○

BRYN JONES

THERE WAS always a flip side to the giant Highbury crowds of the 1930s. It certainly wasn't all bonhomie. As with the modern Arsenal side, continued success raised expectations to ludicrously high levels. George Male recalled: 'When Arsenal lost at Walsall in early 1933, that's when I first noticed a real change. We won the league that year, but I noticed that the crowd was very quick to get on our backs if things didn't go according to the script at home. In fairness, they were picking up on Herbert Chapman's feeling that the team needed urgent rebuilding work. All of us – players and fans – were learning that even a title-winning season might not ultimately be considered a vintage year. The more you won, the more was expected of you.'

Throughout the 1936–37 season, Ted Drake recalled ' . . . my astonishment that crowds were now on Alex James's case. He'd admittedly slowed a bit, and wasn't getting on too well with George Allison, but actually to moan at him? Frankly I was astonished.' The well-oiled Arsenal machine was beginning – ever so slightly – to splutter. Drake also remembered ' . . . the crowds in the last season before the war were particularly demanding. We ended up in fifth place. Not good enough by our standards. Teams like Sunderland, Preston, and Wolves were catching up with us fast. The party was over. Some of the players reckoned it may have been because people were edgy due to the worries about the political situation in Europe. But I reckon that Arsenal fans were simply becoming more and more demanding, and we'd lost our sparkle on the pitch.'

Herbert Chapman was the first to notice supporters 'getting at' underperforming stars. All of Chapman's major signings initially struggled to adapt to life at Highbury. David Jack's chain-smoking worsened during his early days at the club, as he laboured under the expectations of replacing Buchan, and of living up to the enormous transfer fee. Beneath Jack's ice cool exterior lay a worried man for a year or so. George Male recalled: 'None was more confident in his ability than David Jack – but even he fretted about the crowd. I remember him saying a couple of times: "It wasn't like this at Bolton."' With so much resting on his shoulders, Alex James also received occasional abuse from the crowd in his early days, particularly due to his reluctance to shoot on goal. 'At times,' argued George Male, 'Alex seemed to want to pass the ball to death. The crowd didn't always share that desire.'

Via the medium of his *Daily Express* column, Chapman explained that he believed barrackers should be cautioned by club officials, and if necessary ejected from the stadium. His players begged to differ. 'The fans paid their money, and as long as it wasn't offensive, they could grumble as much as they wanted. The players were very open minded on that.' Both Male and Drake concurred on the fact that because of the club's proximity to the West End, and Arsenal's aura as a wealthy club, the traditional view that the Highbury crowd consisted purely of the working man is a nonsense.

'Even then,' argued Drake, 'you'd see well-dressed men in plus-fours in the crowd. They came to the ground because it was the thing to do – to watch the Arsenal – not purely because they were traditional fans. Once, I had a word with a gentleman who was dressed in a really well-cut suit. He had money – you could tell. And after Eddie Hapgood took a throw, he piped up and said to Eddie, "Now get yourself moving to support the attack, because you've not done anything else this game." And Eddie turned around and gave him a real earful. But there are moaners in every crowd, and there will be as long as football is played. I would always argue that the Arsenal crowd is a crowd which needs something to get *them* going, rather than the other way around. It's not like at Newcastle, say, where the fans will cheer if you put eleven dustbins wearing black and white on the pitch. The Arsenal crowd will cheer loudly when *you've* impressed *them*.'

One Arsenal player of that era was 'got at' more than any other. Bryn Jones arrived from Wolves in June 1938 for a gargantuan £14,000. His transfer fee caused shock waves to travel through the football world, and was even discussed in the Houses of Parliament. Several leading journalists of the era claimed that the fee may never be exceeded. In September 2001, the *Observer Sport Monthly* included Jones in their ten biggest 'waste of money in football history list', and cal-culated that, allowing for inflation, Jones would have cost around £28 million in the modern era. A nippy, pacy forward who'd performed well in a decent Wolves side, Jones was dubbed the 'new Alex James'. The well-oiled machine struggled to accommodate a free spirit like Jones.

Ted Drake recalled: 'I thought that Bryn would have trouble at Arsenal as soon as I saw him. It was just a hunch, but I sensed that he wasn't comfortable with the publicity of the fee. He was also used to the team operating around him at Wolves, but at Highbury, he had to fit in with *us*. Within a couple of weeks, it was clear that he was never going to adapt quickly enough. Arsenal were in the process of finishing fifth that year, and very quickly, we all thought he was a luxury player who played well when the team played well, rather than a James type, who could drag the team along by the bootlaces when things weren't going well. After Jones faded alarmingly at Highbury against Derby, the match reporter from the *Derby Evening Telegraph* wrote: 'Arsenal have a big problem. Spending £14,000 on Bryn Jones has not brought the needed thrust into the attack. The little Welsh inside-left is suffering from too much publicity, and is obviously worried . . . his limitations are marked.'

The Highbury crowd soon turned on Jones. George Male recalled: 'Bryn would come in at half-time or at the end of the match in his early days, and he'd be shaking. "They hate me, they hate me," he'd be saying of the Highbury crowds.' The *Islington Gazette* ran a story flagging up 'the sad and, some would say, shoddy sight of Bryn Jones being criticised en masse by home fans'. George Male added: 'Bryn was the right man at the wrong time. He was neat and nippy, but he didn't fit in quickly enough. And for me, he didn't have the mindset for playing at the biggest club of all. Wolves was a big club, but not on a par with the Arsenal. I don't think he really ever took to London life, either. I think the Arsenal crowds viewed him as a convenient scapegoat because things weren't going well. But a number of players had allowed their standards to slip.'

The football world at large claimed that Jones's signing proved George Allison was taking the 'Bank of England' tag too far. Frustrated Arsenal fans sung of the team's big spending: 'No more money in the bank, what's to do about it? Let's put them to bed.' In 1938, Jones was dropped from Arsenal's first team in a bid to pull him out of the limelight. Expecting to run out in front of the proverbial one man and his dog at a reserve game, Jones was astonished to see 33,000 had turned up – simply out of curiosity to see how the world's most expensive player coped in these surroundings. 'Bryn could never find a hiding place from the fact that he cost so much,' added George Male.

Jones was also an extremely unlucky player. Restored to the first-team at the start of the 1939–40 season, his displays drew plaudits from several leading newspapers, including the *Daily Telegraph*. 'Jones is finally showing the Arsenal fans just why he was worth so much money.' Yet all three games are now expunged from official records, after the outbreak of the war meant the suspension of the league programme. At just twenty-seven years of age, the Welshman was forced to take an enforced six-year break from the game, and a sizeable part of his career was lost. When the league programme resumed in 1945, Jones – now a veteran at thirty-three – played for the Gunners for another three years. With the pressure no longer on him, George Male commented: 'Bryn was a changed man, and although the pace had gone, he was a great help to the youngsters. Finally the crowd laid off him, and began to appreciate his skills. But there was always a certain sadness about him, because with his skills, he should really have become an Arsenal legend.'

○ CONFESSIONS ○

THE TERRACE SWEEPER

'Often, apprentices would be responsible for sweeping clean the terraces after home matches, but after the war, the club started to advertise in the local press for sweepers after the games. As a fourteen-year-old lad, it was just a great thrill

for me to be on those terraces at all. The rubbish you found after games was incredible, and it spoke volumes about people's social habits at the time. The first thing you noticed was the fag ends. There were hundreds of thousands of them – quite literally. I reckon pretty much everyone smoked their way through matches back then, and if you consider that the crowds were always around the 50,000 mark, blimey, that's going to be a lot of dog-ends, isn't it? At Christmas it was a bit different. Suddenly, you'd find the remains of cigar-ends, which had presumably been given out as Christmas presents. Then, it would be back to the dog-ends for the rest of the season.

There was also a huge amount of programmes and newspapers strewn all over the place. The terraces were white afterwards. From a distance, it looked like there had been a blizzard over Highbury. Looking back, it's staggering to think how many programmes got dropped during the course of a game. When you consider that nowadays, programmes from that era are sold for for twenty or thirty pounds, it's a bloody shame I didn't pick them up and keep them. It would have been a nice little pension for me.

'Now – you told me to be frank with you – so I'll give you the full truth. You noticed that a lot of the paper, especially in the middle of the Laundry End, was soaking wet, even on dry days. When I first started, I conscientiously picked up everything, but I noticed that it stank a bit. Some of the others laughed at me because all the wet stuff would splatter all over your clothes. It was because blokes had peed everywhere. You could understand why. A packed terrace, a few beers on a cold day, and no way of reaching the toilet. It makes you realise why so few women attended in those days. So that was quite unpleasant – the pee and its smell!

'Blokes would often smuggle in bottles of beer or whisky and pass it around, and down it all during the game. No one frisked you in those days, and you didn't get idiots throwing things like now. And a lot of these bottles were left behind and blokes had peed in those too. So, cleaning up after a game was a slow, old business, because bottles full of urine tend to weigh you down. As much as possible, you'd try to kick everything down the bottom and pile it up in the hope that someone else would finish it off for you. They could deal with all the wet! You found a lot of other strange things left on the terrace. One of my pals claimed to have found a gun once, though I'm not sure I believed him. But you'd get clothing and shoes all the time. I think that maybe they'd got pulled off during crowd surges, and the bloke who'd lost it couldn't fight through to find their stuff.

'I found a few used condoms, which is very odd. It beggars the questions: how? and did anyone notice? I even found an old kitchen tap once. It makes you wonder. But it's the pee I remember most of all.'

Arthur Whatley

THE PROGRAMME SELLER

'My pitch was in the junction between Avenell and Blackstock Road. In those days, you really had to fight for your pitch. You'd collect your bundle of programmes first thing in the morning from the man at the ground, and be there in place for the early birds at eight o'clock. Even at that time on a matchday, the place was buzzing. I think that people just like the feel of being in and around football matches. You need very quick hands to take money from the punters and hand the programme in return. This could be really tricky on cold days. The best part of my job was getting my regulars coming up to me and having a chat with them. They were like my friends, and over the years, Dad would start to bring junior along. It was great how the tradition followed on from fathers to sons.

'Now, I'm not a miserable sod who always goes on about how much better things were in the forties. I think that seeing that era as some kind of golden age is ridiculous. I'll give you an example of why. You'd often get people pushing and shoving to get a programme and some would grab one and then run off. They'd happily do that in an era when the so-called blitz mentality had seen us through the war. Most people were honest though, and someone in the crowd would step out and trip them up or catch them and give them a bloody good clip round the ear. Once it got a bit embarrassing because one bloke had grabbed about ten of them and ran straight past into a copper. The copper just happened to be his brother, so I'd imagine that family relations were a bit strained for a while.

'The thing you really had to look out for in those days was blokes selling pirate programmes. That happened a lot back then, and it was easier to do it when programmes were printed on old white or red paper. There would be tell-tale signs like fainter printing or something like that. You could get in trouble with club officials if any pirate copies were found in your bundle. But there were a lot of "Del Boy" types on the prowl at that time – spivs from the war who couldn't give all that sort of thing up. In the end, someone usually caught up with them.

'I'm a big Arsenal fan, so after I'd sold my bundle, I'd go to the ground to watch the game. You'd often see a lot of the programmes on the road and all the

other mess that a crowd brings with it. The weird thing was that I never actually read the programme at all. I was always more interested in actually watching the match than reading about it, to be honest. I gave up my pitch when the club started charging tax on what you earned. But I'll always remember looking around and seeing all these people moving towards the stadium. I love crowds and it was great to be there on matchdays. On Saturday afternoons, it felt like Highbury was the most important place on earth.'

Clive Rice

○ ON THE SILVER SCREEN ○

IN 1931, a TV crew from Shepherd's Bush rang Herbert Chapman to see if he was willing to allow his players to introduce themselves to the camera, and sing a few songs in order to liven up a rather dull cinema newsreel which was due to be shown in London picture houses. On the face of it, the request was straightforward, but back in an age when moving images of players were very much a new concept, TV crews were often regarded with suspicion. George Male recalled: 'After training one morning, Chapman pulled us to one side and said, "Look chaps, the TV crew want to come along to meet you, and are asking if you could sing a bit of a jokey song or something." It was strange, because Alex James was the one who mixed with the jet set, and he was the one who was anti the idea. "No, no," he said. "I'm not a performing seal." I couldn't understand his attitude, except that he liked to be different. The rest of us thought it would be a giggle, so we agreed to it.'

Two weeks later, a one minute snippet of 'Life at Highbury' was broadcast on newsreels across the capital. Due to introduce his 'fine bunch of lads', Chapman had developed a sore throat and gave the responsibility to Tom Whittaker. One by one, the players were introduced by Whittaker, and then broke into a song: 'Good Company'.

The snippet still survives on the official *History Of Arsenal* DVD, and as George Male commented, the only one who opted out of singing was the uncharacteristically shy Alex James. It wasn't the first time that Arsenal had featured in public broadcasting history. The Gunners' home match in 1927 against Sheffield United was the first BBC radio broadcast of a match, and Charlie Buchan's goal the first ever heard described to BBC radio listeners.

Chapman himself was already aware of the power of media influence. For a number of years, he'd written a *Sunday Express* column, which raised his profile throughout Europe. His autobiography, *Herbert Chapman On Football*, published posthumously in 1934, attracted mixed reactions. Many in the footballing world condemned it for betraying the secrets of the trade. It was a bizarre reaction, given that the book was essentially a collection of his *Sunday Express* articles.

In 1932, Chapman had advocated giving Arsenal players individual numbers. The FA overruled him, claiming it would 'give rise to increasing vanity and ego among the players'. Yet, by allowing in TV cameras to Highbury, and allowing Tom Whittaker to introduce the Arsenal players separately, he'd already taken the first steps towards creating individual identities of his players in the public's eye. George Male commented: 'Chapman used to think that treating all players the same was bad management. Although he insisted we play as a unit, he realised there were different ways of motivating players and, if necessary, disciplining them. So for instance, Alex James got treated a bit differently, but he was the star of the team with all the pressures to perform, so by and large, we accepted it.' Bizarrely, in June 1931, Chapman had agreed with the Arsenal board's suggestion that televised football should be banned in the interests of the game. He argued that along with inclement weather, televised football was a sure-fire way of driving down crowd figures. Interestingly, the meeting took place without Arsenal director George Allison.

Allison had been doing BBC radio commentaries for years. At his height, his clipped tones and deployment of the *Radio Times*' football grid, could attract wireless audiences of over ten million people. Allison was furious with the board, and the manager's decision. George Male claims: 'It's probably the only decision Chapman ever made where you could say he lacked a bit of foresight, but first and foremost, he was a football man.' George Allison was something else besides. 'Frankly, George knew bugger all about football,' explained Ted Drake, 'but with his background in the newspaper industry and in the media, he knew exactly how to keep Arsenal in the spotlight. The world of show business had courted Arsenal for years. Throughout the 1930s, Alex James had proved adept at having his photo taken with assorted sports celebrities. Silent film star Buster Keaton visited Highbury in the early thirties, as did music hall duo Flanagan and Allen. Thanks to Allison's Hollywood connections, Jean Harlow and Mary Pickford also met the players at that time. 'Ah yes, Mary Pickford,' laughed Ted Drake. 'She was a real stunner, and when she came to Highbury she had some shots taken with the players. As I recall, she was quite taken with Eddie Hapgood.'

It wasn't the first time that Hapgood's looks had got him noticed by the rich and famous. George Male recalled that when England visited Italy in 1934, 'You could see Benito Mussolini looking at Eddie with jealousy in his eyes. We had some pictures taken with the Italian supremo, and he kept looking at Eddie's jawline. Mussolini pushed his head back at a ridiculous angle to hide his double chin, trying to out-Hapgood Eddie. But eventually, the Hapgood jawline did finally make it on to the silver screen.'

In 1938, Allison was approached by G & S films to see if he was willing to allow the production company to come to Highbury to film *The Arsenal Stadium Mystery*, based on a novel by Leonard Gribble. Allison virtually bit their hands off, especially when he realised that Inspector Slade – who finally cracks the case – was to be played by his old friend Leslie Banks. Several of the players were more interested in the filthy lucre on offer, and the prospect of working with Hollywood siren Greta Gynt. It also led to some resentment in the squad.

Ted Drake recalled: 'George called all of us into the changing room one day – he did have a lovely, calm voice on him did George – and he said: "Now look chaps, we've had an offer from this film company who want to make *The Arsenal Stadium Mystery*. It's a nice little thriller, and there is an opening for any of you chaps who want to make a few bob over the summer." In those days, you weren't paid as much during the summer months as for the rest of the year. So we said: "How much, boss?" And he said fifty pounds a week. Well, there was nearly a riot in there. The most any of us earned was eight pounds a week. This was huge money for us, which could go towards our pensions, or buying a house! There was a catch, though. George said: "Only seven of you can do it." Straightaway, some of the boys had their noses pushed out of joint. What infuriated people more was when George said, "I've asked Alex James to be in it." We weren't happy about that, because Alex had left a couple of years before. He didn't play for us any more. George reckoned Alex was a world-renowned name, who'd put bums on seats. But we stood our ground, and eventually, he backed down. Alex couldn't have been in it anyway, as it turned out, because we all had to be in genuine playing sequences against Brentford. Once we'd sorted out a few small issues, filming began. It was tremendous fun, and phenomenally well paid for that time.'

The story was based around a mythical friendly match between Arsenal and The Trojans. One of the Trojans' players is poisoned at half-time, and collapses and dies on the pitch. The culprit, as it turns out, is the Trojans manager. Interspersed between the unfolding drama is *bona fide* football action. Visitors Brentford, who played their league game at Highbury on 6 May 1939 sportingly wore an unfamiliar black and white strip in order to simulate the Trojans. Alf Kirchen's and Ted Drake's goals, which gave Arsenal a 2–0 win, are therefore preserved on the film – a rare thing indeed for the 1930s.

Several scenes are shot within the marble halls and Highbury's dressing rooms, and the rest was shot at Elstree Studios. George Allison's acting is a bit on the wooden side, but poor Bryn Jones was unable to escape the burden of his transfer fee even on celluloid. 'He cost as much as the war,' claimed the voice which introduces the Arsenal players. George Male recalled: 'We were in a middle studio. I think there was a western being filmed on one side, and an Egyptian one on the other. We were mixing with cowboys, Indians and beautiful Cleopatra lookalikes. The funniest moment occurred at the stadium itself, when Les Compton did some publicity shots with Greta Gynt, who was a very attractive young lady. Les was only nineteen, but it was the only time I really saw him lost for words when she came across and sat on his knee. Les went bright red. Some of the boys weren't all that happy – because of the money. There was a suggestion that we divvy it up for a whole squad pool, but then we *had* worked through the summer. As it happened, other things intervened, and the matter was forgotten.'

George Allison was always extremely keen on self-promotion. On the back cover of his autobiography, he bills himself as 'the friend of kings and statesmen – the confidant of players'. This was no idle boast. Allison talked tactics with King George V at the 1936 FA Cup final, and via this film, he immortalised many of his players. Allison – who appointed himself technical director of the film – didn't do so well financially as his players. Believing that filming would take a few weeks to complete, he signed a deal which covered him for a month only. The players opted for a deal where they received £50 for five weeks, and ten guineas per day thereafter. Filming lasted nearly three months. 'Every time a scene was messed up,' recalled Ted Drake 'you'd be praying that they would extend the filming so you'd get those extra guineas.'

The Arsenal Stadium Mystery was only a moderate box-office success in London. The main issue was that local residents had other things on their minds than visits to the cinema. George Male recalled: 'Behind the scenes in the film, we knew the good times were coming to an end. Many of us were already considering our options with regard to the imminent outbreak of the war. We knew that our playing careers would be placed on hold. We were concerned about our families, and scared to death about what might happen to our children. The papers were already suggesting the war could be a long one, and if it was, who's to say that our careers wouldn't be over? Or whether we'd return at all? It was a sad and difficult time for the Arsenal team, as it was for everyone in the country.'

Arsenal's 2–0 win over Brentford, now part of celluloid legend, was the team's last first-class game for six years.

1940s

N.5

○ BOMBED OUT ○

IN LATE 1939, Arsenal season-ticket holders received a letter from Gunners secretary-manager George Allison, informing them that the ground had been requisitioned by the public authorities. Lesley Waters recalls: 'World War Two was already well under way, and the letter didn't really come as any major surprise. I remember Allison's letter finished with the line, "I look forward to the time when all Arsenal supporters will be able to foregather on the Highbury ground as they have done in the past." It brought home the full enormity of what was going on. It was the final proof, if any were needed, that normal life was over.'

The requisitioning of Highbury brought home the full enormity of the conflict to the players as well. Ted Drake recalled: 'We all knew that war was coming, of course. As players, we got copies of board minutes, and even years before that, there had been lots of talk about using club buildings for shelter in the event of an air-raid. I seem to recall that someone also came up with a plan to camouflage the stadium and try to disguise the stands as much as possible. Quite how they planned to hide a football stadium, I don't really know.'

Of the forty-two players on the staff, forty joined the forces, and nine would be dead by the end of the war. Arsenal players were scattered far and wide across the globe. George Male spent much of the war in Palestine, Bryn Jones in Italy; and Leslie Compton in India. Arsenal players remained in demand throughout the conflict and made regular appearances in regiment games, and war league contests. Up and coming striker Reg Lewis recalled what life was like at that time: 'As a player it was tough. You dreamed of playing at Highbury in front of thousands, but instead I ended up playing football at White Hart Lane, our adopted home in regional wartime matches. I was stationed at Shoeburyness, and I'd be given leave to come to London to play. They cut crowds at those games to a maximum of 25,000 just in case . . . You got on with it because you wanted to play football, but all the time you were pining for Highbury. What a mess that was in!'

From the moment war was declared, Highbury buzzed with activity. In keeping with the conflict (it was granted the title 'phoney war' during late 1939), the first few months at Highbury were quiet. Highbury was transformed into a stranglehold for the ARP (Air Raid Precautions). The pitch was used twice daily as part of the Islington Borough ARP's training programme. Before he was assigned to Palestine, George Male regularly played in matches against the local ARP wardens. He recalled: 'At first, many of us were still being paid by the club, so we played in some Combination games, and some friendlies. I use the term "friendlies" in the loosest possible sense of the word, as some of those wardens couldn't wait to get stuck into professional footballers. Most of them were Spurs' fans, I reckon! But playing football at Highbury during that time was very odd. The mood of the nation was one of hanging around, in the early months. Playing football was what I did for a living, and yet I'd look around Highbury and see the barrage balloon above the stand, and the bomb shelter furniture under the Laundry End. It was all quite unreal, to be honest.'

With the practice pitch behind the Clock End used for storing building materials; the West Stand as an air-raid shelter; and the East Stand now doubling as a first aid centre, and an air-raid wardens' reporting post, local resident Mark Watts comments: 'The ground was as much a part of the community without the football, as it was when normal service went ahead.' The following extract from the *Warden's Post* proves just what an unnerving experience the night patrol at Highbury was for those whose playing careers were on hold:

> The midnight patrol of the night shift round the Arsenal Stadium is always rather weird to those of us who are so accustomed to the bustle and noise of the vast peacetime crowds. Tom Whittaker has discovered that a run around the ground about eight p.m. is a good time to spot light from those back windows that are such a bane to all wardens who like to do their job as it should be done. From the top of Spion Kop, for instance, one can see the back windows of several streets in our sector so, when a light is spotted, Tom stands and gives the signal when one of the others has found the right house and got the light well doused.
>
> Last week, the moon was nearly full and the night clear. One could see both goals with ease and we paused to look back from the highest point. Memories came crowding in to each of us. What

great matches and what great players are connected with that green stretch of turf that lay so sombre in the moonlight . . . We went back over the years recalling incidents, goals, matches, and above all names: Jack Butler, Dean, Blythe. Suddenly high up in the great East Stand a light flickered and as quickly vanished. Our conversation stopped dead and we stood like statues. The light came again but lower down this time. 'Who's there?' we cried . . . but it was only the nightwatchman on his rounds, so we returned to the post and were soon deep in an argument on the relative menace of incendiary or HE bombs.

The phoney war became devastatingly real to local residents when, on the night of 16 April 1941, around 550 German bombers dropped over 100,000 incendiaries on London. Dozens of incendiaries rained down on the streets around Highbury.

Local resident Harry Stone recalls: 'St Thomas's Road was reduced to a pile of rubble. So was Blackstock Road. It was chaos. People were walking around in a daze. We'd been sheltering in the West Stand that night, and you could tell from the deafening bangs that we were really getting it. You wondered if anything would actually be left standing when you came out. When we did step out next morning, we walked past the Laundry End and we couldn't believe what we saw.

'There was the roof – all crumpled and smouldering. It was the first time we realised what aerial bombardments were really all about. After a while, we all developed a hardened shell to seeing houses flattened, but seeing Highbury like this – I can still picture it now. What had happened was that five incendiaries had come through the Laundry End roof, and fallen on to all the bunks and stuff underneath. Now, I'm no expert, but incendiaries consisted of phosphorous, and although they don't explode, they set fire to anything they touch. All the mattresses went up in flames, and the intense heat had made the roof melt and collapse. When they did some further investigations, they found that the holes in the roof were no bigger than the size of a football – which is ironic really, isn't it? So if all that stuff hadn't been on the terrace, it wouldn't have gone up.

'What was quite funny was that this old fella was having a right go at one of these wardens, and he was pointing to the roof and shouting, "Why the bloody hell didn't you notice and put that lot out when it went up in flames?" And this warden shouted back, "Because we were trying to put out fires near people's houses, and they are a bit more important than your precious bloody football ground." And this old fella came back, "Well you didn't get that right either – my house (he pointed to a pile of bricks) is now just a bloody heap of rubble." And both blokes looked at each other and fell about laughing. This old fella had lost his house, but he still seemed more worried about the Arsenal. Looking back, I suppose it's ridiculous, but that was how it was in the war. You would try and get any kind of black humour from the worst situations.'

A year earlier, a 1,000 lb bomb fell on to the practice ground behind the South Bank, killing two RAF pilots who were sitting in the hut. Two of their comrades walked away with barely a scratch. Genuine tragedy behind the dark humour. Six years of war left Arsenal with a massive problem. With no income from gate receipts, and massive expense required for repairs to the stadium, Arsenal entered the post-war era with a (then) huge £200,000 debt. Admittedly, the club would eventually reclaim the money on insurance. But just like the rest of the country, Arsenal faced an uncertain future. The Bank of England club was bust.

○ WHERE'S MY FOOTBALL? ○

THE ARSENAL PLAYERS who returned after the end of hostilities in time for the 1946–47 season received a rather unpleasant shock. Ted Drake, whose career was in limbo after he damaged his spine during a wartime match recalled: 'We got a letter through the post informing us that league football would resume in August 1946. But the club also informed us that instead of earning the eight pounds a week we received back in 1939, our pay was to be cut to seven pounds a week. On the one hand, it was great to know that things were getting back to normal, but seven pounds a week? I mean, bloody hell!' American baseball star Babe Ruth, who'd labelled Arsenal players 'bloody idiots' for putting up with such meagre wages in the 1930s, was instrumental in ensuring that top US baseball stars received a fifty per cent pay hike at the restart of their new season. 'In fairness though,' explained George Male, 'America didn't receive the same kind of physical damage that Britain had. For most of us, football was a sign that things were righting themselves. And the quicker we could get to Highbury, the better.'

For those Arsenal fans who had been away with the armed forces, the prospect of Division One football at Highbury was greeted with feverish expectation. Stan Chorley recalls: 'Some of my mates and me had been to watch Arsenal at White Hart Lane during the war. We did it when we were on leave. Horrible it was – walking into that place. But we had to do it. At least we got to see Stan Matthews in an Arsenal shirt, because he guested for us a few times. And I suppose they had to get Arsenal fans into White Hart Lane somehow. It's amazing to think that some people hadn't been to Highbury for nearly seven years. In those days, there wasn't the build up to games that there is today. It was announced almost casually in the newspapers. Something like, "The full league programme will resume on Saturday." Can you imagine how long the press would go on about it today? There would be endless supplements. You'd never hear the last of it. But in the pubs I drank in, there was little talk of anything else. These were hard times. Meat and clothes were still rationed. I'd lost two of my brothers. Lots of my pals had lost their lives in the Blitz. It was a dark time. But the thought of watching Arsenal at Highbury again was the light at the end of the tunnel.'

David Baines recalls the atmosphere among Highbury residents: 'We'd helped clear the old North Bank roof away after that had come down, and we then did some work on the Clock End which had taken a pounding during the war. We needed our football club back at Highbury. It was as simple as that.' Even the normally reserved *Islington Gazette* captured the mood of the time, commenting: 'For weeks, the talk around these parts has been of little else. The Arsenal – admittedly with a much changed line-up from the last time they played here – are about to return home.'

On 18 August, the Gunners took on Wolves in the opening game of the season. For Highbury debutant Reg Lewis, it was a time of huge excitement: 'I don't think I slept for two nights after George Allison hinted to me that I would be playing in the Wolves match. All of us knew that on the big scale, wartime football was a case of treading water. For the Wolves game, we were bouncing up and down in the dressing room for ages. It was pure nervous energy. George told me to stop, or I'd be worn out before the game had even begun. We ran out – it was a beautiful day. Highbury was packed. It was a totally joyful feeling, and I scored too. But it wasn't exactly a memorable day for our defence – Wolves thrashed us 6–1.'

The debacle at home to Wolves gave an indication of precisely how much work Arsenal needed to do in order to blend elements of the new team. Arsenal's domination of English football was over, even though more titles and cups would soon be forthcoming. Two factors combined to ensure that the club remained England's most high-profile team. Firstly, the name Arsenal was still world famous, helped by the fact that Male and Bastin – heroes of the thirties – played on. Secondly, demob happy crowds flocked to Highbury, week in, week out. Arsenal's average crowd figure rose by 5,000 on pre-war levels, and throughout the rest of the forties, Highbury crowds rarely, if ever, fell beneath the 45,000 mark. Improved rail connections meant it was increasingly easier for those outside the capital to get to games. Some Arsenal historians have suggested that relatively few away fans attended matches, but as the two following accounts suggest, that wasn't always the case: the first by David Jones recalls the post-war mood of Highbury crowds:

'In the thirties, Arsenal fans got very blasé about the team, and football in general. That changed after the war. Sometimes before the war you wouldn't have gone if, say, Grimsby were coming to Highbury. But now, you had to go. Everyone seems to think these days that we had money to burn in the 1940s. But a lot of blokes still worked really long hours just to scratch a living. People still didn't tend to wear their colours back then. But that doesn't mean we were any less passionate. Although there still wasn't huge amounts of choreographed singing, there was cheering all the time, applause, and rattles. What I started to notice was that the make-up of the crowd changed. Accents were altering. You could tell just from the cut of a fella's suit what background he had. And I often found myself standing next to someone from Hertfordshire or Buckinghamshire or whatever. Even then, Highbury was quite middle-classy in comparison to other London grounds. It wasn't so much the working man who dominated the ground like they had done. I also saw a lot more away fans. There wasn't any segregation then, and you'd see pockets of Villa fans come down. They'd wear claret and blue trousers. Portsmouth also used to have a real following; often sailors, who could be a bit nasty. Mostly, it was quite good-natured. Sometimes, away fans would walk around the perimeter track to swap ends at half-time, and we'd applaud them. There just wasn't that much hassle, because we were all so glad to get our football back.'

David Spencer's recollections are also vivid: 'It was fun at the time, but dangerous in the light of Hillsborough. Sometimes the Laundry End was so full that your arms were pinned to your sides. If you were clever, you'd get to the ground early, so you could stand in front of a crush barrier. That way, no one could do dominoes on you. Sometimes, when Liverpool came to Highbury, pockets of their fans would deliberately shove you down the terraces. They could get quite rough, the Scousers. It's a miracle no one was killed back then at Highbury. There were no real safety measures in place. I think the club finally got to hear about it, because in the programme, and in the *Gazette*, they advised you not to bring your kids. Imagine that now – don't bring your kids to games!

'But it was dangerous. It was a sport to be watched by men with no responsibilities. It was a loud crowd in the 1940s. No chants, but cheering and shouting, and you'd get odd groups singing their own pub songs. I still go to Highbury today, and the crowd is far more choreographed in all four stands. But it was noisier back in the forties on a consistent basis. Lots of cheering and shouting for the whole game.'

○ 'THERE'S WOMEN IN OUR PLACES' ○

AS WITH OTHER forms of social history, women have remained hidden from football's past until comparatively recently. There are several reasons for this. Most football tomes focus on the game played by men – rather than gathering recollections from fans. It is also a fact that many women used to 'accompany their men' to games, rather than attend a match themselves, or with a group of girlfriends. Newsreel footage and TV cameras would invariably focus on events on the pitch, rather than build up the matchday experience, and focus on the fans. And ultimately, it is a truism to say that, until the last decade, the overwhelming majority of those attending games were male.

Back in the 1930s, women played a distinctly peripheral role in football. George Male recalled that at home games, young women would often wait at the entrance to try and gain a glimpse of Cliff Bastin and Eddie Hapgood. 'On one occasion,' Male said, 'a girl gave Cliff a huge smacker on the cheek. Being Cliff, he just waltzed past as if nothing had happened. He was once approached by two little girls in the streets around Highbury, who asked him the score in the Arsenal match. When he told them that Arsenal had won, the girls shrieked, "Hurrah, Arsenal are top of the league," and ran off.' Ted Drake remembered: 'One old dear would stand near the tunnel and shout, "I love you Alex," as Alex James ran by. She sometimes gave him a bouquet of flowers. The lads who played under Herbert knew her by name. I think it was Lil.'

It is extremely difficult to judge accurately how many women attended pre-war games at Highbury. Celia Raparsadia recalls: 'There were pockets of girls who went. It was one of the few places where you could be yourself. You could scream and shout and your mum and dad weren't there to tell you that you weren't behaving in a ladylike manner. The main problem was that the toilet facilities for blokes were bad enough. They were almost non-existent for women. Blokes could go where they stood if necessary. Women didn't really have that option. Then if you think that women tended to have babies earlier in those days, you needed to think, Who will look after the kids? If the bloke was at the game, who looked after the bairns? And there was the whole thing that football was a bloke's thing where they could drink, swear, and smoke, without the missus nagging them. Society's rules were different then. It wasn't the done thing to intrude on a man's thing before the war.'

By the post-war era, social stereotypes were changing. With huge numbers of men away fighting between 1939 and 1945, women were required to do their bit in factories. When the conflict ended, not all were willing to return to their pigeon-holed pre-war existence. Celia Raparsadia recalls: 'For the last two years of the war, I worked in the munitions factory in Finchley. I was single at that time, and the money was good. I liked the feeling of making my own way in the world. I'd been to Arsenal twice in the thirties. You saw some girls there, but it was almost like they were being dragged along by their chaps. After the war, more and more women started to go because the war had encouraged them to have more self-confidence – to do things because you wanted to do them, not because you were being told to do it. Five of us from the Finchley factory would go during the late 1940s. We'd stop in a pub and order a beer each. At first, the barman thought we were from another planet. Women ordering beer and going to football? It just wasn't done.

'But by the 1950s, there were more and more girls going in groups. It became a bit easier to go by then, too. A bit of the post-war football craze had died down, and there was a bit more space on the terraces, as the crowds fell slightly. But football was still overwhelmingly male. You'd get on to the Laundry End and there were clouds of cigarette smoke and the smell of beer. A lot of girls were put off by the testosterone, I think.

'We usually stood on the Clock End, but sometimes on the Laundry End. The Laundry End was always more raucous. People used to say it was the working-class end, where the carpenters and chippies and gasmen from the local area stood. The Clock End was seen as being posher because it was closer to the tube and you needed money to travel in from Hertfordshire or Buckinghamshire or wherever. Whereas North Bankers had walked in from Islington. At first, we'd get a lot of stupid sexist jokes. Some blokes would say: "There's women in our places," or they'd ask sarcastically if we could make them a cup of tea or get them some dinner. Then you'd get your overprotective blokes, who'd try to stop everyone swearing. They'd say: "But there are ladies present." They were well meaning, but it just goes to show that we were like aliens in a man's world. They couldn't cope with women at Highbury! They'd look at us like we had two heads or something.'

The gradual increase of women attending games wasn't the only social change to occur at post-war Highbury. In 1949, the *Islington Gazette* reported that several thousand Islington residents, having been dehoused or evacuated during the war, opted against returning to the district. A steady influx of Italians (many of whom had been POWs), Greeks and Cypriots took their place. Celia Raparsadia recalls: 'You'd walk around the streets and see that the area was changing. Many of the old shops had gone, and in their places, Italian and Greek businesses had sprung up. You'd see specialist Italian bakers and pasta shops all over the place. Inevitably, many of these fellas began going to Arsenal. I think we've always had a fairly cosmopolitan crowd. One day, I found myself standing next to a good-looking Italian chap, with whom I immediately struck up a conversation. He later became my husband.

'What I'm trying to say is that there was much more of a social mix on the terraces than you would think. The other thing was that by the early 1950s, we had the nearest thing at that time to a Highbury anthem. It was called "Anchors Aweigh". In those days, the crowd could be a bit restrained, and it was often the Italians on the Laundry End who started the singing. Latins tend to enjoy the vocals a bit more. And then you'd sometimes have women egging on the chaps, too. "Well sing up then," they'd say. People were much more quiet back then. And without the Italians and us ladies, there would hardly have been any singing at all.'

○ CULT HEROES ○

JOE MERCER

In the late 1940s, Arsenal's team was an eclectic mix of old stagers, ambitious youngsters, war heroes, and cult heroes. For a couple of years, George Male and Cliff Bastin, now in the twilight of their careers, reminded Arsenal fans of the glorious thirties. Reg Lewis and Laurie Scott, having missed a sizeable slice of their career, played the game with genuine ferocity – and hunger. Jimmy Logie – the nearest thing Arsenal had to a new Alex James – scored and provided assists for colleagues on a regular basis. The team was managed by Squadron Leader Tom Whittaker, who received an MBE for his sterling work in the war.

Cult hero status could so easily be granted to several members of that side. The craggy-faced Ronnie Rooke ('He looked like a real thug – almost a dead ringer for Reggie Kray – but in fact he was a teddy bear,' recalled Laurie Scott), was one such candidate. Arsenal's six-foot-three man-mountain plundered goals with aplomb, as defenders literally bounced off him in the process. There was also Denis Compton, the Brylcreem Boy, who clocked up only fifty-nine appearances for Arsenal in a twelve-year Highbury career. 'Denis hardly ever played for us, but he was always there at the right moment in Cup finals and crunch games. Typical Denis, he'd always let the others do the hard work before he finished it off,' Scott commented.

Then there was Dr Kevin O'Flanagan. Reg Lewis recalled: 'Kevin was a man who made everyone feel inadequate, even Denis Compton. He was an Irish sprint champion at school. Then he couldn't decide if he was better at rugby or football, so he decided to have his cake and eat it. He did both. One week he'd be playing for Arsenal, and the next week he'd turn out for Ireland's rugby team. And then he reckoned his best sport was golf, but he never had the time to devote to it. And he was a doctor too – unbelievable!' But the bona fide crowd favourite of that era was Joe Mercer. Signed in November 1946, after the Gunners disastrous start to the season saw them spiral towards the relegation zone, Mercer's stabilising defensive presence saw Arsenal eventually finish in twelfth position.

He didn't look anything more than the shortest of short-term buys when George Allison signed him for £9,000 in November 1946. Already thirty-two, and in dispute with Everton over the terms of his new contract, he appeared to be on the verge of retiring from football altogether, opting to concentrate on his flourishing grocery store in Wallasey. George Allison persuaded him otherwise – with a few concessions. Mercer persuaded him to give consent to him staying in Liverpool and training with the Anfield outfit during the week, and travelling to London or wherever he was needed for away games, on Fridays. 'Joe was a really shrewd operator,' recalled Laurie Scott. 'He knew that if he managed to get away with doing this, he would be in a really strong financial position when he retired. The thing was that Joe didn't need to play football any more money-wise. He joined Arsenal because he loved playing the game, and he loved the thought of joining a team like Arsenal.' George Male understandably made a strong comparison between his friend Charlie Buchan – who twenty years earlier had come to Highbury in the twilight of his career, and kept his gentleman's outfitters in Sunderland running – and the genial Joe. 'Mercer sort of reflected everything about Arsenal at that time. A bit clapped-out – like the East Stand needed a lick of paint in the late forties – but still really classy.'

The former Everton star's arrival had an immediate galvanising effect on the Arsenal dressing room. Reg Lewis recalled: 'In walked Joe on his first day with that massive grin of his. Honestly, he had teeth the size of tombstones. "All right chaps," he said, as he scanned the dressing room. Even if you hadn't met him personally until that moment, you already felt that you knew him. He immediately took loads of stick. Up popped Ronnie Rooke, and with a look of mock horror on his face, said, "What is that bloody grocer doing in here?" And everyone fell about. Even George Allison couldn't avoid poking fun at him. "Joe will usually join us only on a Friday for weekend games, as he is too old and past it to train all week," George told us. Again, everyone fell about laughing, and this was at a time when we hadn't laughed for a while. Joe pretended to look hurt, and said, "Well if that's how you feel, I'll keep my bags of sweets for myself." Joe had brought down some goodies with him, and this was at the time of sweet rationing. Not a bad start, but more importantly, Joe earned our respect on the pitch. He had these bandy legs and knobbly knees. He could barely run, I don't think he had any real pace anyway. But he could organise and cajole. He reminded me of Bobby Moore, in that he always seemed to know how to poke the ball away from an opposition attacker without ever overcommitting himself. Great defenders just know what they're doing, and Joe was a great player.'

George Allison and Mercer decided that he would stay for twelve months at Highbury. Mercer ended up playing at Highbury for seven seasons. 'Joe played until he was nearly forty,' explained Laurie Scott. 'That was pretty much unheard of back then, especially when you consider that attackers would smack into you whenever possible, and that Joe's legs had taken a real battering over the years. Add in all the extra pressure on your joints from kicking those old style balls around, and it's just incredible. He'd come in every Saturday, and you knew that he loved the glory of captaining the Arsenal.'

An unprecedented seventeen-match run at the start of the 1947–48 season saw the Gunners cruise to their first post-war title. Fired by Rooke and Lewis's goals, Highbury was in carnival mood by the time sacrificial lambs Grimsby Town gambolled into town on the final game of the season. Arsenal fan Jim Baines recalls: 'That game was the most hilarious match I've ever seen at Highbury. Arsenal beat Grimsby 8–0 and Grimsby were absolutely terrible. The Arsenal players were virtually queuing up to score. Ronnie Rooke got four, and then late on Arsenal were awarded a penalty. We were at the Laundry End, and the players were play-fighting among themselves to see who would take it. Jimmy Logie pulled the ball out of Rooke's hands and playfully clipped him around the ear, as if to say "You've scored enough son, it's my turn." Then across comes Joe Mercer. He'd never scored for Arsenal, and he never looked likely to either. As captain, he tried to take the penalty. You could see the others telling him to bugger off. The crowd was chanting, "We want Joe, we want Joe," but Logie took it anyway, and scored. Mercer just shrugged and laughed at us. His smile got even bigger when he paraded the trophy around the pitch. The fans and the players lapped it up. It was a brilliant day.'

The Grimsby match also spelled the end of George Male's illustrious career. 'There were tears in my eyes, and in some ways I'm disappointed that I never had a chance to say a proper goodbye, because the Arsenal fans didn't know that I was retiring. But going out by parading the trophy wasn't a bad way to finish.'

Mercer went on to win a further league title with the Gunners, and lifted the FA Cup after Arsenal beat Liverpool in the 1950 final. The end, when it finally came in 1954, was typical Mercer. A horrendous collision with team-mate Joe Wade at home to Liverpool left him with a broken leg. Mercer knew it was over, and as he was stretchered off the pitch, he waved goodbye to the crowd, as they gave him a rapturous ovation. Reg Lewis commented: 'He was an inspiration for all of us on how to conduct yourself on and off the pitch, and play the game with a smile on your face too. It's no surprise that, after he retired, Arsenal hit a rough patch.'

1950s

○ SHEDDING LIGHT ○

IN 1932, Arsenal manager Herbert Chapman travelled to Belgium to witness an historic event. On a pitch near Brussels, two local sides played an evening match, and with the aid of fifteen sets of blazing car headlights ringing the pitch, played a fairly primitive version of floodlit football. With his mind racing, Chapman hared back to London, and, convinced that floodlit games would be a major bonus for English football, informed his team of what he'd seen.

George Male recalls: 'He told us that he believed floodlit football could easily catch on in this country, in the fullness of time. Chapman always liked to keep us informed of what was going on with him ideas-wise. He pointed out that with long winters in England, and with so many men working long days, it was quite restrictive to have to always play matches in the afternoons. During the thirties we tended to kick off at about two o'clock to ensure we finished the game before it got dark. Sometimes, if there was a fixture backlog at the end of the season, we'd play matches on weekday afternoons. The crowd figures were poor, as blokes simply couldn't get time off work to come to the matches. Chapman had pushed for it during the wrong era, though. He was told that during a period of great economic hardship, it wasn't right to waste so much valuable energy on football matches. I think he pointed out that if the club was footing the bill, it didn't matter. He was blocked anyway, but Chapman did manage to reach a compromise. I clearly remember there were lamps set up alongside the pitch at Highbury, and that we'd sometimes train in semi-darkness in the early thirties.'

It was another twenty years before Chapman's ideas came to fruition. In April 1951, the annual Highbury match between the Boxers and Jockeys saw floodlights rigged up and used for the first time. The match, contested by some of the leading stars in their respective sports, usually attracted a crowd of around 10,000. But, lured by a small piece of football history, over 30,000 fans flocked to see the lights used for the first time. The club, and Chapman disciple Tom Whittaker in particular, realised the huge pulling potential of floodlit matches, and began organising a series of friendlies, to test out the new technology. The Gunners looked to the example of league champions Wolves, who, in the era before the European Cup, played the likes of crack Hungarian outfit Honved before crowds upwards of 60,000 at Molineux. The matches clearly increased Wolves's profile around Europe. Inevitably, Arsenal had pioneered the idea of matches against European sides with the series of games against Racing Club de Paris back in the thirties. Although the games usually took place in the French capital, George Male recalls ' . . . the buzz of playing someone completely different at Highbury on a couple of occasions. A big crowd turned up at Highbury to see us play Racing Club. It was the novelty factor more than anything else, and it fitted in with Chapman's view that by playing foreign opposition, we would expand our horizons.'

In 1951, the Arsenal players, including Doug Lishman, were informed by manager Tom Whittaker that they could expect to face continental opposition on a fairly regular basis from now on, as the club prepared to investigate further the possibilities of 'night-time football'. Lishman recalled the feelings among the team when facing sides from abroad: 'We'd heard of the matches against Racing Club from Paris, but they'd stopped due to the Second World War. So I was excited when I heard we'd be playing some different opposition. I'd say that behind the curiosity, there still lurked an overall feeling of arrogance. It wasn't until Hungary beat England in 1953 that we really began to see that foreigners' technique was far superior to our own. Even though the Moscow Dynamo side had beaten Arsenal back in 1945, we hadn't learned our lesson. Football-wise, we thought would still triumph because we were English. During my time at Arsenal, I think many of us learned our lesson. The two matches I remember most were the games against Berlin, and a representative side from Brazil, and I was struck with how much more organised the Germans were, and how much more technically gifted the Brazilians were. The Highbury crowd realised that too. Sadly, I was too old to have played in the European competitions, but I distinctly remember playing a game against Hapoel Tel Aviv, and it was the first time an Arsenal side had played under the floodlights.'

Swelled by huge numbers of fans from London's Jewish community, over 40,000 supporters flocked to Highbury to see the match. Arsenal fan Leonard Green recalls: 'It was the biggest Jewish gathering London saw in the 1950s. Anyone who was anyone was there that night, and if you weren't, you were dead, or something. This was the first Israeli side ever to play in England, so you *had* to be there. As an Arsenal fan too, it was a very exciting night for all of us. I've always laughed when it's said that Spurs are the "Jewish" club. Arsenal have a huge number of Jewish supporters. I've also come to love night games. I find them more intimate, and I love the idea of sitting in near darkness and watching the players perform in the light. It makes it more of an event. But, of course, back in the early fifties, no one had ever seen floodlights at Highbury. We filed into the ground in near darkness, and then, shortly before kick-off, the announcement came through that the floodlights were about to be switched on. When they did, there was a massive "Ooohhh", as if we'd witnessed a miracle, which I suppose, in a football sense, we had. Everyone spontaneously applauded, and loudly cheered. As for the match itself, it was really just a training match for Arsenal, and Hapoel were totally outplayed, losing 5–1. But as a Jewish Arsenal fan, it was an unforgettable night.'

Largely thanks to the success of the match – the crowd figure and the fact there were no technical hitches – the Football League soon allowed Arsenal to play floodlit league games soon afterwards. Reg Lewis, who came on as a substitute against Hapoel and scored twice, recalls 'an entirely new world was being opened up to football and footballers'. A few days later, Glasgow Rangers visited Highbury for a friendly match, and the floodlights were officially inaugurated. Lewis recalls: 'Now that night-time matches were going ahead, it meant that we could avoid the bottlenecks which occurred at the end of seasons where you'd have to cram in games that had been postponed in the days before undersoil heating. That made it better for fans and players. More important in the long term was that midweek games could be scheduled, and because clubs could swap information on floodlights, they were more likely to play each other. The European Cup was set up soon afterwards, and it just wouldn't have been possible without floodlights, because clubs were occupied in their domestic leagues at weekends. And for players, and fans, there was initially a real wow factor when you played under the lights. It was a new kind of football.'

Floodlights had indeed opened up a whole raft of possibilities in the world of football, but it would be a few years before Highbury regulars sampled the delights of European competition.

○ BY THE SKIN OF THEIR TEETH ○

ARSENAL HAVE a habit of making life extremely difficult for themselves. Just as championship races appear won, and FA Cups bedecked in red and white ribbons, the team threatens to implode. Then, just as defeat seems to have been snatched from the jaws of victory, the team comes through, after fans have endured squeaky buttocks and heart palpitations for ninety minutes. Of course, it doesn't always turn out that way – it just seems like it. One such 'Alamo' scenario occurred at Highbury at the climax to the 1952–53 season. In fact, the whole campaign was a roller-coaster experience, dominated by rumbling discontent over 'blown Doubles', and players' anger with sections of the home support.

In the previous season, Arsenal – beaten by Newcastle in the FA Cup final and 6–1 at Old Trafford in the last game of the season – lost out on both the League title and the FA Cup at the final hurdle. The 1952–53 season didn't start especially well. The Gunners had some excellent attacking players in Logie, Lishman, Goring and Holton, but the team seemed incapable of gelling effectively until a run of victories around Christmas time. When Sunderland came to Highbury and won 3–1 in January, the crowd voiced its displeasure. Peter Goring walked out of Highbury after the game, only to be confronted by a disgruntled fan. Goring recalled: 'This chap was completely drunk, but he started telling me that he'd seen the Arsenal team of the thirties, and we weren't fit to lick their boots. I wasn't the only player to be confronted in such a way. Some of the other boys also got hassle from fans, which wasn't at all nice. The ironic thing was that I agreed with the bloke. We were a battling team, rather than a side to be compared with the thirties' vintage. But the fact was that we were never lower than third in the league throughout the 1952–53 season, and some of those Arsenal fans were very hard to please. We felt that they didn't know they were born.'

One of Goring's team-mates snapped and told a *Daily Mail* journalist – anonymously – that he was 'ashamed of the crowd and considered them the most unsporting collection in the country'. Goring informed me that he knew who said this, 'but he still has the right to remain anonymous.' Arsenal continued to play inconsistently, as did their nearest rivals Preston and Wolves. With just two games remaining, the Gunners could seal the title with a win at nearest rivals Preston. Tellingly, Arsenal had garnered 52 points from 40 games, the lowest number of points any potential champions had gained at that stage of the season. The nervous Arsenal lost 2–0 at Deepdale, succumbing to the brilliance of Tom Finney, and left themselves needing to win the final game of the season at home against sixth place Burnley, in order to pip Preston to the big prize.

As Don Roper recalled, this would be no easy task: 'By the end of the season, we were very tired. The pitches became really heavy. I remember Wolves' and Preston's pitches were total quagmires, and your legs felt like they weighed a ton. For the Burnley match, I'd say that the Highbury pitch was the worst of the lot by a long way. I don't think there was a blade of grass on it, and when we went out for the pitch inspection that morning, it was obvious that the edges were completely unplayable. Either the ball would get stuck, or you'd fall over. It was terrible. We felt the pressure. We had the chance to win the League in front of our own fans at Highbury, which would be a huge honour. Even Joe Mercer, who was normally the life and soul of the group, was noticeably quiet when we ate our eggs on toast at King's Cross station. It was always our meeting place, and for many, it was the biggest day of their lives. What was funny was that lots of Blackpool and Bolton fans were milling around because the FA Cup final was being played the next day. And all of them were coming up to us and wishing us well, because Preston were the local enemy. And they weren't overly keen on Burnley either!'

The match kicked off at the early time of 6.30 p.m. on Friday, 1 May. This was due to the absence of floodlighting at Highbury. Arsenal fan

Harry Wright ensured that he got to the ground early: 'People were milling around the ground from midday onwards. You sensed this would be a great occasion. Weather-wise, it was a very odd day. There were constant showers, and in my mind's eye, every man jack seemed to be wearing a raincoat. But they were happy to be standing out in the rain as well. I think many people believed that the game would be a sell-out, so they were ready to rush in and have a beer when the gates opened. When it got to about six o'clock, the atmosphere got really intense. For the first time in what seemed an age, the Arsenal crowd seemed as one that night. There was a big crowd – around 50,000 – but it wasn't full to capacity, which amazed me and my pals.

'Lots of fans wore rosettes and colours, which was quite rare for those days. The crowd actually worked *together* to produce the atmosphere. All of us clapped "Arsenal, Arsenal" in unison – that's the North and South terraces. Even the stands joined in. It was a marvellous atmosphere.' Doug Lishman concurred: 'The crowd was at their best that night. The noise they made was unbelievable, it was really ear piercing – enough to make the hairs on the back of your neck stand on end. However much the players and fans were in conflict that season, I can't deny they were superb on that night.'

The action was frenetic. After six minutes, Burnley's Des Thompson put Burnley ahead against the run of play. Midway through the first half, Arsenal found their attacking rhythm. Alex Forbes – courtesy of a huge deflection – equalised, and two minutes afterwards, Jimmy Logie ducked out of the way to allow Doug Lishman ('I just smacked the loose ball as hard as I could. It was the greatest moment of my life when it went in') to put Arsenal 2–1 up. Just before half-time, Jimmy Logie pounced from five yards out to snaffle a poacher's goal. At half-time, Harry Wright recalls: 'There was this horrendous downpour. It absolutely teemed it down. The buoyancy of the crowd suddenly disappeared. From talking about how many goals we might score, the talk was "Would the game be abandoned?" You could see the puddles developing.' After the restart, Burnley proved they weren't dead and buried. If they won, they would finish fourth – no mean achievement for a team which had laboured around mid-table until March. Five minutes into the second half, the Clarets' Billy Elliott pulled the score back to 3–2.

At that point, the Arsenal players attempted to shut up shop; a risky strategy with forty minutes left. Don Roper recalled: 'I noticed that Joe Mercer's legs had gone. And the thing was that Joe later admitted that they went for good that night. (He reckoned it was the last time he operated as a top-class player.) Half the team were now struggling as the ball weighed about twice as much as it did at the start of the game, due to the wet pitch. Every time you kicked the ball, your whole body ached. I had a knee injury, and at one point I thought I'd collapse with pain when the ball caught me on the side. It later turned out I'd torn a ligament, but these were the days before substitutes, so you had to carry on. Jimmy (Logie) and Pete (Goring) were virtual passengers by now. They could barely walk, and so we just stuffed them behind the ball. We had no option but to stand firm in the final half-hour.

'Tom Whittaker couldn't stand the tension. He walked out and poured himself a double brandy. Arsenal fans told me it was just unbearable to watch. A single Burnley goal would have finished us, because there was no way we could have summoned the energy to come back at them. By now we were all defenders, and we knew that one careless tackle could be curtains for us. With about a minute to go, I caught Billy Elliott in the box. These days, he'd have gone straight to ground and won a penalty. To his credit, he stumbled and carried on. He said, "There are better ways of denying you the title than that Don." I still smile at the sportsmanship of that moment, today. Then he hit the bar with a minute left, and I think all of us nearly filled our pants! "Bugger," he grinned. "I should have dived when I had the chance".'

Finally, at 8.01 p.m., the referee blew his whistle. Arsenal had won the title on goal average, by 0.099 of a goal. Harry Wright recalls: 'The rain had eased off, and the sun was trying to break through. The sky was red, which I thought was very symbolic. All the scarves and rosettes were being thrown up into the air. Most of us invaded the pitch in search of the Arsenal players. My friend chaired Joe Mercer off the pitch. Some of the players like Jimmy Logie couldn't get off the pitch. They just stood and chatted to fans. It was fantastic.' Don Roper recalled: 'Whenever I see reruns of Liverpool v Arsenal in 1989, or Spurs v Arsenal in 1993, I always think our achievement was equally as dramatic. What a shame there were no TV cameras. I still often think of what we achieved that night. I'm proud to be part of such a backs-to-the-wall display. To me, it summarises what it's like to play for Arsenal. And to do it in front of our own supporters too. Marvellous!'

It was just as well that the players and fans lapped up the celebrations. Tom Whittaker's health was starting to fail, as had Chapman's and Allison's before him. It was further evidence that the job of keeping Arsenal at the top was proving an intolerable strain, and something had to give. There wouldn't be another Highbury night like that one for another seventeen years.

○ THE BABES ARE BACK IN TOWN ○

FIFTY YEARS AGO, the employees of Arsenal and Manchester United quite liked each other. So much so, that Matt Busby's team would occasionally stay down in London for the night, after a game, so they could have dinner and a few beers with the Gunners team. By 1958, it was clear that the likes of Edwards, Charlton and Taylor formed the core of a team which seemed poised to dominate English football for years to come. This was in marked contrast with Arsenal, for whom memories of the glorious thirties were fading fast, with the passing of Alex James in 1951; Tom Whittaker, 1956; and George Allison, 1957. The good old days – at least for the time being – were over.

After the last-ditch title triumph of 1953, Arsenal had slipped into decline. Gerry Ward, who became Arsenal's youngest ever debutant when he took his bow at home to Huddersfield aged just 16 years 322 days, in August 1953, recalled: 'There was a belief at the club that directors wouldn't splash out on huge bids for a player. That feeling was all well and good, but football was changing. If you wanted top players, you had to pay top money. Arsenal's directors weren't willing to do that. It wasn't a great time to be an Arsenal player, to be honest. The fans used to get on our case. For example, when Vic Groves arrived, he really struggled for form, and he got booed by the Arsenal fans, and then he received abusive letters. The crowd could also be difficult with me. I was hyped as the next big thing because I was home-grown and so young, but I didn't really progress as well as I, or the crowd, had hoped.'

The Arsenal team of the late 1950s had some fine performers, including David Herd, Derek Tapscott and Jimmy Bloomfield. But there was a feeling that too few were genuinely top-class performers, and that 'Gentleman' Jack Crayston, who took over as Arsenal manager from Tom Whittaker, wasn't a great manager either.

Arsenal fan David White is blunt in his assessment of the team of that era. 'We'd gone right down the pan. In one game, we had Gordon Nutt and Danny Le Roux. Jesus Christ – they sounded like a dodgy drag act. When you considered what class players we'd had before, it was all really embarrassing. Crowds dropped off alarmingly, but for the United game in 1958, suddenly everyone reappeared. All the Arsenal fans knew about United's reputation. It wasn't like the press built them up or anything. They didn't used to do that in those days. It spread via word of mouth. I was at school in Holloway at the time, and boys in my class would talk about Duncan Edwards like he was some kind of god, and they'd never even bloody seen him play. They might have seen his photo in the newspaper or on cigarette cards, but no one really owned a telly in those days, so his legend grew via word of mouth really. I think that was the time when a lot of people "down south" started supporting United – because of the aura surrounding the Busby Babes. If we're being honest, most of the crowd that day went to Highbury to see United, not Arsenal – 63,000 were there to see the opposition. They were legendary even before then.'

For ninety minutes only on 1 February 1958, the good times returned to Highbury. 'I've been going to Highbury since 1945,' recalls Bruce Smithers, 'but that United match was the best I've ever seen there, no question. There was none of the unpleasantness between the two sides which you see today, and the crowd was there to marvel at the power of Edwards and skill of Charlton. Not many fans admit these days that they are impressed by the opposition. Times have changed.'

The game began according to the form book. United's devastating blend of speed and power ripped Arsenal's suspect defence to shreds. Duncan Edwards and Bobby Charlton thumped two scorchers from the edge of the box to put United 2–0 ahead, and when Tommy Taylor notched United's third after thirty minutes, 'half the crowd would willingly have walked out,' comments Bruce Smith. Miraculously, Arsenal mounted an astonishing six-minute onslaught on United before half-time, and Bloomfield (2) and Herd struck to pull Arsenal level.

Gerry Ward recalled: 'The crowd was in total uproar. None of us had ever seen anything like it before, and nor had the players! At half-time, when the players came off, we just couldn't concentrate. United's stars looked dumbfounded, and some of the Arsenal lads couldn't believe we'd pulled it back against this great side. To be honest, we lost concentration in the second half, and United taught us a football lesson – how to attack like a panzer division.'

Viollet and Taylor put United into a 5–3 lead, before Derek Tapscott tantalised the home crowd by pulling another goal back. With the crowd screaming for an Arsenal equaliser, the Gunners poured forward in the final ten minutes. Gerry Ward recalled: 'We could have equalised. Jimmy Bloomfield and Tappy (Derek Tapscott) came really close. We threw everything at them, and the Arsenal crowd went completely bananas. But it wasn't to be, and United held on. When the final whistle blew, I went straight to Tommy Taylor and shook his hand, and he winked at me. We all knew that it had been one of the great games. There was some talk of us all going up West in the evening to have a bite to eat, but Matt Busby said they had to go back to Manchester on this occasion, as they were playing in the European Cup that following week. We were disappointed, because going out with the United boys was always great fun. Boy, could they drink and smoke! As everyone knows, this match had an even greater significance in the history of the game, and things that had happened – or not happened – live long in various people's memories.'

The match at Highbury was the Busby Babes' last match in England before the Munich air crash, in which United's entire backline of Byrne, Coleman, Jones and Edwards (fifteen days later) died. The tragic news totally stunned the Arsenal players. Ward recalled: 'It shook me to the core to think that, less than a week before the fellas died, we'd played them at Highbury, and had a couple of pints afterwards. I always think of Tommy Taylor and Duncan Edwards when I think of that game. I can picture Tommy winking at me like it was yesterday. And God only knows what Duncan would have gone on to achieve. I know that Dennis Evans always looked back to the match, and regretted not taking out Duncan when he had the chance. Earlier on, Edwards had lamped his mate, Danny Clapton, on to the gravel. Late on, Duncan went through, and Dennis could have got in his retribution, and chopped him down.

'Dennis used to say, "If I'd done that, maybe Duncan wouldn't have got on the plane and he'd still be here." Dennis said he pulled out of the tackle because it was Duncan Edwards – a very special player. But there were other incidents too. Like I had a fifty-fifty on Taylor, and he whisked the ball away. And you think, If I'd caught Tommy, he might not have gone either. But it's all ifs and maybes, and Arsenal players weren't really in the business of booting other players. That was part of our problem.

'The game also showed the hard side of Duncan. You almost felt guilty about tackling him, because of who he was, and how young he was. But Duncan didn't need protection. He was a man with legs like oak trees before he was seventeen – I reckon. And boy, could he swear. After he took out Danny Clapton, he stood over him and shouted: "Oh fucking get up." I was really close to him when he said it. And some of the crowd looked staggered because most of them hadn't heard a player swear before. They looked amazed. So we also saw Duncan's hard side that day, too.'

Bruce Smithers recalls the end of the game: 'The whole crowd was cheering both sets of players and the teams came off with their arms around each others' shoulders. Edwards and Taylor came off and applauded the Arsenal fans. And a lot of the Arsenal fans had a soft spot for United, so they applauded back. It had been a beautiful experience, and no matter how many Doubles we win under Wenger, I'll always look back on that game and picture Duncan Edwards smiling and waving at the crowd. It is a very poignant memory for me – and Arsenal had just lost!'

1960s

N.5

○ EMPTY SPACES ○

THE WARNING signs had been there for some time. From the guaranteed 50,000 plus gates of the late 1940s, Arsenal's crowds at Highbury crashed to a hard-core 20,000 by the early 1960s. For the bigger games against Spurs and Manchester United, the hordes miraculously returned, only to disappear again when the likes of Cardiff or Stoke came to town. By the 1965–66 season, the situation reached crisis point. With Arsenal mired in mid-table, just 8,000 attended when West Bromwich Albion visited Highbury. The *Islington Gazette* commented: 'It is a symptom of the times that so few attend games, where once so many would fill Highbury.' The nadir arrived in April 1965, when Arsenal entertained Leeds United. Admittedly the weather was poor, and Liverpool's Cup-Winners' Cup final against Borussia Monchengladbach was being televised live – a rare event in the 1960s. However, no one could have predicted that just 4,554 would show up to watch the Arsenal v Leeds clash.

Steve Hart was one of the chosen few. He recalls: 'You could tell in the pub that the crowd figure was going to be really low. We got to the Gunners pub at seven o'clock, and literally, no bugger was there. Honestly, we threw open the doors and there were about five bar staff with their arms folded. No punters to serve except us. "Have we got the wrong evening?" my mate John asked the barman. But we hadn't. So we finished our beer, set off towards the ground, and it was pretty much one man and his dog. Hardly anyone at the turnstiles, none of the usual clickety-clicking as you entered. When we walked on to the North Bank, it was almost deserted. It was a really weird atmosphere, and you could hear the players' shouts echoing around the ground. I remember Bob McNab shouting at Ian Ure to "get your bloody head up", which was pretty much what the crowd always used to tell him!

'The thing I remember most was that some lads at the front of the North Bank started up a little bonfire with paper and all this rubbish, and were dancing around it like Red Indians. There was nothing else to do. We used to quite like it, in a masochistic sort of way. It was like our last stand or something. We were the only loyal fans left, all the others had deserted the cause.'

The reasons for the empty spaces at Highbury are numerous. One of the main problems was Tottenham's success, culminating in their Double triumph of 1961. Ironically, Arsenal had attempted to sign flying winger Cliff Jones before he moved to White Hart Lane, and John White too. But George Swindin's Arsenal was seen as a club which could be tight with the readies. Another example was when the Gunners matched Huddersfield's asking price for Denis Law, only to be gazumped by Manchester United. Joe Baker recalled: 'It wasn't exactly the best time to be an Arsenal player. Everyone heard about the "grand theatre" that Highbury had been, but in the 1960s, it was often really subdued. Funereal, almost. And it was so hard to take Spurs' success. They were a wonderful side admittedly, but you knew that Arsenal fans were really hurting.'

Many Arsenal fans remain scathing of manager Billy Wright, as do some of his former charges. Arsenal supporter Billy Hayes recalls: 'He was a nice guy – Billy Wright. But he was a bloody disaster for Arsenal. Couldn't engender team spirit. Couldn't get players working as a team at all, in fact. It was embarrassing. But the biggest embarrassment of all was his association with the fucking Beverley Sisters. Rumour had it that the board appointed him to make Arsenal a more modern and trendy outfit. There were loads of pictures of him with his wife Joy Beverley in their stupid bloody outfits. We were a bloody laughing stock. Young kids weren't listening to the Beverley Sisters, they were into The Rolling Stones or The Who. It got to the stage when lots of fans stayed away. On a couple of occasions we got to the ground and people would be saying: "Turn back, we'll boycott the games until we get this clown out of the job. It was rough, to be honest. You'd hear chants of "Wright Out, Wright Out". I don't think I'd ever heard that sort of thing before at Highbury. But he really was a disaster.'

The late George Armstrong said of Wright: 'A lot of us young guys owed Billy a lot, because he brought us through and gave us our chance. He knew how to talk to us young players. But he could never get us to gel with more senior players, he couldn't get the two elements together. For instance, Joe Baker was a great player, but he never saw the need to defend; nor did George Eastham. Everyone did their own thing on the pitch, rather than work together. Then there were the little things, like when he shook his fist at Chapman's bust. Fans got to hear about that, and it suggested that Billy couldn't cope. And they blamed him for changing the red and white shirts to all red. (Even though it was actually Frank McLintock's idea.) No one really thought Billy was an Arsenal man.'

Arsenal's on-the-field underachievement aside, there were other reasons why attendances were plummeting. Joe Baker recalled meeting a group of disaffected Gunners fans in a pub, who told him: 'Frankly, Joe, we'd rather get ourselves some wheels instead of watching you lot.' Then there was the advent of television – one of the very things that contributed to the record low attendance against Leeds. In January 1966, the *Islington Gazette* noted: 'A large number of bowling alleys, cinemas and music venues are springing up in the capital, which are pulling young men away from watching football.' A 1965 *Times* survey stated that on average, household incomes had risen by fifteen per cent in ten years, but that money was spent on luxury items like fridges and washing machines, rather than on sport.

Arsenal fan Rory Hinds comments: 'Yeah, there were things like cars and records to spend your money on. But it wasn't just that. As the team got worse, you started to question things at Highbury. Like the bogs. They stank, and overflowed with piss. Why couldn't Arsenal have done something about that? When I went bowling or went to see a film, the loos were okay. So why should a football club let that happen? Then there was the catering, the beer was clearly watered down – it was horrible. Or you'd get a cup of tea in a plastic cup and it was so bloody hot that you'd drop it. And I started thinking, I'm not putting up with this any more. Already, we were a generation who expected more than our fathers had. We hadn't had the experiences of fighting in a world war, and we wanted more from life than slavishly following a team which wasn't very good, and whose players didn't always appear to be giving it their all. And, remember, that by now the maximum wage was abolished. These guys were on good money, and we expected them to perform.'

◦ THE GREATEST ◦

IN EARLY 1966, Highbury was chosen as the venue for the rematch between the new star of heavyweight boxing Cassius Clay (who was in the process of changing his name to Muhammad Ali) and Henry Cooper. At Wembley Stadium three years earlier, Cooper became the first boxer to knock Clay to the floor, but our 'Enry's tendency to cut easily meant that he was eventually beaten in the sixth round. Yet Cooper's punch had made its mark. At a press conference prior to the Highbury rematch, Clay commented: 'Cooper hit me so hard it shook all my relations in Africa.' By 1966, Clay was already heavyweight champion of the world, and in the build up to the Cooper fight, several Arsenal players came within close proximity of 'the greatest'.

The Clay v Cooper fight wasn't the first time that Highbury had been selected to host a non-football event. In 1949, as part of Denis Compton's testimonial, the stadium hosted an Arsenal v England All Stars cricket match. Reg Lewis recalled: 'Yes, that was a strange episode. Cricket pitches tend to be square, rather than oblong. So you had all the batsmen trying hard not to smack the ball too hard, otherwise it would travel with some force into the crowd, and that could get a bit dangerous. But everyone took care, and it was a brilliant occasion for Denis, who was a real giant of football and cricket.'

A more bizarre proposal for the stadium came in 1955, when US evangelist preacher Billy Graham embarked on his tour of North London. It was widely reported that Graham would address his audience from a raised platform in the centre of the pitch. Graham was the first US media-savvy preacher, and there was a huge wave of interest around Highbury.

Local resident Clive Barnett recalls: 'I opened up my door one morning, and I was a bit drowsy and thought it might be the milkman or something. But I was greeted by the sight of two smart men in suits. "Good morning my brother," they said. "Is the good Lord shining on you today?" I must have looked fairly nonplussed, because they carried on and said: "Take courage son, take courage. Mr Billy Graham plans to help you embrace the Lord and come to know him. Are you ready to embrace the Lord, my son?" I told them that I didn't think I was, actually. And I tried to shut the door on them. But before I could do so, they told me that Billy Graham was doing a gathering at the Arsenal ground later that week. But as far as I know, it never happened. But Billy Graham's men were around for quite a while. We used to nickname them "the God squad".'

It says a great deal for Arsenal's lack of success in the 1960s that the Clay v Cooper fight was the biggest event at Highbury during the entire decade. It also provided an opportunity for young apprentices like Charlie George to earn some extra cash. He recalls: 'The fight took place after the end of the season, and so we had the chance to renovate and transform the ground. I think that Ken Friar said the entire turf was reseeded, and then the wooden boards were put down on top of the pitch. Along with other apprentices, and outside help, I was assigned to put down the boards, and build the ring. It was very exciting, and it made a nice change from scrubbing all those bloody boots for the first-teamers. The whole place was swarming with the media, because they had to sort out all the TV stuff and lay down hundreds of yards of cables. The club's officials were going nuts because they had to hire all the seats – all 46,000 of them. But I loved it. We got paid a few extra pennies, and best of all, we got to see the fight for free. Henry was a big Arsenal supporter, so there were loads of Arsenal fans cheering him on that night.'

Although Jon Sammels and Bob Wilson recall being snapped in a sparring pose as part of local newspaper coverage, the Arsenal team did not attend the fight, as they had flown away on tour the day before. The injured Joe Baker opted to attend on his own. He recalls: 'It does seem strange that we didn't all attend the fight. You'd have thought they could have delayed their flight for a couple of days. You can imagine that if the fight had taken place at Stamford Bridge, the entire Chelsea side would be there, with Raquel Welch in tow, no doubt! And a lot of the Arsenal players were big boxing fans as well. Just before the fight, Ali held one of his press conferences at the Park Lane Hotel, and one of my mates who was a journalist smuggled me in at the back, warning me that I'd never seen anything like this guy before. He was right, Ali was wild and on fire. He was up and about shouting: "I'm pretty" and "I'm so great" and, "This chump ain't got no chance. He gonna get his ass whupped." Then he tried some of his poetry, boasting that he was, "Gonna put Cooper into a stupor."

'What was interesting was that Henry just sat there – a bit bemused – laughing as Ali put on this show. I tried to meet Ali afterwards, but his entourage ushered him away. But his show for the press – which included the line "soccer players are ugly – they ain't pretty like me" was unforgettable. It was a bit too much for most British people, who tend to like their heroes to be modest and understated. But I'll never forget it.'

The fight took place in front of an expectant 46,000 capacity crowd, which included Hollywood stars Burt Reynolds and Lee Marvin. Arsenal trainer Bert Owen was fortunate to be in Clay's dressing room – which would normally be occupied by the Arsenal side. As he informed Jon Sammels, he was impressed by what he saw: 'Bert had been a trainer since the thirties, and he'd worked with all the biggest Arsenal names like Bastin and James. But he was bowled over by Ali. He told me that Ali was doing the famous shuffle before the fight, and his "Pah Pah" shadow boxing. But with the warm-up, Ali just did a couple of shoulder shrugs, and then after the fight slipped on his bomber jacket, and was gone. As for Henry, he was a great fella. He trained with us for a while after he picked up a cartilage injury. But being honest, most people would always have expected Ali to win the fight.'

A large number of those present in the crowd were Arsenal fans. Henry Cooper later described the atmosphere as ' . . . crackling with electricity. It was probably the best I'd experienced at a fight, and the crowd were chanting "Cooper, Cooper". It was just like a football match, and I thank those present – a little belatedly perhaps – for making it so memorable.' The 36-year-old Cooper held Clay at bay until 1 minute 38 seconds into round six, when a right-hand jab above Cooper's eye left him requiring twelve stitches. The referee stopped the fight, and as Cooper later admitted: 'My curse, which was my tendency to cut easily, did for me again.' His consolation was a £40,000 purse. Afterwards, Clay's manager described his fighter's jab as 'a wonderful punch', although Ali claimed: 'I hate to spill blood. It's against my religion.'

The watching Joe Baker had mixed feelings about the fight. He recalled: 'On the one hand, it was a privilege to see such an event at Highbury, but on the other, you just wished the Arsenal side could induce the same kind of passion at Highbury. I felt a bit sad, in certain ways.' Eighteen years later, Ali's great rival Joe Frazier visited Highbury for a home clash with Luton in late 1984. After the game, the team met Frazier in the players' lounge. Charlie Nicholas recalls: 'He was a giant of a man, but really friendly and interested in what we were doing. He asked me if this was where Ali beat Henry Cooper. I had to check with Ken Friar, who confirmed that, yes, this was the place. Then Frazier does this mock spit on the floor and whispers: "Goddam son of a bitch. Ain't nowhere I can escape that man." And this was twenty years, or so, after the fight!'

⌒ A TALE OF TWO ENDS ⌒

BY THE MID-1960S, the Clock End and the Laundry End (now officially called the North Bank) began to acquire their own distinct identities. It is impossible to affix a definitive date as to when Arsenal fans began to adopt the 'North Bank' title, but ex-BBC researcher Tony Watts believes it coincided with the BBC's Kop Choir competition, which ran in 1964.

He recalls: 'It was a bit of fun that we had with clubs to see which fans could generate the most noise. It was an interesting time because, as a football goer in the mid-sixties, I noticed that fans didn't generally sing en masse. Now they started to. Lots of the newspapers attributed the change to our competition, as fans, and especially teenagers, saw that if they worked together, they could produce a tremendous racket. But I think that's a bit simplistic. I think you need to look closely at Beatlemania. Suddenly, young kids went around singing songs which became anthems, which hadn't happened before. And this spread to football. At Anfield, they started to sing 'She Loves You' and stuff like

'Ferry Cross the Mersey'. It started there, and it spread to other grounds. And with the advent of *Match Of The Day*, it was easy to copy what was going on elsewhere.

'A lot more teenagers were going to gigs around the country. People began to sing more than they had before. Kids decided that one end of the ground was theirs too. It was their fortress – the place to be. Football became much more tribal. For United fans, their patch was the Stretford End; for Chelsea it was the Shed; and for Arsenal – the North Bank. It sounded a bit meaner than the old-fashioned Laundry End, didn't it?'

In 1963, Arsenal drew 4–4 with Spurs, in front of 67,986. At least, that was the official figure. Arsenal fans who attended the match suggest the real figure was closer to 75,000. Arsenal had trailed Spurs 4–2, but late goals by Joe Baker and Geoff Strong tied up the result. The subsequent crowd surge at the Clock End led to crushing, and over 100 fans required treatment by the St John ambulance medics. Reports have always suggested that the incident was simply due to Arsenal's late heroics. But two new pieces of evidence suggest otherwise.

Joe Baker recalled: 'When I scored the third goal, I went to the Clock End to celebrate. I noticed that there were a lot of Arsenal fans at the front going bonkers, but at the back of the Clock End there was hardly any movement, which suggested there were a lot of Spurs fans in there. Then, I could see the Spurs fans do the dominoes thing, and the Arsenal fans at the front got violently pushed forward. That's when people began to get hurt and I noticed for the first time that standing at matches could be a very dangerous experience. But, more worryingly, that other fans would sometimes deliberately try and hurt you in a crowded situation. It was also becoming clear that away fans were gravitating towards the Clock End. In that same game I saw that, when Spurs scored, there was virtually no movement at the North Bank end – apart from a few pockets of white. Up till now both ends were usually quite mixed. But already by 1963, you could see that opposing fans didn't mingle as much any more. Away fans really only penetrated the North Bank if they wanted to cause grief.'

John Stubbs concurs with Baker's view: 'What started to happen was that the North Bank became the place for the kids. In most cases, our dads originally suggested going there because it wasn't so crowded in the mid-1960s, and there was a roof so you wouldn't get wet. Gradually, it became *the* place for kids, and soon the dads themselves stopped going. The North Bank was now *our* place, where you could sing, drink, and swear as much as you wanted. I likened it to when you were at school, and the teacher isn't there. You can do what you want, can't you? And after a while as you got older, the dads would say, 'Well, you're old enough to be by yourselves now.' and they'd go and stand on the Clock End or sit in the East or West Stands, or just not bother coming. I think that's why going to football became a bit dodgy; there wasn't that controlling adult influence.

'Some would say it's another symbol of family life breaking down. But really, who wants to stand with their old man when they're sixteen? And once you're free from your dad's influence, you're also free to drink. In those days, the pubs around Highbury began to open their doors early to get people off the streets. Now think . . . if there's no adults about, what will kids do? Get roaring drunk. So the North Bank is suddenly full of drunken teens who are singing songs. It started off fairly straightforward with 'Arsenal, Arsenal'. Then we started to greet the players individually. At first it was good-natured, but later on you'd get trouble.'

The numbers of away fans in the Clock End grew rapidly in the 1960s. This was due mainly to the 'football specials' laid on by British Rail and the FA. Liverpool and Everton fans began to arrive as late as possible via Arsenal tube station, and could take their places on the Clock End within five minutes. John Stubbs recalls: ' . . . huge numbers of red or blue Scousers mouthing off, and singing and dancing. You could hear them a mile off. When they came back into Division One in the early sixties, their influence changed what it meant to be a supporter on a terrace.'

In Darren Jarvis' eyes, the North Bank was the only place to be for hip young Arsenal fans in the mid-1960s. 'It was a rites of passage type of place. My dad got to hear about what it was like on the North Bank and said, "Oh Gawd, you're not going in there are you? It's rough. Why don't you go and sit with your uncle in the East Upper?" There was no way I was doing that. The North Bank was the only place I could get a drink and a smoke without Dad knowing. Then when we went back to school on Monday, and people asked me what I'd done with my

weekend, I could say I've been on the North Bank. And people looked at
you with respect. That's a big thing when you're a kid.'

○ BENDING THE RULES ○

ALTHOUGH THERE had been isolated incidents of violence at
Highbury during the previous decades, the situation worsened
rapidly during the 1960s. Eyewitness accounts tend to suggest that
the Arsenal v Liverpool clash in 1964 saw the first serious incidents
in and around the stadium.

PC Robert Cooper was on patrol at Highbury at the time. He recalls:
'You could see it starting to change outside the ground. Travelling
Liverpool supporters tended to be much more volatile and outgoing
than your average Arsenal fan. They'd pile out of the Arsenal tube
station, and start pushing and shoving to let people know they were
there. You'd give them a warning, and they appeared to heed it. Then,
before you knew it, they'd give you the verbals halfway down the road
and start acting up again. We'd get lots of reports from locals about
Liverpool fans doing damage to fences and gates, and occasional
reports of smashed windows. There were plenty of witnesses claiming
that they sang Beatles songs as they did so. It wasn't long before they
began to make their presence felt in the ground.

'When Arsenal played Liverpool back in 1964, a few supporters at
the Clock End had to be treated for cuts to their heads, because
Liverpool fans had thrown coins with serrated edges at them. During
the following year, Arsenal fans responded in kind, and you'd notice
things going on which hadn't happened before, like young Arsenal
fans giving you backchat and stuff. My colleagues and I spent a lot of
time discussing why this might be happening. Was it because
National Service had been abolished and there was a lack of discipline? Was it because this generation had no experience of war,

unlike their dads? It was very hard to put your finger precisely on the problem.

'I think those things were partly to blame, but young people were just changing, generally. I used to patrol the Goldhawk Road in the sixties before I got a transfer, and you'd see the "pill heads" spill out of the pubs and clubs. They'd copy groups like The Who, who were into amphetamines called purple hearts. And this was going on across London, with that particular generation. A lot of kids on the North Bank, and on the Clock End were more aggressive. They'd either drunk something or popped something. You could see it in their eyes; it made them far more aggressive. I remember when Everton fans pinched a line from The Who song 'My Generation' and taunted Charlie George with it. 'Hope you die before you get old,' they'd sing. I couldn't understand people who behaved like that. But more and more joined in with it.

'Then there was the trouble that took place away from the ground. It was particularly bad at Manor House tube station, which always seemed to be a war zone if Arsenal played any of their main rivals towards the end of the sixties. Or at the back of Finsbury Park tube. You heard that something was happening, but by the time you got there, it had finished. Scores were settled away from the eyes of the police.

'Kids pushed the boundaries in other ways as well, where they hadn't done so before. The club had a policy where they would let them in to the East Stand for a reduced price, and then they were allowed on to the North Bank if they met up with their parents. There was no paperwork needed or anything. It relied on trust. So many kids spotted "imaginary dad" on the other side. "There he is, there's my dad," they'd shout. Before you knew it – and you couldn't really stop them – they were through the gate with their mates laughing at you. On one occasion, a gang of ten kids charged past me, knocked me out of the way, and got through the gate. In the end, the club locked the gate because so many kids were wilfully bending the rules. Obviously, the vast number of Arsenal fans were fantastic people, but more and more were willing to abuse our trust.'

The mid-1960s witnessed the return of slumbering giants Leeds United (managed by Don Revie) and Liverpool (under Bill Shankly) to the top flight. With their teams dominated by such 'iron men' as Smith, Yeats, Hunter and Bremner, both sides came to reflect a new brand of cynicism and a 'win at all costs' mentality in football. George Eastham recalls: 'Leeds had a vicious little so-and-so called Bobby Collins in their midfield. He was tremendous player, but Jesus did he dig at you. Then, when he retired, Bremner and Giles took over the role. At the time, I was quoted as saying something like, "Well if they're going to play like that, then maybe we should give them the title." Or words to that effect. What I meant was that several players couldn't stand Leeds' attitude to games. They decided to win games 1–0, and boot opponents off the park. Leeds were a fantastic side, but they sacrificed flair and creativity for brute-force tactics. And then players at other clubs wised up and began doing the same. Everyone seemed to be bending the rules. You'd get clobbered from behind all the time in the sixties. The game was becoming more brutal.'

Football writers are on dodgy ground when they try to find a connection between trouble on the pitch and off it. In truth, changes in society are reflected by behaviour in both places. It is important to remember that the word 'teenager' wasn't in general use until the late 1950s, by which time Marlon Brando's and James Dean's films – *Wild Things* and *Rebel Without A Cause* – were shown in cinemas nationwide. Several Arsenal supporters from the era spoke of their belief that the influence of film and on-the-pitch violence, led to more aggressive behaviour in and around Highbury.

Terry Moore recalls: 'By the mid-1960s, it started to matter which little group you belonged to when you went to games. There was the Holloway Posse, the Islington Angels, and the Finchley Boys. There were probably lots more, but those were the ones I knew of. And even if you didn't belong to one of them, blokes would claim they did, just to look like they belonged. A lot of it was down to what you saw in the cinema – I really believe that. Kids were going to flicks and seeing Marlon Brando's gang on motorbikes, and James Dean's crew illegally racing cars. And at gigs with groups experimenting with instrument smashing. All causing trouble – looking for it. And the way guys portrayed themselves: moody, diffident, arrogant, aggressive. If you were young, and up for things at that time in your life, that was the way to be.

'So when you saw, say George Eastham being booted around by the likes of Bobby Collins, you'd swear and feel more aggressive. The best example I can give you is that when you watch Arsenal play United, you feel a lot more aggravated and pumped up than if you're watching Arsenal play Charlton, don't you? Because you're expecting trouble, and the testosterone is flying around. And really, football is handbags compared to what it was. By the sixties, teams were kicking lumps out of each other every week. Football was violent, and it was getting worse, and this was transmitted onto the terraces. So, for a lot of Arsenal fans, Peter Storey was the man, because he was the terminator – or whatever. He went hunting down the opposition until he got retribution for what had happened to our guy. He was the fella who'd stop Billy Bremner or Tommy Smith taking liberties. It could be like a war out there, sometimes. And that pumped you up even more.'

○ CONFESSIONS ○

THE TROUBLESHOOTER

'In the late sixties, Arsenal were really concerned about the growing instances of trouble on the terraces, especially the North Bank. There had been some horror stories when Rangers came to Highbury for a friendly in 1967. One of my police colleagues said that local residents had their milk bottles stolen, and smashed against the sides of their houses. Arsenal fans were injured because Rangers supporters were throwing potatoes with razor blades stuck into them. Then, at Manor House tube station, the police had confiscated swords and bayonets from more Rangers fans. They were big guys too – fellas in their thirties – unlike Arsenal troublemakers, many of whom were barely out of their teens. The club called us in primarily to protect Arsenal fans, because many of the mouthy ones were getting in serious trouble when rival gangs infiltrated the North Bank. In those days, there was an unwritten rule that crowds were basically supposed to police themselves.

Arsenal Football Club decided that their fans needed the extra help.

'When we volunteered for the undercover work, we were informed that we were to dress in so called "hooligan" code. So I had to put on braces, big black boots, and then I had to shave my head. It was actually quite exciting. I don't think anyone who does undercover work enters into it if they are averse to some danger. And then we had to gravitate towards Arsenal's bad boys, and become one of them. It was pretty hair raising stuff, because undercover work also means you need to socialise with them. It was eye opening – many were completely out of control in their own lives with drugs, drink . . . everything. Some were in respectable jobs, and just went along for a Saturday afternoon thrill. I know that some of them later became coppers themselves. One name stood out above all others. All the skinheads claimed to know Johnny Hoy. "Johnny's gonna get you, Johnny's gonna get you," they'd sing, as if he was some kind of Robin Hood figure. I doubt if many of them would have known Mr Hoy if they fell over him. It was pure posturing.

'After a few weeks, we were ready to get to work within the ground. We'd be primed, and manoeuvre ourselves into position near the group just before kick-off. The spotters – the guys with the binoculars – would be scanning the crowds all the time from their vantage points inside Highbury, in order to see where the trouble spots were. You'd be told, via walkie-talkie, to keep moving round the terrace, until a spotter saw trouble flaring up, or maybe evidence of weapons being played around with. If you got the signal – bang – you'd move in and make the arrest. Policemen in uniforms would usually assist.

'It wasn't really a job you could do for very long, and it could be extremely stressful. It was very hard to disguise the fact you were using a walkie-talkie, and you lived in fear of blokes discovering that you were an impostor. When you finished your stint as undercover, you had to lie low in another area completely, for fear of bumping into the group you'd busted. After a while, some of the Arsenal hoolies cottoned on, and it was virtually impossible for an outsider to join their group. I think we were quite successful in what we did, and we began compiling records on known troublemakers who supported other clubs, and went regularly to away games. We also raised the problem of hooliganism in the public consciousness. Even by the late 1960s, when things were often quite rough at games, the public perception was that everything was still fine like it had perhaps been ten years earlier. I think that without us, the trouble would have been far worse, and that we nipped many problems – and kids – in the bud before they became big-time hooligans. The most difficult part of the job was distinguishing *between those kids on the North Bank who simply egged others on, and those who were genuinely involved in fighting, because kids do like to mouth off – especially at football after a few beers.'*

'Richard' – Undercover Policeman

THE BAND MEMBER

The Arsenal fans were used to a band at Highbury since 1913. I was part of the Metropolitan Police Central Band. First and foremost, I was a copper, but I used to look forward to Saturdays at Highbury because I was a big fan. It was great. I could do both my hobbies in one afternoon – watch football and play music. We'd do our stuff before the game, but what the crowd really used to enjoy was the band marching at half-time. Our drum major's party piece was to throw his mace up into the air and catch it. It became a tradition. He was a fella who could best be described as "up himself".

'He always used to do it in front of the North Bank. It was as if he needed to prove himself – the musical equivalent of taking a penalty, almost. The whole terrace would be going "Oooo-aaah" as they prepared for him to throw it up in the air. Like they do now when a goalie prepares to take a goal kick, hoping that something goes wrong. Ninety-nine times out of a hundred he'd get it spot on. But one day, up went the mace, down it came, and he dropped it. The whole of the North Bank was wetting itself. They were celebrating like they'd scored a goal. They'd finally seen something they could tell their grandchildren: "The mace that fell to earth story."

'He was absolutely distraught afterwards, and the whole band was hardly sympathetic, and we were all shaking with laughter. It was like his life was over. "I can't carry on now. I'm finished," he was saying. You half felt sorry for him, but it was so funny. I mean . . . people in the world were dying from starvation, but this guy has gone to pieces because he dropped his stick. I think that even by the early sixties, we'd become a bit of an embarrassment to younger Arsenal fans. We'd march on the pitch, and you saw that although the crowd found our presence funny, we were well past our sell-by-date. They might as well have put Gracie Fields out there. You could see their point about the band, and it fitted in with how many fans saw the team going at that time. A poor team, whose glory days were long gone, watched by old men going on about Alex James. How was any of that relevant to younger fans? We were stuck in the past, and a lot of supporters made no bones about telling us.

'And then, of course, Billy Wright turned up with Joy Beverley, and things got even worse at the club. I mean, it was a bit of a joke. Liverpool fans went on about The Beatles, and United had Bestie with all his girls. Arsenal had a marching band and the Beverley Sisters. The club kept a band marching at Highbury until the mid-eighties. And the strange thing was the number of complaints they received about it. They couldn't live with us, and they couldn't live without us. Nowadays I take my grandson to games, and I find that the tannoy music is way too loud and intrusive. And thankfully, in my days with the band, we never had a stupid green dinosaur marching along with us, either.'

Clive Spencer – Band Member

○ COCKNEY REBELS ○

BY THE MID-1960s, football fans started to take more of an interest in what they wore at football matches. Pictures from before the early sixties reveal a blur of grey and brown suits and raincoats in football crowds. The older working man continued to wear his staple clothing to all social events, complete with hat and smart shoes. But when the footballers' maximum wage was scrapped in 1963, leading stars had oodles of cash to splash out on designer gear, and terrace fashions quickly changed.

Joe Baker recalled: 'I was talking to some supporters in the Marble Halls after a home match. It was about 1965, I reckon. And my eyes quickly fell on their clothes. One guy was wearing a light brown suede jacket, a dark polo neck, pinstriped trousers, and white shoes. He was wearing the same sort of gear that George Best wore, and I remember seeing a magazine with a picture of Roger Daltrey from The Who in it, and he was wearing the same outfit. It was the first time I noticed the growing connection between fashion – in this case mod clothing – and football. You started to see it more and more. Guys were coming to Arsenal and spending a fortune on their gear. I put it down to Bestie's influence. Blokes really started to care about their appearance in a way they hadn't done before. That went for players *and* the fans.'

By the late 1960s, John Simon's Ivy shop in Richmond was attracting a great deal of attention from 'hard mods' and it soon spawned numerous other outlets around London. The skinhead era had arrived, and the press believed that the amount of terrace violence at football matches was in direct correlation with the increasing number of skinheads inside grounds.

Arsenal fan Dave Squires – a 'hard mod' in the late sixties – claims that the appearance of skinheads at Highbury didn't tie in with the increasing amount of trouble in and around the ground: 'A group of around thirty of us would meet at Highbury and Islington tube station and get to the ground at around 2.30 p.m.. People got scared of us because they'd heard all the negative stuff about us in the news. And I don't deny that it felt good to walk towards Highbury with people staring at you and backing off a bit. You'd see other lone skinheads going to Arsenal games, but they weren't in gangs. It was mainly about image for them. We had our particular garb that we wore to games. You'd have your DM boots – some of the lads wore cherry colour boots if they wanted to stick out – Levi jeans or Sta-Prest, the braces, and most of the lads wore the old-style grandad shirts. And we'd stick the Arsenal scarf around our wrists, or just wear one around our necks. A lot of people wrongly cast us as villains who brought trouble to football. The only thing we really did was to encourage others to wear their colours. I don't think there's too much wrong with that.

'The problem was that most people resent change – especially in those days at staid, old Highbury, which seemed to be perpetually grey. We were the first to look different. The problem was that we were different, and because we were in a big group we got quite loud at games. The police would therefore drag you out first if there was trouble. Other Herberts got away with it because they *looked* more like an Arsenal supporter *should* in those days – grey and drab!

'Within the ground, I think that our lasting legacy was that we encouraged others to sing at games. People tentatively joined in, before they really got going. Then when Charlie George first arrived on the scene in the late 1960s, he was the original football skinhead, and he played for the Arsenal. So because of that, he became an icon to me and my mates.'

The arrival of Charlie George in Arsenal's first team had a sensational impact on the aura surrounding the club. Arguably, his biggest influence was to make the club a bit more hip for would-be younger fans. The two stars of Arsenal's sixties side – George Eastham and Joe Baker – were very much in the mould of late fifties footballers. Highbury crowds labelled Baker the 'laughing cavalier', but Baker recalls some fans nicknaming him 'Elvis' due to his quiff and passion for rock 'n' roll. With the full Brylcreem treatment, the fragile Eastham appeared to hark back to the Denis Compton era of the late 1940s. Joe Baker recalled: 'Before Charlie George arrived on the scene, the Arsenal team didn't really even consider fashion. Players had a short back and sides and even when we socialised, we wore old-fashioned suits. One of the Arsenal directors had words with me about my quiff. He said it made me look rebellious. In my time at the club, it didn't do to stand out from the crowd!'

For a couple of years before he made his first-team debut in 1969, the *Islington Gazette* had shown pictures of George glowering at the back of youth team photos, looking bored and broody. Already, his reputation for leery behaviour had been noticed by more established Arsenal professionals. 'Charlie had no qualms about calling me a wanker or a prick, and I was the bloody club captain,' recalls Frank McLintock. 'His attitude as an eighteen-year-old was far different from that of players we'd had at Highbury before. That's why I think the Arsenal crowd – especially teenage fans – loved him right from the start.'

Dave Squires talks of Charlie George displaying the full skinhead attitude: 'Charlie stuck two fingers up to the world right from the off – literally and metaphorically. He did whatever he wanted, both on and off the pitch. I was in a Highbury pub with some mates after a home game, and he strolled in. This was in the late sixties, and he still had his skinhead haircut. In he walked with that impudent manner of his. Then he shouted to his mates: "Right, which one of you wankers is gonna buy me a drink?" And his mates came back to him and said: "Who are you to call us wankers, after the way you played today?" And

Charlie grinned, admitted that he had played badly, and bought all his mates a round. There was no pretence or pomposity about him at all. He was grounded. Charlie influenced so many of us in the crowd to be different. If someone had a go at him, he'd have a go back. He really stood out in a team which wasn't all that glamorous, to be honest.'

To a degree, George agrees with Dave Squires' comments, but as for the suggestion that he was a style leader, he's *not* having it. In fact, he positively bridles at the suggestion. He recalls: 'I was different as a player; I'd take the piss. I'd nutmeg people, and if I felt like it, I'd swing round and nutmeg them again. I could turn the game into a show, and I think people could identify with that. It's what people wanted to see at games. They pay to be entertained, don't they? But as for being an icon for skinheads – that's a lot of old bollocks, really. I didn't set a trend at all. I got me hair cut short because others were doing the same. I never woke up one morning with the idea, I'll turn myself into the first skinhead footballer. And I never wore cherry boots or a Ben Sherman shirt, either.

'Neither do I think there's any mileage in the view that I was some sort of guiding light for skinheads through my behaviour. I'd have a go back at people if they annoyed me because I came from a tough part of London, where I had to be like that to survive. I resent it when people try and pigeon-hole me.'

Although Charlie refuses to play ball on this issue, Dave Squires argues that from the moment George made his debut, the North Bank found a kindred spirit. 'Right from the start, Charlie knew what it was like to play to an audience. And so he should, he'd stood there as a kid, hadn't he? Whenever he scored a goal, or a team-mate scored, he ran to us – there was the connection right from the start. He dragged Arsenal out of the dark ages. All those mid-table finishes, all that bollocks under Billy Wright. Then Charlie arrived and shook us all awake.'

1970s

○ REBIRTH ○

BY 1970, seventeen painfully long years had passed since Arsenal had lifted a trophy – and didn't the players know it. Frank McLintock recalls: 'You'd play your game, and all the guys from the thirties and forties would be there afterwards. You know: the Mercers, the Drakes, the Comptons. All Arsenal legends. And it made you feel inadequate, to be honest. They'd won things. And we'd won nothing. And you'd think to yourself, Christ, this isn't good enough. You'd see pictures of the thirties side all around the stadium, and it would fill me with this feeling: We've got to strive to equal what they did. Some people suggested taking the pictures down, but Don Howe always argued that we *had* to be aware of their achievements, in order to try and match them.'

By March of the 1969–70 season, Arsenal had a golden opportunity to bring to an end the trophy famine, because the team had reached the semi-finals of the Fairs Cup – the prototype of the UEFA Cup. Unlike the modern version, which has largely been sucked dry of talent due to the ever expanding Champions League format, the last four teams were Arsenal, Inter Milan, Anderlecht, and red hot favourites Ajax. 'Of all the teams in the last four that we wanted to avoid, it was Ajax,' recalls Jon Sammels. 'They had a young Johann Cruyff, and Dutch football was really on the up. John Radford actually wanted Ajax in the semis because his wife Engel was Dutch. We just wanted to avoid them like the plague. Guess what? We drew Ajax. And to add to the challenge, the first leg was at home, which is another thing we didn't want.'

Inevitably, the hype surrounding the Arsenal v Ajax clash centred around Cruyff. George Armstrong recalled: 'He was a beautifully balanced player. Those in the game realised he was Europe's rising young star, and our defence needed to be on their toes, as he was an absolute magician. Ajax also had guys like Krol, Keizer and Muhren in their team, so they were a formidable outfit. Their style of play was typically Dutch, where they'd defend deep, and hit back on the counter, and we rose to the challenge. We sensed at Highbury that they were backing off us too much, and our performance that night was outstanding.' Ultimately, Charlie George stole the show. His passing – often delivered with the outside of the foot – and his superb low shot for the first goal drew admiring comments from Cruyff himself, who claimed, 'George can become as good as Di Stefano.' Two more strikes from Sammels and Graham gave Arsenal a 3–0 win, and the Dutch side could only muster a 1–0 win in the return leg. The Gunners had reached their first final in twenty years.

Belgian outfit Anderlecht awaited in the final, after they unexpectedly overcame Inter in the semis. In front of a hostile Belgian crowd, who whistled and jeered every time an Arsenal player touched the ball, the Gunners were summarily destroyed by Dutch star Jan Mulder during the first leg of the final. 'He taught us a new kind of football that night,' confessed George Armstrong. 'We learned that if you gave guys like that too much room in games, they'd kill you.' Anderlecht won 3–1, after Kennedy's late header gave the team – in the *Daily Mirror*'s words – a 'Ray Of Hope' for the second leg. But that was about all.

A week later, 57,000 packed Highbury for the return leg. Arsenal fan Peter Swift recalls: 'In my opinion, that night was the best ever at Highbury. The crowd was really up for it, in a way they probably hadn't been for years. The North Bank was heaving. For the entire game, both the Clock End and the North Bank chanted 'Arsenal, Arsenal'. It was like at Spurs in 1987, when the crowd and the team just merged as one. It is the sort of occasion which happens once in a generation, and you can sense the enormity of it all as the game unfolds. You could tell on that evening: This is it. It has to be the start of something. The rawness of the evening came from the fact that not a single Arsenal player – and increasingly few in the crowd – had seen any degree of success in recent years.'

It's clearly not simply a case of fans viewing the game through rose-tinted spectacles. Frank McLintock recalls: 'The crowd was like a twelfth man that night. You could feel the hunger in the air. It got right through to the players, and energised us even more. In the press, all the players had urged the fans to give us the kind of reception that Anderlecht received from their fans in Belgium. You know – feisty and intimidating. And believe me, the noise really was ear splitting back at Highbury.' Jon Sammels adds: 'No one inside Highbury will ever forget that night.' Added impetus to the game was given by McLintock's rousing speech in the aftermath of the first-leg defeat, where he came out screaming from the showers, 'We can win this,' and UEFA's ruling just a few hours prior to the second leg that in the event of a tie, away goals would count double. Arsenal knew that a 2–0 win would suffice. Not that that would be an easy task.

For twenty-five minutes, Anderlecht backed off Arsenal, threatening briefly when Jan Mulder and Paul Van Himst ventured forward. McLintock recalls: 'Mulder was an outstanding player. Different from anything you saw in England. You had to keep him under guard all the time, as he could – in the blink of an eye – make runs off you and drop deep. One touch – and bang – he could make killer passes or hit you with a great shot. They said Cruyff was the best, but if Mulder hadn't got an injury which ended his career early, he could have been equally as famous.' Arsenal exploded into life on the half-hour mark. From a Sammels pass, Eddie Kelly sidestepped his marker, and smashed an unstoppable shot past Anderlecht keeper Trappeniers. 'Although we were halfway there,' recalls McLintock, 'I said to the lads at half-time to keep it tight, and keep hounding the Anderlecht players.' As the Arsenal players jogged back for the start of the second half, the captain decided to take matters into his own hands. 'I ran over to the North Bank, and did this...' (At this point, McLintock jumps up from his chair, and starts thumping his fists together – his leadership skills just as potent thirty-five years later.) '"Sing up, come on!" I was shouting at them.'

Peter Swift believes McLintock's gesture could be the most significant intervention made by a club captain at Highbury. 'McLintock's gesture was amazing. Inevitably, you go a bit flat during the half-time break, and it can take a while to get back into the swing of things. But Arsenal didn't really have the time, so he was saying to us – and the team – to stay focused on the job. Immediately, the crowd noise rose to the level it had been in the first half.' In the seventieth minute, the non-stop chanting finally paid dividends as a mud-splattered John Radford headed in a George Armstrong cross. Two minutes later, Jon Sammels blasted home a third. 'It was a beautiful moment, absolutely mind blowing,' Sammels recalls. Arsenal were within touching distance of the trophy.

'The last few minutes were like Chinese water torture,' explains McLintock. 'The work the defence had to do was amazing. You needed eyes in your arse to see Van Himst and Mulder. In the last minute, Mulder hit this great half-volley which skimmed the post. Fortunately for us, it went the wrong side, but it was a warning. If that had gone in, it would have tied the scores up at 4–4. Who knows what would have happened then?' The referee blew his whistle after four minutes of added time. Arsenal had landed their first trophy since 1950. The scenes were astounding. Peter Swift recalls: 'I was just at the front of the North Bank, and when the whistle went, the instinct was to run on to the pitch. I got to Bob Wilson, who told me that he would do the lap of honour if it killed him. It was a fantastic night. Afterwards, the fans congregated in Avenell Road, and were chanting the Arsenal players' names. Eventually, they emerged from the main entrance, and were greeted like superheroes. I spent the whole night thinking about how good it felt to stuff the Spurs fans' jibes up them, as they had taunted us for years about being second-class. Arsenal were back!'

For Bob Wilson, the memories of that evening remain as fresh as ever: 'The final whistle brought an outpouring – a release. All that pent-up frustration in the fans and players was gone in a flash. If you think about some of the older members of the crowd, they had seen the great sides of the thirties and forties, and finally the slumbering giant had awoken. All the crowd – it seemed – came over the barriers at the final whistle, and the police knew that it was a friendly pitch invasion. So they turned a blind eye. I was determined to do the lap of honour, because it had been such a journey, and we were all so fed up with being runners-up. Now we'd actually won something. For a goalkeeper, it's nice to get to both ends of the ground as well, because obviously, I spent equal time at both ends, and they were equally as supportive to me. Confidence is crucial for goalies, so I felt I had to do it.'

The sense of relief felt by Arsenal players was unbelievable, and to a man, they were delighted for their captain. Jon Sammels recalls: 'Highbury is such a special place, and it's wonderful to win a trophy in front of your own supporters. Above all, I was so pleased for Frank, because he'd had so many disappointments, and he was an inspirational captain. You can never underestimate the importance of his speech after the first leg. He set a captain's example.' And how did McLintock feel in the aftermath of the Fairs Cup victory? 'Like I wasn't jinxed any more. Like I'd delivered, and that my team had finally delivered. Now I could finally look people like Joe Mercer in the eye. And I think we all realised that finally, Arsenal was awake again, and that the millstone had been lifted from around our necks. I also think it shows the desire we had within us that we weren't content simply to sit back and rest on our laurels. We believed this could be the start of something massive for Arsenal.'

So it proved. As the nation prepared itself for the beginning of the 1970 World Cup, the vibes emanating from Highbury were positive ones, at last. 'Now, we'd like to go and win the League,' was the overriding message. The 1970–71 season would prove to be one of the most dramatic and remarkable in Arsenal's history.

◦ NO HALF MEASURES ◦

THESE DAYS, the Halfway House (so-called due to the fact that it lies halfway down the tunnel at Highbury, and because it is situated more or less on the halfway line) has been converted into a mini-TV studio. Players and managers gather there for post-match interviews, in front of a cardboard backdrop bearing the Sky, BBC or AXA logos. 'It's a pretty scruffy place really. It looks quite nice on the television, but it isn't like that at all,' explains Bob Wilson. As if to prove what an eyesore the Halfway House is these days, it doesn't even warrant a mention as Wilson conducts his 'Legends' tour of Highbury, and the door to the room remains locked. Yet forty years ago, the team meetings which took place in the Halfway House played a crucial role in the club's return to trophy winning ways. The gatherings were not exactly for the faint-hearted.

There has always been a rich tradition of 'no-holds-barred meetings' at Highbury, dating back to the 1930s. To the astonishment of the club's directors, Herbert Chapman originally introduced team meetings as far back as 1925, an idea he'd used to great success at Huddersfield. It fitted entirely with Chapman's view that far from being ignorant serfs, players should be taught to reflect on their performances, and bond with team-mates. George Male commented: 'It was part of Herbert's general philosophy that footballers shouldn't be treated like fools, and that they must reflect on their performances to help them improve.' The tradition was carried through into the post-Chapman era.

Newcomer Ted Drake couldn't quite believe it after he'd arrived in 1934. He recalls: 'I scored both goals in a 2–0 win over Sheffield United in the last game of the season. I was feeling pretty pleased with myself. Arsenal had won the league, it was time for the summer break, and I'd settled in well. I'd changed, and was just about to go, when George Allison and some of the senior players decided to call a team meeting. They reckoned that even though Arsenal had won the league, some of the performances hadn't been good enough. I couldn't believe what I was hearing, and in any case, I wasn't really used to team meetings at Southampton, because our manager just told us to get on with it. What was stranger was that Alex James came in for criticism – to his face – by team-mates. The greatest player in the country at the time was actually being accused of being a bit lazy.

'George asked me directly how I thought I'd played, and I made some flippant comment about scoring two goals – so I must have done something right. Big mistake. I got ripped into by team-mates like Alex, and Cliff Bastin, who argued that I should be contributing more to the team. I obviously appeared a bit bewildered, because George Allison looked at me sternly and said: "Ted, look around you, and walk around this great stadium. It's here because so many people have worked beyond the call of duty for this club, and have bettered themselves. That's what we expect from you – you need to reflect on your performance, and strive to improve." From that day on, I realised that Arsenal was different. Highbury crowds don't accept 'OK'. Self-satisfaction could have been the start of the slippery slope. Those meetings kept us hungry and focused.'

Thirty years or so later, Frank McLintock, who became captain in the mid-1960s, decided that something was fundamentally wrong with the team. He decided – along with manager Bertie Mee – that no-holds-barred team meetings would focus the team's minds. He recalls: 'Under Billy Wright, everything was a complete mishmash. On their day, the team possessed some world beaters, like George Eastham or Joe Baker, but the team never worked as a unit. Players did their own thing. So, after a weekend match, when we were back at Highbury for a running day, we started to meet in the Halfway House to discuss where things had gone wrong – or right – at the weekend. Occasionally, Don Howe or Bertie Mee would chair the meeting, but often it was done behind closed doors – players only. If Don did it, he'd have a magnetic board with stick-on figures, and he'd plan tactics or matches.

'If I was chairing it, I'd sit at the front and invite comments about the game, and how we could improve things. It could get quite savage, I suppose, but everyone had a chance to air their grievances. I'd say (McLintock jumps out of his chair at this point), "Hey, *you're* not doing it, and *you're* not doing it." And I'd swear at them, and they'd swear back. I remember once, Peter Storey took exception to my comments, and he shouted at me: "Well how the fucking hell do you think you're playing?" and I said, "Probably as crap as you, but at least I'm trying to sort things out." It was hard and it was frank, but I believe very much that without such an approach, the players wouldn't have had the success they did. And no one really bore a grudge for long. I recall that Charlie George got me by the throat once and threatened to throttle me, but people's tempers cooled off pretty quickly.'

On other occasions, team meetings would take place in the dressing room. Bob Wilson recalls: 'Bertie Mee gave his famous speech with about two months of the season remaining. To be honest, I thought he'd lost it at first, because he was shaking so much. He told us that for the remaining six or eight weeks, we needed to put our family life on hold because we had a great opportunity to achieve the Double. And he was absolutely right. Then, he started giving us warnings about discipline, and he did it quite pompously, so I said to him, "Oh for God's sake Bertie, get off your high horse." And that provoked quite a lot of laughter, because little Bertie would have struggled to get on a horse in the first place!' It should be added that the Arsenal squad reacted in different ways to the meetings. Some, like Bob McNab, would shout back if they felt they were being singled out, as did Charlie George and Ray Kennedy. John Radford admitted to 'falling asleep' in Bertie Mee's meetings, and doesn't actually remember Mee's motivational speeches at all.

The Halfway House also served another purpose – as a players' room where they could meet wives, girlfriends, and other friends after matches. Jon Sammels describes it as ' . . . a narrow room, maybe eight feet wide, and no longer than fifteen feet – at the most. At one end, there was a bar which served tea and coffee and sandwiches. But it was tiny. After games, it was a real hub of activity though.' Bob Wilson recalls: 'One day, I met this really mad keen Arsenal fan in there, and he seemed a really good bloke. When he left, I asked Frank McLintock who he was. Frank told me he was "Mad" Frankie Fraser. "He's a hit man for the Richardsons," Frank said. I was a bit naïve in those days and didn't know what a hit man was. Frank looked at me oddly. "A bang-you're-dead type hit man Bob." It took a while for the full meaning of what Frank had said to sink in.'

It wasn't the first time that Wilson had a brush with the London crime scene: 'In the late sixties, there was a chap who offered us players really good deals on shirts and other goods. He'd wait outside the stadium, and you could get five really high-quality shirts for a tenner from him. Literally – it was from the back of a van, and yet I don't think I ever realised that it might not be strictly legitimate. One time, I was offered some Kodak films for virtually nothing from his shop just down the road from Highbury. The chap knew that I was often the official photographer on Arsenal's tours abroad. So I practically bit his hand off, and got hold of these films. A couple of weeks later, Bertie Mee summoned us to the Halfway House, and told us that the police wanted a word. We were told that there was a great deal of stolen merchandise in circulation in the area, in particular camera equipment and films. I think I went the colour of Arsenal's shirt, and slid down in my chair, trying not to look too obvious. I wised up a bit afterwards!'

Bobby Gould's memories of the Halfway House are also decidedly mixed: 'The player I always remember from those meetings was Peter Storey. He was such a quiet lad you barely ever heard a peep from him. He was one of those intense, brooding types. Anyway, I mentioned once that I didn't think he'd played very well in a game, and that he wasn't getting stuck in enough. Imagine saying that about Peter Storey. I remember that he was sat in the chair in front of me, almost like he wasn't listening. When I had said my piece, he sort of casually glanced behind me, and then looked me up and down. He said nothing, but I got the distinct impression he didn't like what I'd said.

'After the meetings, we used to go and play five-a-sides on the pitch behind the Clock End. Peter was on the opposite team to me that day, and as we kicked off, he smirked at me. Jesus Christ, I got the full Storey treatment: slammed off the ball, crunching tackles . . . the lot. Clobbered left, right, and centre. The lads were doubled up laughing, and years later, I can see the funny side too. But if you bore a grudge against a team-mate, for what had been said in the meeting, it didn't last longer than that five-a-side match. You sorted it out like men on the pitch, and it was over. It made team spirit ten times better. I'll never forget the Halfway House. I'm convinced it was one of the key reasons for Arsenal's success in the early seventies.'

○ HEAD FIRST ○

LIKE MANY of his contemporaries, George Best made his money during the final years of his life by reliving experiences from his playing days. Judging from his comments at 'An Evening with Best and Greavsie', he didn't particularly enjoy Manchester United's games with Arsenal very much. Best's most difficult opponent? Peter Storey. 'He breathed up my arse for the full ninety minutes, every game. I couldn't get a kick. He'd have booted his own granny up in the air if it would have stopped an opposition goal.' The worst moment of his career? 'When I was clean through against Arsenal in 1970, with just Bob Wilson to beat. I did what I used to do all the time – feinted to the left and moved to the right. But this time, Bob snatched the ball from me. I can remember it like it was yesterday. Sometimes, I would wake up at night and wonder how I didn't score. And it was over thirty years ago!'

The BBC's *Match Of The Day* cameras covered Arsenal's opening match of the 1970–71 season against United, who were playing in uncharacteristic blue shirts. As always, it was one of the most eagerly anticipated games of the season, and after the Fairs Cup victory three months earlier, hopes were high. An enormous 55,000 crowd packed Highbury that day, for a game which gained huge significance as the season passed. After the underachievement of the 1960s, hope was once more restored among the crowd.

Steve Ashford recalls: 'The start of the 1970–71 season was great. It felt like Arsenal were big-time players again, after years of nothing. By now, the players were really individuals. Of course, they were team components, but you began to look at them as different people. When the teams ran on to the pitch, it wasn't like nowadays, when both teams come on together and then shake hands to promote good sportsmanship. The opposition used to run on first, and normally they'd run to the Clock End. But if teams fancied cranking up the atmosphere, they'd run towards the North Bank, and everyone would roundly boo them. United, Spurs, and Liverpool sometimes did it. But usually, they'd head towards the North Bank. First out would be Bob Wilson. He'd always jog across and throw his cap and gloves into the net and we'd chant "Wilson, Wilson, Wilson" at him.' ('I'd never clap the supporters until I reached the penalty area. I enjoyed hearing the crowd building up the chanting. Then I'd clap back – I milked the moment. But all of us would listen out as the crowd sang your name. Of course we did. It was important,' recalls Wilson.)

'Then came Pat Rice,' continued Steve Ashford. After 1972, we'd shout "Pat Rice, tasty goal!" at him, because that's how he described his goal at Reading in the FA Cup. Then it would be "Geordie, Geordie Armstrong, Geordie Armstrong on the wing," which we then sang at Brian Marwood years later. For George Graham, it was "Graham, Graham, Graham", Peter Marinello's chant was my favourite: "Hey, hey, hey, hey, hey, hey, hey, na, na, na, Marinello," after the song by Steam. There was, "Storey, Storey, Allelujah", and, "Born is the King of Highbury" for Charlie George. And if they didn't respond and clap back, we'd boo them!'

The United game was also a crucial development in the relationship between football and television. George Armstrong recalled: 'We'd just had the 1970 World Cup, and I don't think Brazil would have made the impact they did if it hadn't been for colour TV. Those sunshine yellow shirts on the lush green pitches . . . it was a very powerful image. A lot of Arsenal fans have since spoken to me about the Arsenal v United match, as it was the first time they'd ever seen Arsenal on telly in colour. We had the classic red and white tops, and United were in dark blue. The colours contrasted really well. And to see football in colour was a real novelty. Then add in John Radford's hat-trick, Bob Wilson's save, and Bestie. Just the guy's presence added to the aura of the game. We were in the modern era now.'

Arsenal fans' response to Best's presence was mixed. Steve Ashford claims: 'I was never interested in other team's big stars. Never interested me when Keegan or Chivers or Best came to Highbury. No sense of awe at all. I was an Arsenal fan who was there to watch Arsenal. It wasn't a case of wanting Best to play well just so, in years to come, I could say I saw Best play a blinder. I wanted him to play badly so that my team would win. That myth about people wanting the opposition to play well is a load of old bollocks, really.' Arsenal fan Frank Standen disagrees: 'There was an aura surrounding Best that you've not really had with a footballer since. When he used to trot over to the touchline to take a throw or whatever, you'd boo him, but in the back of your mind you'd be thinking, Bloody hell, George Best is standing a few feet away from me. I never had that with Beckham, but I did with Bestie. He made football cool and attracted so many to the game. He made Arsenal v United clashes even more spicy than they would have been already.'

To Steve Ashford's delight, and Best's disgust, the Irishman was brilliantly shackled by Peter Storey that afternoon. 'He stuck to me like shit to a blanket,' Best admits. John Radford's three strikes, and George Graham's cleverly headed goal gave Arsenal a 4–0 win. As Frank McLintock points out, it was a blueprint for the rest of the season. 'The quality of our attacking was excellent, with Ray Kennedy and John Radford leading the line powerfully. We also had the skill there from guys like George Graham. The Arsenal team I was in always had a great record against United. We'd always put Peter Storey tight on Bestie. And Snouty would always grunt and snort when he played in that destructive role. Basically, he didn't really like playing there, and he'd swear and make noises, anything to put Bestie off his game. None of the team gave Bestie the chance to express himself. He was a beautifully balanced player who could glide past you – if you let him – and then he was gone. Some said he was quite chatty on the pitch, but I don't really recall that. Besides which, I was always too busy breathing through my arse trying to catch him.'

Despite the 4–0 scoreline, Bob Wilson's save remained the talking point of the game. He recalls: 'Attackers would come through at full pelt, but I knew that at some point, they would knock the ball a little bit too far ahead. It was like an in-built computer, but I knew there was a split second where I could pounce. People said I was mad, because I went in head first. But that was the aspect of my game which lifted me out from the pack. It was the diamond in my game, and I really would go like a torpedo at players' feet. My attitude was that I was the last line of defence, and if I ducked out of the challenge, the opposition would score. Eight times out of ten, George would have scored that day. He dropped his shoulder, and tried to go to my left (his right) and for a moment, the ball was out of his control. I shocked him by scooping the ball away from his feet, and he looked back in horror. He jogged away, but I got up on my feet, and was elated. It remains my greatest save, because it was from George Best. When it happened, there was this amazing noise from the crowd, because it happened so early in the game – twenty minutes in. It was a crucial turning point in the season, even though it was only the third game in.'

In Wilson's study, he has a framed sequence of photos recording the moment. Over these Best has written: 'Kind regards, Bob. Sooner or later you get a lucky one – George.' The game's importance went deeper than that, as Wilson recalls: 'The fact was, we beat a United side which contained Best, Charlton, Law and Stiles. And even if United were going into something of a decline, Arsenal's victory that day sent out a message that, following on from the Fairs Cup win, the club was moving forward in the right direction. It was the best of omens for a wonderful season.'

○ **FORGOTTEN HERO** ○

As is the case with any crop of emerging youngsters at a football club, it is inevitable that one or two will fall by the wayside. Yet as the Sammels, Armstrong, Storey, Simpson and Radford cohort gained their first-team chances under first, Billy Wright, and then Bertie Mee, it appeared that the group would prove the exception to the rule. 'It's remarkable,' explained Bertie Mee to the *Islington Gazette* in 1966, 'that this group of hard-working youngsters seem set to be at the core of Arsenal sides for years to come.' Initially, John Radford bore the brunt of home fans' wrath. Frank McLintock recalls: 'The crowd initially saw him as a bit slow and cumbersome, but he soon got them off his case, with a hat-trick against Wolves back in 1968, and he never really looked back. He was a tough character, was John.'

With Jon Sammels, the case was reversed. He enjoyed ten-and-a-half happy years at Highbury, before the crowd began to turn on him. Bob Wilson claims: 'Jon was a fantastic player, who had great peripheral vision. He could also ping a ball with minimum back lift. This was no mean feat considering the ball weighed twice as much then as it does now. I remember his great goal against Manchester United, when the ball seemed to swerve in all directions before going in. He had genuine class, and was a bona fide Arsenal boy. He was arguably the most naturally gifted of all Arsenal's midfielders. He was the thinking fan's favourite player.'

Arsenal fan Miles James recalls: 'With many of the Arsenal players, it was easy to pick out their strong points. George Armstrong galloped up the wings, and put in great crosses. Peter Storey took out opposition defenders, and John Radford scored and set up lots of goals. The problem with Sammels was similar to the one with Gilberto these days. People started to ask, What does this guy actually do? How does he actually contribute? Looking back, I think that Sammels would have done well in the modern game, as he liked to take his time on the ball and deliver killer passes. And in the Double season, it got very unpleasant towards him. Arsenal fans turning on one of their own is never pretty. And it wasn't just from isolated pockets either. It began in the stands, as a lot of moaning does, and it spread like a disease. Maybe we were too thick to understand, but whenever I saw him play, I asked the question: "What do you actually add to the team Jon?" But now I look back and think, Christ, we destroyed a good player by what we did.'

Although most books on Arsenal suggest that Sammels had borne the brunt of the fans' wrath for a number of years, it wasn't always the case. Throughout the late sixties, as his silky midfield skills drew admiring glances from rival managers, the 'Sammels for England' lobby had a strong presence in the media. He was one of the first Arsenal players to have a song dedicated to him. The Highbury crowd chorused: 'I'd walk a million miles, for one of your goals, Jon Sammels,' whenever he scored. By his own admission, he remains ' . . . a huge Arsenal fan. I loved playing for the club. And when you break through with other youth team players like I did, you think that life couldn't get any better, and you've got the world at your feet. The goal I scored against Anderlecht in the Fairs Cup Final was just the icing on the cake. But definitely breaking through with Raddy and the others was very special, because it forges team spirit and togetherness. It's such an important part of your development as a player and a person. You're going from being a boy to a man. My bond with the club – and the other players – was very strong.'

Frank McLintock believes that – despite Sammels's undoubted potential – the bond was possibly too strong: 'Jon was a great lad who loved playing for the club. And he was a genuine Arsenal fan. Maybe that was part of the problem. He was quite sensitive, and took things to heart very easily. At different times, all players got some grief from the fans, but most were tough characters. If anyone had a go, say, at Charlie George, he'd threaten to "nut ya". Bob McNab would call you a "wanker". They could rise above it, or maybe have a few drinks and forget it. Jon was different – he'd brood on things and let it bother him.'

Sammels's problems began in earnest in late 1970. An ankle injury kept him out of the early matches of the Double season, and his place in the side was taken – at different intervals – by George Graham and Peter Storey. When he returned, the Gunners were already into their stride, and appeared capable of coping without him. He returned in

October for the home game against Liverpool, but admits to sensing 'a different mood from the fans towards me', although he opts not to elaborate further. Steve Ashford recalls: 'Sammels returned for the Liverpool match, but it really wasn't a case of "Nice to see you back Jon". Football fans are cruel. We say that footballers have no sense of loyalty, but often fans are just as bad. Once someone's out of the loop, they're forgotten. So Sammels came back and you think, What's he doing here? We've been fine without him. Cruel, but true.'

Frank McLintock also believes that his playing style didn't help: 'Jon was a very languid and elegant player. A good-looking lad as well. But he could get panicky on the ball. So if you got at him, he'd lose the ball. The general rule is that if you're having a nightmare on the pitch – and we all do from time to time – then do the simple things. Jon felt he had a responsibility to do his job properly, and he tried to carry on sweeping these long raking passes forward. And just as he shaped to do so, he'd pause and someone would whip the ball away from him. The one night it really got to him was in the Fairs Cup quarter-final against Cologne in March 1971. It was one of those nights when everything he touched ran away from him. Don Howe brought him off at half-time, and lo and behold his replacement comes on and scores. I suppose when luck turns on you like that, you know that the writing is on the wall. The crowd groaned every time he received a pass, and it was bloody terrible for him. By then though, the crowd had new favourites, like Charlie George and Ray Kennedy. Things had moved on by the time Jon came back.'

Bob Wilson confirms the sense of annoyance felt by the team as Sammels was barracked by the crowd: 'We hated it. Of course we did. I always thought it odd that Jon should get booed like he did, whereas Bobby Gould, who couldn't trap a bag of cement, seemed to be adored by the fans in the late sixties. Now Gouldy is a great mate of mine, but even he would admit that Jon was twice the player he was – skill-wise.'

Bertie Mee picked Sammels for the next game – an away clash at Crystal Palace. Yet by the following Saturday, he was omitted for the home game with Blackpool. It was an unsubtle message that Sammels was no longer seen as being strong enough to contend with the vagaries of the Highbury crowd. He was an outsider looking in when the season's big prizes were won.

He politely declines to put forward his version of events during those difficult early months of 1971, opting to put a positive spin on events instead: 'The first ten years at the club were great. It's the last six months which weren't so fabulous. I left to join Leicester where I had six good years, so my playing career lasted nearly twenty years. Not bad at all. I also think that by talking about those last few months, I'm diminishing the achievements of the lads who won the Double. The main thing for me is that we're still all friends today, which shows that we were a great group together. The bizarre thing is that when I did go back to Highbury, with Leicester, I got a huge ovation, which brought tears to my eyes. Life can be strange.'

Bob Wilson adds: 'Jon was my room-mate and the night before the FA Cup final, he was seriously choked up. I can't even begin to imagine what it must have been like for him to miss out on the climax to the Double season, after he'd been at Highbury all those years. You hate to hear one of your team-mates receiving criticism from the crowd. Fans have a much bigger influence on players than they think. In some cases, they can make you – but they can also break you.'

As the club's fortunes fluctuated wildly over the next fifteen years, Jon Sammels wouldn't be the last to suffer verbal abuse at the hands of fickle Arsenal fans.

○ THE CULT OF CHARLIE GEORGE ○

FROM BEING the original skinhead footballer in the late sixties, Charlie George was labelled the first 'footballing hippy' by the *Daily Express* in December 1970. Not that Charlie's approach to the game appeared to enshrine the values of peace and love. In an interview with the *Evening Standard* earlier that season, he'd already admitted: 'If anyone thumps me I just nut them.' In the era before all-pervasive camera angles prove it to be the case, an assortment of testimonies from Arsenal fans vouch for his habit of seeking retribution against the hatchet men of seventies football. A sly rabbit punch behind the referee's back, often followed by a wink to the crowd, and a torrent of foul language directed at the officials defied the, 'Where's your handbag Charlie George?' taunts which he received each week.

Yet Charlie remained enigmatic and – on the surface at least – inarticulate, compared with fellow seventies' mavericks Marsh, Bowles, Hudson and Worthington. It didn't prevent others from attempting to fathom out just what Charlie George stood for. In the early seventies, Alex Soles ran a barber shop in Holloway – Charlie's birthplace. He recalls: 'A lot of young Arsenal fans came in here to get their hair cut at the time Charlie George played for Arsenal. At first it was straightforward. "Give us a Charlie George," they'd say as they came through the door. And that was easy, because you set the clippers on 3 and off you went. Then, in late 1970, all these fellas didn't come by for a while. I thought I must have offended them or something. Then, one day, I popped out for lunch, and a group of these fellas now had long hair, platforms and flares. I said to them, "I thought you were a bunch of skinheads, what's with all this flower-power garb?" And they laughed and said, "We're done with all that. Charlie George grows his hair long these days." And I realised that young men were more interested in image rather than genuine values. I mean, skinheads and hippies aren't generally known to have much in common. At that point I realised just how much footballers can influence fashion. These days Beckham does it with his haircuts. But Charlie was one of the first.'

Steve Ashford believes Alex Soles' comments are rather too simplistic: 'Guys in the crowd grew their hair long because Led Zeppelin and Pink Floyd did it. I don't think you can credit Charlie with that.' Thirty years later, the man himself emphatically agrees with Steve Ashford: 'Here we go again. People talking about me hair and what I stood for. At the time, The Beatles and the Stones grew their hair long. If anything, I was just following them. But I suppose if you're a young footballer, you have to accept that people do tend to follow what you do.'

During the first four months of the 1970–71 season, the Highbury hippies who'd avoided the barber's razor were disappointed. Their hero had suffered a broken ankle on the opening day of the season, courtesy of Everton goalie Gordon West's flying challenge. The only action he saw at Highbury was by endless running up and down the North Bank in his mission to rebuild the muscles in his leg. It wouldn't be the last time in which a freak injury would hinder his progress at Arsenal. When he returned to the side early in the New Year, he was greeted like a returning messiah. Frank McLintock recalls: 'We always resented the fact that we were labelled a boring side. You could never call George Graham, Ray Kennedy or George Armstrong dull. We were also an incredibly fit team, because we trained so hard. Much harder than many modern sides – a fact which is often overlooked. But when Charlie returned to the side, he added something extra to the team. He was our X-factor. He could spray passes around all over the place. He could shoot from distance with minimum back lift – no mean feat given the weight of the old-style footballs. Just as importantly, he could also look after himself, which you really had to do in those days. Having him come back midway through the season was a bit like signing a new player. His impact on the team was amazing.'

Established professionals had been astonished by George's impact at the club from the minute he joined Arsenal. McLintock recalls: 'In Charlie's eyes, people are either great guys or wankers. There's no in between. He's totally black and white on such matters. The thing was, he was like that from the minute he arrived at the club. He thought nothing of turning around and calling me a wanker. "That was a shit pass, Frank," he'd snarl in that cockney accent of his. And I was club captain and about ten years older than him. But that was Charlie. He had no fears at all.' Bob Wilson originally joined Arsenal as an amateur, as his original aim had been to become a schoolteacher. Wilson recalls: 'I suppose that I was Charlie's teacher for a while. I'd go into his school in Holloway and take coaching sessions. All the boys would address me as "Sir" or occasionally "Mr Wilson". Not Charlie, though. He'd come up to me in that impudent manner of his and say, "Hiya Bob, how's it going?" He didn't mean to be rude, it was just his way. Then I'd be in goal, and he'd cut through and shout at me "Which way do you want me to put it Bob? To the left? The right? Or through the legs?" So cocky! But he had the talent to back it up.'

In 2005, football writer David Winner provided an intriguing insight into George's footballing brain. The following extract was cut from an interview with the player which Winner conducted for *The Times*, but it offers a previously unseen glimpse into why his talents shone so brightly at Highbury, and why he was never able to forge an effective working relationship with Bertie Mee.

> Self-taught, he honed his skills on the unconventional pitches of childhood: park kickabouts, gravel, a patch of grass behind the flats on his estate. His favourite pitch was the local playground. 'It was only sixty yards between the goals, but there were obstacles: swings, roundabouts, a tree, railings. You weren't just playing against other players, you had to dodge all the other stuff as well . . . I could hit the ball whatever way it came to me. I was always able to correct where it had to go. You have to adjust yourself. I could hit the ball completely off balance. People told me, 'You're not supposed to do that. You've got to be like this,' which was crazy. No one could ever teach me how to play football.

His impact on the team was never better illustrated than against Newcastle at Highbury, in April 1971. Still trailing Leeds by five points at this stage of the season, Arsenal began to show signs of battle fatigue. George was being effectively shackled by Newcastle captain Bobby Moncur, and was becoming distinctly hot under the collar. Bob Wilson comments: 'Charlie was often more nervous than he looked, and he was sick with nerves before a game. Sometimes, he appeared to drift out of the game completely, and you'd have a word with him at half-time. But his major strength was his ability to remember the one good thing he might have done. Even if he was quiet, he always had the ability to believe he could do something special later in the match.' George Armstrong recalled: 'In that game, it just wasn't happening for us, and the crowd was getting edgy. Charlie was getting more riled as time passed, and Moncur was digging into him more and more. Eventually, Charlie flipped, and put his hands around Moncur's throat. "Don't keep fucking pissing me off, or I'll nut you," he shouted at him. I was right by Charlie when he did it, and was amazed, because Bobby could look after himself. But on this occasion Bob did as he was told!'

Ten minutes from the end, George received a loose ball on the edge of the box, played a one-two off Moncur's legs like it was a deliberate rebound off a tree, and scorched a left-foot drive into the bottom corner of Newcastle's net. As the North Bank celebrated, George ran towards them, hair flapping all over his face like a lace curtain. It remains one of *the* Arsenal images of the seventies, but George remains typically taciturn about the whole thing. 'My aim was to belt it as hard as I could. And I did just that. You could say I was quite pleased.'

The match was televised live on *Match Of The Day*, and after his long injury lay-off, it proved to fans from other clubs that he was well and truly back. From now on, the abuse he received from opposition supporters grew by the week. George Armstrong recalled: 'There was the match against Stoke at Highbury towards the end of the season, and Stoke always took a big following to away games. I reckon about 4,000 Potters spent the entire game barracking Charlie. The whole lot of them shouting "Where's your handbag?" at him. Then the Arsenal supporters responded back, "Born is the King of Highbury". So we had this vital game which we scraped 1–0, but the backdrop is one of fans shouting about Charlie. It's the fate of players like him. No one ever thinks you're just OK. They either love or hate you. And Charlie travelled everywhere by tube. So after the game, he'd be there on the train with the fans, still very much on their level – not like today's players.'

A few weeks later, George's winning goal against Liverpool in the FA Cup final elevated his cult status on to an even higher plane. But it would be ten long months before he scored again at Highbury, and Arsenal's brightest star was already fading. As well as being 'unteachable', Charlie George would rapidly become unplayable.

○ CULT HEROES ○

TERRY MANCINI

To say that Arsenal fans had a tempestuous relationship with their centre halves in the early 1970s would be an understatement. There was cool respect for the classy Peter Simpson, and genuine adoration for Frank McLintock. Then there was Jeff Blockley . . . The Birmingham City stopper arrived for a (then) gargantuan £200,000 fee. Standing at six foot three inches, the imposing Blockley certainly looked the part. Just two days after arriving in 1972, he made his one and only England appearance. Blockley was supposed to be the long term replacement for McLintock, who had just celebrated his thirty-third birthday. The Scot found himself phased out of the side quicker than he bargained for. Within two weeks of taking McLintock's place, Blockley was already giving the Highbury crowd the jitters.

One of Blockley's former team-mates, who prefers to remain anonymous, comments: 'Blockley was utter crap. He was a staggeringly useless defender. A group of us went to Bertie Mee and said to him "Come on Bert, this guy is shit, get Frank back in the team." But as usual, Bert got all stubborn and pompous and we somehow got lumbered with "the Block" for two years, and Frank was allowed to go to QPR. Ridiculous. What we needed was the Highbury crowd to give Blockley the sort of grief they gave poor Jon Sammels. But they were surprisingly patient with him. They let us down!'

Within two years, even the stubborn Mee had had enough, and Blockley was bombed out to Leicester City. It left Mee with a gigantic hole in the centre of defence. The promising David O'Leary was progressing, as was Brendon Batson, but an experienced campaigner was required to stabilise Arsenal's backline. Mee opted to sign a balding thirty-two-year-old from QPR, Terry Mancini. On the face of things, it was a baffling decision – further evidence that Mee was losing his grip on events.

Mancini takes up the story: 'I could well understand why the Arsenal fans wouldn't have been overly thrilled to see me. I mean, Bert had got rid of Frank in his early thirties, only to replace him with someone who was just a fraction younger than him. And the club was in dire straits. By the time I arrived in January 1974, they were in the bottom three. That was practically unheard of for Arsenal. Let's be honest, I was no world beater, and I was aware that under normal circumstances, I'd never have been an Arsenal player. But when a club like that comes knocking, you have to say, Yes! The fans probably expected Sunderland's Dave Watson to come instead of me, but the club felt that Watson would block David O'Leary's progress. I was always a short-term option. The crowd expected very little from me, and in hindsight that helped me.'

The Arsenal fans in the Bailey pub near Highbury, raise their thumbs and thump the table at the mere mention of Mancini's name. 'He was great,' enthuses Steve Ashford. 'He had heart, and got stuck in.' Mancini says: 'I didn't have some of the skills that Arsenal defenders normally have. But in my last year at QPR, I learned a lot from Frank McLintock about positional play. I also never gave up. Bertie Mee knew that although I spent much of my career in the lower leagues, I'd never been in a relegation side. And make no mistake, Arsenal needed those qualities in the mid-seventies, because they were in a real scrap.'

It wasn't simply Mancini's appetite for the battle that made him a cult hero at Highbury. He also had a reputation for being a larger than life character off the field. In the early 1970s, he'd been part of The Clan – a group of wide boy footballers which included Alan Ball, Alan Hudson and Malcolm Macdonald. The Clan was supposed to cash in on the growing commercial opportunities for footballers. Mancini recalls: 'I was known to enjoy the occasional glass of wine with Huddy and the others. Terry O'Neill, the photographer, did some publicity shots of us where we were in our suits sat around a table heaving with champagne. Even more strangely, I've never smoked anything in my life, and yet there I am chomping on a cigar.'

Then there was the story of Mancini's Republic of Ireland debut, at home against Poland. Mancini qualified on account of his grand-parents' Irish connections, but he speaks with a broad London accent. As the two sides lined up and the national anthems began, legend has it that Mancini sung along enthusiastically with the Poland players. 'Oi, that's their national anthem you prat,' hissed Don Shanks – his former QPR team-mate. Did this really happen, or is it just another example of a seventies urban myth? 'No, that's absolutely true,' laughs Mancini. 'I suppose I got carried away and was keen to make an impression.'

Steve Ashford and friends argue that Mancini 'got what it meant to be an Arsenal player'. His brothers were well-connected in London's boxing world, and Mancini's interaction with the crowd also endeared him to the Highbury faithful. 'In those days, Arsenal players didn't really tend to applaud the crowd like they do today,' argues Steve

Ashford. 'But he did. It was like he knew how lucky he was to be at Arsenal. All of us would shout "'Enry, 'Enry" at him, after the guy who wrote the *Pink Panther* theme tune [Henry Mancini], and he'd rub his bald head and slap it a bit as well. I seem to remember him talking to the crowd on a couple of occasions, as well. He wasn't a bad player either, and he was much quicker than a lot of people gave him credit for. But he got stuck in, and that was crucial. When you were in the mess we were in, you needed that mentality. Get stuck in or piss off.'

Two matches aptly sum up his time at Highbury. One is preserved for prosperity on BBC's *Match of the Seventies* series. As Arsenal's defence laboured on a cabbage-patch pitch, in a 1975 home quarter-final FA Cup-tie with West Ham, Mancini can clearly be seen cajoling his fellow defenders; to little avail. From a Mervyn Day punt, Mancini was deceived as the ball landed flat on the mud. When Billy Bonds swept the ball into the Arsenal penalty area, three more defenders failed to anticipate the ball not rolling. 'The mud deceived them all,' screamed commentator David Coleman. But not Hammers' striker Alan Taylor, who poached his first goal. After a piece of Brooking magic, West Ham, who'd started the game in a pristine white away kit (now an attractive shade of brown) scored a second, with Taylor again on target, and reached the semi-finals. 'Apart from the money, of course, the standard of the Highbury pitch is what has changed most of all, since my playing days,' Mancini comments. 'On the day, Alan Taylor and Trevor Brooking were too good for us, but the Highbury bog really took its toll.'

His finest hour in an Arsenal shirt came with just four games left of the 1975–76 season. The Gunners faced Wolves in a crunch relegation match. With just a few minutes left on the clock, Mancini trotted forward for a corner, and as the ball sailed across, he connected perfectly to head Arsenal's winner. But for Mancini's goal, Arsenal would have been playing Second Division football. What Mancini did next is open to debate. Steve Ashford claims: 'He ran behind the goal at the Clock End and did his head slapping routine. All of us went mad.' Dave Summers remembers it differently: 'He ran to one of the corner flags and did a jig around it, then he wiggled his bum at the crowd.' Emphatically untrue, claims the man in question. 'I think I just shook hands with everyone and ran back to the halfway line. I don't think that a goal against Wolves would justify that sort of celebration, and besides which, I'd have been too tired to do that kind of thing by such a late stage in the game. I wouldn't have had the energy!'

With Arsenal now safe, and manager Terry Neill installed, Mancini moved on to Aldershot for £25,000. 'Along with Brian Marwood,' argues Frank McLintock, 'he was probably the best short-term buy Arsenal have ever made.' Mancini remains awestruck by his former club. 'Playing for Arsenal gave me that extra stature at the end of my career. Whatever happened from then on, I could always look back and say that I played for the Arsenal.'

○ HAMMERS AND TONGS ○

BACK IN THE 1970s, there used to be a green shed at the rear of the North Bank which served tea, Dundee cake, and beer. Fans wishing to embrace the entire terrace experience made a beeline for the green shed, and its notoriety spread among football fans from further afield. British Rail now laid on Football Specials for travelling supporters. In reality, it was the worst rolling stock available, and was no place for those who wished to watch England's beautiful countryside roll by.

Manchester United fan Chris Terry caught the Football Special from Manchester Piccadilly every year in order to make the pilgrimage to Highbury: 'The "Specials" were rough. The seats were ripped up and they were covered in graffiti. The bogs were disgusting and over-flowing, or just simply overflowing. If they were closed, you can imagine the state of the carriages by the time the train got to Euston. Everyone, it seemed, went armed with their Party Seven (beer pack), but you'd normally get stuck into the catering trolley as well. So if you had a three hour trip to London or however long it took in those days, you'd be absolutely slaughtered by the end of it. But somehow through the haze, you'd remember, "We've got to get ourselves into the

Green Shed." If you were up for a tear up, that was the only place to go.'

'I used to walk past it with my dad,' explains Arsenal fan Steve Chambers, 'and something always seemed to be happening inside. You'd hear "Give me an A . . . " right through the spelling to "The Arsenal, The Arsenal", and everyone would spontaneously clap. Or there would be a silence, and then roars of laughter. Often the chant would go up "We're gonna, fight, fight, fight, fight for the Arsenal!" and blokes would thump the walls. I would sometimes ask my dad if we could go in, but he'd just look at me strangely and pull me away. Once, he went to the toilet and as I waited for him, I popped my head round the door. You could almost smell the testosterone. Tattoos, beer bellies, fag smoke, booze. A man's place.'

Steve Ashford was a regular in the Green Shed. 'It was like a Tardis – so tiny from the outside, but when you made it inside, there were loads of people. There was a great atmosphere inside, and usually it was just heaving with Arsenal fans. Then, after a few beers, you'd stumble on to the North Bank to watch the match. Following Arsenal in the seventies was very different, but it was still the Arsenal, and I loved it. I mean, we were crap in the mid-eighties, but in the mid-seventies the standard of football was much worse, and most of the "hoof it" merchants who came to Highbury weren't much better. And for some games, the North Bank was sparsely populated. Then, the big crowds would return for the big attractions, and you'd get the buzz back.'

The mood changed when the likes of Liverpool or Manchester United came to town. Arsenal fan Jim Knight recalls: 'There was no segregation back then, and it was easy for away fans to infiltrate the North Bank. Most of the time, it was really about willy waving, though. Liverpool fans would turn up and they'd be in the Green Shed talking about how they'd nicked stuff from the West End that morning. They larged it a bit, but really they were much worse back in the sixties. Some of them would flash Stanley knives about, but they didn't actually use them, to my knowledge. It was the same with Manchester United. A lot of talk and swaggering, and maybe an occasional flare-up. But United tended to like gathering at the Clock End, and fighting after the game had finished. But when Chelsea or West Ham came to Highbury, there was always serious trouble. They were the first sets of fans to really wear their colours, and they'd tie their scarves around their wrists. They were saying, "We don't give a shit if you know who we are." It became a code of honour that they'd try to take the North Bank. About five minutes before kick-off, up would go the chant: "Zigger, oi, Zagger, oi, Zigger Zagger, Zigger Zagger Oi, Oi, Oi" and a group of about 300 Chelsea fans would charge down the steps with their scarves, Donkey jackets and DMs kicking and punching as they went. I've always been a coward, and the noise was thunderous, mainly from people trying to get out of their way. The police would come and encircle the crowd, and hundreds of coppers would stay there for the whole game. There was one match where the Chelsea mob was taken by surprise after Arsenal fans waited at the top of the steps for them. Chelsea had to back off, and basically, they walked straight out, as they were so humiliated. As a dad of two, I look back and wonder how we ever put up with that every week. Football then was the preserve of single young blokes, who were up for a piss-up and didn't object to some fisticuffs.'

The most infamous case of North Bank trouble occurred when Arsenal hosted West Ham in the 1975 FA Cup quarter-final. Conservative estimates suggest that 20,000 Hammers fans infiltrated Highbury that day, around half of whom watched the match from the North Bank. 'I lost count of the number of games I watched through rows of policemen's helmets,' recalls Steve Ashford. 'In those days, there weren't really any stewards at games. You more or less policed yourself, which was a pretty dangerous situation. The police were there to *contain* trouble rather than prevent it. But with that West Ham game, there were just too many West Ham fans to cope with.'

Terry Clarke recalls: 'In those days, West Ham had the Mile End mob and the ICF, who were always really up for it. They were as bold as brass, and often used to invade the Green Shed, which was provocative enough anyway. You had to be impressed at their efficiency. They'd get into the middle, and ring the outside as well. They'd encircle you in a pincer movement. There must have been some invisible sign between them, because all of a sudden, their arms would go up and they'd shout "United, United" and then it would kick off. And with West Ham, it really kicked off. A lot of their boys brought hacksaws with six-inch blades secured by insulation tape. And they had no qualms about using them either.'

Jim Fisher watched the game from the North Bank: 'The atmosphere was seriously edgy. By three o'clock, I was surrounded by hundreds of West Ham fans. I don't think I heard a single Arsenal chant that day. It was all West Ham, mocking the Arsenal fans with a rendition of "You're gonna get your fucking heads kicked in". When Alan Taylor scored their first in front of the North Bank, there was this huge stampede and we all got shoved down the steps. It was on *Match Of The Day* that night and you can see those at the front go down the terraces like dominoes. It was so dangerous. I'm a fairly big guy and I told this West Ham fan to stop shoving me in the back. He pulled out a knife and told me to "Shut up or I'll do you". I spent the rest of the game praying for the final whistle. It was a really crap day. I'd been threatened, and the Arsenal team was abysmal. It's my overriding memory of Highbury in the seventies. It could be a really violent place when London derbies came around.'

○ WITHOUT PREJUDICE? (1) ○

BY THE EARLY 1970s, a significant number of Afro-Caribbeans began to attend Arsenal matches. Many of these were the children of parents who'd arrived in the United Kingdom during the immediate post-war era. Their experiences of visiting Highbury were decidedly mixed. Collins Campbell's father arrived at Tilbury in 1953 ('My Father was obsessed with coming to the mother country – as he called it – and believed it would be a magical land of opportunity') and soon found work as a warehouseman in Finchley. Collins developed a passion for football through watching BBC's *Match Of The Day* and ITV's *The Big Match*. It wasn't until 1973 that he decided to go to a live game. By this time, he had embraced the Rasta lifestyle.

'The two guiding lights in my life were Bob Marley, with Charlie George slightly behind,' he recalls. 'Before I went to Highbury, I'd tried out several other grounds in London. I'll never forget the time I told Dad I was going to watch Chelsea at Stamford Bridge. His eyes were like saucers on sticks. "No way man, you can't do that. They'll eat you alive. You're not going there." So off I went – totally ignoring him. But I wish I'd followed his advice. Even as I approached Stamford Bridge, I was getting hassle from them. "Give us a spliff man," they were shouting in their worst Jim Davidson-type accents. Once inside the stadium it was worse. "Get your hair cut man," they shouted in their mock Jamaican accents. Other fans moved away from me, like I was some sort of criminal. Others whispered about me, and turned around to take a peek, like I was some kind of circus freak. One of my friends told me that going to Upton Park was even worse – and bizarre. At that time, Clyde Best played for them. Yet, even though he was one of their players, they were no more advanced in their vocabulary. "Give it to the nigger," they'd call out. Some even indulged in a spot of monkey calling.

'Going to Highbury was really the final shot in the dark to be honest, and I was nervous about what reaction I might receive. As I walked down the road from Finsbury Park, I noticed something rather strange. No one was looking at me. They didn't appear shocked or startled because a black man was walking towards the ground. What I also noticed – which I didn't see at Chelsea – was that there was more of a genuine ethnic mix in the streets around the ground. There were plenty of guys who were from southern Europe – Italians and Greeks, you know. It just felt different. Funnily enough, my first time at Highbury coincided with Brendan Batson's home debut against Sheffield United in March 1973. To be honest, I didn't know anything about him before he ran out, so I was quite shocked to see him. I was also a bit nervous as to what reaction he'd get from the crowd. But again, they were great, chanting: "Batson, Batson," and he applauded them back. Everyone was cool about it.

'There was a really positive reaction to Batson among my friends during the following week. He was a big inspiration for many of us – a shining example of what black guys could achieve. Because you have to remember that, at the time, it was like it is now with Asian footballers. A lot of talk about why they're not breaking into teams. It was also a time when commentators would come out with stuff on the telly which was bordering on racist nonsense. I remember pundits going on about black players with their "natural sense of rhythm" and magazines labelled them the "ace of spades" and all that rubbish. So, seeing Batson play for Arsenal was a big moment in my watching football.

'From then on, I was hooked. I tended to sit in the upper deck of the East Stand. The old fellas up there – I don't think they'd seen a black man before. One guy complained loudly to his friend that he hadn't paid his admission money to sit next to a "golliwog". People were also far more liberal with their use of the "n" word. You'd also be amazed at how many people reckoned the best way of breaking the ice with me was to talk about *Love Thy Neighbour* – the supposedly hilarious comedy in the seventies about a white guy living next to a black guy. But there was always this defence mechanism at Arsenal. If anyone did mouth off, they'd get told to sit down and shut up pretty quickly.'

Brendan Batson made six appearances for Arsenal between 1972 and 1974. He recalls: 'I wasn't aware of any form of racist abuse directed at me during my time at Arsenal. When I left and went to Cambridge, there was a bit. And then when I went to West Brom, me, Cyrille (Regis) and Laurie (Cunningham) used to get a lot of abuse at away games. I don't think there are any straightforward reasons as to why the Arsenal crowd is more open-minded than others. Maybe it's because there's always been a tradition of Greeks, Italians and Cypriots at Highbury. Maybe it's due to the club's proximity to Hackney Marshes. What is odd, is that of all the London clubs, West Ham was the most high-profile in the mid-seventies in nurturing black players. And yet Clyde Best eventually left because of the abuse he received. Whereas at Arsenal, I was the only black kid on the books, and it was a few years before the Chris Whyte-Paul Davis-Raphael Meade generation broke through at Highbury. So there is no real rhyme or reason as to why Arsenal crowds are more open-minded than other clubs at that time. They just were.'

It would be a gross over-exaggeration to claim that racial harmony persisted in and around the ground. When I placed an advert in the *Islington Gazette* for information on aspects of Highbury history, I soon received three virtually identical testimonies, citing problems at the exit to Arsenal tube station, and in the maze of streets nearby. In the mid-1970s, National Front leader John Tyndall admitted: 'We hope to swell our ranks by launching a recruitment campaign outside football grounds.' The National Front clearly made its presence felt around Highbury at the time.

Lloyd Packer had been going to home matches for a number of years, before he had a first-hand encounter with a member of the party: 'I walked out of Arsenal tube station, and headed away from the ground to meet some friends near where the Emirates Stadium is being built now. There was just a trickle of people walking away from Highbury, and I noticed a guy standing at the side of the road. He saw me and sneered. "Oi mate, fancy joining the National Front," he said. In his hand, he had a pile of leaflets or flyers with Union Flags on them, and there were also copies of *Bulldog*, the far-right magazine. My friend Ade told me afterwards that round the other side of the ground – up towards Highbury and Islington tube – there were copies of *Bulldog* being sold there too. And the scary thing was that people were buying them. That struck me as being weird, because I'd never experienced any problems inside the ground at all.

'Anyway, when the bloke made this comment to me, I threatened to hit him. And I'm a big guy, so he scarpered quickly, although he called me a string of racist names as he went. It made me feel very angry and shocked at the time, because my father – when he first came to the UK – had to put up with all sorts of abuse. When he tried to find digs he came across signs like, "No dogs, no blacks" and it was deemed OK for his workmates to call him derogatory names. He also told me and my sister that as part of the "Windrush generation" – as he described it – he had to put up with all sorts of hassle, but *we* didn't have to accept it. This incident outside Highbury was the first time I'd encountered a serious racist incident, and I was twenty at the time. What knocked me was that it happened at a place where I was supposed to enjoy myself, and where people forgot their differences. In fairness, the police were excellent about it and took my complaint seriously. A couple of weeks later, I received a call from them telling me they'd seized a large quantity of racist literature near the ground. The National Front was obviously on a serious recruitment drive at the time.

'By the early eighties, their presence outside games – at least those at Highbury – had almost gone, and the police clamped down quite a lot. But back in the seventies, those streets around the ground could be dodgy. They seemed to be far more dimly lit back then, as did the stadium, and it was all quite sinister at times. It was often like something out of Dickensian London. Ticket touts, guys flogging dope, and people just hanging around looking a bit iffy would sort of step out of the dark. There was far more of an edge around Highbury back then.'

○ GETTING CONNECTED ○

FEW ARSENAL PLAYERS – past or present – are able to explain their personal relationship with the Highbury crowd as articulately as Malcolm Macdonald. And as for espousing the virtues of the club and Highbury in particular, Macdonald is in a league of his own. After breezing into Highbury for an eye-catching but, bizarre fee of £333,333.33 in the summer of 1976, the bandy-legged, swashbuckling striker quickly lived up to his reputation for outlandish promises, and outrageous goal-scoring feats. At the press conference which rubber stamped his move South, he claimed: 'My aim is simple. To score thirty goals in a season, and to make Arsenal the very best team in the land.' Looking back on his tendency to make such bold predictions, he comments: 'Sometimes, the policy worked. I used to do it to motivate myself. It's the way I operated. Sometimes my predictions flew back in my face and made me look rather silly. But I had to motivate myself. And remember, I'd joined a wonderful, wonderful football club. I owed it to everyone – the fans, my team-mates and my manager – to give my absolute very best.'

During Macdonald's first few months at Highbury, his form had at times been rather patchy. The fans took to him immediately though, and sang the 'Supermac, Superstar, how many goals have you scored so

far?' chant whenever he received the ball. Yet Macdonald remained dissatisfied with his form, and that of the team's. In part, he explains,
this was due to 'Terry Neill's revolving door policy as regards players.
There was a defender called Pat Howard, who also arrived from
Newcastle. He played around nine games for Arsenal, and then he was
gone. In Neill's opinion, he didn't fit in. It was a bit like that with the
whole team. A hotchpotch of ideas with no one really knowing their
place. Several wonderful players couldn't really get along with his
tactics. Alan Ball and Alan Hudson, for instance.'

As Arsenal prepared to take on Macdonald's former club Newcastle
on 4 December, the team languished in mid-table, the early season
optimism had faded, and Arsenal's striker had scored just six goals in
fifteen games. 'Unacceptable in every way,' explains Macdonald. 'It was
an insult to Highbury supporters. When my former club came down, I
decided to lift the mood. I'd left Newcastle because I didn't get on with
Gordon Lee, the new manager. I never understood what he wanted
from me. My role – plain and simple – was to score goals. But that
wasn't enough for him, and then he said in the press, "I wouldn't have
paid that amount of money for Macdonald, he's not worth it." So I was
very keen to rise my game on that afternoon. The big problem was the
pitch. We'd had the 1976 summer drought, and now we had a big
freeze, so the wings of the pitch seemed virtually unplayable. Geordie
Armstrong seemed to cope OK, though!'

Armstrong recalled: 'Malcolm had a tendency to sulk if he didn't
score goals. And he'd had a bit of a slow start at Arsenal. Basically he'd
been a bit unlucky – things not bouncing for him and that type of
thing. But in the Newcastle match, Malcolm got it absolutely and
totally right. And his team-mates, and the Arsenal fans, saw that day
precisely what he could do.' Macdonald dispatched his first goal when
he bullet-headed an Alan Ball free kick into the top corner of Newcastle
keeper Mahoney's net. ('I loved that goal, it was the delivery you dream
of, and the product you train for,' Macdonald recalls.) Midway through
the second half, he pounced to score his second after Frank Stapleton
had miskicked his shot. Macdonald completed his hat-trick with a
simple tap in. But it was his reaction to the goals that summed up the
'Supermac' (a nickname he doesn't much care for) persona. He ran
straight to the crowd at the North Bank and the Clock End, rather than

thanking his team-mates, who'd put all three goals on a plate for him.

Macdonald explains his single-mindedness and connection with the Highbury crowd: 'I knew in my head that I would score the goals which would transform Highbury into a perfect arena for me. I knew that goals would enable me to connect with the crowd. Goals are an incredibly powerful thing. They make people love you. I knew that I was a goalscorer, who delivered the goods and made people happy at the weekend. Everything else to me on the pitch was secondary. Arsenal fans were a little different to Newcastle supporters. Less vocal perhaps, but very canny and savvy about their players. I remember the Newcastle game as if it were yesterday, and in their eyes, it meant that I'd really arrived. If a goal is a powerful thing, then a hat-trick is stellar. A gift from above, almost. It puts you on an entirely different plateau.'

Yet Macdonald's approach occasionally put him at odds with his team-mates. George Armstrong winced at the thought: 'Malcolm was a goal junkie. And if he didn't get his fix, he went bananas. An example of that was when we played Manchester United at home in the same season as the Newcastle match. Malcolm scored a good goal, and then Frank Stapleton, who was only a young fella at the time, rolled one slowly over the line past Alex Stepney. But just as it was crossing the line, Malcolm slid and then tried to claim it was his. How ridiculously single-minded was that? And afterwards, he says to Frank "That was my goal," even though TV replays clearly showed it was Frank's. But Malcolm just wanted more and more goals. That was around the time that he referred to Frank as "my dog", in that Frank was expected to do all the fetching and carrying for him. Mind you, I don't think we complained too loudly to Malcolm, as he secured our win bonuses on several occasions!'

If team-mates were bowled over by Macdonald's supreme confidence, the man himself was staggered at the grandeur of Highbury: 'You walked in and saw the Marble Halls and Chapman's bust – and the whole place screams quality and history at you. Newcastle was a big club, but at St James's Park we had cold, old dressing rooms which could be a nightmare in winter. At Highbury, there was underfloor heating and a bath warmed for you before the game if you wanted one. When I was at Newcastle, the dressing room had a huge crack in the window which let in the draught, and we had an old electric fire to warm us up. I mean, how dangerous is that with water sloshing around everywhere? It's amazing how much a stadium can reflect the type of club you're at, and Highbury completely sums up the type of club Arsenal is.'

Macdonald narrowly failed to meet his first year target, scoring twenty-nine goals. In his second year, he scored a further twenty-five, but the cartilage problems which conspired to end his career were already hampering his progress, and he was forced to retire in May 1979. The memories remain vivid: 'Highbury was a beautiful, special place and when I arrived there, I knew that I'd arrived. But when I got the news from the doctor that I had to retire, I walked through the Marble Halls for the last time, and looked down St Thomas's Road. I felt terrible. All the glory was over. It was the loneliest feeling in the world. You're walking out of a temple and going into the real world. I'd felt completely at one with the whole place.'

○ CULT HEROES ○

WILLIE YOUNG

Highbury regulars with long memories believe it's a toss up as to whose Highbury debut – Ian Ure's or Willie Young's – was the worst. Back in 1963, Ure made his first appearance in an Arsenal shirt against Wolves. The former Dundee defender, who'd arrived for a gigantic £62,500 fee, was now officially the country's most expensive defender. With his shock of blond hair, Ure was one of the most distinctive figures in sixties football. He certainly stuck out like a sore thumb against Wolves, as their pacy defenders nipped around him like speedboats around an oil tanker, and the Midlands side ran out 3–0 winners. Ure recalls: 'My first game, shall we say, wasn't a complete success. I don't know what it was down to – new surroundings maybe –

or perhaps my mind was still partly on the move – and the fee. But you often find that Scottish players who are new to the English top-flight have teething problems.' Ure slowly recovered after his disastrous start, and became respected, if not adored, by Arsenal fans.

Thirteen years after Ure's debut disaster, fellow Scot Willie Young made his Highbury bow against Ipswich in March 1977. Their quick forwards, Trevor Whymark and John Wark, had made life difficult for most Division One defenders that season, and Young hadn't actually played a competitive match for two months. Throw in the aerial threat of Paul Mariner, and the omens weren't good. Young had a nightmare, as his manager Terry Neill recalls: 'He tried to play like Pele, Best and Gerson rolled into one. He should have remembered that he was a fourteen-stone Scotsman.'

Young – through gritted teeth – recalls his debut. 'I had a bad feeling beforehand about the game, because I was lacking in match fitness. I hadn't actually played for a while, and although I could run and stretch OK, if you're rusty with your sharpness, you have a real problem. And Ipswich were a good side, but I think you could say that three of their goals were down to me. For their second, I totally misjudged the bounce of the ball, air-kicked it, and John Wark sneaked in and scored. It was one of the few occasions that I wished the ground could have swallowed me up.' When Willie and his new team-mates slouched off at the end, a cacophony of booing greeted him ('understandable in the circumstances, I suppose') as he disappeared down the tunnel. Highbury crowds are rarely so harsh on debutants, but just ninety minutes into his Arsenal career, he'd already broken two codes of conduct. First, he hadn't acknowledged the crowd when they applauded him prior to the game. Young admits: 'I could never hear what the crowd was singing or chanting. I was often too focused on the game. But I accept that not responding to them was a pretty major faux pas.' And second, and more glaring, Willie had signed from Tottenham.

Arsenal fan Trevor Barlow recalls his feelings when he discovered that Young had arrived at Arsenal: 'I got home from work and my brother-in-law phoned. He says, "Arsenal have signed a central defender – you'll never guess who it is." So I trot out the names. Terry Butcher? 'Cos he was the emerging star at the time. Dave Watson? Alan Hansen?

Because every club was after him from Partick Thistle. So I went down the list and in the end my brother-in-law says, "Oh, you'll never get it. I'll tell you – Willie Young." "Willie Young . . . " I said. "Willie fucking Young!" I couldn't believe it. Here was the guy who'd got sent off for taking out Frank Stapleton in a north London derby match. Spurs had dropped him because they didn't rate him, and now he signs for us! I thought, What is going on here? Then there was his debut against Ipswich. All of us thought he was another Jeff Blockley, only less mobile. We reckoned that Young would last about two weeks, then he'd bugger off back to Scotland.'

After the Ipswich match, Young was walking back to his car which was parked behind the Clock End, when an irate Arsenal fan appeared from nowhere and began hurling verbal abuse at him. 'This guy started calling me all sorts: a prick; a Scottish wanker. "Why don't you fuck off back to Spurs, you useless bastard?" he asked.' Lesser men may have been intimidated, but the fighter in Young rose to the surface. 'I had my family with me, and there was no way I was going to be spoken to in that way. So I told him that if he didn't bugger off, I'd throttle him. The guy backed off and scarpered. Although I'd proved my point, I realised I had a massive job on my hands to win over the Arsenal fans.'

Three weeks later, as Arsenal prepared to take on Spurs, Young's form hadn't noticeably improved. The *Islington Gazette* predicted that Young would be 'rested for the match, in order to give him time to adapt to the rigours of life at Highbury'. Yet when the Arsenal team trotted on to the pitch at 2.55, Young was there. The reaction from both sets of fans can best be described as 'unique'. 'I was the first player to be booed by both sets of fans at a north London derby,' explains Young. 'Arsenal fans had their heads in their hands because they thought that with me in their side, they'd lose their biggest game of the season. And I was told that the Spurs fans were questioning my parentage. But looking back, that game was the turning point for me at Highbury. It's strange, because Arsenal fans only really warmed to Sol Campbell after he played a blinder at White Hart Lane. But fans expect big performances.'

The Gunners won the game 1–0 thanks to Malcolm Macdonald's last-minute goal. But no one doubted that Willie was the star of the show. After ten minutes, Spurs strikers Peter Taylor and Gerry

Armstrong mysteriously found themselves sparked out on the turf after Young's unique blend of thuggery and combativeness saw them off. Half an hour later, his head was split open after an aerial clash with Glenn Hoddle, and the Scot departed for medical treatment. Ten minutes later he returned to the fray with a white bandage wrapped around his head. 'I looked like Basil Fawlty in "The Germans" episode from "*Fawlty Towers*",' he recalls. Upon returning to the fray, he once again proceeded to lay into Spurs players at will.

'Willie was immense that day,' explains Terry Neill. 'Arsenal fans could see that if they were patient with him, he could prove to be a great foil for David O'Leary. On the deck, David's pace would sort out most problems, but if anything was in the air, Willie would clear the danger. And with Willie you knew he'd get stuck in all the time. After that Spurs match, he got the message from Arsenal fans – you're in!' As Arsenal chased a UEFA Cup place – to no avail as it turned out – Young was granted a selection of chants. 'We've got the biggest Willie in the land' was one variation, but many of the fans preferred the simpler: 'Willie, Willie,' especially as the Scot prepared to wreak havoc at corners.

Not all Arsenal fans appreciated Young's habit of smashing the ball away at the first sign of trouble, though. Lee Chilvers recalls: 'There was a home match against Birmingham and Willie Young had been belting balls into the lower East Stand all game to clear the danger. With about a minute to go, I turned away from the action for a split second to talk to my mate, and then suddenly – BANG! I got smacked by the ball full in the face by one of his clearances. Glasses smashed to pieces and blood streaming from my nose. I remember my head was buzzing, and everyone around me was killing themselves laughing. All very embarrassing. I got home and my mum went mental. She didn't believe that a ball had done that. She banned me from going to games for a while, because she was convinced I'd been in a fight and wasn't telling her the full truth. Nearly thirty years on, she doesn't believe me. Bloody Willie Young!'

Over the next few years, as Young's legend grew off the pitch ('A pint, a fight over nothing and a bust up with Terry Neill, and Willie was happy,' recalls Alan Hudson), his cult hero status grew. 'Let's be honest,' Young argues, 'You don't get ginger Scotsmen playing for

Arsenal any more. Nor do you get bald blokes like Terry Mancini. Modern players are identikit. I was very different.' He certainly was – not least in the fact that Arsenal fans were forced to do a dramatic U-turn in their assessment of him. Occasionally, villains become heroes.

○ A FECKIN' GENIUS ○

ACCORDING TO a 1999 study conducted by the *Islington Gazette*, an estimated thirty per cent of Highbury residents claim Irish ancestry. Several nearby districts, including Camden and Kilburn, also contain a thriving Irish expat community. So it comes as little surprise that a fair proportion of Arsenal regulars have their roots across the Irish Sea.

The onset of World War Two accelerated the process of Irishmen flocking to Highbury, as East Stand season-ticket holder Michael Flynn explains: 'In 1939, unemployment in Ireland was very high. In some places like Cork and Dublin, it had reached levels of around sixty per cent. When the war began, English factories were crying out for manual labour – especially in the munitions workshops – and Irishmen from Dublin, Cork, and Belfast flocked across in their droves. I reckon that eighty per cent of the shells made in the Second World War had shamrocks on.

'I got a job in the munitions factory near King's Cross, and I can't honestly say that the reception I received was a friendly one. Some of my mates couldn't find lodgings. They'd see signs up like "No Irish" and in the factories, some of the English boys didn't seem too keen to see us either. "Why don't you fuck off back to Paddy-land, you fucking navvy?" they'd say. It was difficult, because you tended to stick together in certain groups, and a lot of Englishmen seemed to dislike us because we were often far more outgoing than they were. We'd have a sing song and have fun at work, whereas they would seem very uptight to my way of thinking.

'As the war progressed, attitudes changed a bit, and they began to get used to us, and we got used to them. It also helped that women began to come into the factories, as many of the men were away fighting in the war. Some of the English lads suggested we go and see some football with them. "We're off to watch Arsenal at White Hart Lane, you coming?" they'd ask. That was their home ground during the war, and me and my friends were hooked immediately. And I'll tell you something else, we taught those English boyos to sing. Jesus, I know there was a war on, but we came from backgrounds where you'd sing your hearts out at Gaelic football. So we started to do the same in England. Those bloody stiff-upper-lipped English. They wouldn't rouse themselves to sing up for the lads.

'After the war, it was the same when we went back to Highbury. It was the Irish in the crowd who got them singing – and the Italians too. Highbury's always been a very cosmopolitan crowd, and it's a good job. Left to the English, it would have been the Highbury library years ago!'

By the late 1970s, Highbury was a virtual home from home to many Irish Arsenal fans. Managed by Ulsterman Terry Neill, Eire internationals David O'Leary, Frank Stapleton, John Devine and Liam Brady played alongside Northern Ireland stars Pat Jennings, Pat Rice and Sammy Nelson. 'It wasn't a deliberate case of positive racial discrimination,' laughs Terry Neill. 'Most of those players would have walked into any First Division side. It was more to do with the excellent scouting network which the club had set up in Ireland. Those lads were coming through the ranks when I took over as manager. So the view that I favoured Irishmen is a convenient one I know, but it's simply not true.'

In 1978, London-based tabloids began to label Arsenal as 'The London Irish'. They also perpetuated the myth that the dressing room was dominated by an Irish mafia, and that the clan regularly argued with one another. Pat Jennings denies the accusations: 'There was a lot of talk about being a clique, and that we somehow controlled the club. It was a story run by lazy journalists who wanted to stir things up. In truth, we didn't really socialise as a group. Myself and David O'Leary were good pals, but Frank Stapleton pretty much kept himself to himself. Liam Brady's best pal was Graham Rix. So the Irish mafia thing is nonsense. A journalist once asked me – and this was at the height of the troubles – "Don't you all disagree over politics and religion?" That was nonsense also. I'm the least political person you could meet, and I struggle to remember the religions or leanings of the others. It was never discussed. We were team-mates, and we got on fine with each other.'

The club was happy to play on the 'London Irish' nickname. The 1979 FA Cup final song, 'Super Arsenal', was based on a popular Irish ballad, and after defeating United in the final, the BBC cameras joined the Arsenal players on the team bus, where the whole coach indulged in a spot of close harmony Irish singing. In Arsenal fans' eyes, one member of the London Irish stood head and shoulders above the others.

'I'm going to go all Father Ted on you now,' explains Michael Flynn: 'Liam Brady. A feckin' genius. The man was a feckin' genius. In an amazingly Irish way, as well. He was a poet. He was a creator. He was the footballing equivalent of George Bernard Shaw or James Joyce. He almost spoke a different language on the pitch because his intelligence stood out like a beacon, and at times, he appeared to be on a different plane from those around him. In the dressing room, he followed in the Irish tradition of men like Johnny Giles, who were known for their articulate nature, and outspokenness. Even down to the left foot, he was an idiosyncratic Irish genius. The Irishness was crucial. If you look at other Highbury heroes like Charlie George or Tony Adams, what distinguishes them is their Englishness. They were what I call "heart on sleeves" players. Their body language was one of Englishness. They seemed to shout "Get in there" and "Get stuck in lads". It was almost the language of the trench. His relationship with the crowd was different too. Whereas Adams was all fist clenching and thumbs-up, and Charlie was V-signs and aggression, Liam played hard for the team in a less "in yer face way", and rather than screaming for him, like the Highbury crowd did with those two – and Ian Wright – it was more a controlled appreciation; still a love for him, but a different way of showing it. The late seventies was *the* time to be an Arsenal fan if you hailed from my neck of the woods. The North Bank seemed crammed full of Irish tricolors. To be honest, it was often like an Irish social club.'

Brady burst into Arsenal's clique-ridden side in 1973, and quickly established himself as a first-team regular. The young Brady also became an expert in dressing room politics, an essential gift as Bertie Mee's ailing side began to disintegrate. Terry Mancini another Eire regular – recalls: 'Liam was never backward in coming forward. He reminded me a lot of John Giles. He was self-confident in his ability on the pitch and off it.' With Mee's departure imminent, the Ball-Mancini faction favoured the appointment of Bobby Campbell as coach, whereas Brady and others favoured the 'new broom' approach. In the eyes of Arsenal fans, Brady's emergence, together with that of Frank Stapleton, partly assuaged the sense of disappointment felt when the bubble-permed Charlie George left Arsenal. Football writer David Winner comments: 'Although Charlie was very street-smart, he was never wise. He wasn't able to adapt to changes around him, hence his ridiculously early departure from Arsenal at just twenty-four years of age. He wouldn't compromise with people.' Brady, on the other hand, was an extremely smart operator.

Brady's former team-mate Malcolm Macdonald is especially gushing in his praise of Brady's skills: 'Liam was a dream to play alongside, because he could deliver a perfect through-ball to you – which is your dream if you're a striker. Right foot, left foot, and with that brilliant skill he had of making the ball backspin on impact. Like all true greats, he had fantastic balance. He wasn't blisteringly quick, but he *was* amazingly smooth to watch. You could give the ball to Liam, and the rest of us could dawdle forward to the opposition penalty area, have a chat, and we knew that the ball would find us. Then there was that shot of his. The deceptive swerve he was able to put on it was something else. I remember one of his goals at home to Leeds at the start of the 1978–79 season, when he made the ball arc into the net. It was beautiful. Like a lot of Irishmen, he was extremely articulate, who operated with his brains as well as his feet. The thing about Liam was that like any top player, he wanted the biggest prizes. And when success doesn't come, problems arise.'

Throughout the late seventies, as Brady's stature grew, concerns among the Highbury faithful increased, after a *Sun* article linked him with possible moves to Liverpool or Manchester United. Despite Arsenal's re-emergence as a potent cup force, culminating in the 1979 FA Cup final victory over Manchester United, the feeling was that it might not be quite enough to quench Brady's thirst for a League championship medal, or European success. After the *Sun* article, the *Islington Gazette* suggested: 'Maybe Arsenal fans should stop worrying about the situation, and enjoy watching him while they can.' The *Gazette*'s cautionary statement was well founded.

1980s

N.5

◦ GLADIATORS ◦

'TRUE ARSENAL PLAYERS – those who love playing in big games against the very best and biggest – realise that European football and big finals is where it's at. When I heard the news that Arsenal had been drawn against Juve in the 1980 Cup-Winners' Cup semi-final, a surge of excitement went through me. They were arguably the biggest name in European football at the time.' Willie Young's excitement at the prospect of playing Juve was matched by that of his colleagues. Ten years after Arsenal had won the Fairs Cup by defeating Anderlecht, Highbury once again heaved in expectation, the crowd swelled by the huge numbers of Juve fans who joined the throng from various parts of London.

The game was a welcome distraction from the growing sense of unease at Highbury. In the previous summer, Liam Brady decided he wished to leave Arsenal, and move abroad at the end of the 1979–80 season, when his contract expired. Although this was a blow of solar- plexus-smashing proportions, the financial recompense for his departure was equally as galling. Due to EEC regulations, the maximum price Arsenal could get for the player would be £600,000. 'That wasn't a lot of money,' admits Willie Young. If anyone was worth £1 million, it was Liam. But I would argue that it was better to sell him to a Spanish or Italian club for less, than to allow him to go to Liverpool or United. Not only would that have put the title on a plate for them, but you'd have had the indignity of Liam coming back to Highbury every season. To be honest, neither option was pleasant, and whatever happened, it was very bad news for Terry Neill.' Throughout the 1979–80 season, tabloids suggested that if Arsenal were to garner a trophy or two during the season, Brady might do a U-turn. According to Neill, the tabloids were 'indulging in a spot of mischief making'.

In some quarters, the mood towards Brady began to change. Steve Brennan recalls: 'It began in the seats, actually. Whereas once there had been this adrenaline rush when Liam got the ball, there was a distinct lack of buzz. And if there was a lull in the game, or he started to drift out of it, shouts would go up of "Come on Brady, earn your money", and, "You haven't left us yet". One guy sat near me merely said, "Brady, why don't you just fuck off *now*?" I think that his performances did drop off a little bit, but when that guy said what he did, there was nearly a fight about it in the seats. It was sacrilege. But as soon as you say that you want to leave a club, your relationship with the fans changes. It was another example of how Brady and Charlie George differed, because Charlie was virtually forced out of the door by Bertie Mee. You got the impression that if Mee hadn't been the boss, Charlie would have loved to stay, whereas Liam came out and said, "I've had enough." Then the mood began to spread from the seats to the North Bank. I noticed that the reception he received was more muted than before. People often underestimate the fact that this sort of negativity starts in the seats, and assume it all comes from the terraces. Not true.'

Brady remains candid about the change in mood displayed towards him from some elements of the crowd: 'The Arsenal side I was in had the potential to achieve great things. It reached three FA Cup finals in three years, but still wasn't ever really in the running for the League title, which is the benchmark for success. I'd got to the stage where I wanted to sample life and football abroad. I wasn't prepared to wait any longer. I never really sat down with Terry to discuss terms. If the club had paid me the going rate in England at the time and promised me that they would build a team which would challenge for the title, things might have been different. But I don't think he believed I ever would leave, and when the club did start to talk terms, it was too late. It was a bit of an unsettling time, because I announced at the start of the season that I wanted to go. I still believe that it was the right decision, to make my intentions clear. But there were a few disgruntled individuals who voiced their opinion about my impending departure. To be fair, that was expected. It was a minority, but I did notice it, and it was clear that some Arsenal fans really held a grudge, which was a shame.'

A further issue that his likely departure would throw up, was whether Frank Stapleton and David O'Leary would be tempted to follow Brady's example, and be tempted by pastures new. The Irishman almost came to be regarded as some kind of agent provocateur in some quarters. 'Arsenal fans were worried,' recalled Paul Vaessen. 'There were lots of concerns about what could happen at the club, and even Terry Neill, who was always chipper, looked a bit stressed about how things were going. Mind you, that could have been because we seemed to be playing about five times a week at the end of that season. The Juventus semi-final match was probably the biggest game many of the players had ever been involved in.'

In the press releases prior to the game, Neill warned that Arsenal would need to guard against Juve's skill at playing 'quick, quick, very slow' football. The Juve side contained the backbone of the Italy side that went on to win the 1982 World Cup. Dino Zoff marshalled the defence which contained Gentile, Cabrini and Brio. Scirea, Causio, and Tardelli ran the midfield, and were all capable of dictating the pace of the game. The star of the team was the silver-haired striker Roberto Bettega, who'd virtually single-handedly beaten England in Rome two years earlier in a crucial World Cup qualifier. The golden boy of Italian football also hosted his own chat show on Italian TV.

For the first twenty minutes of the tie, the two sides indulged in a phoney war. Tardelli and Causio probed Arsenal's defence while Bettega went close with a rasping drive. The game exploded into life after twenty minutes – quite literally. Firstly, Willie Young was struck by a Roman candle which belched out purple smoke ('It would have to be Willie!' laughs Terry Neill) and seconds after the candle had been doused, Bettega tore into David O'Leary's shin with a two-footed lunge, ripping open his sock and cracking his shin-pad. 'It was the worst tackle I've ever seen,' recalls Neill. 'It could have ended David's career. We had to take him off and get him stitched up. It did bring the game to life though. Our supporters were outraged, and Juve began to resort to type. From time to time, Juve players would hurl themselves to the floor in mock agony: clutching their faces and making doe eyes at the ref.'

'Italian sides had a bad reputation for doing that at the time,' recalls Willie Young. 'English players didn't tend to do that sort of thing back then. I remember that I brushed Scirea's shirt in the first half, and he went down like he'd been hit by a lorry. The ref booked me immediately. Then, five seconds later, he's up on his feet laughing. I remembered that for the second leg.'

The action was fast and frenetic. In the first half, Brian Talbot brought down Bettega in the box, and Cabrini smashed in the rebound after Pat Jennings saved the initial spot-kick. Marco Tardelli was sent off after a scything foul on Graham Rix. With five minutes remaining, Willie Young nodded down a Brady cross and as Bettega tried to clear from Stapleton, he inadvertently sliced the ball into his own net. Highbury erupted. Later, Neill really went to town, labelling Bettega 'a disgrace', and claiming 'we had to take the studs out of O'Leary's shins'. The press war raged. Juve players claimed that Neill had insulted their national pride, claiming they would be 'ready' for him in two weeks.

Conventional logic suggested the game was up, despite Arsenal's late equaliser. *The Times* argued: 'That goal will give only the optimists hope for the return leg in Turin . . . ' Willie Young recalls: 'That was the point at which the true competitors at Arsenal came to the fore. Everyone told us we'd never make it through, but it's so often Arsenal's way to fight against the odds. It's also a thing that Arsenal tend to do the donkey work at Highbury, and then grab the glory away from home. I'll always remember a journalist telling me: "No foreign team has won in Turin for thirty years. How do *you* expect to win?" It was the kind of challenge that I always liked to hear. And Paul Vaessen's winner in Turin a couple of weeks later proved that my instincts were right!'

○ THE TRANSISTOR MATCH ○

IN THE MODERN ERA, it's extremely rare for both sets of fans to leave the ground ecstatic, especially after one of the teams has lost, but this is precisely what happened after Arsenal beat Aston Villa at

Highbury in May 1981. Gunners players of that era still speak with awe about the crackling atmosphere inside the ground, as a 55,000 strong crowd – swelled by an estimated 20,000 travelling Villa fans – saw the League title decided in dramatic circumstances. Arsenal knew that a victory would guarantee them a UEFA Cup spot, and Villa knew that if rivals Ipswich slipped up at Middlesbrough, they would be crowned champions whatever the result at Highbury.

On the day of the match, Arsenal Football Club took its first tentative steps towards commercial expansion. Those who bought the official programme that day would have seen none other than Pele grinning maniacally at three red and blue dots on a screen with a white blob in the middle. He was promoting 'an exciting new video game cartridge' on behalf of Atari, and as the players warmed up, Pele did a lap of honour around the pitch. The crowd – only half joking – yelled 'Sign him up' as 1,000 balloons were released into the air, to herald the Atari revolution. The Arsenal players remained distinctly unimpressed by all the hullabaloo. Willie Young recalls: 'Those bloody balloons put me right off in the warm-up. People don't realise how much the players are focusing at that time. They don't need all that nonsense in the background. I'm glad I retired before all that pre-match stuff became popular.'

Although several of the players were delighted to receive free Atari games for the kids ('I could never get the bastard to work,' Paul Vaessen admitted, 'but it must be added that I was always a complete techno retard'), the real kudos lay in a photo opportunity with the Brazilian master. 'The cameraman decided that it would be a good idea if we could pick Pele up and support him in our arms,' continued Vaessen. 'I recall that Willie Young decided that, as he was the biggest, he should have the privilege of lifting the maestro. Terry Neill wasn't having any of it. "Oh no, you don't, Willie," he said. "Imagine if you dropped him. It would be all over the press, and you'd be even more unpopular than you are already with people. I can see the headline now: WILLIE YOUNG KILLS PELE. Let someone else do it Willie." We all fell about laughing – Pele included!'

The real business was taking place on the pitch. Villa fan Dave Webber recalls: 'It was easily the biggest game in Villa's recent history. That season, it hadn't really sunk in that we could win the League until May. At that point, travelling support went bang. For the Arsenal match, *everyone* seemed to be making arrangements to travel to London. I never expected so many to actually keep their promises. The trains from New Street to Euston were absolutely heaving. The atmosphere was unforgettable. When we got to Highbury, I was worried that we wouldn't actually make it into the Clock End, which by half-past two was a heaving mass of claret and blue shouting 'Villa, Villa,' in unison. It was a wonderful moment. The carnival atmosphere soon stopped when Arsenal went 2–0 up. The Villa boys were very nervous. I bumped into Gary Shaw and Tony Morley at a Villa convention, and they said they were so uptight they could barely put one foot in front of another.

'During the game, I'd say that every one in two Villa fans had a radio glued to their ears, listening out for what was going on at Ayresome Park. In the second half, when we heard that 'Boro had done the business for us and beaten Ipswich, you couldn't beat the atmosphere in the Clock End. It was unbelievable. The Arsenal fans were great to us because, by winning, they'd secured their UEFA Cup place. They chanted "Champions, Champions" at us and applauded our lads when they walked around the pitch. I think everyone was glad that Liverpool hadn't won it again! Being honest, if it was Liverpool or Spurs doing that on their patch, they'd have disappeared pronto at the end of the match.

'At the final whistle, we piled on to the pitch, and I managed to grab Gary Shaw and some of my mates lifted him shoulder high. The funny thing was that Ron Saunders was walking around the pitch and his miserable expression hadn't changed at all. He was being mobbed by lots of Villa fans – something he wasn't comfortable with at all. Everyone was saying to him, "Well done Ron, isn't this fucking wonderful?" And he grudgingly said, "Thanks", before adding, "I've told them they've got to win the European Cup next year." We all laughed, but Ron was right, as Villa did just that. It's a shame he wasn't around to see it.'

Willie Young has equally fond memories of the day: 'When I was playing, it really was possible for teams like Villa and Ipswich to win the big prizes. From an Arsenal player's angle, the Villa game was great as we beat the champions. I got the first, and Brian

McDermott the second, so I was delighted. What was very odd was that both sets of fans were cheering, because the Villa fans had their radios and were following the match at Middlesbrough. I don't recall playing in another game where both sets of fans were so over the moon.

'To be honest, Villa looked shot on that day. We played well, but guys like Tony Morley – who'd been destroying defences all season – seemed to have run out of steam. Our players felt that, on balance, Villa just about deserved it over the season. Looking back, it was the last really great atmosphere at Highbury for a long, long time. The mood was already changing anyway. Liam Brady's departure subdued the whole place, and with Frank Stapleton also about to go, things were changing. But the Villa game was a great memory for all of us, and we joined them for champagne afterwards in their dressing room.'

Several Arsenal fans claimed that the Villa match was their outstanding memory of the 1980s. Reading-based fan Dave Chambers recalls: 'What makes it so memorable is that you just don't get enough away fans at Highbury any more. They talk of the Highbury Library, but you need more away fans to crank up the volume. For that match, there were nearly 20,000 more people in the same area as you get inside Highbury today. That is a hell of a lot of fans. The whole North Bank was like a sea of humanity with everyone swaying around and pushing and shoving. On one occasion, I got lifted clean off my feet. All very amusing back then, but not when you consider what happened at stadia during the eighties.'

As Willie Young commented, Brady and Stapleton's departures ushered in a difficult spell for the club, and the grim realities of eighties football and the economic recession were about to hit home. Highbury's Dark Ages had arrived.

○ BOO BOYS ○

THE H BUMS

After the million pound transfer madness which pushed the likes of Wolves and Manchester City to the brink of extinction in the early eighties, the game entered a far more regressive era. Having sold Brady to Juventus and Stapleton to Manchester United, Arsenal fans were painfully aware that their club was no longer a 'major player' in the grand scheme of things. Not without good reason, there was talk of a 'crisis' enveloping Highbury. Paul Vaessen recalled: 'When Arsenal let Liam and Frank go, the atmosphere around the club went flat, to be honest. Everyone tried to put a brave face on things, but when your two best players leave, and you replace them with the players Terry Neill brought in, you know there is a problem.' Since becoming Arsenal manager in 1976, Neill had gained a reputation for gambling on a series of low grade stopgaps whom he hoped would 'come good'. Almost to a man, they immediately lived down to Arsenal fans' expectations.

The Ulsterman's bargain basement shopping habit began in earnest during the late 1970s, when he dipped his toe into the burgeoning Antipodean transfer market, bringing Australian international John Kosmina to the club for 'a nominal sum'. Kosmina, supposedly the brightest prospect 'down under', was an unmitigated flop. Willie Young described him as being '. . . the only Australian I've ever met with a self-confidence problem'. Terry Neill later revealed that such was his dread of the English winter, Kosmina would don huge sheepskin coats to training. His most infamous moment in an Arsenal shirt arrived during a UEFA Cup clash with Red Star Belgrade. As the referee beckoned substitute Kosmina on the pitch to replace Mark Heeley, he noticed the Australian had disappeared. With Heeley off the pitch, and Arsenal down to ten men, Red Star scored a crucial goal and won the tie. There is one story behind Kosmina's disappearance. He claimed: 'I'd needed a leak for ages.'

In 1981, with Alan Sunderland's goal tally falling in the wake of Frank Stapleton's departure, Neill invested a fee of £50,000 on the combined talents of John Hawley and Ray Hankin. In fairness, both had once been twenty-goals-a-season top flight strikers, but their day was long since gone. Hankin, now two stones over his optimum playing weight, lasted barely two games. Appearing as a substitute against Liverpool, he proceeded to trip over – much to Kenny Dalglish's amusement – as he jogged towards the opposition penalty area. After a month at Highbury, Hankin soon disappeared back to America. Hawley's stay was rather more successful, as he eventually scored three goals in fifteen games. It didn't stop Highbury regulars from booing him at regular intervals. Terry Neill had left Hawley open to ridicule, when he openly admitted that Hawley had found goals hard to come by recently in the Second Division. The general rule is that ailing lower division strikers do not find a new lease of life at the top level. As Brian McDermott recalls: 'The crowd was on his case right from the start. They paid their money, didn't like what they saw, and told him so.'

Both players declined to give their version of events. Hankin released a simple 'no comment', although Hawley's reason for not wishing to contribute is more revealing. 'I barely made any kind of impact at Highbury during their "Dark Ages". I knew – and the fans knew – that I was never really an Arsenal player. So I'd rather not say anything.' Arsenal fan Graham White recalls the 'Dark Ages' all too clearly: 'You'd get to a run-of-the-mill game like Coventry or Birmingham, and there would be 20,000 there, tops. Looking back, the atmosphere could get pretty hateful at times. You mentioned John Hawley, but take your pick from Peter Nicholas, Lee Chapman, Paul Vaessen . . . among others. Just seeing those guys on the pitch reminded us how bad things were. Admittedly, singing "There's only one Liam Brady" probably didn't boost their confidence, but we booed them because they made us feel bad about ourselves. It was like – is this really the best we can do? I always thought the biggest carthorse of all was Lee Chapman. Absolute donkey, he was. We bought him for £500,000, and Terry Neill laughably dubbed him "The Boy Wonder". Half a million was about what we got for Brady. I remember the blokes around me in the East Stand used to moan and throw up their hands in frustration whenever he got the ball. His first touch was awful. In fairness to him, he improved massively as he got older, but he was an absolute disastrous signing for Arsenal.'

The nadir was reached on the night Arsenal lost a UEFA Cup-tie to Belgian part-timers Winterslag, in October 1981. Having lost the first leg 1–0 in Belgium to a team consisting of accountants, bakers, and carpenters, Arsenal scraped a 2–1 home win, but went out of the competition on away goals. Even the normally reserved *Times* commented the next day: 'Now is the Winterslag of Arsenal's discontent.' On the bench, Willie Young and Terry Neill had the last in a catalogue of arguments. Neill had dropped Young – who was in dispute over a new contract – and opted to play Chris Whyte instead. Over in Belgium, Young had put the ball in Winterslag's net, only for the header to be ruled out due to pushing. As time ebbed away at Highbury, and the crowd chanted: 'Willie, Willie', Young urged Neill to send him on as substitute. The Arsenal boss refused to budge. The defender recalls: 'I said to Terry afterwards that his stupid pride lost us that tie. Winterslag's defenders were scared shit of me, and Terry knew it. And at least me coming on would have put Paul Vaessen out of his misery.' The wall of hatred encountered by Vaessen (large sections of the crowd chanted 'Vaessen off, Vaessen off,' each time he received the ball) shocked his team-mates, several of whom openly criticised the fans in the *Islington Gazette*.

Speaking years later, Vaessen, by this time a recovering heroin addict, remained bitter about his treatment from the Highbury crowd: 'Some blokes are born to play football. I'm not simply referring to their talent – I'm also talking about mental toughness. As you can see (at this point he lifted his shaking hands – a sure sign of drug addiction) I've never been the strongest of people. It was very strange – the thing with the crowd. When I first came into the team, and was understudy to Frank Stapleton, the crowd was great with me. There was no real pressure on my shoulders. My goals in Turin, and the header against Spurs bought me time with them. In my mind, after my winner against Juventus, I thought I'd made it. All the press started to make a fuss of me, and with hindsight, I took my eye off the ball, so to speak.

'When I needed to make the next step, and become a first-team regular, things changed. The relationship changes ever so slightly in the crowd's eyes. You're no longer a boy learning his trade, you're expected to deliver, and come up with the goods. And part of being a first-team regular is learning to cope with terrace complaints. The problem was that the Arsenal crowd of that time was a fairly unsettled one. Many were pissed off that Liam and Frank had gone. Suddenly the good feeling was gone. It was a case of "Why isn't Vaessen as good as Stapleton? Frank wouldn't have done that . . . " if I messed up a chance. Their patience with me had vanished. The night of the Winterslag game – I have to say that at the time it was complete and utter humiliation. What they didn't know was that my knee injury – which ended my career a year later – was already restricting my movements on the field. It was also a pretty poorly kept secret that I'd cut my wrists the Christmas before. The pressure to succeed at Arsenal was huge. For years afterwards, I was very bitter at what happened with the suppoters. Some of the lads at the club like Kenny Sansom were great, and gave me some cash when I packed up. Having graduated from the youth team, I never made much money from my career. I finished up with nothing – at only twenty-three.

'But I hated Arsenal fans for a long while. I was very bitter that they could turn on one of their own like they did with me. At the time, fellas like Graham Rix and Kenny Sansom would tell me to ignore the barrackers, and go home and forget it. That's what I'm saying. They had the mental strength to get through things like that, but I was different. Fourteen years on – I don't bear a grudge any more. Fans pay their money, and are entitled to their say. For me to remain bitter for ever about the Winterslag match is ludicrous really. Now, I try and focus on the early days when the crowd cheered me. The thing is, it's hard to remember back to those days.'

Paul Vaessen was, tragically, found dead in his Bristol flat in August 2001. He'd been undergoing a Methadone programme; the local paper noted high levels of drugs were discovered in his blood.

○ MORE THAN JUST A GAME ○

ON MAY DAY 1982, Arsenal prepared to take on West Ham at Highbury. For years, the Upton Park outfit's notorious Inner City Firm

(ICF) made it their business to infiltrate the North Bank, and spend the match attempting to annex areas of it completely. Before the latest clash between the Gunners and West Ham, word spread that the ICF was poised to launch another huge onslaught, and that they were preparing to smuggle in potatoes stuffed with razor blades, in order to cause maximum mayhem. The speed at which the rumours spread suggests that even in the pre-Internet and mobile phone era, violence at matches was far more organised than first believed. The attendance – a comparatively low 34,000 – proved that many simply stayed away, fearing the ensuing chaos.

In the hours before the match, North Bank regulars plotted their tactics. Simon Delaney recalls: 'Most Arsenal fans with half a brain knew exactly where to stand, or not, during matches. Over the years, the ICF tended to pour into the North Bank from the edges, especially the Gillespie Road entrance. They'd often attack in a pincer movement. I heard they'd copied it from *Zulu*. Whatever it was, it worked. Everyone knew the rumours going around, that they were planning a mass invasion with flags and everything – it sounded like cavalry charge. Sounds pathetic – grown men uptight about where to stand at games, but a lot of us got to the stage where we thought, We're just not going to take this any more. We decided we would make a stand on this occasion, and it was amazing how many blokes, who ordinarily wouldn't get involved in such things, decided to make a stand too.

'I couldn't decide whether it was all about rights, or not. You'd often get blokes standing with their little lads near where they knew trouble could start. And then when it kicked off around them, they'd say it was a disgrace and all that. Up until that West Ham match, I'd always taken the view: "What sort of father are you if you're prepared to endanger the safety of your son?" Then I began to think that no one should have to move, or feel endangered watching a football match. Why should people's day at the football be ruined by ICF cretins? So for once – and for the only time – we decided to meet fire with fire. We decided to fight them, and play them at their own game.'

At 2.45 p.m., David Gerrard entered the North Bank from the Avenell Road entrance: 'Right on cue, there were hordes of ICF gathering at the top of the North Bank, ready to charge down the steps and join the throng. They were unfurling this huge white banner, which had the hammers painted in claret and blue. They were making it obvious that they planned to leave it as a giant calling card. I'd say there were at least five hundred at the entrance, and I'm told it was the same from the Gillespie Road turnstiles. All the Arsenal fans stopped climbing the steps, and watched. Suddenly, this cry of "United" went up, and these guys got ready to charge. I remember clearly that many of them had wedge haircuts, and they were wearing those grey, "West Ham Pride Of London" sweatshirts which used to be all the rage. As they started to move down the steps, they were quickly encircled by a large group of Arsenal fans. There was one Arsenal guy dressed in all the mod gear who looked like Paul Weller, and he shouted, "Not this time, you East London slags." And him and his mates started laying into the West Ham fans. In the distance, you could see similar outbreaks all over the North Bank. The West Ham fans must have synchronised their watches beforehand. It was a major operation.

'On the North Bank itself, there were isolated pockets of West Ham fans surrounded by formations of Arsenal supporters. There were Arsenal boys fighting who'd never have got involved in trouble under normal circumstances. As I moved down the North Bank, there was one incident which seemed to have come from a film. There was one respectable balding chap being hassled by an archetypal West Ham thug, with serrated earholes and all the jewellery. "You West Ham mate?" the guy screamed. "No, I'm Arsenal actually," came the clipped tone reply. Then, quick as a flash, the Arsenal man kicked him in the bollocks. The West Ham fan went down like a sack of spuds, and this Arsenal fan looked gobsmacked that he could bring down someone just like that. The police had simply lost control. They were trying to make sense of what was happening, and were asking North Bankers "What did you see? What is going on?" And pretty much to a man, they were stonewalled. There was a feeling that this was a private battle.'

With trouble raging at the mouth of the North Bank, en masse fighting raged in the centre, and on the wings. Colin Philpott recalls: 'I had my little lad with me there that day. You thought you'd be safe on the edges, but that wasn't true. It was like the scenes from Heysel, where hundreds of people are streaming across terracing, screaming as loudly as they can. Liam, my son, was saying "Dad, why do people do that at football?" As a dad, what can you say? I hoped that things might calm down when the teams ran out for the start of the game. If anything, it got worse.'

At 2.55, an enormous smoke bomb was detonated in the centre of the North Bank, which engulfed the terrace for a good five minutes. Over the next few weeks, the tabloids mistakenly reported that West Ham fans were responsible. In fact, Arsenal fans set it off. Simon Delaney comments: 'I don't know precisely who was behind the bomb going off, but it was designed to show the West Ham fans that the North Bank belonged to Arsenal fans. It really was a pitched battle. A few Arsenal fans jumped on to the pitch to escape the smoke, but many opted to stay on the terrace and carry on fighting. You could see their silhouettes through the mist. The fighting really lasted only several minutes, and the game kicked off just a few minutes after three o'clock. In one way, the game was a turning point for the North Bank, because in future, the ICF never invaded again. At least, there was no en masse attempted invasion. You'd always get pockets trying to infiltrate and cause trouble. And shortly afterwards, the club built these steel fences to prevent the wholesale surging and running we saw that day. So, on the one hand, it was the welcome end of an era. We'd done our job, and policed ourselves. But because of other events later that day, what happened was tragic.'

After the match had ended, an Arsenal fan was stabbed to death in Arsenal tube station. Once more, tabloids spiced up the story, alleging that a calling card with the message 'Congratulations, you've just met the ICF', was left on his corpse. The subsequent inquiry found this to be untrue. The fact remained that football violence had reached a new pitch at Highbury that day. Colin Philpott recalls: 'The cameras weren't at Highbury that day, but if they had been, they'd have shown a series of events which could easily have resulted in the deaths of many, many people. Imagine being with your boy and all this is going off around you, and you realise "Football just isn't safe any more". I didn't take Liam for a couple of years after that, and I don't think we went back on the North Bank until George Graham became Arsenal manager. It just wasn't worth the risk. I needed to wait and be certain that football was safe again.'

Simon Delaney and a few of his friends also stopped going to

Arsenal matches for a while: 'I felt disgusted and ashamed of myself. We'd believed we were sticking up for our rights and then you learn that as a direct consequence of the trouble, someone has died. At that point, you have to hold up your hand and accept that things have gone too far. It almost seemed that after the West Ham match, the North Bank purged itself of trouble. We realised that football had become too tribal, and that all the posturing could have devastating effects. It was time to grow up, really.'

Despite the history of terrace trouble on London derby day, this was the first, and last, time that the ultimate cost of hooliganism became apparent at Highbury. With hindsight, it was the beginning of the end of the North Bank.

○ CULT HEROES ○

VLADIMIR PETROVIC

These days, Vladimir Petrovic is boss of the Serbia and Montenegro national side. He's a tad more jowly than he was as an Arsenal player, his standard of English much improved, but his gaze remains as intense as it was a quarter of a century ago. In the early 1980s, Terry Neill earmarked the Red Star Belgrade midfielder as the playmaker who might alleviate the gloom which had descended on Highbury. But the negotiations to bring Petrovic to Highbury dragged on . . . and on.

He recalls: 'Terry first watched me in 1981, when I was at Red Star. At that time, with the Iron Curtain down, clubs in Eastern Europe could tie up the deal in red tape for months, if they felt like being awkward. The transfer looked like it would fall through. Then Terry got the negotiations up and running again in the summer of 1982. The problem was, I'd played for Yugoslavia in the World Cup, but we'd had a poor tournament, and as a punishment, our Football Association blocked anyone's proposed moves to the West. I was devastated, and I'd been training with the Arsenal players that summer anyway, but to all intents and purposes the deal was dead. I returned to Red Star with a heavy heart. Then, just as the winter took hold, Red Star said, "You can go to Arsenal." I was thrilled, but in hindsight, it was all a bit late and rushed.'

Back in his homeland, he was regarded as a mercurial and fragile talent. He joined Arsenal at a time when the crowd was restless, and with the team mired in the bottom half of the table. The onus was on the Gunners to win at all costs. There simply wasn't the scope – or the talent in the side – to play the type of game which suited Petrovic's cerebral approach. He made his Highbury debut against Swansea, and a sublime through-ball put Tony Woodcock in to score a great goal. But the warning signs were there from the first minute. 'The crowd was great with me and gave me a rousing reception. Not a minute had gone before one of their big defenders went right through my ankle. My English wasn't very good at all back then, but I think he said "Welcome to England".' A few weeks later, he curled home a spectacular thirty-five yard free kick against Stoke.

But Petrovic flattered to deceive, as his team-mate Stewart Robson recalls: 'He had a tendency to drift out of games completely. I would argue that he was probably the most talented player I've ever played alongside, but he was often outmuscled and intimidated. It's odd, but he'd be ideally suited to modern Arsenal, because his passing was on a different level, and of course these days, you can't clobber attackers like you used to be able to. So I think he'd have flourished in today's climate.'

Petrovic comments: 'If I'd joined Arsenal in the summer, I'm convinced I'd have done well there. I did my pre-season training and felt that I was starting to adjust to the pace and rhythm of the English game. But then I went back to Red Star, where the pace is slower, and got a knock on my ankle. So when I arrived at Highbury, I was well off match fitness. It was all too rushed; the heavy pitches took it out of my legs, and I was expected to deliver straightaway. Most foreign imports these days are granted a season to prove themselves. I was judged from the start. It's funny now, but the first thing I remember at Highbury was when an Arsenal fan shouted at Graham Rix, "Get rid of it!" when he was about to deliver a measured pass. Nowadays, the Arsenal crowd would hammer you for aimlessly booting the ball. It just goes to show how much the Highbury crowd has changed over those years.'

Former team-mates remember 'Vladi' with great affection. Brian McDermott recalls: 'He was a great guy who loved London. Every time I spoke to him, he always had something planned with his wife and two girls, and they'd go exploring. He fitted in immediately, in the sense that he liked living in England. The problem lay in the fact that he couldn't communicate very well. On the pitch, Tony Woodcock and Alan Sunderland would shout "Vladi, Vladi" and stretch out their arms pleadingly. Vladi was a bright guy, and if he'd stuck around a bit longer, you never know. But Red Star wanted around £400,000 to secure a permanent deal, and these were tricky economic times in football. You could tell fairly quickly that he'd be bombed out.'

Scant evidence exists to prove that Petrovic ever played for Arsenal. His startled face peers out of a few old programmes, either as part of a team group or with wife Zaga. His finest hour in an Arsenal shirt arrived in the 1983 FA Cup quarter-final with Aston Villa. Petrovic ran the show. Stewart Robson recalls: 'Straight after Terry made the decision to get rid of Vladi at the end of the season, he turned in a blinder against Villa. When he scored his goal, he turned Dennis Mortimer and Ken McNaught – both European Cup winners – inside out. He cut in from the right and just launched one. We were really pleased for him, and he lapped it up. Then, in the next game, he was anonymous again. Maybe with a Wenger in charge of him, he could have been cajoled and pushed into playing more of a role. But as I said, it was a different era. He was seen as just another flaky foreigner who didn't have the stomach for the fight.'

When Terry Neill announced that Petrovic would be leaving Arsenal, the news was greeted with a resigned acceptance. 'There were hardly armed uprisings in the streets around Highbury when it was announced I was going,' chuckles Petrovic. 'I got some fantastic letters when I left – ones that made me cry, you know. One said: "Maybe one day we'll watch an Arsenal team where skilful players flourish, and where we accept that we can learn things from foreign players. Maybe one day Arsenal fans will enjoy watching a skilful team, rather than a bunch of runners and kickers." I wonder if Arsène Wenger wrote the letter?'

Arsenal fan Steve Duffy sums up the prevailing mood at the time: 'Eastham, George, Marinello and now Petrovic. There was this growing feeling among cynical fans – and I was one of those – that Arsenal were so entrenched in their style that it could never adapt to having mavericks in their teams. People who have only followed Arsenal since Wenger took over won't know what I'm on about, but in the early eighties it felt like we'd be stuck with this kind of underachievement for ever. No place for talent, only runners and grafters. The crowd would be chanting "Vladi, Vladi" and he'd give you something different. Nowadays, we have a team full of players who can do just that, but in 1983 you only had Petrovic and Woodcock – if the latter could be bothered. But when he went, we didn't argue. Foreigners weren't right for English football back then.'

When I first spoke to Petrovic back in 2000, he commented: 'I always got kicked. There was no time on the ball in England.' Brian McDermott claims: 'He was delicate looking. He appeared like he would collapse at any minute. But he was an outrageous talent. He was like a messenger from the future – letting us know that one day English football will be ruled by players like him. But we were too entrenched to be aware of it. The message was, "You don't fit in with us, so on your bike."'

Vladimir Petrovic played sixteen times for Arsenal, scored three goals, and reckons, 'Not many Arsenal fans will remember me at all.' Yet the image of the Yugoslav spraying passes around in the troubled early eighties burns long in the memories of those who witnessed it. Arsenal's first true foreign star had left his footprint.

○ THE TAO OF BONNIE PRINCE CHARLIE ○

AS THE ARSENAL players waited patiently in the tunnel before the opening game of the 1983–84 season against Luton, new signing

Charlie Nicholas' mind was racing. 'I was conscious that already people in the media seemed far too keen to attach labels to me. Firstly, because of "Charlie", there were parallels drawn between me and Charlie George. Then, because of all the hype which went with my transfer, I was dubbed "London's Kenny Dalglish". And then the guys in the media, who already tracked my every move, claimed that if I wasn't careful, I'd turn into the new Peter Marinello, who'd never really adapted to English football after he joined Arsenal in the late sixties. He had the looks, and the hair, and the connections with music, but he proved that if you're not doing the business on the pitch, you won't succeed. Already, people seemed to expect me to be something, or someone, I wasn't.'

The 40,000 crowd sensed the dawn of a new era. There was far more of a razzmatazz surrounding the game than a contest against Luton justified. The new loudspeaker system (agent Jerome Anderson was the man behind the music) blared out Wham and Duran Duran hits, and the newly launched Junior Gunners club was being frantically advertised by Anderson at every available opportunity. It was the twenty-two-year-old Nicholas whom the crowd remained frantic to see.

'I had Rixy next to me in the tunnel, and he gave me a tug on the arm and says, "Right man, let's go,"' Nicholas recalls. 'So the team is about to emerge en masse from the tunnel, when a club rep said "Hang back fellas, you're gonna run out separately. You're gonna go out one by one." Some of the lads looked at each other. Some were annoyed, because players can get tense before a game, and are ready to get on with it. None of us were too comfy with what was going on. On reflection, it was a bad, bad move. This wasn't American football, and really, no one should be billed as being bigger than the rest of the team. And I was thinking: "They're doing this because of me." I didn't like it. I wanted to be part of the club, and integrate slowly. Like I said, it was a weird thing to do because, naturally, as the big signing, I'd get a bigger cheer than the others. It wasn't what I wanted.'

Despite Nicholas' misgivings, the crowd gave him a thunderous reception. Brian McDermott scored the second goal that day in a 2–1 win, and recalls the mood of the crowd: 'Delirious. What I'd call seriously up for it. And it was all because it was the first day of the season, and they couldn't wait to see Charlie. He was young, glam, and cool – in an eighties way. As I recall, he played quite well in that first game. A few decent passes, a few decent flicks. Nothing out of this world, though. Immediately, there was a ridiculous pressure on him to succeed. The club and the fans were desperate. And he *had* to produce immediately. There was no settling-in period.'

Two days later, Nicholas scored both goals at Wolves in a 2–0 win, and Arsenal were sitting at the top of the league, after two games. The media frenzy grew. But Nicholas failed to score in an Arsenal shirt for another three months, and his first Highbury goal was a penalty against Birmingham on 27 December. The glittering image of Charlie Nicholas as Arsenal's saviour was a false dawn. Although his impact on the pitch was fitful, Arsenal fans from that period speak gushingly about his influence upon fashion.

Having signed for Arsenal wearing a custom made Italian suit, which bore a startling resemblance to Emma Peel's outfit in *The Avengers*, Nicholas proceeded to appear in numerous tabloids as a cowboy, a soldier, and a fireman. He also landed a modelling contract with Top Man, and admits he was happy to wear 'any label going'. Fashion-conscious Arsenal fans looked on. Steve Edwards recalls: 'Before Charlie arrived, the vast majority of Arsenal fans made no effort to look good when they went to matches. It was a sea of nothingness, with possibly a few scarves and hats standing out. But Charlie stoked up interest in what you wore at games. For that Luton match, the North Bank was crammed with Casuals, or so it seemed. It was a casual invasion, there's no other way of describing it. You started off with the Charlie haircut, the mullet. Later on you might get a back perm added, and maybe even some highlights . . . and an earring, obviously. Several of the chaps standing near me on the North Bank seemed to have got it done at some dodgy place a few days before the game, because there were a lot of infected earholes, I can tell you.

'Arsenal fans had a huge advantage due to the proximity of designer shops. From the bottom up, you'd start with a nice pair of jeans – usually Levis. Or perhaps a pair of pinstriped trousers, like Charlie was wearing at the time. Trainers were a must too. Most wore Pumas, but I recall that if you thought you were some kind of hard nut, you might wear a pair of Reeboks. You'd also have a polo shirt by Ralph Lauren or Hugo Boss, maybe. What separated Arsenal's Casuals from the others was the jacket. Lots of Arsenal fans splashed out on Armani jackets – often rolled up at the sleeves – or if you didn't fancy spending all your money on just a jacket, you might settle for Berghaus or Goretex. At that time, lots of blokes were more concerned with looking at what others were wearing, than actually watching the game. Mind you, the way Arsenal were playing back then, it was hardly surprising. There was one guy who used to come to games with us dressed like George Michael. He wore white suits, with his jacket sleeves rolled up. I always remember his trousers were rolled up to just above his ankles, and he wore no socks. He always used to get wolf-whistled whenever we walked past the pubs. "When *you* can afford to wear Armani jackets, then you can wolf-whistle," he used to shout back. All of us thought we looked the dogs' bollocks, to be honest.'

Not all Arsenal fans are convinced that Nicholas was responsible for altering terrace fashions. David Winner comments: 'To be honest, Bono and Duran Duran were behind the image change. When he was signed from Celtic, a phrase did the rounds which was, "That's a lot of money for a haircut." But with or without Nicholas, changes would have happened anyway in fashion. Footballers don't have *that* much influence over what people do.' Steve Edwards disagrees: 'He was the first footballer of my era at Arsenal that really affected the way you looked. Maybe there were other influences at work, but primarily, most of us looked as we did because we wanted to look like Charlie. To look like him was to look cool. It's no different from kids wanting to look like Beckham now.'

In his own way, the man himself is as obstreperous as Charlie George in assessing his influence: 'A lot of people have claimed I was a leader and a revolutionary in the fashion stakes. But really, I was just following what a lot of young teens were into. My hair was copied largely from Bono – I was a massive U2 fan – and clothes-wise I just went with what I liked. The label given to me as football's first Casual was weird too, because I'm not even sure I knew what a Casual was back then. It wasn't something I actively sat down and plotted. I didn't set out to start a trend. I'd get guys twice my age coming up to me, pulling back their mullet to show their earring, and they'd tell me, "I got this done to copy you". Then later, when people like Chris Waddle started getting back perms and stuff, it was written that he was copying "the Nicholas look". Christ, I was already trying to move away from all of that. But I do accept that I did have some sort of a role to play. If you're a young footballer, people do copy you. But that doesn't make me the Casual king.'

One thing that cannot be denied is that he wore the tightest fitting Arsenal home kits in living memory. 'People talk these days about the skintight tops worn by teams like Wales and Spurs, and say that if you have a bit of a tummy on you, it's pretty obvious. But those Umbro kits from twenty years ago were much worse. And those bloody pinstripes too, and the bollock-crushing shorts! You look back now and you wonder how you agreed to wear them. I mean, tight nylon is the worst thing for making you sweat during games. It wasn't too good for your nipples, either. You couldn't really wear a T-shirt under your kit, so what we used to do was cover our nipples in Vaseline, and then put plasters over them. Otherwise, the friction burns on them would be worst than Luton's or QPR's bloody plastic pitches.'

○ THE ARSENAL ACTION GROUP ○

If you're enough of a masochist to enjoy compiling a list of worst ever Highbury matches, then the early to mid-eighties is the richest seam of all to mine. Several Highbury regulars, including Nick Hornby in *Fever Pitch*, argue that a goalless draw against Birmingham, scraped out in front of just 17,000 fans, was the grimmest of all. Charlie Nicholas claims a 0–1 defeat at home to Coventry was 'utterly soul destroying – a dire experience'. Then there was the 5–2 hiding dished out by Spartak Moscow in November 1982. Arsenal fans, who'd been ironically cheering each time a Russian received the ball, then genuinely applauded when each Spartak thrust cut through the Gunners' defence.

But if there is one home match which encompassed the mood of the time, and proved to be the straw that broke the camel's back, it has to be a Milk Cup debacle at Highbury, against Walsall in October 1983. Fifty years previously, Chapman's Gunners had been beaten by the Midlands side and that defeat had spelt the end for five of the Arsenal team. This Milk Cup result also led to heads rolling.

After Stewart Robson blasted Arsenal's opener, the Gunners inexplicably panicked. Walsall swarmed forward in the second half, and Mark Rees equalised after sixty-one minutes. With six minutes to go, Chris Whyte miskicked, allowing Ally Brown to slam in the winner. After a crescendo of boos greeted the final whistle, 3,000 converging fans in Avenell Road bayed for blood, their vocal protests captured for posterity on radio and television. Stewart Robson recalls: 'The dressing rooms at Highbury face Avenell Road, and believe me, the dressing room was really quiet after the Walsall match. You could clearly hear the fans chanting "Neill out, Neill out". It was a weird situation, because Terry did his best to ignore it, but you could see that his time was coming to an end.' Neill clearly couldn't comprehend the disaster, saying 'I'll never know how the team that beat Spurs at White Hart Lane in the last round could then go out and perform like a bunch of pantomime horses.' He described the defeat as a 'night of shame' and 'humiliation'. It was the second time in a fortnight that the air had turned revolutionary. After another Highbury disaster at home to West Brom, a game which Arsenal lost 1–0, the Arsenal Action Group first made its presence felt. Gunners fan Stewart Marney recalls: 'I hadn't seen anything like it since the 1960s. At that time, there were guys going to Arsenal who wanted to see the back of Billy Wright. They'd stand near the turnstiles and encourage fans to turn back and go home. They reckoned that by not turning up at matches, the board would get the message that Wright had to go. They did a good job. The Arsenal Action Group's tactics were different. They were far more organised with their petitions, and they seemed to have the ear of important people at the club.'

One of these 'important people' was new director David Dein, who was already on the way to changing the matchday atmosphere at Highbury. The precise influence of the Action Group on Dein has always been something of a mystery, but the group's spokesman, Alan Esparza, claims their impact was far-reaching: 'These days, because football is such a high-profile business, any fans' Action Groups will get a lot of attention. Obviously, football back in the eighties didn't receive all the headlines it gets today, but we were still fairly high-profile at the time, and we made our mark. Basically, we set up the group because we were dissatisfied with Terry Neill's management. Since we'd done the Double in 1971, we'd won one FA Cup and we were mediocre to say the least in the league. This was Arsenal and it wasn't good enough. It was time for a change. I remember I waited outside the Rotherham ground after they'd beaten us in the late 1970s and I slaughtered Neill. He said, "Oh but I haven't seen my family for two weeks and we're trying to sign the Van Der Kerkhoff brothers." I wasn't interested – he got paid to deal with that – it wasn't my fucking problem.

'In 1983, some of us in a café on Gillespie Road formed the Action Group and we stood with clipboards outside pubs and stations, and the ground, getting names on a petition against the management. There was a lot of ill feeling and I tell you what, there were nearly 25,000 names at the end of it. So, yeah, we were definitely representative. Anyway we tried to arrange a meeting with Hill-Wood and eventually got to see Ken Friar. He tried to waffle, saying, "Let me show you our new sprinkler system." As if *that* was what we wanted to talk about! We also met David Dein on more than one occasion. I'm not gonna tell you exactly the nature of what was said, but he listened . . . he sat and listened to what we had to say.

'There was some misrepresentation about what happened back then. Although we got the petition together, the crowd congregations outside Highbury after the Walsall and West Brom games were spontaneous gatherings, after a run of four defeats. They weren't specifically organised by the Action Group or anything like that. It was just the overriding mood of the time. There was the growing realisation that people like Nicholas and Woodcock, for all the hype, were never really going to land us the big prizes. Things just came to a head. What I remember most is Terry Neill on the radio after Walsall. He goes, "Oh, there's one or two fans shouting". It was more like four thousand – he hadn't got a bloody clue. I waited for Dein, Friar and Hill-Wood afterwards, and said to them, "Are we no better than this?" They said, "What do you think we've been talking about up there? We haven't been playing cards." Obviously, Neill got sacked soon after this. I think you can say we brought some pressure to bear and brought it to the forefront of the press.'

It is recorded in Neill's book that Dein took members of the Group 'for a burger' at around the time of his sacking, and it is public knowledge that Dein attended a public meeting after Neill had gone. Esparza says that the meeting had been arranged before Neill was axed. Significantly, Neill claims that he believes his bosses were paying 'too much attention' to the group. Stewart Robson recalls: 'As players, you live in a fairly cocooned world, and to be honest, as long as you're fit and playing in the team, you pay little attention to what is happening away from the pitch. But I thought at the time, and I still believe, that although Terry had to shoulder some of the blame for what happened, the players tended to get away with it. That Walsall match really was the end for him, especially when you consider how well we'd played against Spurs in the previous round. I remember that around the time when Terry was sacked, Tommy Caton joined us from Manchester City. He kept saying in the press: "I'm so pleased to be joining a stable club like Arsenal." because he was so used to instability at City. Then, within a few days of him joining us, the boss who signed him got fired! Fans who used to watch us back then never knew what was going to happen. We could be brilliant one week, and plumb the depths the next. They were strange and unsettling times for all of us.'

○ CONFESSIONS ○

THE MASCOT

'When I was selected to be the Arsenal mascot for the opening game of the 1983–84 season, I was chosen from a group of around 300 Junior Gunners members. It was the first year of the scheme, and it was designed to get more families to come to games at Highbury. In order to be in with a chance of qualifying, you had to have joined the Junior Gunners by 1 June. These days, there are about 15,000 members, so statistically, the odds are stacked against you for being a mascot. I remember the day I was chosen very clearly. I was seven years old, and the headmaster at my school came to fetch me from my lesson to tell me I'd been picked. My mum and dad received the call at home, but they were so excited that they called the school immediately.

'On the day, there was tremendous excitement because Charlie Nicholas had just been signed from Celtic. In those days, the mascots would meet Debbie Wakeford an hour and a half before kick-off, and she looked after Mum, Dad and me really well in the East Stand. I then got changed into my Arsenal kit in the referees' room, and was shown around the Arsenal directors' box. I also got to look at the trophy cabinet. It had been a while since Arsenal had actually won anything, and it needed filling up a bit more, I thought! The mascots didn't run out with the players at that time. And anyway, for that game, all the players ran out separately so that Charlie Nicholas could be introduced to the fans properly. Terry Neill carried me out in his arms, and I had to go near where the family enclosure area was. There were some footballs lined up, and I was supposed to kick them into the crowd. But because I was so little, I ended up throwing them over the advertising hoardings instead. And that was it really, at least until after the match. I didn't warm up with the players, or shake hands with the captains like they do these days. I went and sat in the East Lower, and watched the game from there.

'After the match, I was allowed into the players' lounge, which was known as the Halfway House back then. I got the matchball signed by the players, and also had the chance to get some autographs. The club was great, and made me feel extremely welcome. The big thing on the day was catching a glimpse of Charlie Nicholas. To actually see him in the flesh was amazing, considering all the media hype there had been about him all that summer. I suppose that the memories have faded a bit with the passage of time. I remember that afterwards my parents took for me for a Chinese meal as a treat. These days I work in the club offices, and help organise fans' travel arrangements for away games.

'I also come into contact with lots of Arsenal mascots, and I'm able to pass on plenty of information and advice in advance. They get more of what I'd call a "sustained session" now. They walk on, get a round of applause from the crowd, and have a decent few shots at Jens Lehmann, or whoever is in goal. Even so, most mascots tell you that the day goes by far too quickly. That season was also the *first time the club really made a conscious attempt to get families into games, so I think it was a very important day in the club's history. It certainly was in mine!'*

Daniel Quy

THE 'MAKE MONEY' GIRL

'By the early 1980s, clubs realised that they needed to pull in other forms of income rather than just relying on gate receipts. Crowd figures around the country, except for really big matches, was falling rapidly. Clubs like Arsenal had to wake up to the fact that other methods, like sponsorship, were needed to swell the coffers. I remember the year before I became a Make Money girl, there was a story in the tabloids that, due to financial cut backs, the club wouldn't be giving out free turkeys to its employees any more at Christmas. It was a silly story, but it proved that even the mighty Arsenal were feeling the pinch.

'I can't remember exactly how I became a Make Money girl. I think my boyfriend saw details about it in the Islington Gazette. One of the perks was that I got to watch the game for free, and as a devoted Arsenal fan, that was great. A lot of the girls weren't particularly fussed though, and just drank endless cups of tea until half-time, and then they'd start work again. This was still the era when women and football weren't supposed to mix. The blokes in the crowd tended to be a bit patronising towards you, like they are these days in the North Bank concourse with the promotions girls. But they were never as bad towards us as they were to the Sky Dancing Girls in the early nineties.

'I don't recall anyone telling us why we were doing the job. We were told that the Make Money With Arsenal scheme was like the Arsenal lottery, and that it gave the fans a chance to win some money. If their numbers came up, they could claim a cash prize, and would be presented with their cheque at the next home game by an Arsenal player; usually one who was crocked. It was blindingly obvious to most of us that it was a way for the club to make some cash.

'Judging by some of the old photos I have, we looked like a bunch of trolley dollies on a plane. We all wore tight, white T-shirts, although I'm not suggesting that the size of your boobs affected whether or not you got the job. Before the start of the game, and at half-time, we'd wander around in front of the North Bank, and mill about at the back of the stands or terraces and sell the cards for 50 pence each. I've seen a picture of myself back then, and I look like Carol Decker out of T'Pau with my hair all lacquered back – very eighties. As I said, some of the blokes, in fact most of them, got a bit leery. Pack mentality set in. "Get your tits out love," was a pretty obvious one, as was, "Do you take it up the Arsenal?" And, of course, we got wolf-whistled a lot. A few of the girls ended up dating some of the blokes, and I heard that there were a few weddings too.

'The big thing in the mid-eighties was to see whether you could pull some strings, get yourself into the players' lounge and meet Charlie Nicholas. Most of us fancied Charlie – in an eighties sort of way. I managed to wangle myself in on one occasion, and there he was, wearing an all-white leather suit, with a black tie. He looked like something out of the band Berlin – I thought he was great! Bear in mind I was twenty-five at the time, and was behaving like a pre-pubescent schoolgirl. I found myself standing next to him, and was just about to say something – I'd no idea what that was – when in walked Suzanne Dando. She was a well-known TV presenter at the time, and is married to Andy Gray now. She shot me a look, whispered something to him, and they swept away. I never did like her much after that!

'I stopped doing the Make Money promotions in the early nineties, and the whole scheme folded soon after that anyway. I think that by the time the club had introduced the executive boxes, and developed the corporate side, the money raised through the Make Money cards was really irrelevant, and it looked outdated. But it did prove that clubs were actively seeking new ways to make money. I like to think that I played my part.'

Sarah George

○ 'GO OUT AND BE THE ARSENAL' ○

BEFORE GEORGE GRAHAM's young side took the field against Manchester United at Highbury on the opening day of the 1986–87 season, the new boss gave his players a rousing team talk which encompassed both tradition and ambition. It was arguably the most effective clarion call in the history of the club. Stewart Robson recalls: 'There we were – sat in the dressing room, waiting for the season to start. The tension was audible. Some players like to stretch their legs.

Some like to go to the toilet, or read the programme. But when George Graham called us to order, we all listened: "Go out and be the Arsenal," he urged us. "This club has been asleep for years, and you have the opportunity to make history, and awaken a sleeping giant. Look around you (he waved his hand at the walls and the marble) and you'll see that this place was built by great men who did more than they had to. They went beyond the call of duty for the Arsenal. They're legends. At the moment, you're nobodies. But you can become legends too if you win things. And I think that you can. But to do so we'll have to work as a team, and you'll all have to work hard. It all starts here.'

Throughout the close season, Graham's crisply ironed white shirt and natty ties had been splashed across the media, as were his comments about 'rebuilding this great club'. Stewart Robson recalls that Graham referred to Highbury on more than one occasion during his rousing pre-match speech. He recalls: 'He talked of the tradition of the place, and of Chapman, James and Bastin. He said that we should appreciate our heritage, but not to fear it. He claimed we should aspire to what they had done. Graham reckoned we were playing in one of the most famous stadia in the world, and that players from across the globe would give their right arm to play in such a place. He was using Highbury to motivate us. Even right down to the size of the pitch. The fact that the pitch is so small lent itself to his vision that we should squeeze, harry and snaffle the ball off visiting teams. "Squeeze them, hussle them, don't let them play," he urged us before the United match. He told the midfielders to help the defence so that United were smothered. It worked a treat. It may not have been pleasing on the eye, but it worked.'

Paul Davis – who had been an integral part of the underachieving Arsenal team for six years – recalls: 'Before George arrived, the club was going nowhere. In the first two weeks, he put a bolt of electricity through the whole place. The most startling aspect was his individual meetings with players. He'd make you sit in a chair outside his office and wait for your appointment, probably so that you'd overhear what was going on inside. When a new manager arrives, most players try and go for an improved contract with improved terms. There was no chance of that with George. From his office at Highbury, you'd hear all these shouts and ranting and raving, as players were told they weren't going to get better terms. I remember Tony Woodcock wanted to talk to George about a new contract. I don't think George even said hello to Tony. But that was how the club was going. Most were given their chance, but the emphasis was on youth, and if you didn't like it, you could go. When we took the field against United, I felt that at last, we had a game plan, that we'd stick to no matter what. It wasn't a great game. It was 0–0 until very late, and then up popped Charlie to get the winner. He always did save his goals for the big occasions. The crowd celebrated like we'd won the Double or something. Within a few weeks, fans were coming up to players almost shaking with excitement because they felt that we were on the move again. It was a very exciting and fulfilling time to be around the club. What made it extra special was that it was *my* club, and I'd graduated from the youth ranks. And finally we were on the right track. History shows that the birth of modern Arsenal began on the day we beat United.'

The goalscorer – Charlie Nicholas – is equally enthusiastic about the new Arsenal spirit shown under Graham: 'My goal that day was the icing on the cake, but everyone knew that with or without me in the team, that Arsenal side was about to go places. Let's face it, I wasn't George's kind of player. I'd been brought up in the atmosphere of Glasgow derbies, and I always loved the big occasion. If you look at my record in derby matches against Tottenham, I often seemed to come up with the goods. George wanted hard working, versatile athletes. And in training, when you saw guys like David Rocastle, Tony Adams and Michael Thomas coming through the ranks, it was clear we had the basis of a great side. The result against United was a microcosm of how things were under George for a while. The scoreline was prophetic, and the fact we'd shackled great flair players like Olsen and Whiteside pleased George no end. In fact, I always joked that George took more satisfaction from that game because we'd kept a clean sheet, than the fact I'd scored the winner. I still reckon I'm right!'

In the aftermath of the United result, the next few home games – including 0–0 draws with Tottenham and Oxford United – were as dire as the dark days of the mid-eighties. Arsenal fan Kev Wright recalls: 'How does that phrase go? Life has to be lived going forward, but you can only understand it looking backwards. I think you can only understand George's early weeks by thinking of it that way. No one at the United game came away thinking, This is it – we're on to something. And I remember at the Oxford game, we were all moaning as loudly as we had in the worst games under Don Howe and Terry Neill. It was so appalling that for a while we reckoned nothing had changed. It wasn't until late October and through November, when young lads like Rocky and Quinny broke into the team, and we went on that great run when we topped the league for a while that it dawned on us that we might be seeing something great unfold at Highbury. And they really were just a bunch of kids. You'd see Quinny and Hayes run about and they were so skinny and gangly looking. It probably didn't help that they were running around in those tight eighties kits. But it's no surprise that as soon as they became established in the first-team, younger fans started to return to Highbury. The club was worth watching again.

'I remember there was a game against Manchester City, where we beat them 3 0 at home. The attendances had gradually been creeping up, from the 20,000 mark to the 35,000 mark. You could sense the crowd was regaining its confidence, and getting its swagger back. Then this chant began in the North Bank, and it spread around Highbury: "Arsenal are back, Arsenal are back!" And it was so infectious we sang it for the entire second half. I remember Kenny Sansom coming across to take a throw-in, and he was grinning like a Cheshire cat because the team was winning, and he knew that things were changing. Then Tony Adams ran across and gave us the thumbs-up sign. It was a great moment. Let's be honest though, most of those eighties chants like "Here we go" and "We'll piss all over you", deserve to be shoved in the dustbin of history, but you can't beat the feeling of realising that your team, after years of being in the doldrums, are finally on an upward curve. Because of the money in the game these days, that chant seems really quaint, but at the time it was a fantastic feeling. Arsenal were back!'

○ CULT HEROES ○

PERRY GROVES

'It's amazing how many Arsenal fans now come up to me and tell me how much they used to like me,' laughs Perry Groves. 'Out of a crowd of 40,000, I'm sure that 20,000 of them used to call me "wanker" every week.' After inquiring as to whether I've got a letter wrong in the 'cult hero' status afforded him, he's happy to talk about his six-year spell at Highbury. Groves was George Graham's first capture in the transfer market, and arrived at Highbury in September 1986. As first signings go (he cost £75,000 from Colchester United), he was as low key as it gets. Groves admits: 'At Colchester, I was their top boy, but at Highbury, I was just a ginger nobody.'

The manner in which he arrived at Highbury reflected much about George Graham's early years there: financial parsimony and a dogmatic vision that things should be done his way. Groves recalls: 'Crystal Palace were also in for me at the time. A lot of people said that I should go to Selhurst Park and bide my time, but when a club like Arsenal swoops, it's an opportunity which is far too good to miss. When I arrived at Highbury to sign for Arsenal, I was taken upstairs to George Graham's office. It was like a headmaster talking to a pupil, even down to the fact that he was in a big chair and mine was a smaller one. There was no negotiation over terms or anything. It was a case of, "Here's your contract – sign it." I did as I was told. It was George's way of doing things. The money – which wasn't great – was irrelevant to be honest. That turned out to be George's way with many players, and very successful it was too! A lot of the lads who came in, like Steve Bould and Lee Dixon, were lads from the lower leagues who were grateful to George, and probably felt they owed him a favour. Building a team like that just can't be done these days at the top level.'

Although team-mates were unaware of Groves' background, he quickly began to make himself known at the club. He recalls: 'I'll always remember my first training session. I bowled up in a red MG BGT which had steam pouring out of the engine because I'd pelted down the M25. Guys like Viv Anderson and Kenny Sansom – who were driving BMWs and Mercedes – were looking at me as if to say, "Who the fucking hell is this?" It was a great time to be at Arsenal. George Graham was second to none as a trainer. He had the image of being hard nosed, and up to a point he was. Some of the lads called him Gaddafi behind his back. But in training, he was ten years ahead of his time. When he demonstrated shooting and passing, he was perfect every time. And his heading ability was better than anyone else's at the club. He'd walk along, strutting like a demented chicken, making a pecking movement, saying, "This is how you do it lads, this is how you do it." Sometimes he'd join in five-a-side matches, and as soon as his team started losing, that would be the end of the session. There was a story doing the rounds which claimed that he used a piece of rope to get the back four of Bould, Adams, Dixon, and Winterburn to perfect the offside trap. That's bollocks. He used to say: "*Imagine* there's a piece of rope there." It was a myth created by journalists who wanted to perpetuate the "Boring Arsenal" label.'

After making his full home debut – and scoring – against Watford in October 1986 ('I was a right winger but George told me frankly that I would play on the left-hand side. I wasn't about to argue.'), Groves began to appear more regularly, and developed a habit of scoring vital goals. It would be an exaggeration to say that he was universally popular at Highbury. Considered distinctly 'blue collar' in comparison with the likes of Paul Merson and David Rocastle, Groves' ginger quiff, and his tight shorts afforded him several nicknames. '"Tin-Tin" was one. So was "Kinnock", "ginger nuts" and "carrot head",' he confirms. 'It's true to say that I wasn't the greatest player Arsenal ever had. I couldn't really complain about the treatment I received, and at first, they gave me the benefit of the doubt because my Uncle Vic had played for the club; so that helped. But the crowd always knew that I'd work my arse off, and no matter how badly I was playing, I never hid during a match. Some players will create angles on the pitch to avoid getting the ball. I never did that, and sometimes that wasn't always the most sensible course of action.'

Groves' finest hour in an Arsenal shirt – his run which set up Charlie Nicholas' winner in the 1987 Littlewoods Cup final – was ironic, bearing in mind he was Nicholas' direct rival for a place in the team. Groves recalls: 'Nothing was ever said between me and Charlie, but there was a bit of tension in the air. I had been bought to replace him, and from his angle, I wasn't on the same level skill-wise. It was one of those things. You're not going to be best friends with all your work colleagues, are you?' But it was activities away from the pitch which – rather like Willie Young – sealed his reputation as a cult figure. 'Things happened to me which didn't happen to the other lads,' he confirms. 'When Nigel Winterburn got the winner up at Sheffield Wednesday, everyone on the Arsenal bench jumped *out* and *upwards* to celebrate the goal. I just jumped *up*, and smacked my head on the dugout roof. I almost knocked myself out, and couldn't come on as sub. George wasn't amused.

'Then there was a home match against Liverpool in 1989 when the St John ambulance team were wheeling me off on a trolley. As they banged over the touchline, I ended up falling flat on my face in front of all the Scousers. They were extremely sympathetic, as you can imagine! So I shouted, "Get me back on the fucking stretcher." When we reached the Arsenal bench, they were all wetting themselves, because I had red grit marks all over my face. Finally, in the dressing room, they bloody dropped me again. These stories got back to the Arsenal fans, and that's when the "Perry Groves world" chant began – based on The Beatles' song *Yellow Submarine*. I like to think of it as being half-complimentary, half-taking-the-piss. I'm not sure who coined that idea, but I quite liked it. Sometimes, the fans chant it nowadays during quiet periods in a match. My sons come with me to games, and it's nice for them to hear the crowd still remember me. If you think how many better players there have been than me, I'm quite honoured, really.'

Arsenal fan Nick James claims: 'Even though he played for us as recently as 1992, it's as if he belongs to an entirely different era. He was quick, but he was very limited in terms of skill. That's the sort of player we used to sign in the Graham era. Players could look different back then too. Nowadays, they're all identikit, primed athletes. Perry Groves was a bit tubby, he had flabby thighs, and he liked a drink. Everyone knew that. It's why you can't really call modern Premiership player's "cult heroes". They earn far too much, they're too fit, and they live life like monks. There is no place for idiosyncracies any more. There's nothing quirky about them. Back in the late eighties, you could take the piss out of them in a fanzine, and then see them in the pub after a game. No more. Perry Groves was one of the last of a dying breed.'

Groves remains in awe of the club: 'The red shirt, the tradition, the marble halls, the professionalism. The whole place is awe inspiring,' he explains. 'Whatever else I do in my life, no one can take away the fact that I used to play for the Arsenal. And, as with most former players, it's a case of once a Gooner, always a Gooner. As I said, my sons come up with me to games now, and I hope their sons do the same. Every day I was here, I counted myself privileged to be at Highbury.'

○ STICKS AND STONES ○

The rivalry between Arsenal and Manchester United was deepening by the late eighties. Admittedly, they were only the early signs of conflict, but the seeds were sown for the fractious relationship which exists today. There had always been needle there, partly due to the huge numbers of London-based United fans, which grew during the Busby Babes era. There was also the issue of the so-called 'North–South divide'.

United fan Colin White recalls: 'Up until the era of all-seater stadia, United took a minimum of eight thousand fans to Highbury for any match, and it was often more than that. Apart from London derbies against Spurs or Chelsea, I don't think any other club could get close to that. It meant there was a genuine level of needle in the ground. We tended to sing songs about our side, whereas Arsenal fans, aware that United contained bigger names in those days, often sang songs about our individual players. Frank Stapleton used to get it in the neck. "You fucking Judas", Arsenal fans would shout at him. One time, we went to Highbury and hammered them in a Milk Cup-tie, and Frank scored. He put two fingers up at the Arsenal fans. What he meant to say was "I've scored two goals". It seemed as if he was throwing them an insult.

They'd tell Mike Duxbury – who wasn't the best-looking player in the world – to "Take your mask off Duxbury". And most opposition fans hated Whiteside in those days anyway. Add in the huge number of cockney reds, and you always had the potential for an explosive cocktail.'

By 1988, seventeen years had elapsed since Arsenal had won the league, and twenty years since United had lifted the Division One trophy. Liverpool had dominated the league for the past fifteen years, but by the late eighties, Dalglish's side were showing signs of battle fatigue. In part, this was due to the arrival of George Graham at Arsenal, and Alex Ferguson at United – two Scottish managers who took losing football matches as a personal affront. With English clubs banned from Europe, domestic clashes took on an added significance. When the Gunners drew United in the FA Cup fifth round in February 1988, it was an ideal opportunity for Arsenal's youngsters to deliver on the biggest stage of all.

The Highbury FA Cup clash with United was the last of its kind. Over 55,000 crammed in, with space at a premium on the North Bank. Dave Cameron recalls: 'That was the last time you had a truly buzzing terrace at Highbury. We arrived at the ground at two o'clock and already we were struggling to get on to the North Bank. By half past, there were still no United fans on the Clock End, and yet you could see them being held back by the police on the edges, dying to get in. Then, twenty minutes before kick-off, the police moved out of the way. It was one of the most amazing sights I've ever seen. They swarmed on to the Clock End and dashed around looking for the prime spot. Within ten minutes, there must have been more than ten thousand United fans in place. The thing is, we complain about the poor atmosphere at games these days, but you have to have a decent number of away fans to crank up that atmosphere. When I look back at the most memorable Highbury games in the 1980s – Villa in eighty-one, Juve in eighty and the United game – it's because away fans made a massive contribution to the whole event. I did miss that side of things at Highbury after the ground went all-seater.'

The Arsenal team took to the field with George Graham's instructions ringing in their ears. Alan Smith recalls: 'George told us that this was our chance for glory. "Don't give them any space. Hit them on the break as often as you can," he said. George also said this was our chance for glory. The club had won the Littlewoods Cup the year before, so why not add the FA Cup this time around? We really went at United in the first half. Some of the Arsenal fans weren't too happy with my form early in my Arsenal career. My goal against United that day certainly helped me to win them over. I remember Nigel Winterburn clipped over a great cross, and I was able to flick it over Chris Turner's head. It was a fantastic sight to see it hit the back of the net. The noise was something else – probably the loudest roar I ever heard at Highbury. Then Mike Duxbury helped us by nodding into his own net, and it seemed like we'd got the game won.

'Our relative inexperience crept in by the second half though, and we let United back into the game. Brian McClair pulled one back for them, and then United laid siege to our goal for about the last twenty minutes. They won a penalty, and some of our lads were really unhappy with the way in which Whiteside won it. They felt he wrapped his leg around Mickey Thomas and took a dive. The ref was never going to change his mind though. So we were 2–1 up against United in a crucial game, and they had the chance to tie it up and take the replay to Old Trafford. The exterior pressures on McClair were immense. The Arsenal fans screaming at him . . . Arsenal players shouting in anger . . . Too much time to think about it . . . And here was a guy who I don't think had ever missed from the spot for United. So despite all the pressure, his confidence must have been quite high as he stepped up.'

Dave Cameron recalls: 'McClair's penalty miss is one of my all-time Highbury memories, and it goes back to what I was saying about football being an interactive event. There was some delay before the kick was taken, and it gave us the chance to put McClair off. Shouting: 'McClair – you're a wanker' and 'Miss, you Scottish bastard', were two ways of doing it. But, as we all know, the best way to distract a penalty-taker is a crescendo of whistling. Preferably so loud that your ears nearly split. And the whistles got louder and louder, and McClair looked edgier and edgier. Then up he comes, and blasts the ball over. Unbelievable. Better than one of our players scoring and making it 3–1. Because you can see Lukic's joy, and McClair's fury. It's theatre. Conflicting emotions. Then the final whistle went. At that moment the relationship between Arsenal and United changed.'

The highlights of the match were shown on ITV's *The Big Match* the following day. Footage showed Nigel Winterburn 'console' McClair after he'd missed the penalty by informing him, 'You're fucking crap, you are.' Brian Moore understated the point by claiming, 'McClair wasn't too happy about that.' But as an anonymous Arsenal player explains: 'Nigel doesn't discuss that incident at all. He used to pass it off by saying that not all players can get on. Down the years, there have been so many clashes between individuals: Keane v Vieira, Keown v van Nistelrooy, but this was the first real personality clash. You could say that battle lines were drawn that day. Things happened then that could never be changed. It coincided with the growing realisation that clashes between us meant rather more than a squabble over 'who would finish fourth or fifth'. They were now having an important bearing on the title. Add to the mix the fact that the media now began to hype up the games, and things were starting to simmer between the two.'

○ CONFESSIONS ○

THE FANZINE EDITORS

'When I started the Arsenal Echo Echo in 1987, I was heavily influenced by the approach adopted by When Saturday Comes. It was the most original magazine on the market, at a time when it wasn't really the done thing to say anything controversial in football writing. I wanted the fanzine to discuss issues which were of importance to Arsenal fans, but primarily, I aimed to produce a fanzine which made supporters laugh. For the opening print runs, I ran off around a thousand copies and gave a mate of mine cash in hand, to run them off. I stapled the pages together myself. When I tried to sell copies of the first fanzine in late 1987, I wandered around at the top of the steps which led down to the North Bank. As fanzines were practically unheard of, I received some very strange looks. Most people just didn't know what to make of it. I sold two or three before a Chelsea game, and things felt a bit flat, to be honest.

Then, at half-time, I sold a few more and suddenly loads of people swarmed forward to buy a copy. It was a "eureka" moment! Then, the police noticed the large numbers of people, saw what I was selling, and didn't like the look of it. So I was carted off to the club office. The headline on the front was something like: SHOCK. GEORGE GRAHAM CAUGHT SPENDING A FIVER – INTERPOL ALERTED. It was a tongue-in-cheek reflection on his parsimony in the transfer market. The official's attitude was that, "We can't have this sort of thing going on," and I was banned from selling it inside Highbury. He suggested that George would find my humour offensive. I reckon George would have risen above it, but there was little I could do. I wasn't personally banned from games, although I didn't get to see the rest of the Everton game that day.

'From then on, I rented a stall by the turnstiles at the Gillespie Road entrance, and I used to sell around three thousand copies a game. Not too bad at all. But some people clearly didn't get the message. There was one spoof headline which said: LESTER PIGGOTT NAMED AS NEW TOTTENHAM BOSS. It was at the time when he'd been jailed for tax evasion. People didn't understand that it was a spoof – it's like failing to understand that Alan Partridge isn't a real chat show host! You either got it or you didn't, I suppose.

'We would ape things in the media. In all our issues, we ran a, "Herb gives it to you straight" column, based on John Sadler's writing in the Sun. Some of the columns took digs at Tottenham. I remember once "Herb" said: "Hoddle found God, Waddle found music. Neither found the barbers. Scruffy buggers." The shorter the sentences, the more effective. At least that was our view. Some of the headlines – like: CHELSEA MANAGER JOHN HOLLINS SAYS THERE'S NO CRISIS AT THIS CLUB, and STEVE WILLIAMS ATE MY HAMSTER, BLASTS BRIAN CLOUGH, were based on typical Mirror or Sun headlines. But the Echo also made some serious points, like questioning the club's gradual gentrification of the ground, Thatcher's proposed membership scheme, and George Graham's decision to sell Charlie Nicholas. That was never going to happen in the matchday programme, was it? So I like to think that the Echo helped make Arsenal fans – at least those who bought it – more critically aware of what was happening. It was the first sign that fans did have the right to reply.

'From my own point of view, it was a great time to be a fanzine editor. That generation of players – Merson, Rocastle, Thomas, Adams – felt like my generation. *The club was aspiring to better things, and was trying to recapture former glories. Some of the things we regarded as great, feel quaint when I look back. Like winning the Littlewoods Cup seemed such a big thing and now that tournament is derided in so many quarters. The biggest change is in the levels of expectation among Arsenal fans. These days, the team is expected to finish in the top three every year, but we had no such lofty ambitions back then. We could have won the title, or we might have finished mid-table. It was far more fluctuating in the late eighties. You'd come to Highbury genuinely not knowing what could happen. With hindsight, it was a more refreshing experience. My best moments as the editor came when I caught the tube on the way home from a game, and some fans who were reading the fanzine, started to laugh. On one occasion, a guy pointed out what he'd found funny, and his friend laughed too. That was wonderful.*

The Echo ran until 1991, when I found that working as a Liverpool-based journalist and editing the fanzine led to a conflict of interest. I'd be criticising players in the Echo one minute, and interviewing them the next. Something had to give. We'd run for four years, which was pretty good going, and I like to think we were one of the better Arsenal fanzines at a time when the movement was just getting going. My first editorial began with: " . . . no tits, no horoscopes, no Joan Collins. The aim of the Echo Echo is to discuss the things that really matter." I think we did that, and I'm still very happy with how things went.'

Guy Havord – *Arsenal Echo Echo*, Editor 1987–1991

'In the late eighties, I think many Arsenal fans felt that the match programme was pretty poor, and someone needed to be bold, decisive and vent their spleen. At the time, there wasn't really a fans' voice in the game as such, and media coverage was a fraction of what it is now. These days, most newspapers have a separate sports supplement, but back then, there were no sixteen-page pull-outs. It's quite hard to remember where Arsenal fans were "at" in the late 1980s. We hadn't done very well at all for a good few years, and by 1988, there was this intoxicating feeling that we were on an upward curve. Back then, any degree of success was brilliantly new, and for a success-starved eighteen-year-old like myself, it was an amazing feeling.

'We genuinely felt that we were marching with George's army, as the song went. I think that Arsenal fans were a good deal less uptight back then, and we were able to laugh at ourselves a bit more. The game in the late eighties wasn't so money orientated. Losing ten games a season wasn't so unusual, and it certainly didn't feel like the end of the world if we did. Possibly that was because we didn't

have the pressure of having to qualify for Europe, as English clubs were currently banned.

'At the time, I planned to become a sports journalist, and I regarded the Gooner as a launch pad into that. Then I quickly realised that editing a fanzine carried with it a large degree of responsibility, and that fans actually took notice of what I said. For the first edition of the Gooner, I ran off three hundred copies. It had risen to eight hundred by issue six. The fanzine had a very "spit and sawdust" look about it. I'd run off the copies myself at work, and often slaved through the night at the weekend, sorting out the fanzine when a deadline loomed. For those first few issues, I'd often spend some time outside the ground explaining to fans what a fanzine was. Sometimes they would buy it, and on other occasions, they'd say, "Oh, I don't think so," and then walk off. In many ways, I was probably a bit too shy, and didn't like to push it on punters too much. Nowadays, Gooner sellers are dotted all around Highbury, and have become part of the matchday experience for many fans, I think. Even in the early days, we never sold it inside the ground, and I wasn't pulled into the Highbury offices like Guy at the Echo. We always had the feeling that the club would rather we didn't exist, but history shows that the birth of the fanzine movement led to a more critical and questioning fan base, which I think is a good thing. You could even suggest that groups such as REDaction wouldn't exist today if it weren't for the fanzines.

The Gooner is the only one of those early fanzines to survive. The Echo and One Nil Down are long gone, and Highbury High rarely appears these days. I think our strength has been that, although we've always had a core team of contributors, there are numerous other writers who are happy to submit articles now and again. It keeps it fresh. Despite all that, I still look back to the late eighties as the golden era for fanzines. The players, for instance, were good players, but not physically perfect specimens like they are now. You could laugh at members of your team, like Groves or Gus Caesar, a bit more. And players led normal lives, but that kind of access has been taken away. And there were so many issues to debate back then, like the move to dismantle the terracing, or the increasing influence of television on football. Then, there was the discussion over whether George's Arsenal was boring, or not! Many of these issues have either resolved themselves, or have been debated to death in the modern era. Even though Wenger's team plays great football, the late eighties was still my favourite time as a fan because Arsenal's success was so novel. It was great to start the Gooner at a time of massive change in the club's fortunes, and in football generally.'

Mike Francis – Gooner, Editor 1987–2001

○ CORPORATE IDENTITY ○

AS VISIONARY BOOKS go, Bob Wall's *Arsenal From The Heart* is in a league of its own. The late Arsenal general manager's autobiography, published in 1969, is a literary essential for those interested in club history. After reminiscing about Chapman's thirties team, and discussing Arsenal's stature in world football, Wall bravely contemplates the possibility of redeveloping Highbury. He ponders the feasibility of putting a roof over the (then) uncovered Clock End, and of phasing out sections of terracing in favour of seats. Wall then enters a 'brave new world' by advocating a 'super season-ticket scheme' where wealthier fans would pay for additional facilities such as improved views of the game, and a higher standard of food and drink. In other words: corporate hospitality.

Back in the 1930s, with the Gunners being England's most successful club, a growing number of affluent fans were already part of the 'Ascot club'. Ted Drake recalled: 'After a match at Highbury, I was pulled aside by George Allison and informed that someone wanted to have a chat with me. As players, we spoke to fans all the time, but on this occasion, I was introduced to this extraordinary looking chap, who was so ridiculously plummy, it was as if he had stepped out of an episode of *Jeeves and Wooster*, or something. He was wearing plus fours, top hat, monocle, and carried a cane. He surprised me because he was actually very knowledgeable about the game, and unlike other wealthy fans, didn't talk down to me. I must have chatted to him for about fifteen minutes, in between him sipping his champers! He was coming out with such terms as "old chap" and "absolutely spiffing", and all the rest. You couldn't make it up, honestly. George Allison told me later on that he was called Sir Greville something or other, and that he was a member of the Arsenal Ascot Club. Members paid a bit extra for a meal and some drinkies. Very nice too. But as players, we didn't mix too much with more affluent fans. The corporate side of things was fairly low key back in the thirties. Times were too hard for it to really take off.'

Further evidence of Wall's vision is evident when he advocates the construction of a retractable roof over the stadium, and of an 'entertainment complex' at the back of the ground. Bobby Gould recalls: 'I used to love chatting to Bob Wall. He was such a great fella, and genuinely cared about the players. He was always enthusiastic about his ideas for how Highbury should be redeveloped, and used to talk about casinos and bowling alleys, and shops and all this type of thing. To me, it sounded like pie in the sky. It was like something out of an H.G. Wells' novel. All very interesting, but this was football. I never thought anything would happen like that. And as for corporate hospitality, I don't believe any of us reckoned that would happen – not in the working-man's game. It's a shame Bob Wall isn't alive now, because I would shake him by the hand and tell him that he was clearly a man ahead of his time. Everything he predicted has come true. Fans now *expect* all the things that Bob Wall advocated forty years ago. So Bob, if you're reading this now, I apologise for laughing at you! You *were* the man.'

In February 1988, the club finally announced the redevelopment of the Clock End. In the official programme for the Manchester United FA Cup clash, the club revealed: 'Our plan is to erect a new ultra-modern stand, which will house forty-eight boxes, with the very latest in executive and catering facilities; an exciting prospect as we head towards the 21st century! There's good news for our Clock End regulars too. The arrival of the boxes will mean most of our Clock End terrace fans can stand under cover.'

The recently formed fanzine, the *Arsenal Echo Echo,* took issue with the club over how the entire matter was handled. Editor Guy Havord recalled: 'It annoyed us that the club failed to make its intentions crystal clear for the Clock End. Through the medium of the fanzine, I asked whether the Clock End should have a "skullcap" or a "ten-gallon hat". This was because most Clock Enders believed they were entitled to be kept dry by a roof that covered the entire terrace, not just a bit of it. We realised that corporate hospitality was an important revenue stream for the club. The problem is that the South Stand has never really looked right. At the time, the club was disconcertingly vague about the whole scheme. They mentioned something about planning permission preventing them from turning the Clock End into a genuinely impressive construction – like the Witton Lane End at Villa Park. They missed out there, I think.'

Football consultant Alex Fynn is even more outspoken over the redevelopment of the Clock End, and believes the club missed out on a golden opportunity. He comments: 'Arsenal had a straight choice. They could prioritise boxes, or they could prioritise seats, and thus create a double-decker stand at the south end of the ground. Other clubs had done this in recent years, so it wasn't as if the Arsenal board didn't have a blueprint from which to work. Obviously, they opted to prioritise boxes, as they believed this was a vital source of income that the club needed. That's true, but with a degree of forethought, they could have had the best of both worlds. If the club had gone for a double-decker stand, they could have had five thousand extra seats, plus the boxes, and virtually no extra cost. If we project the impact of that forward, the extra revenue those seats would have brought in over the last sixteen years would have put Arsenal in a far more comfortable situation financially than they are now.

'They wouldn't have needed to take such a quantum leap when it came to a new stadium. The Americans have a phrase which I rather like, when they talk about "bells and whistles". It refers to the addition of luxurious extras. Arsenal would still need a new stadium, but it could be based on the more functional Parc des Princes model than on the state-of-the-art Stade Français idea. The new stadium, if Arsenal had pulled in the income from five thousand extra Clock End seats, wouldn't need all the bells and whistles which are going with it, and which is costing an exorbitant amount of money. As we know, the cost of the new stadium, whatever the board says, has clearly affected Wenger's dealings in the transfer market over the last two years. It's easy to be wise after the event, but if clubs like Aston Villa had the foresight to build in extra seats, why couldn't Arsenal? The Clock End redevelopment was a missed chance – in my humble opinion.'

For Arsenal fan Jim Knowles, the development of the new Clock End was a significant turning point in Arsenal's history: 'I remember its official opening really clearly, because it took place before our game with Spurs in early 1989. George Graham and Terry Venables cut the string, and this blue sheeting fell down to reveal the famous clock. The game – which was being shown live on *The Big Match* – was put back an hour or so by ITV to ensure that *Coronation Street* could be shown on time. So the signs that football could be dictated to by TV, and that

Highbury was changing, were pretty obvious. What irritated many of us was how we found out about the plans for the Clock End in the first place. I read about the club's ideas in the *Mirror*. It made me feel that the club wasn't all that bothered about keeping its supporters informed. It seemed that we were often the last to know what was happening. "Disenfranchisement" they call it. I think we all realised the club had to pull in extra revenue, but it wasn't being done especially overtly.'

In *Arsenal From The Heart*, Bob Wall touched on the biggest problem of all. 'Due to the large numbers of houses surrounding the ground . . . the only way to develop the stands is to build skywards. It's quite a problem.' It proved an insurmountable one, and ultimately, spelt Highbury's doom.

○ EVERYTHING CHANGES ○

ON THE FACE of it, Saturday, 15 April 1989 was a crushingly archetypal Highbury afternoon in the George Graham era. The Gunners, who'd been labouring in the league of late, were struggling to get past Newcastle United's obdurate defence. The underachieving Geordies, struggling against relegation, almost took a shock lead when ex-Arsenal defender Kenny Sansom rattled his shot against the post in the second half. Part of the problem was Highbury's dreadful playing surface, none too fondly referred to as the 'mud flats' by Perry Groves.

Paul Davis recalls: 'We were a young team anyway, and by March, a number of the players were completely drained. The last thing you want is your own pitch draining your legs away from you. It was like the opposition had a twelfth man, at times. Nowadays, it's like a croquet lawn, but back then, there was mud and sand dumped everywhere. It was a terrible surface. It levelled things out, and teams like Millwall or Luton, who usually came for a draw, knew that we couldn't flow as well because of the pitch. It was disappointing, because we finally won the title that year, but our best performances tended to be away from Highbury. I'm convinced that the state of the pitch contributed to some dodgy performances. Interestingly, our best performance at home that year was against Norwich, when we thrashed them 5–0. It happened to be played on a really hot day, when the pitch had finally dried out.'

In the Newcastle match, winger Brian Marwood netted a late winner. The relief was palpable, especially as the Gunners had seized the opportunity to narrow the gap on a Liverpool side who were playing in the FA Cup semi-final against Nottingham Forest at Hillsborough that afternoon. Marwood recalls the events of that afternoon all too well: 'As we went into the game, I was in good spirits, because I felt I was starting to play well again after a series of niggling injuries. There was some good banter with the crowd before the game too. I was with the mascot, who was taking pot shots at John Lukic, and every single one of them was pinging into the back of the net. The crowd gave him a rousing reception. "We all agree, mascot is better than Marwood," they were singing. The crowd also started going through each player's name and shouting – in my case – "Marwood, Marwood, do the twist". And unless you wiggled your bum at the North Bank, you'd get booed. There was no option. I thought that my winner put the icing on the cake that day, and the crowd went bananas. Everyone knows that title winning sides need to win their fair share of games 1–0. But then I sensed that the crowd seemed a bit distracted in the last few minutes. There was a strange buzz, and it was clear something wasn't quite right.'

Arsenal fan Frank Saunders recalls: 'These were the days before mobile phones, so unless you had a radio clapped to your ear, you were completely cut off from the outside world. But obviously, some guys did have radios, and it was clear that something bad was happening at Hillsborough. At first, the reports suggested some fans had been injured. Terrible as it sounds, most of us didn't even bat an eyelid, because those sorts of incidents were frequent in the eighties. But after Brian Marwood scored, we all knew that something was seriously wrong, and that several fans had died. The crowd was quite subdued afterwards. We all went for our customary post-match pint, and when

'As the [West] stand began to go up [pictured here in July 1932] you got some sort of indication of what an incredible structure it would be' builder Robert Hume (*Getty Images*).

'He had genuine star quality and was the first Arsenal player to make people think it was worth getting out of their chair to go to Highbury.' The legendary Charles Buchan leads the team out in 1926 (*Empics*).

The 'spit and sawdust' Highbury of the twenties, with the rickety old East Stand in the background (*Colorsport*).

The first floodlit game at Highbury, v Hapoel Tel Aviv, September 1951 (*Empics*).

The North Bank, v Sheffield Wednesday, August 1959: 'It was now our place, where you could sing, drink and swear as much as you wanted' (*Empics*).

George Eastham (left) and John Barnwell (right), both central components of Billy Wright's sixties team, emerge from the tunnel. 'Billy Wright was a nice guy, but a bloody disaster for Arsenal' (*Empics*).

'You realised the East Stand [here pictured in 1967] was a message to the rest of football that Arsenal was number one for style' construction engineer, Stephen Lowry (*Empics*).

'Highbury, beautiful though it was, was beginning to seem very small' (*Tony Davis*), complete with 'the mural', with necessary daubs of brown and black paint, in 1993 (inset; *Colorsport*).

Classic art deco: the famous West Stand entrance (*Tony Davis*); (below) watching Arsenal at the Clock End, 80s style: 'Open terraces, segregation, and lots of mullets and dodgy jackets' (*both Colorsport*).

the doors to the Highbury Barn swung open, it was almost deserted. I thought to myself, Shit, if people are actually abandoning their post match beers, things must be much worse than I'd imagined.'

Brian Marwood recalls the aftermath of the Newcastle match: 'We got into the dressing room, but before we arrived, there were some uneasy looking faces in the tunnel. George Graham delivered his verdict on the game, and was very focused, as always. It was only when we left the dressing room that we heard what had happened. To say that it put things in perspective would be a slight understatement. 'One member of the Arsenal team, who has contributed to this book elsewhere, comments: 'I've been asked on many occasions how I felt on that day. I would say – an overwhelming sense of sadness, and a sense that football was irrelevant. You couldn't think anything else, really. But the feeling that the game didn't matter any more couldn't prevail, despite journalists writing things like, "Well, the league is unimportant this year." I could see what they meant, but as professionals, we all knew that we had a job to do. We had ambitions to win the title. We owed it to ourselves, and to the fans who paid to watch us. But we were all aware that something fundamental in football had to change after Hillsborough.'

For those Arsenal fans who watched the Newcastle match, there was an uneasy period of reflection on past experiences. Those with long memories recalled the weekly crushes on the terraces in the 1930s, and regular spillages on to the pitch if things got too cramped. In recent times, there were numerous other events which could have gone horribly wrong – like the West Ham match in 1981, and the crushing on the North Bank a year earlier, when over 50,000 watched Arsenal take on Everton in a Littlewoods Cup semi-final clash. There were countless other incidents which never made it to the headlines, but nonetheless left some supporters with an extremely eerie feeling. Steve Ashford recalls: 'There was an FA Cup game against Chelsea back in 1973, when over 60,000 turned up. They were queuing right down the road to get in. It was so tight on the North Bank. Your arms were pinned to your sides throughout the match, and there were blokes around me who had their coats pulled off by the pressure of rubbing up against others. But because you couldn't actually raise your arms, you couldn't get your clothes back. At the Chelsea match, I got into a crush, and through sheer force, my shoes were pulled off. Can you believe that? There was no way of getting them back, so I had to walk home barefoot.'

Andy Nicholls recalls a League Cup clash with Manchester City in the late 1970s: 'The crowd seemed to be concentrated in the North Bank. It was a warm April night, and it was absolutely sweltering in there and dangerously tight. Some were visibly distressed. They managed to jump on to the pitch, and get away from the crush. Thank God Arsenal stuck to their guns and never put cages on the front of the North Bank, or we could have had a disaster on our hands. Some made light of it and shouted "I'm being crushed to death". They made these gurgling sounds, and everyone passed it off as a great joke. Of course, we did that because we were of the opinion that football was safe.

'When the Hillsborough tragedy happened, we were all acutely reminded that the safety net had been removed – football terracing could be deadly. And you know what the most worrying thing of all was? The safety net was never there in the first place. We just assumed that it was.

1990s

○ FIN DE REGIME ○

ON 2 DECEMBER 1990, Arsenal prepared to take on league leaders Liverpool at Highbury. It hadn't been the best of weeks for the Gunners. Trounced 6–2 at home by Manchester United in the Rumbelows Cup, and deducted two points by the Football League after the rumpus at Old Trafford back in October, Arsenal went into the game trailing the Anfield side by a massive six points. The *Sun*'s headline typified the tabloids' response: GAME OVER. David O'Leary commented in *The Mirror*: 'They might as well hand the title to Liverpool on a plate.' The unequivocal message appeared to be that Arsenal's title chase was over.

In the build up to the match, George Graham's tone with his players was anything but defeatist. Anders Limpar recalls: 'The way in which George used the events of the week to our advantage was him at his best, in my opinion. Before the Liverpool game, he told us that we owed it to ourselves and the club to come up with a massive performance. I'd never seen him so impassioned: "We're playing Liverpool, and we all know of their reputation. But I think we've got the measure of them. They think they've already got the league won. They think we're down and out. Subconsciously, they feel we've relaxed. We've been hammered by the tabloids all week, and by United, so now you boys need to go out and hammer Liverpool." Then he rounded off in classic George Graham style by telling us to, "Go out and be the Arsenal." It was inspiring stuff. When we walked out for the start of the match, the fans made an unbelievable noise. It really fired us up for the game. Even their chants had a "fortress mentality" spirit about them. Especially the one which even some of the players began to sing: "You can stick your fucking two points up your arse." It was a fantastic atmosphere in which to perform.'

Intimidating racket or not, Arsenal's players were acutely aware that defeating Liverpool would not be an easy task. Alan Smith recalls: 'Rather like United in the nineties, Liverpool often seemed to have games won before they stepped out on to the pitch. The fear factor they engendered in other sides stemmed from their success over many years.

When we played them, they were reigning champions, and had fantastic players in their team like Rush and Barnes. But as our win at Anfield showed, the machine was starting to creak a bit. We thought that if we got at them in the match, we could get some joy. We also felt a raging sense of injustice going into the game after the points deduction.'

Strictly speaking there is no such term, but the Liverpool game is often regarded as the high point of 'Grahamism'. The game, broadcast live on ITV's *The Big Match*, also signified a fundamental power shift away from Liverpool, permanently. Arsenal fan Tim Kenworthy recalls: 'Yes, 1990 was a long time ago, but the memories of the game are still very clear in my mind. It was a time when you'd see home-grown players play out of their skins in a great team that worked as a unit. And we were a club which had a fortress mentality spirit, right up from the fans to the players. Beating Liverpool in those days meant so much to us, because everyone inside Highbury that afternoon had grown up with the feeling that Liverpool were almost invincible. But their days at the top were nearly over. I can't remember seeing a game at Highbury where you can look back and recognise a power shift had occurred. Maybe when we lost to Chelsea in the Champions League in 2004. But that's about it.'

With George Graham's rousing words ringing in their ears, Arsenal laid siege to the Liverpool goal. Paul Merson squeezed home the first after his half volley was adjudged to have crossed the line before Barry Venison desperately tried to clear. 'You could see they were rattled,' recalls Anders Limpar, 'because they knew they'd be harried every step of the way.' Midway through the second half, Lee Dixon scored from the penalty spot after Limpar had been brought down by Gary Gillespie. The Swede received criticism for the way he went to ground, but Limpar argues: 'That's nonsense. Gillespie caught me with his trailing leg. TV rarely conveys just how fast the attacker is running.'

There was a spectacular finale. With Arsenal pushing forward for a third goal, Paul Merson back-heeled the ball into the path of the onrushing Alan Smith, who smashed his shot past Bruce Grobbelaar. 'It was probably the best goal I scored that season,' confirms Smith. 'It was a fantastic team goal, and as others have said, destroying Liverpool so convincingly – and on telly too – sent a hell of a message out to other teams. As footballers, you rarely think about "what ifs", but it's true to say that if Liverpool had won that day, they would probably have cruised to the title. They would have been nine points clear at Christmas, which would have been very difficult for us to chip away at. As it was, the lead was cut to just three. It was a classic six-pointer game. They became jittery after that and history proves it's been sixteen years since they've won the league title. For someone like me, who was brought up in an era of Liverpool domination, that seems incredible. Our 3-0 victory proved they'd run into a team which could match them in all departments.'

There is a lingering feeling among several Arsenal players of that generation that the team never received the credit it deserved for taking Liverpool's crown away from them. Anders Limpar comments: 'I don't know whether it is because many people seem to be unable to remember events before the Premiership era began, but history seems to have been rewritten. Alex Ferguson and Manchester United seem to be taking the credit for ending Liverpool's dominance. Correct me if I'm wrong, but wasn't it Arsenal who beat Liverpool at Anfield in 1989, and then we won the title again in 1991. Even Leeds won the title before United got it in 1993. I suppose it doesn't matter too much any more, but it was Arsenal who broke Liverpool's stranglehold.'

Limpar's team-mate, Perry Groves, believes that in early 1991, Arsenal were in an ideal position to dominate the 1990s, just as Liverpool had dominated the 1980s: 'At that time, money didn't come into the equation as much. If you look at how George built his two title-winning sides, he did it efficiently and effectively. He was never quite the same after 1991. Whether he simply began to lose his edge, or whether he simply found it impossible to rebuild, is difficult to fathom. But when I think back to that Liverpool game at Highbury, I always remember walking off the pitch with the feeling that we could dominate football for years - like Chapman's team did in the thirties.'

○ THE BEST OF TIMES ○

'FROM AN ARSENAL FAN's perspective,' explains Anders Limpar, 'I'd imagine that the latter stages of the 1990–91 season represented the high point of George Graham's era at the club. The team was playing fantastic football, and eventually won the title comparatively easily. That's a rare thing in the club's history. All the components of the side integrated superbly, and some of the games at the end of the season were unbelievably fantastic to play in.' The most comprehensive Highbury display was a 5–0 destruction of Aston Villa. At the time, Arsenal looked odds-on to become the first English club to complete a historic double Double.

Arsenal fan Jo Selby recalls the rocking atmosphere around Highbury as the season neared its climax: 'The atmosphere in the ground got more and more intense. I remember that season's end for the chants that were going around. Before the Villa game we were in the Clock End just bouncing up and down to "We're gonna win the Football League again". What I still recall to this day was the feeling that we were about to do the Double. My dad used to go on about Charlie George and Bob Wilson, but I really thought that we were going to match that achievement in 1991. The Villa match was practically a procession. We just annihilated them in an unbelievable half-hour blitz. I can remember the goals even now. Limpar was in brilliant form and he slipped Campbell in for his first. At that time, Kev was one of the most promising strikers in the country. Alan Smith got two really good goals. But the best of all was from Paul Davis. He was having his best ever season for us, and he got the ball on the edge of the area. He sort of flipped it over his head and back volleyed it into the roof of Spinks' net. It was unbelievable. He was a player who you sort of knew was bright, intelligent and alert and that goal showed amazing vision and skill.

'You had to be in Avenell Road after the game to appreciate the atmosphere. Everyone was singing "We've got that Double feeling". It was a shameless rip-off of the Righteous Brothers' "That lovin' Feeling" which had been re-released. It sounded crap, and yet fantastic at the same time, which is how most football chants are, isn't it? The Highbury Barn rocked to it! We'd stuffed Villa 5–0. We were cruising in the league and we had the Spurs match coming. We just felt invincible. I know that Arsenal fans get criticised a lot for not making as much noise as we used to, but those final games of 1990–91, all of which seemed to be evening games, were just amazing. I didn't think we could fail to do the Double. Then Spurs and Gazza wrecked our Double chances, and got us back with "You've lost that Double feeling" whenever they could. But even that semi-final defeat couldn't stop our progress in the league.'

Anders Limpar recalls George Graham's fury in the Wembley dressing room after the Spurs match. "You've let me down," he was wailing. He made it abundantly clear that we were expected to bounce back and win the league for him after this. We stuttered a little after Wembley. There was a home game against Manchester City where we went 2–0 up, and ended up drawing 2–2. But what helped us was that Liverpool couldn't sustain their challenge, and faded away. I recall that Ian Woan, a guy who actually came from Liverpool, scored the winner for Nottingham Forest against Liverpool, and as their game was shown earlier on telly, we knew that we were already champions, before our home game with Manchester United. It was strange. For me, I was elated that we'd won the league in my first season, but some of the guys who were involved in the win at Anfield a couple of years before, reckoned it was a bit of an anticlimax. I think that Tony Adams and the others got a real kick out of the do-or-die stuff. The atmosphere was fantastic. I heard later a story that Arsenal played under the influence of champagne. It may have flowed afterwards, but can you really imagine George Graham allowing that to happen? "Go out and be the Arsenal," he ordered – as always. He never let up, even in celebration. And the boys turned on a great show.'

After the trauma of the season – including the points deduction, and Tony Adams' jail sentence – the relaxed Gunners tore United apart. Alan Smith thumped in a hat-trick to secure the Golden Boot award. He recalls: 'It was the kind of evening which all players long to be part of. Clearly, it was vastly different to Anfield in eighty-nine, but I was quite glad that we could actually relax at the end of a season for once. It was wonderful of Lee Dixon to allow me to take the penalty to get my hat-trick, and it reflected the team spirit we had. That side of ninety-one was a fantastic outfit.' The defence, with Adams and Bould majestic, easily repelled Hughes and Robins. Only the Football League sullied the occasion, keeping the championship trophy locked away in their cabinet at Lytham St Annes until the following Saturday. Still, on that memorable May night in 1991, trophy-lifting wasn't needed to confirm that Arsenal, two years after the Anfield triumph, were once more the best in the land.

The final game of the season, at home to Coventry was, in truth, nothing more than a championship parade, with the match itself a mere sideshow. Yet, it attracted several exiled fans from around the globe. Mickey James, who'd moved out to Boston, USA, from Finsbury Park in 1983 takes up the story: 'When I heard that Arsenal had won the league, I went straight to a pub in Boston that is really popular with British expats. There were a couple of other Arsenal fans in there and we had a fantastic night. I remember getting really plastered, and the three of us walked home past the Cheers bar shouting "Champions, Champions" at top volume. But even in my inebriated state I knew what I had to do. I had to be at Highbury on the Saturday to see the Arsenal play Coventry.

'I hadn't seen a game for two years – when we'd beaten 'Boro 3–0 at Highbury. But once I told my girlfriend what was happening, she knew I had to go. I frantically made some phone calls to my boss to book a few days off work; to my mates in London to fix me up with a ticket and a place to crash when I got there. The flight to Gatwick on the Wednesday seemed to take an eternity and a mate was there to pick me up when I arrived. We spent the next couple of days inside pubs and various curry houses, making sure we were ready for Saturday.

'Highbury looked packed and magnificent that afternoon. My mate had got me a ticket on the North Bank and, as it turned out, it was the last time I'd stand at Highbury. Coventry were really just "lambs to the slaughter", weren't they? I'd heard and seen on TV lots about Anders Limpar and he turned on a brilliant show. He scored a superb hat-trick and tormented his marker all afternoon. Alan Smith and Perry Groves scored too. The final score was 6–1. We just totally destroyed them in an awesome fashion. In a way, I was a bit annoyed that I'd been abroad for the whole season. But I'll never forget Tony Adams lifting the trophy about five yards in front of me, and posing for a picture. I've still got it at home. I just call it, "The Class of '91", which is apt isn't it?

'It always amazes me to think that the team won the title that season with all those tribulations. Most sides would have folded under the pressure. But then, that Arsenal side wasn't just any old team, was it? Now, I have every video from each game sent out to me by my mate. It's expensive, but who cares?'

The 1991 Arsenal side, labelled by John Roberts in the *Independent* as 'masters of adversity' had been defeated just once in the league that season. Only Preston's 'invincibles', back in the days of Queen Victoria, had matched that feat. Such a monumental achievement appeared unlikely to be equalled again. Another point worth making, as Limpar points out, is that: 'With the exception of myself, the rest of the side was entirely British. Looking back, that seems incredible, but George Graham built the entire side from youth team products and shrewd lower division buys. It goes without saying that you can't win a title like that any more, but I still feel an immense sense of pride that I was part of that side. I honestly didn't feel that any team would ever equal that achievement of losing only one game in the entire season, but I'm glad that another Arsenal side ended up doing just that.'

○ THE WORST OF TIMES ○

IN THE MIDST of Arsenal's record breaking triumph, a large black cloud hove into view. It was announced in the souvenir Coventry City programme, that the club had decided to finance the cost of making Highbury all-seater (around £22.5m) through a bond or debenture scheme. The club eventually hoped to sell £16.5m worth of bonds to fans, while the rest would come from within the club's not unsubstantial coffers. Rangers had redeveloped Ibrox through such a scheme, as had several clubs in America. Doubtless this was where

David Dein got the idea from. It was announced that, for an outlay of either £1,200 or £1,500, buying a bond would entitle a fan to 'exclusive rights' to a season ticket for up to 150 years and a Bond Certificate signed by Peter Hill-Wood and George Graham.

The battle to save terracing had been lost. Clubs were informed that if they refused to comply with the findings of the Taylor Report, their safety licences (i.e. rights to stage matches) would be revoked by season 1994–95. It was a *coup de grâce*; over a century of tradition was all but over. Fans were saddened by that, but what rankled most of all was the manner in which the club went about the whole all-seater process. Vice-chairman David Dein quoted several sections from the Taylor report to fans, but demurred from trotting out the part which recommended that clubs should involve and 'consult' fans on any pending decisions. In his report, Taylor said: 'As for the clubs, in some instances, it is legitimate to wonder whether the directors are genuinely interested in the welfare of their grass-root supporters.'

Rumours about the bond had already leaked out via the *Evening Standard*, but the 'consultation process', which Taylor advocated, consisted of a few vague public meetings and a thin questionnaire in the Arsenal v Leeds programme. The half-baked questions were unlikely to gauge public opinion on the 'all-seater' debate. In truth, the most important information the club received through the survey was contained in the box after the word 'Address'. Those who responded (an estimated 15,000) were sent a glossy brochure on the merits of the scheme. As for the findings of the questionnaire – they were never made public.

Immediately, it became clear that, if pursued, the bond scheme would have a major impact upon the social make-up of the Highbury crowd, due to the necessary outlay – in instalments (around £100 a month for a year or more), or as a lump sum of over one thousand pounds. This was *on top* of the price of a season ticket. Football consultant Alex Fynn comments: 'That's the key point: should football fans actually be charged for the privilege of buying a season ticket?' One band of Arsenal fans spent the summer of 1991 establishing the Independent Arsenal Supporters' Association (IASA). In the words of one of its founders, Ian McPherson: 'We were incensed that the club thought that they could push through these proposals at the last minute, unchallenged, and hope that everyone would forget about it over the summer. It was unforgivably arrogant on the board's part.'

Fans' moods were not improved with the news of a 33 per cent price hike in matchday tickets around the ground at the start of the 1991–92 season. In the final season of the old North Bank, some crowds slumped beneath the 30,000 mark, due to inflation-busting ticket prices and discontent over the bond scheme. David Dein, now the majority shareholder with his 42 per cent stake in the club, was unquestionably the driving force behind the new initiatives. The day before the 1991–92 season began, the First Division chairmen, with Dein at the forefront, announced that, in the following season, they would form a breakaway Premier League.

After deciding to press on with the bond scheme, the board stood accused, by its own fans, of two heinous crimes; namely social engineering, and high-handedness in dealing with supporters. The anti-bond IASA, had already achieved notable success. Early in June 1991, a *Time Out* article publicised the movement, which prompted David Dein to threaten legal action against the group. Dein had obviously calmed down a few days later, because the movement's leader, Dyll Davies, and *One Nil Down*'s editor Tony Willis were invited into the inner sanctum to meet with Dein and Friar and discuss their differences.

The meeting was heated but fairly good-natured. The transcript from the meeting was reproduced in *One Nil Down* some weeks later. One question/answer in particular summed up the gulf between fans and the board. They were asked the question: 'What provisions are being made for loyal fans who cannot afford a bond?' (Namely, the majority of teenagers, students, OAPs and the core of the North Bank.) Friar and Dein apologised for the chaos that was likely to occur, but said that '. . . the club is not run as a charitable institution'. A fair point, but in a nutshell, they'd admitted that no provision was being made for lower income fans.

Dein and Friar's responses at the meeting were terse and sharp. The reason for this was, that out of 16,000 bonds up for sale, only an estimated 5,000 (£5m worth) were sold by Christmas 1991. The IASA's campaigning was proving to be a serious pain for the club.

Ian McPherson wrote several articles for *One Nil Down* and helped put together the IASA newsletter. He recalls the prevailing attitude among many fans at the time: 'I don't think that the club ever *really* understood what our grievance was. The North Bank had always been the traditional stronghold of our support. In general, it was populated by the lower income sections of our support. It was, therefore, of real symbolic importance. The bond scheme was an exclusive, elitist scheme, which asked those people to shell out a large sum of money. It was money which many did not have. In effect, the club was telling people on the North Bank that money was more important than loyalty. They were constructing a new kind of football audience; a well-heeled, middle-class audience who would then be able to spend a fair proportion of their cash on club merchandise. In effect, it *was* a form of social engineering. I remember that Tom Watt said at the time that the club was afraid of its own supporters. Look at the way the club dealt with the whole issue. In effect, they used threats all the time. They said that if they were forced to take the money from the club's coffers, then they wouldn't be able to afford any decent players. Then they said that in order to attend games, you had to have a season ticket and in order to get one of those you needed to have a bond. Someone told me that the club, allegedly, used to call us the "intelligentsia" – which kind of hints that they found the IASA intimidating. That's actually quite amusing, but it just goes to show that for all their claims of being a "progressive club", it was actually being led by an archaic elite, with no public relations skills at all.

'We saw it as our responsibility to come up with an alternative plan for financing the conversion of Highbury into an all-seater stadium. We proposed that, first, a debenture scheme should guarantee season tickets at a *reduced* rate, which meant that fans would get a *real* return on their investment. We suggested issuing a maximum six thousand of these. Second, we suggested setting up a membership scheme which, for twenty pounds a season, would enable fans to obtain an option on buying a ticket for every home match. Third, we put forward the idea of a *limited* share issue – raising between £2m and £4.5m. Added together, this would have brought in between £12m and £14m. The membership card scheme mysteriously appeared in the following year. This was the *club's* idea, of course!'

It soon filtered through that over the next two years, when the capacity was to be slashed to around 28,000, the club hoped to sell all

16,000 bonds. It also hoped to make 'up to' 12,000 tickets available to fans on matchdays. By the time the away side had received their share and the touts had got their hands on some of them, closer to 6,000 tickets would be available to non-bond holders for each game. It would, in effect, turn Highbury into Fort Knox, with sufficient cash to buy a bond seemingly being a prerequisite for regular entry to the ground. Once fans comprehended this news, letters of support and cash donations flooded into IASA headquarters. Here are extracts from two of the letters:

> I'm not against making Arsenal the best in the land, but not all people can afford such a sum to pay for a bond. And the sad thing is I have already had the sad duty of telling my son (twelve) that this is probably the last season for some time that we can attend all matches, if any. My son and I love this club with all our hearts. I don't think the club's as loyal to us, just our money.

> As the father of two children who are devoted to Arsenal, I'm appalled at our exclusion from any thinking into restructuring plans. It is simply way beyond my means to pay for bonds for the children. Will we ever be back after this season?
>
> *(names withheld from both letters)*

Ian McPherson recalled that 'for every bond that wasn't sold, it meant that a loyal fan who couldn't afford the bond, could get into games over the next two years. It would be interesting to find out exactly how many supporters never returned to Highbury after the bond fiasco. It must number into the thousands.' Alex Fynn concludes: 'Hindsight is a wonderful thing, of course. What is true is that the Taylor Report was a revolutionary document, and the quicker the club adhered to it – in their eyes – the better. Where the club went awry was the manner in which they proceeded with turning Highbury all-seater. Fans were taken for granted. The club carried out insufficient research into the whole issue, knowing full well that, unlike in the case of supermarkets or cinemas, the "customers" wouldn't take their loyalties elsewhere. There were some alternatives to the bond scheme. The club could have taken out a straight loan for around £16.5 million, although there are some clear arguments against doing that. They could also have taken out a loan as collateral. The returns would have come from season ticket sales and revenue from the hospitality suites. Either of these ideas would have given the club the money it required, without incurring the wrath of its supporters.'

○ SAYONARA NORTH BANK ○

THE IMPACT OF Ian Wright's arrival at Highbury from Crystal Palace in September 1991 cannot be overestimated. During a routine phone call, Arsenal's David Dein casually enquired of Palace's chairman, Ron Noades, if striker Mark Bright was available for transfer. Noades said that he was not, but within two minutes the conversation had been turned on its head, and a bemused Palace chairman agreed to sell Bright's striking partner, Ian Wright. Arsenal shattered its transfer record, signing him for £2.5m. There were some initial doubts when he first arrived. Some said that capturing him was unnecessary and that he mightn't even get a place in the side. Other 'tactical experts' claimed that rather than playing up front, he might function in midfield or even on the wing. Spectacularly wrong on all counts, as it turned out.

The reasons why Wright wanted to leave Palace are fairly clear. The press highlighted the fact that Noades said in a TV documentary that black players lacked 'bottle' and didn't 'like the cold'. This outburst probably made up his mind for him, but Wright had long since realised that his genetic make-up 'required a larger stage'. The maelstrom that was Ian Wright was all too much for Palace – a club whose limited fan base often meant that Selhurst Park was semi-deserted, despite Noades' protestations that they were about to become a big club. Thus George Graham had signed a star who felt, as he later commented, '. . . that I was born for the really big occasions – Arsenal gave me that stage'.

In order to fully understand the extent of Wright's burning desire when he arrived at Highbury, one only needs to look at his background.

Originally considered too lightweight and flimsy to make it as a pro, he seemed to be headed on a road to nowhere. Jailed for seven days in Chelmsford for non-payment of car fines, and burnin' rubber in London without MOTs, tax or car insurance, he was in with a 'bad crowd'. By age twenty-one, he was certainly no over-nannied or cosseted young star; he was up to his knees in filth, repairing and constructing tunnels for Greenwich Borough Council, struggling to make ends meet in order to support his young family. He drifted around the non-league circuit, playing for Greenwich and all-black side Ten Em Bee. He finally turned professional at twenty-two with Palace, quickly transforming himself into their cult hero. When he arrived at Highbury, he was twenty-eight years old and, realising that his shelf life was limited, he knew he had to make up for lost time. As Arsenal fan George Towner comments: 'We instantly fell under Ian Wright's spell because he fitted in perfectly with our perceptions of what being a Gunner is all about, and a great deal more besides. The passion, the intensity, the fury. That's the way I'd play if I ever got to pull on an Arsenal shirt.'

Wright was the nearest thing Arsenal had at the time to a bona fide superstar. Alan Smith – often considered a casualty of the 'Wright effect', explains the phenomenon: 'When Ian arrived, he became the life and soul of the dressing room. He was a really funny lad, with a strong personality on the pitch too. He wanted the ball all the time and, to be honest, we started to play to his strengths too much. We seemed just to give it to him all the time which made us far too one-dimensional and too focused on him. The affect on my game was immediate. I'd always scored lots of goals, but they dried up almost straight away. My strength was holding up the ball, and allowing others to come into the game. But with Ian, he wanted the ball "now", and so I saw less and less of the ball. Subconsciously, I think that some players thought "if we give it to Ian, he'll do the business for us", which I don't think is too healthy for a team. The effect didn't really kick in on the others until the following season. After all, towards the end of the season the team played some of the best attacking football I ever saw. Within a couple of years though, watching Arsenal often seemed to be more about watching Ian.'

The growing sense that Wright was willing to go to extremes to plunder goals was already evident to some of his colleagues. Anders

Limpar recalls: 'Off the pitch, Ian was a lovely man, but on it he could be a total animal. I wouldn't say that he was bigger than the team, though. It just happened that we started to rely on him too much. That wasn't his fault.' Steve Morrow remembers 'a walking, talking, swearing, raging inferno of goals. That was Ian Wright.' As the 1991–92 season reached March, the Gunners treated fans to regular goal fests. The 7–1 destruction of Sheffield Wednesday ('That was an absolutely staggering scoreline, bearing in mind we were drawing 1–1 at half-time,' recalls Limpar) was the most newsworthy. Alan Smith claims a 4–1 trouncing of Wright's old club, Crystal Palace, was 'the most complete team performance of the season to date'. Yet for Arsenal fan Harry Jones, Ian Wright's brace of strikes against Liverpool in a 4–0 hammering was the most eye-catching scoreline of all, quite literally.

He recalls: 'When Wrighty scored his first goal against Liverpool, he did so by latching on to a great pass by Limpar, and he swept it past Mike Hooper with the minimum of effort. Those last few home games of the season were very special to me because I'd been a North Bank regular for over twenty years, and I was very unhappy with what was going on at the club. Luckily, the team was whacking in goals left, right and centre, and Wright was getting most of them. When he scored that goal, we all went ballistic. I took my eye off what was going on, only to glance back a couple of seconds later, and see Wrighty bearing down on the crowd at a rapid rate of knots. "Fuckin' yeah," he yelled, and piled in on us, poking me in the eye as he did so. So everyone else is enjoying their few seconds of fame and are hugging the great man, and I'm stood there like a prat with one eye shut. All very embarrassing. We'd never had anyone at Highbury quite like that before. Because that gap between the touchline and the terrace reflected the gap between players and fans. To cross that line spells either danger – in Cantona's case – or riotous celebration. And Wrighty regularly crossed the line for all the right reasons. What made it extra special, as I said, was that it all happened in the last days of the old North Bank.'

Of all Wright's achievements in an Arsenal shirt during the early years, none were more significant than his hat-trick in the final match of the season at home to Southampton. On an emotion packed afternoon, fans flocked in to pay homage to the end of an era, and bid farewell to the North Bank. It was a game which demanded drama, and with Ian Wright aiming to win the Golden Boot award, the match lived up to its billing.

Save for several choruses of 'You'll never take the North Bank', the cries were for 'Ian Wright, Wright, Wright' and his whirlwind display. The media hyped up Wright's and Gary Lineker's contest for the Golden Boot. With five minutes to go in the Southampton game, it looked as if Lineker had won after his strike at Old Trafford. Arsenal made heavy weather of beating the Saints with scrambled goals from Smith and Campbell, and Wright's penalty. With five minutes to go, and Southampton tiring, Ian Wright took centre stage. Harry Jones takes up the story: 'The crowd was singing a rather mournful tribute to the old terrace, feeling slightly deflated about the whole day. Before the game, in the pub after a few beers, blokes were suggesting sit-ins, and demos after the game. One pissed old sod was rabbiting on about lying in front of the bulldozers to stop them pulling the place down. "If they crush me to death, I won't give a shit, because it will prevent them pulling it down." All pub talk bollocks, but it was how many felt. It was a sad day. And I was stood there thinking, Come on, this should be a day of celebration. A happy day for all the great times I've had here. Then Wrighty struck. Furious at the thought of losing the race for the Golden Boot, he dropped back into his own half and Seaman threw the ball out to him. Wrighty galloped at full pelt deep into Saints' territory, brushed past Terry Hurlock and slammed the ball past Tim Flowers. If the scenes that goal produced were chaotic, then, what came thirty seconds later was fucking orgasmic. Campbell squared a ball to Wright. He shinned in his hat-trick and got hoisted high by Campbell in front of the maelstrom that was now the North Bank. It was mad in there. The best day at football for me, because it all meant so much. And blokes around me were in tears, because they knew the significance of what was going on. It just showed that Wright always picked the right event on which to rise to the occasion, and on that May weekend, he gave us memories we'll always remember. I'll always love Wrighty for what he did that day. Whatever happened after that, he was my hero. And I was an old sod of forty at the time! The North Bank couldn't have had a better send off.

'Wrighty's goals took the sting out of a situation that could have turned a bit nasty. Funnily enough, I saw the bloke afterwards who'd threatened to lie down in front of the bulldozers. He seemed quite happy now, and he decided to give suicide a miss on that occasion. Afterwards, most fans drifted away. A few demonstrated, chanting 'You'll never take the North Bank,' but it was all a bit hollow, and the police moved them on. Some, including me, lingered for a bit, and thought of all the great times I'd had there. Then I went to the Highbury Barn, got really hammered, and forgot about it. Thank God for alcohol.'

Perry Groves recalls events that day: 'It was an emotional occasion for the players too, because you automatically run to the North Bank and listen out for their chants. The game happened at a time when Ian was doing the Nike ads. It was amazing how it all turned out, because some footage from the match was used in his ad. After he scored the penalty, he ran up to the North Bank, and tapped his boot. On all the posters, he said 'Sayonara Lineker San'. He was saying farewell to Gary, who was off to Japan. And the ad suggested that Ian was taking over as the lead striker in England. So it was ironic that he beat Gary to the Golden Boot that day. But that sort of thing happened to Ian. He had a great sense of drama, and knew exactly how to play to the crowd. Then the Nike ads appeared on telly, with Wrighty scoring goals to the backing of a sampled version of Lou Reed's 'Walk on the Wild Side'. It was a good ad.'

The final day in the life of the North Bank was unforgettable in every way, with the crowd spellbound by Wright's persona. It wouldn't be the last time either.

○ ANNOYING THE NEIGHBOURS (2) ○

IN LATE MAY 1992, David Carson and three friends dressed up in grim-reaper garb, and walked to Highbury from Carson's nearby flat.

When they arrived at the stadium, they saw a crowd of over 300 people had already gathered to see the definitive end to the North Bank's existence. At 10 a.m., five huge yellow caterpillar bulldozers made their way into spaces to the sides and at the front of the North Bank. 'All of us,' explains David Carson, 'were looking through the open gates as the caterpillars tore down the North Bank. When the bulldozers ripped into the posts holding up the North Bank, the whole structure collapsed, and the roof crumpled up and fell in on itself. Pretty quickly, a fleet of lorries began to drive in, and remove all the debris. It was horrible. I stayed for a while, and walked home, still in my grim-reaper outfit – I felt like death, actually. We thought that by dressing up as grim reapers, we were making some huge point about the death of the terracing, but the sight of them tearing it down like that was horrible.'

Over those summer months, souvenir hunters successfully managed to salvage pieces of the old terrace, with the help of some friendly demolition experts. Dave Carson is the proud owner of a crush barrier from the North Bank, which has pride of place at the foot of his garden. 'I went back a few days after,' he recalls, 'and security wasn't all that tight, because there had to be access for the trucks to flow in and out. There were all sorts of bits and bobs lying around, and several of these crush barriers. I started to try and lift one of them up, but it was pretty bloody heavy. One of the workers came across and asked me what the bloody hell I thought I was doing. He didn't seem too pleased when I told him, pointing out quite forcibly that he'd be sacked if the guvnor caught him, and that it was dangerous – not to mention illegal – for me to be on the site at all. Then he recalled that the guvnor wasn't in that day, so between us, we pulled it to one side, and I was able to pop home, get my van, and we loaded it up. I've heard that I wasn't the only one to do that, and that some fans bribed construction workers for slabs of concrete and all that, but I've never actually met anyone else with a piece of old North Bank memorabilia in their house. I felt a bit guilty – like a tomb robber in some ways – but it would only have been used for scrap, so why not? I occasionally walk by that barrier and tap it, to remember all the years I enjoyed standing at games. I'm fully aware, by the way, that most people reading this are probably thinking that I'm a bit of a weirdo.'

Within a couple of months, new ground beams and drainage were completed, and the club announced that 'one of the finest stands in Europe was in the process of being constructed'. Quickly, the super-structure of columns rose up from the ground. On the face of it, the whole process appeared to be running very smoothly, but behind the scenes, bitter battles had been fought over the design of the new North Stand. Back in March 1991, AD Construction – the company responsible for the redevelopment of the South Stand – was invited by the club to draft proposals for the new North Bank Stand. The model for the proposed 12,750-seater stand was revealed to Islington residents at around the same time.

Larry Parker was horrified by the proposal: 'As an Arsenal fan, and an Islington resident, I was frankly, appalled. The original plan looked – as Prince Charles might say – like a "monstrous carbuncle". The first thing that struck me was the height of the bloody thing. It would mean that if you included the trusses, you'd have thirty metres worth of stand. When you consider that the old shed on the North Bank was only around fifteen metres high, it would make a huge difference light-wise around the north side of the stadium. The other thing was that the materials they planned to use were totally out of character with the rest of the stadium. It would have looked like some great hulk of ugliness, with its wraparound corners. Imagine that – sandwiched between two beautiful art-deco stands, both listed buildings and the envy of the football world. It was at precisely the same time that masses of Arsenal fans were getting shirty about the whole manner with which the new stand was being funded. So, as well as all the "stuff the bond" groups, the club also had a battle on its hands with the plans for the North Stand. We formed the GAAS (Group for an Alternative Arsenal Stand) action group from local residents. A lot of the members of GAAS were also in the IASA. So we were fighting a battle on two fronts. It always amazed me that the club seemed so baffled by our opposition. We'd always formed the impression that they weren't overly interested in what we had to say, but in the early 1990s, they were forced to sit up and take a bit of notice at last.'

After a particularly stormy meeting on 5 November inside Islington Town Hall, the council gave the club six weeks to come up with an alternative design to the AD plans, preferably one that blended aesthetically with the East and West Stands. Ultimately, Norwest Holst, along with architects from the Lobb partnership (including one, Rod Sheard, who led the design team for the Emirates Stadium) and engineers from the Jan Bobrowski firm put forward a design which was nearly four metres shorter than the original AD design and, with its use of modern materials, looked far better juxtaposed between the two existing East and West Stands.

Larry Parker recalls: 'GAAS was able to make suggestions to the Lobb Partnership which bore some fruit. We ensured that pressure was brought to bear on the club's high-handedness, and that the council threw out the original AD Construction proposals. Through our actions, the height of the new stand was reduced by a further couple of metres. We also worked with Lobb to ensure that the stand was set further back from Avenell Road, and that a crèche was provided inside the stand. I thought that the architect Paul Sheard emerged with a huge amount of credit, because as he said, the new construction was a subtle blend between the 1930s' art-deco style espoused by Claude Ferrier – who designed the East and West Stands – and the need for a more modern design, and up to date materials. The fanning effect on the side windows is great, as it espouses the principles upheld by Ferrier. Arsenal is all about tradition and history. If we lose sight of that, we lose our soul.

'Charles Thomson was also a great ambassador for GAAS. He made a very pertinent comment when he said: "The Taylor Report requires all-seater stadiums. It doesn't require massive, badly designed stands." There were clear parallels between what was going on with the bond scheme, and what was happening with the North Stand. The club, if they could have done so, would have tried to push through the AD company's plans with no consultation with fans. Like the IASA, we forced their hands. I'd like to think that the club learned its lesson after those difficult times, and realised the need for full consultation. But I'm not too sure that they did. When Arsenal finally received permission from Islington Council for the construction of the stand (this was the third attempt), the relief on the club's part was huge. Yet they could have avoided all that trouble if they'd engaged in some proper discussion beforehand.'

The bad feeling among local residents towards the club regarding the new North Stand wasn't the only 'own goal' that Arsenal scored throughout the rebuilding process. In order to mask the building work at the 'construction end', the club commissioned a giant mural which stretched the entire length of the North Bank, and depicted a sea of faces which looked out across the Highbury pitch. The problem was that none of the faces were painted black or brown. Paul Sheehan comments: 'I wouldn't describe myself as politically correct or anything like that, but it was a bit of a faux pas on the club's part. I read somewhere that the artist said the brown and black had faded over time, but I'm not sure whether that's true or not. Arsenal have always prided themselves on being a cosmopolitan club, and on nurturing black players. Not to reflect that – a cursory check would have meant the situation could have been avoided – seemed a bit clumsy.

'Purely from a fan's angle, that season was weird. A three-sided stadium didn't help, and neither did being forced to migrate to the Clock End for a sort of 'last stand'. It came as little surprise to me that our best performances that year tended to be in the cup competitions – away from Highbury. It was the first time that the "Highbury Library" jibe started, and visiting supporters joked that the painted people made more noise than the Arsenal fans. Part of the problem was that any noise we made sort of drifted up into the sky, although as we know, there are deeper reasons as to why Highbury has become quieter over the years. Anyway, the mural was useful for blocking Jensen's and Hillier's shots, so I suppose there were some benefits to it.'

Alan Smith recalls the curious mural effect: 'People reckoned there was a curse on the mural. It took us about six games before we scored at that end of the ground, when Ian Wright netted a header against Manchester City. There obviously wasn't a curse, but it did seem very strange without the North Bank cheering us on. Not scoring at that end became psychological in the end. You'd run out at Highbury, and it just wasn't quite right. But I still think that having a mural there was better than having nothing at all. When you went to other grounds at the time, it was surprisingly off-putting when the backdrop to the goal and the touchline was a building site. At least the mural gave the ground a more intimate feel. Our league form wasn't great that season, but you can't put that down, as some did, to the absence of the North Bank. The team simply wasn't as strong as it had been – it was on the wane – especially if you think about the way in which we had won the title in 1991.'

○ THE DOG'S BOLLOCKS? ○

BY THE START of the 1993–94 season, George Graham's Arsenal was showing distinct signs of battle fatigue. Having already signed two Scandinavians, Lydersen and Jensen – thereby, already, indirectly signing his own death warrant – his team became widely criticised for their style of play. The opening of the new North Bank Stand drove home the uncomfortable reality of life at Graham's Arsenal in the Premiership. The hi-tech, all-singing, all-food dispensing North Bank Stand was unveiled for the opening game of the season, against Coventry. It wasn't quite finished, and with the Clock End a mass of concrete slabs and cement, as it was being converted to all-seater, Highbury remained more of a construction site than a football stadium. Still, the all-seater era was here and even some sceptics were won over. One fan sought out David Dein and admitted: 'If I have to sit, then this (North) stand is the business. It's the dog's bollocks.' Those who didn't keel over from vertigo after clambering all the way up to the new Upper Tier would have had a bird's eye view of Mick Quinn belting an unbelievable hat-trick past Seaman in Coventry's 3–0 win.

Arsenal fan George Talbot explains his reaction to the start of the all-seater era: 'I'd always been a terrace boy, for twenty years, and I wasn't keen at all to sit at games. I had to admit that the North Stand was impressive. You could actually get decent food at the football for once, like bagels, and Nachos. And the tea and coffee was actually decent quality stuff, not the powdered stuff which used to stick to the side of the cup and burn your bloody hand whenever you touched the plastic container. Then there was the band in the concourse, and there were penalty shoot-outs and stuff to do with the kids. And I think all that is great, if you're a father who is taking the missus or the kids. Maybe I'm a bit selfish – and, of course, the club had to adhere to the Taylor Report – but I wasn't always too comfortable with the move to football becoming a family-orientated event. I was brought up with the notion that football wasn't meant to be nice and genteel; Highbury was a place where I could come and shout and swear, after a working week when I had to be nice to lots of customers whom I didn't much like. I remember that Coventry game, because I happened to be sitting right at the front when Mick Quinn scored the second of his goals, and he came right up close to the stand. I shouted to him, "Where's Spit the fucking Dog?" because he looked like Bob Carolgees, who was on the telly at the time. And he grinned at me and gave me the finger. I found it funny, because he had the last laugh, didn't he?

'Now on a terrace, I'd have been standing with guys through choice, who would have joined in with me, but instead, I got a foul look off some mum who was there with her kids. She asked me if I could tone down my language, and then spent about half an hour handing out sandwiches to her family and explaining to them who Spit the Dog was, instead of actually watching the game. The problem is that I more or less did as I was told, and felt self-conscious about swearing in front of families. And I had no one around me to sing with, for that particular game anyway. At the end, the woman was going to tell a steward about Quinn giving me the finger sign, and I just thought, That isn't how football works in this country. It ain't meant to be nice and sugary sweet. So, apart from the diabolical result, I also came away a bit worried, thinking, Is that how it will be from now on? For big games like United and Chelsea, the atmosphere goes back to what it once was, but overall, you have to admit that although it's much safer at Highbury now, the edgy side has more or less been taken away, and that the atmosphere has suffered as a result.'

The Gunners suffered a dire October, drawing four consecutive blanks against the likes of Oldham and Norwich. These disasters were not helped by the fact that George Graham rested some players for Europe. In the press, Graham admitted that the Cup-Winners' Cup represented the club's best chance of success. After a month, he let slip that he considered a routine home league game against Norwich to be 'less important' than the Cup-Winners' game with Odense. His obsession for European success was admirable, but with fans in the North Bank paying an average of £15 for a seat, his tactlessness didn't go down particularly well with Arsenal fans. A clump of them unfurled a cryptic banner at the home game against Norwich – an appalling goalless draw: GIVE THE SUCKERS THEIR MONEY BACK. Was this an unsubtle reference to the bond fiasco, or the poor fair on show?

George Talbot summed up the mood: 'The fact is that football wasn't cheap any more. The club were expecting us to pay big money for matches, and they had a duty to entertain us. Things had moved on. We were no longer standing on wet slabs of concrete, and paying peanuts to get in. They expected *us* to up the ante by paying more to get in, so they had a duty to entertain. It might have something to do with the fact that a more middle-class audience was attending games, and that many of the old North Bankers just didn't come back. I know of around ten who never set foot in Highbury after the whole bond issue. People expected more for their money.'

The home match against Manchester United in April demonstrated the urgent need to set up a workable membership card scheme at Highbury. During the season, black marketeers had been able to buy up wadges of tickets and sell them to punters at inflated prices. At the United match, there were thousands of United fans (with obligatory Home Counties accents) in the North Bank, having bought tickets from touts outside. The club was inundated by irate Arsenal supporters who'd been to *all* previous home league games that season, but were forced to miss out on the match against the eventual Premiership champions.

According to Andy Daniels, the match also spoke volumes for the merchandising revolution that was developing inside mid-nineties Highbury: 'That United match was bizarre. It was the one where Cantona got sent off for the second time in a week, on this occasion he clashed with Tony Adams. What was apparent straightaway was that there were as many United fans in there, as there were Gooners. When Ian Wright had a perfectly good goal struck off in the last minute, which would have given us a 3–2 win, there was nearly a fight in there. It came as little surprise when the club announced plans for the membership scheme in the few days after. The other thing about the match that struck me, was that I was sat next to a very well-spoken guy who was the prototype of the Arsenal fan from the *Fast Show*. He didn't seem especially interested in what was happening on the pitch, more on the contents of his plastic bag. By the look of it, he'd bought the entire contents of the Arsenal World of Sport. There were mugs, videos, posters, you name it. He told me he'd got the ticket from a bucket shop in the West End, and that he'd be going to Stamford Bridge that weekend to see Chelsea. You can't blame him, I suppose, but that was symptomatic of what was starting to happen at Highbury. The clientele was becoming increasingly middle class and affluent, and you needed to spend a fair portion of cash both to get in, and buy merchandise. I think it's the type of fan the club wanted by the time the mid-nineties came about. And I don't think that kind of fan – by definition – is the type who will sing their heart out at games. Things were changing.'

◦ CULT HEROES ◦

ANDERS LIMPAR

When George Graham signed Anders Limpar from Italian side Cremonese, he had secured the services of a star player – complete with a stubborn streak and mesmeric skills. Limpar, an unpredictable mixture of Swedish and Hungarian blood, combined East European feistiness with Scandinavian logic and coolness. Case in point: rather than play against Chester in the Rumbelows Cup in October 1990, he defied managerial orders and skipped off to play for Sweden against Germany. His contract stated that Arsenal had to release him for internationals, but Limpar recalls that Graham was never happy about the situation: 'Do you *have* to go Anders? It's Arsenal who pays your wages, not Sweden.' Graham would say. Perhaps a less strong-willed player would have backed down, but Limpar exercised his right to go. Some would argue that he had made a foolish move. Certainly his decision to shoot from the hip to any Scandinavian journalist on the trip who cared to listen, was less than shrewd. The Swedish press reported on alleged bust-ups at Highbury. George Graham, apparently, was always shouting at players and Mickey Thomas was alleged to be fuming about the limitations of his midfield role in the team.

Limpar later apologised for his actions and claimed that he'd been misquoted. Of course, George had to continue picking him, but perhaps by the end of November 1990, Limpar had already sown the seeds of his own destruction in George's mind. From now on, GG classics on Limpar such as 'he needs to impose himself more on the game', became *de rigueur*. The number of substitutions also told their own story (similarly, these fates later befell David Ginola at Spurs). The situation would become far more unpleasant over the next three seasons, and Anders was on the route to a Highbury nightmare with GG as his chief tormentor. In the meantime, the Swede was by far the most potent attacking force in the old First Division. Alan Smith recalls: 'Anders added a touch of the unexpected. He combined pace, a great finish, and basically, a different way of thinking about the game. He was on fire during those early few months of the season, and I have to thank him for putting so many chances on a plate for me.' In Graham's eyes, Limpar's unpredictability and maverick genius was his greatest strength (in terms of match-winning ability) and at the same time, his Achilles heel (he found Anders hard to fathom). It was a bizarre situation, which led Graham to admit in his book that, 'Anders and I could never get on the same wavelength.' A criticism of Limpar, or an ironic admission of George's inability to man-manage true flair players?

Throughout the following season, Limpar's influence on the team waned considerably, although his spectacular fifty-yard lob against Liverpool at Highbury is still regarded as one of the most outstanding goals of the 1990s. Limpar describes the goal: 'I looked to pass to Ian Wright, but he was offside so there was really nothing else on. I looked up and thought I'd give it a go. It was an amazing sight as it hit the back of the net. It's a once in a career moment – it's still a great memory for me.' Anders was hoisted up into the air by Kevin Campbell, and the Swede clutched his hands together in mock prayer. Arsenal fan Greg Hinds recalls Limpar's trickery against Nottingham

Forest: 'There was a moment in the game which I'll remember for ever. I'm sure that most Arsenal fans, if they're close enough to the action, have an almost photographic recall of a Wright or Henry surge of pace. It's only if you're right up close that you can gauge just how fast they're moving. We were playing an evening game at home to Forest, and Limpar, all in one movement it seemed, lurched left to dodge Roy Keane, and then right to beat Stuart Pearce. Both of them were left kicking air, and ended up in a tangle. And Keane and Pearce are no fools, are they? It was one of the most amazing things I've ever seen at a football match.'

As the 1993–94 season got under way, Limpar became more of a peripheral figure. During a painful 0–0 draw at home to Manchester City in October, East Standers boomed out the chant of, 'We want Anders.' Season-ticket holder Tim Yates recalls: 'George Graham turned around with a face like thunder, and shook his head at us. We carried on calling for Anders, who was a sub, and George turned back and shook his finger at us. It was like a teacher telling off the class for talking out of turn. With hindsight, that probably banged another nail into Limpar's coffin, because the more we moaned about Limpar not playing, the less likely George was to pick him. He was too bloody stubborn for his own good.'

In his autobiography *The Glory and the Grief*, Graham paints a portrait of Limpar which is rather disturbing: a ball juggling wing wizard who began as 'my new match winner', who slowly lost the plot and the confidence of his team-mates through an increasing lack of effort both on and off the pitch. In Amy Lawrence's book *Proud To Say That Name*, Graham does a hatchet job on Limpar again. He is portrayed as someone who lacked real confidence in his own ability and who enjoyed the 'high life' rather too much. In short, he was a figure who would have been more suited to playing for Arsenal ten years earlier – a Charlie Nicholas or Tony Woodcock type member of the 'song and dance brigade'.

After talking to several of his ex-team-mates, there are some grains of accuracy in Graham's version of events. (Paul Davis recalls that Limpar had a tattoo of a mouse on his lower back which had a caption: Nobody's Perfect. '. . . And that probably summed up Anders as a team player'.) But in truth, Limpar was the kind of player who was becoming *persona non grata* at Highbury in 1994. Alan Smith commented that George was still adept at 'getting the best out of mediocre players'. He was not, however, able to get the best out of Arsenal's two greatest talents of the mid-1990s – Merson and Limpar. Add that to his cold shouldering of Paul Davis, and one could present a fairly watertight case that the real reason why Arsenal were floundering at times was down to Graham himself.

By 1993–94, George virtually declared open warfare on Anders, saying to Joe Lovejoy that, 'Limpar doesn't work hard enough.' So Anders began to cut an increasingly lonely and unhappy figure. Speaking about his final days at Highbury, he commented: 'By the time the 1993–94 season arrived, I was fed up with the whole fucking situation. I decided to write a letter to Graham to ask if we could sit down and sort it out. I sent it and waited a couple of days and then he came to me, with the letter. He said: "Anders, you don't need to send me a letter, you know you can come and talk to me at any time." But every time I did try to catch him after training he'd say, "Oh I'm in a rush – I've got to go", or, "Come and see me tomorrow". And, as we know, tomorrow never comes. It was ridiculous. He treated me like a kid – he just wouldn't communicate properly with me at all.

'In my final season, I started just nine games. Those guys who replaced me – Carter and McGoldrick – they were runners. They had good engines and all that to get up the wing, but that's all they were, runners not wingers. In my last two appearances for Arsenal we scored nine goals in two away games. I'm not being arrogant, but I was excellent against Ipswich and Southampton. I thought I set up Ian Wright really well. The Arsenal fans sang my name during those games – all the time – and I think Graham hated that.

'I went to him because in those two games, I really felt as if my form was coming back. I told him that I wanted to stay and said, "It's up to you if you want me to stay." He said, "No, Anders, it's up to *you*." The conversation went nowhere.

'In the end, he told me that he'd got an offer from Everton which was too good to refuse. That was it. The end of my Arsenal career. I've never been so heartbroken in my life. I just sat there, thinking about how much I wanted to stay with all my great Arsenal memories. But it was finished.'

○ THE TWILIGHT ZONE ○

TO DATE, no Arsenal fans have confessed to the crime, but when Arsenal lost 3–2 at home to Newcastle United in October 1994, the unthinkable happened. 'There I was in the East Stand,' recalls Arsenal fan Colin Wingrove, 'and I heard some blokes behind me shout, "We want Graham out." although the vast majority of East Standers opted against joining in, a few did. And, more tellingly, those who started the chant weren't told to shut up by those around them. Although it was a few months before the axe fell, you could tell that things were starting to move against George, and that defeat to Newcastle pushed us into the bottom half of the table. After the success we'd become used to under him, that wasn't good enough.'

Events behind the scenes were already out of Graham's control. During a mundane training session late in the previous season, Danish TV reporter Henrik Madsen emerged from a gaggle of hacks and asked: 'Mr Graham, do you know Rune Hauge? Have you ever taken money from him?' Snorting contemptuously, Graham responded: 'Those are very serious allegations,' and walked off. Tellingly, he didn't deny the claims. As Arsenal's league form collapsed during the 1994–95 season, and the tabloids buzzed with rumours of 'bungs', 'sweeteners' and 'kickbacks', it emerged that Graham had received a payment of £140,000, allegedly his cut from signing Norwegian defender Pal Lydersen, and £285,000 in return for snapping up John Jensen. As Alan Smith recalls, the Scot's famed motivational powers were also waning: 'By the 1994–95 season, George had said pretty much all he had to say to us. We'd heard it all before, and I think that even he realised it was all a bit stale. We used to run out at Highbury with fire in our bellies, but now things had gone flat.'

There had been a bad feeling in the air before the season even began. Another substantial hike in ticket prices, coupled with Arsenal's poor form, left even Graham loyalists questioning what was happening. Colin Wingrove comments: 'Everything unravelled before us. You could tell that Paul Merson was in a very bad way. At the first game of the season, at home to Manchester City, he was doubled up, completely knackered after ten minutes. Problem. Ian Wright was doing it all alone up front in most games. No wonder he was pissed off. Problem. And the quality – or lack of it – on the pitch was abysmal. McGoldrick, Hillier, Jensen . . . I could go on. If you consider that the only bright spot that winter was Jensen's goal against QPR – in a game which we lost 3–1 – you knew we were in the shit. And George had lost his ability to dig us out of it.'

After allowing Graham to spend a total of £8m on the combined talents of Glenn Helder, Chris Kiwomya, and John Hartson, he was eventually fired on 21 February 1995, after his financial irregularities came to light. His final signing – Glenn Helder – recalls the bizarre events of that day: 'We had a morning training session to prepare for the game against Nottingham Forest at Highbury that evening. Some of the lads heard that George had been sacked. They went a bit quiet, and the training session had a strange feel to it. Personally, I was stunned. As a player, alarm bells always ring when the manager who signed you loses their job. I was in a pretty vulnerable position, especially as I hadn't made my debut yet. Before the Forest match, Stewart Houston gave the team talk. He was calm about it all. He told us to go out and perform in a manner of which George would have approved. When we ran out on to the pitch, I feared what sort of a reaction we'd receive. Would Arsenal fans boycott the game? Would we get booed? And by that I mean, would Arsenal fans blame us for his dismissal? As it was, the crowd gave us a fantastic reception, as they always did. In fact, there was an added intensity to that night. Some of the English lads like Tony Adams and Steve Bould admitted they felt almost relieved that the whole saga with George had drawn to a close. In his book, I saw that Tony Adams likened the atmosphere to a classroom where a feared teacher had gone. Everyone could relax a bit now. It was a very strange night – surreal really – a bit like being in an episode of *The Twilight Zone*.'

In the event, Arsenal played well, defeating an understrength Forest side which was missing Stan Collymore and Bryan Roy. Chris Kiwomya had the privilege of netting the first Highbury goal of the post-Graham era. Glenn Helder recalls: 'Chris scored a great goal, and I played quite well on my Highbury debut. At one point, I did this little shuffle, and I found out later that Arsenal fans expected really big things from me. Things didn't really work out as I'd have liked though, and I got labelled a "one-trick pony" pretty quickly by the fans. Things noticeably cooled, which was a shame because they used to shout "Lionel Richie on the wing" at me on account of my hair. The crowd did a few renditions of "One Georgie Graham", and "Georgie Graham's red and white army", and that was it really. I've played for a few clubs, and they claim that players blow hot and cold, but fans can be equally as bad. Their players can be heroes one minute, and forgotten the next. Things move very quickly in football, and in fans' eyes, the club is paramount. It's bigger than all of us. So in some ways, Graham going was the bitter end. But at the same time, it was also a new beginning.'

For Arsenal fans who attended the game, the occasion was even more bizarre, because the match programme – printed before Graham's sacking – contained his pre-match notes. One line read: 'Rumours of my departure have proved somewhat premature.' Any lingering traces of Graham at Highbury were quickly erased. His voice in the Arsenal museum was replaced by Bob Wilson's. Arsenal chairman Peter Hill-Wood refused to comment on the affair. George's ambition to have his marble bust placed alongside that of Herbert Chapman was permanently dashed.

Colin Wingrove recalls the Forest match very clearly, as earlier that day, he had a brush with the man himself. 'I'd just heard about his sacking on the car radio, and pulled up to buy a newspaper on the parade. I couldn't believe it when George Graham walked out of an Italian restaurant with – it turned out – his daughter. I was in my Arsenal shirt, and he clocked it and did a double take. He looked a bit embarrassed, and tried to look away, but I went up to him and shook his hand, and said thanks for everything he'd done. Again, he looked embarrassed, and strode away, still looking like the old stroller. Later that day, I went to the Auld Triangle pub before the match, and expected the place to be like a morgue; it was anything but. More like a millstone had been lifted from around our necks. We'd had a terrible time, and we knew that, barring relegation, this was as bad as it would get. Inside the ground, we all did a few renditions of George Graham songs, but not too many, as I recall.

'George always had a cool respect thing going with the Arsenal crowd. It wasn't some mutual love-in between us at matches. We'd politely clap him, and he'd maybe give us a little wave or a nod of the head. There were no tears when we learnt he'd been sacked. Arsenal fans just sort of get on with it, knowing that the long-term future of the club is what really matters. I think he'd have appreciated that too. And we all knew his time was coming to an end. When someone with his aura goes, there is this irrational fear that the whole club will collapse with him. But players and managers come and go, even those like George. But the fans are the one constant. I have to admit though, that during that Forest match, I kept looking at the Arsenal dugout, expecting to see him there in his raincoat, barking out orders. It took a good few weeks to accept that George was no longer our manager.'

○ CARDIAC ARREST ○

BY THE MID-1990s, it was clear that the Gunners – at least for the time being – were unlikely to mount a serious challenge to Manchester United's Premiership dominance. With flair players like Limpar and Rocastle sold, many Arsenal matches turned into grim wars of attrition, with the emphasis on muscle, tight defence, and midfield harassing. Limpar recalls: 'In my final season at Arsenal, George Graham replaced me in the side with Eddie McGoldrick, who wasn't really a winger at all. I'm not knocking players like that, but if you have a team loaded with players like that, then you're starting to place too much emphasis on power and strength rather than skill. The team was also far too over-reliant on Ian Wright, and if you're so dependent on one player for your goals, there's no way that you'll win the title.'

Although the Gunners faded badly in the Premiership, by the middle of the decade, the Arsenal side was ideally suited to cat and mouse European contests. Graham's Arsenal had learnt a very painful lesson about how to play European football, after being defeated 3–1 at

home by Benfica in the European Cup in the 1991–92 season. Paul
Davis recalls: 'After drawing 1–1 in the Stadium of Light, we were in a
better position, but we panicked a bit, got carried away, and ended up
playing helter-skelter football, which George always hated. He
withdrew into his shell after that, and realised that winning in Europe
required a great deal of control, patience, and possession.' By the
1993–94 season, the team had mastered the art of grabbing tight
victories in the Cup-Winners' Cup. After Arsenal – fielding the
equivalent of a 9–0–1 formation – grabbed a 0–0 draw in the Stadio
Delle Alpi, a game notable for David Hillier's limpet-marking of
playmaker Venturin, Torino indulged in their own blanket defending
at Highbury two weeks later. With two defenders chained to Ian
Wright all night, the game appeared to be headed for extra-time, until
Tony Adams popped up to head the winner from Paul Davis's free kick.
'Tight, tense, sinewy,' was how Steve Morrow described the game. 'You
couldn't really claim the matches were fun to play in, it was more a
case of doing your job, and praying that you didn't make a mistake.
With the team we had at that time, we couldn't really open up the
play, as we didn't have the attacking players for that kind of game. Or
rather, George Graham believed that to be the case.'

A month later, Paris St Germain visited Highbury in the second leg
of the semi-final, and with red-and-white cards on the seats, were
greeted with a deafening rendition of 'Georgie Graham and his red
and white army'. Arsenal's defence and midfield got to work quickly
on David Ginola and Valdo, with John Jensen under strict instructions
to 'soften up' the Brazilian. Arsenal's tight 1–0 win – the goal courtesy
of Kevin Campbell – was overshadowed by Ian Wright's tears of rage
after a booking meant he'd miss the final. At the end of the game, the
relief was palpable, as the Gunners reached their first European final
for fourteen years. The players, as Morrow recalls, were '. . . totally and
utterly drained. The concentration level required to play like that was
phenomenal.'

Of all the titanic Highbury Cup-Winners' Cup clashes, the semi-
final tie with Sampdoria in April 1995 was the one which, in Stefan
Schwarz's words, 'nearly caused me to have a cardiac arrest'. *Daily
Telegraph* journalist Henry Winter comments: 'George Graham's
Arsenal knew exactly how to approach European matches. Skill-wise,

they didn't come close to Wenger's teams, but they knew how to defend across the pitch, and in Ian Wright, they could always grab a vital goal. That team was expertly drilled.' Schwarz, signed by Graham after the 1994 World Cup, admits: 'I can't say that my season at Arsenal went particularly well. It was great to play in the Premiership, especially for a team like Arsenal, but it was a difficult time to be at Arsenal. If you had any ambitions of being creative in midfield, it was very difficult because of the over-reliance on Ian Wright. My job was to protect the back four and try and deliver the killer pass for Ian to latch on to. Pressure at both ends. I went on record as saying I was unhappy because my neck ached due to watching so many balls sail over my head. It was a spot of poetic licence, but I did feel like that. I'd imagine Arsenal fans can't really claim to have been entertained very well during my year at Highbury. When it came to the Samp matches though, caution was thrown to the wind, and the players and the fans proved that on the really big occasion, we could all rise to the occasion. Even though George Graham had gone by the time we played Samp, it was still very much his team. I'm not sure that he'd have approved of the style in which the game was played.'

The matches against the Genoan outfit reflected Arsenal's ability to raise their game against Italian opposition. As with the final against Parma the year before, the Gunners were clear underdogs, but were assisted by the absence of David Platt and Ruud Gullit – both suspended. 'Before we went out on to the pitch,' recalls Schwarz, 'Stewart Houston, who was caretaker manager at the time, told us to stick tight to Attilio Lombardo and Roberto Mancini, and try and get in among them. He insisted that we dictate the pace of the play from the off. We did just that, but not quite in the way which Stewart expected. We went at them right from the off.'

After just five minutes, Lee Dixon's swerving shot was tipped over by Walter Zenga, before Arsenal finally broke through. As the ball broke loose in the Samp box, David Hillier's drive was parried by Zenga, and Steve Bould rammed in the rebound. Ten minutes later, Bould's flicked header looped all the way over Zenga to double the lead. 'Two goals from Steve was amazing, although I'm not too sure that he intended the second one,' recalls Stefan Schwarz. 'I heard that some guy had put down ten pounds on a Bould double, and that he won somewhere in the region of £10,000. We were all delighted for Steve, and he took his first goal like a master craftsman.'

In the second half, Jugovic pulled a goal back for Samp, before Ian Wright latched on to Paul Merson's through ball to put Arsenal 3–1 up. 'It was typical Wright,' comments Schwarz. 'He'd hardly had a chance all night, but top strikers only need one opportunity. That's why he was in the side. I remember there was total bedlam in the stands.' Another Jugovic goal pulled the score back to 3–2, and ten minutes later, as both sides went for late glory, the final whistle blew. Those present at the game vouch for the combustible atmosphere within Highbury. The Samp end could have been sold out several times over, given the interest generated among London's Italian community. Steve Morrow recalls: 'Arsenal fans couldn't complain that they didn't get value for money that night, and we felt a renewed sense of purpose when it came to Europe. It allowed us to leave behind the pressures of the league. We enjoyed pitting our wits against opposition deemed "better" than us. It was the kind of challenge which George Graham had always relished too. The second leg in Italy was equally as staggering. This time we lost 3–2, but won on penalties to get to the final. It's tended to be the way Arsenal have done things in their history. We draw at Highbury or scrape a win, only for the real glory to lie away from home.'

Stefan Schwarz confesses: 'Of all my games for Arsenal, those two matches stand head and shoulders above the rest. They're probably the best of my entire career. It's interesting, because these days I see a lot of Arsenal games on telly, and I think the Arsenal side of ten years ago might have done better in the Champions League than Wenger's team. Even with the talent they have, they do seem to be at a loss to deal with tough defences and attackers who spin turn in order to create space. The Arsenal of my generation realised that you needed a degree of flexibility and compromise in order to succeed. On the other hand, it must be far more pleasurable to play in the modern side, so there are pros and cons to every situation.'

○ A BERGKAMP WONDERLAND ○

AS ARSENAL prepared to take on Southampton in September 1995, serious questions were being asked (by the press, at least) of the club's new signing – Dennis Bergkamp. After arriving for a £7.5m fee from Inter Milan, Bergkamp had already gone seven games without a goal. After failing to score against Hartlepool in the Carling Cup, the *Sun* labelled him 'Hartlefool'. Other tabloids were already comparing him with Charlie Nicholas (who failed to live up to his eye-catching transfer fee thirteen years before). After the staleness of the final days of the Graham era, this wasn't what had been expected. The Dutch star – charged with dragging Arsenal into the more global Premiership – was failing to impress the gentlemen of Fleet Street.

Bruce Rioch, the new Arsenal manager who'd signed Bergkamp, recalls: 'The hype surrounding Dennis was massive, as you'd expect. The atmosphere at his first home match against Middlesbrough was unbelievable. And remember that David Platt, recently appointed England captain, was also making his Arsenal debut. Although Arsenal had signed star players before, Dennis represented something different. Signing him was a gesture of intent by myself and the Arsenal board. In those first few games, Dennis took time to find the right form, and adapt to the new tactics. The press, who often have their own agendas about things, claimed he might struggle to adapt to the pace of English football. It was a non story, and patent nonsense, but it got printed anyway. His team-mates, and I'm pretty sure the Arsenal fans, knew that at some point he would explode into life, and show everyone what he could do. The flicks, the control, the perfect balance . . . it was all there. But they all wanted to see him score goals. I'm glad for everyone that it finally happened at Highbury.'

As soon as the news spread that Arsenal had signed Bergkamp, it was clear that perceptions of the Gunners (and the 'boring Arsenal' label which journalists still regularly affixed) were changing. Steve Morrow recalls: 'The fact that we'd signed Dennis and David resulted in two things. First, it showed that after a spell in the doldrums, and with the club accused of not opening the purse strings, the board was willing to spend, in order to have a genuine tilt at the title. By the mid-1990s, you had to accept that without a degree of financial outlay, you had little chance of winning the title. Second, it proved that the club was embracing the Premiership era. Fans now had higher expectations. Beforehand, it had been acceptable simply to win. Now, fans expected to win with a degree of style.

'Dennis was the kind of player who could take the club to the next level. When you saw him in the flesh, he even looked different from everyone else at the club – he resembled a blond god. Bergkamp trained differently to most English-based players, he approached life differently – Dutch players don't really embrace the booze culture – and he played the game differently. I count myself in on what I'm about to say, but we had a very workmanlike team by the mid-nineties. That was certainly our reputation. We were a hard-working "no frills" outfit. That was George's Arsenal. Bergkamp's arrival opened up a whole new world. It was the first sign of what we were about to become.'

Arsenal fan Chris James recalls: 'Unbelievable though it sounds, many of us were more excited about David Platt's signing than Bergkamp's. It showed that we were still quite insular at that time. But as soon as you saw him in that Middlesbrough game, there was a buzz every time he touched the ball. The sense of anticipation when he ran out against 'Boro was palpable. I always feel that you need some exciting signings to get the crowd geed up at the start of a season, but fans of my generation remembered Charlie Nicholas, and all the accompanying hype, so I suppose we were a bit cautious. The difference with Bergkamp was that he was already a quality world-class player. In those early weeks of the season though, Arsenal stumbled around a bit, and everyone was saying about Dennis: "Well, I think he's going to be great, but at the moment, we can't really tell."'

For the first half-hour of the Southampton match, the Dutchman's form mirrored the rest of his early-season displays. He underhit a couple of long range shots, and a couple of sublime flicks were hoofed away by attentive Saints defenders. Chris James recalls: 'At first, you wondered if Dennis was a bit too cerebral for those around him.' Then, on the half-hour mark, fellow Dutchman Glenn Helder – recently shorn of his locks – intercepted a loose ball on the left-hand side. He says: 'Southampton gave us a lot of space in which to play that day, which suited me perfectly. When I got the ball, I looked up and spotted Dennis loitering on the edge of the box. No one had really picked him up. When I crossed to him – it was a decent cross – I expected him to control the ball first, and then shoot. It seemed a tall order to accurately volley that ball into the corner of the net. But Bergkamp is a master of making the difficult look ridiculously simple. So, he volleyed a beautiful shot into the far corner. There never was any real pressure on Dennis, but every striker wants to score goals, and his sense of relief was visible. The crowd went mad, but he was only just getting started.'

Shortly before the interval, the Saints struck two sucker punches which pulled the scores level at 2–2 (Tony Adams had scored Arsenal's opener), and as Glenn Helder admits: 'We went in at half-time angry with ourselves.' With the Saints pressing forward for an unlikely third in the second half, Bergkamp began to run the show. Late on, he feinted to Ken Monkou's left, shifted his balance to the right, and blasted in an unstoppable thirty-yarder. His team-mate Steve Morrow watched on in awe: 'You'd be hard pressed to find a more beautiful goal scored at Highbury. I was right behind the shot, and it was stunningly executed. That kind of goal became his trademark. He had the ability to dummy one way, dart in the other direction, and curl in a shot. That was an aesthetically beautiful goal – right from the way it arced towards goal, and then flew in sideways as it rocketed off the post. Dennis is a very understated guy, and on subsequent interviews, I've heard him describe that kind of goal as being "fairly simple to execute", or words to that effect. The way he ran around punching the air afterwards proved how much it meant to him.'

After six barren weeks in an Arsenal shirt, Bergkamp had finally made his mark at Highbury, and a goal from Ian Wright gave Arsenal a 4–2 win. Manager Bruce Rioch recalled: 'Dennis was delighted, and so were his team-mates. It made a mockery of those who claimed he wouldn't make it. Yet he was always very hard on himself, and it took a few weeks before he felt really at home at Highbury. It was around Christmas time when the players ran out, and the crowd began to sing the "Bergkamp Wonderland" song for him. Some of them had their Santa hats on, as he warmed up, and did his usual thing of jumping and heading an imaginary ball towards the North Bank. The chant was infectious, and it's stuck. Players generally know they're "in" at a club when they're granted their own anthem. I'd say that, arguably, Bergkamp later developed into the most influential Arsenal player since Alex James.'

○ DEMOLITION DERBY ○

DESPITE THE Arsenal board's official vow of silence at the AGM in September 1996, the fact that Arsène Wenger was primed to become Arsenal's new manager was the worst-kept secret in London. There had been rumours that Johann Cruyff, Bobby Robson, and 'people's favourite' Frank Clark, were favourites for the job, but the conspiracy theorists claimed that Arsène Wenger – contracted to Japanese club Grampus Eight until September 1996 – had a hand in bringing Bergkamp and Platt to the club a year earlier, meaning that in reality, Bruce Rioch was merely a caretaker manager. These allegations remain unfounded, but the beginning of the 1996–97 season (when Arsenal played their opening home match against West Ham, the only new signing was thirty-seven year old John Lukic, on a free transfer from Leeds) was an unsettling period. After Rioch's resignation, there was a frantic interregnum when both Stewart Houston, and then Pat Rice, had spells as caretaker boss.

Midfielder Steve Morrow recalls: 'Early that year, we had a chaotic 3–3 draw with Chelsea at home, which mirrored the times. We'd gone 2–0 down, Ian Wright scored a goal which looked set to give us an unlikely victory, and then Dennis Wise popped up in the last minute and pinched an equaliser. The place went mad, but things were all over the place. Some players didn't really know whether they were coming or going. As professionals, you get on with it. It was also the time when Tony Adams admitted he was an alcoholic, and fans were wondering whether Wenger really was going to arrive. When the board confirmed that he was installed as the new boss, it was announced that he couldn't actually take over straightaway, because of commitments in Japan. So he communicated with us from afar via video link-up. Strange times indeed.'

From the fans' angle, matters were about to become stranger still. With tabloids booming out Arsène Who?, after the Frenchman was officially unveiled in September, he communicated with Arsenal fans his thoughts and hopes about the job through the medium of the Jumbotrons screen before an evening home match with Sheffield Wednesday.

Arsenal supporter Kev Blake recalls: 'That was a weird old night. The game kicked off really late because the electronic turnstiles failed, so I don't think we actually took our seats until about nine o'clock. I remember queuing outside the ground, and everyone was saying, "Who the fuck is Arsène Wenger?" Most of us wanted Robson or Cruyff as boss. Someone we'd actually heard of. I hold my hands up and admit that I wanted Frank Clark as boss, who was doing really well with Forest at the time. I thought after the farce with the end of Graham, followed by Rioch, that we needed a good old-fashioned English influence. I reckoned that Clark looked a decent chap, and that he was a better bet than some French geezer I'd never heard of. Lots of people are wise after the event, but I don't honestly believe that many Arsenal fans reckoned Wenger would be anything less than another failed experiment from the board. These were different times. We hadn't won the title for five years, and after the bond fiasco, and what had happened with the last two bosses, we wanted the club to get it right, for once. And I don't think we believed that the club *had* got it right with Wenger.

'As we streamed into the Wednesday game, Arsène's face appeared on the big screen and he started talking. The sound quality was so poor, and apart from him saying "Let's win tonight", I didn't understand a word he said. Lots of people were doing Clouseau impressions, but to be honest, I thought he sounded more like Marlon Brando in the *Godfather*, due to the mumbling sound quality from the speakers. When the game started, Arsenal destroyed Wednesday 4–1. Ian Wright got a hat-trick, and in the process his 150th Arsenal goal. To be honest though, I was more impressed by the little present Wenger had delivered us. Midway through the second half, just as Arsenal looked like they were starting to flag in the centre of midfield, on came Patrick Vieira in place of Ray Parlour, and immediately you could see that we had a midfielder with the kind of presence we hadn't seen since Liam Brady. So I left the game, obviously delighted with the result, thinking, If Vieira is anything to go by, maybe Wenger knows what he's doing after all.'

Vieira recalls his first Arsenal appearance: 'The crowd was positive, but I sensed a feeling of "Who is this tall man coming on?" I had a lot to prove after not doing well at AC Milan. I think I did quite well [on my debut] and I saw at first hand the passion of the Arsenal side when Wrighty grabbed his hat-trick.'

The new manager's first full-on experience of English football arrived with the North London derby in late November. (He'd already endured his first experience of the press, when he was forced to stand on the steps leading into the main entrance, and confront assorted hacks over allegations about his private life.) 'Because of the nature of the game,' recalls Steve Morrow, 'it was the first game in which Wenger was really under the spotlight. The atmosphere inside Highbury that afternoon, as it often is for games against Tottenham, was amazing. It was the first indication of the positive effects he was having on the club. It was completely different from the type of regime which George Graham ran.'

After Ian Wright put Arsenal in front with a penalty (and pulled up his shirt to reveal a T-shirt with 'I Love The Lads' scrawled across it), Andy Sinton levelled the scores. 'We weren't happy about that,' recalls Morrow, 'because Spurs should really have thrown the ball back to us after we kicked it out of play because one of their players was injured. It happened later in the season against Blackburn, as well, when Chris Sutton refused to play the ball back to us. But that incident really fired us onwards. Under George Graham, it's possible that we might have shut up shop, but already under Wenger, the shackles on individuals were loosened. Arsène Wenger's team talks are always very measured, and before the game he encouraged us to think about the passion of the event, and deal with the threats which Spurs posed. Very much in control. It was the same at half-time. He likes a period of silence for a few minutes, so that players can gather thoughts and reflect on the first-half performance. Some of the lads at the start weren't entirely convinced about whether or not his appointment as boss would work. By the end of this match, though, I think we could all see that he was already on the right track.'

After Sinton's equaliser, Arsenal surged forward in an attempt to win the match. Morrow recalls: 'We were treated to the sight of Tony Adams and Steve Bould galloping forward. This was unbelievable, as they'd been pretty strictly marshalled under Graham.' With ten minutes left, Adams latched on to a loose ball, and thumped a half volley past Spurs' goalkeeper Ian Walker. 'It was one of the most intense moments I've ever had at Highbury,' recalls former *Gooner* editor Mike Francis. 'Everyone was thinking – what is Adams doing *there*? It was the first sign that we were developing into a far more attack-minded side. As it went in, there was a tremendous release among Arsenal fans. With the rain lashing down, and everyone going mad, it was an incredible moment. Five minutes later, Ian Wright turned Clive Wilson inside out on the right-hand side, and delivered a cross which Dennis Bergkamp controlled and blasted past Walker. 'Dennis' reaction said it all,' explains Steve Morrow, 'because Spurs' owner, Alan Sugar, had suggested that in the winter months, Dennis might not be interested. And here he was, sliding on his knees in the mud, with the rain slashing in his face, having driven home a fabulous goal. Any lingering question marks over him were well and truly answered.'

The scoreline – 'We beat the scum 3–1' as the departing Arsenal fans sang – was symbolic. Ever since a Paul Gascoigne-inspired Spurs had defeated Arsenal in the 1991 FA Cup semi-final by the same scoreline, travelling fans had delighted in travelling to Highbury and chanting, 'We beat the scum 3–1'. Over recent years, the 'Nayim from the halfway line' mantra had also been aired. Paul Davis recalled: 'In the mid-nineties, there was still the general feeling that although Spurs weren't doing as well as Arsenal in the league, they were still the team to watch for pure entertainment, and they certainly weren't going to let us forget the FA Cup semi-final win in a hurry, even though it had happened six years earlier. So when Arsenal beat Spurs in late 1996, it felt like revenge, and also Arsenal's record at home against Spurs had been pretty patchy. History shows that since that win over Spurs, they've only beaten us once.'

The sheer gusto with which Arsenal dispatched Spurs was equally as important. Steve Morrow recalls: 'Beforehand, it was always a case of – in the media's eyes – "boring Arsenal" grinding down "entertaining Spurs" and squeezing out a result against them. But from now on, you couldn't honestly describe Arsenal as boring, and it wasn't good news for Spurs. Arsenal were top dogs in London, and it was clear that we also played the most attractive football. So it was a significant shift that day.'

Dashing away from Highbury in torrential rain, Kev Blake felt a surge of adrenaline. 'For the first time, the Arsenal fans were shouting: "We're on the march with Arsène's army." Winning that North London derby proved what was possible. My mate Adrian, walking alongside said to me, "I reckon Wenger could be a good 'un, Kev." He hasn't done too badly, I suppose!'

○ JUST DONE IT ○

BY 1997, there was a feeling among many of his team-mates that with the prolific Ian Wright in the Arsenal side, the chances of the Gunners winning the elusive Premiership title were slim. The uncomfortable sense that too much was being channelled through Wright led *One Nil Down* editor Tony Willis to comment in his editorial that; 'It would be more of a team without Wrighty in the side.'

The Arsenal striker went public, and, referring to Willis' comments, claimed: 'Some comments from Arsenal fans have hurt me badly.' Wright's former Arsenal colleague Glenn Helder recalls: 'Ian's hunger for goals remained undiminished, even as he approached his mid-thirties. It was staggering, and as his career at Arsenal progressed, two things worked in his mind. First, he knew that age was catching up with him. Second, he knew that he was in sight of the goals record, and it became a point of focus. Strikers like Ian use targets to motivate themselves, and keep going. It's in their make-up. Equally as amazing was the ferocity with which he craved the ball. Even before I had received the ball, sometimes, it was a case of "Oi Glenn, pass it here". Some people have suggested that guys like me, John Hartson and Kevin Campbell may have had longer Highbury careers if Ian hadn't been so single-minded, and that the team would have benefited as a result. That's a very simplistic view. No one could argue with Ian's goalscoring record, and as for how many times he got us out of jail, I lost count. From my point of view, I never felt intimidated by him, although I'm sure that many players had the view: "We must give it to Ian." That's not really conducive to a healthy team ethic. If you look at the reasons for why Wenger's teams have been so successful, one big factor is that all the strikers are also great providers of goals for others. Great scorer that he was, Ian didn't really fall into that category.'

Although Wright declined the opportunity to be interviewed for this book, his agent was willing to allow me to print his response to my question backstage at *Friday Night's Alwright* back in 1998. I'd asked him about his approach to the art of goalscoring, and he replied: 'I've always got a buzz from scoring goals, dating right back to when I was a little boy playing in the streets. The bigger the game, the bigger the buzz. We used to play a game called "Wembley" as kids, where you had to score to get through to the next round, and if you didn't, you'd be out. Scoring in that gave me a real buzz every time. Scoring goals is often described as a selfish pursuit, and to have got as many as I have in my career, I've had to be pretty single-minded. But nothing beats the feeling of scoring goals, nothing.'

By the time September 1997 arrived, Wright was on the brink of writing himself into the history books. Having scored at Leeds on the opening day of the season, a brace at Highbury against Coventry took him to within a goal of equalling Cliff Bastin's record of 175 Arsenal goals, which had stood for half a century. The hype surrounding the (imminent) event was unbelievable. The Arsenal programme had been running a countdown chart for the last six months, and the Jumbotrons had been showing a selection of his goals prior to each home match for the last year. 'It was all getting fucking ridiculous,' reckoned Arsenal fan Nick Saunders. 'You'd go to matches, and there were players of the quality of Bergkamp and Vieira, and some muppets were still singing "And it's Ian Wright FC". Bloody stupid. That song harked back to the mid-nineties when we were really struggling to create chances. We'd moved on, and I don't think I was the only one who was thinking: Let's get this record out of the way, and focus on everyone else. The sideshow was still the main event. And that wasn't right. I don't think it was great for Wrighty either. He missed a couple of sitters at home to Tottenham, and began to play crap, to be honest. What was apparent was that skill- and team-wise, Bergkamp was light years better than Wright. On a different planet. But, typical Wrighty, he eventually got himself up for the big event, and proved that he was a real showman.'

On a blazing September afternoon, newly promoted Bolton frustrated Bergkamp's creativity, and even took the lead through an Alan Thompson goal. Then Wright finally got to work, as he blasted an equaliser into the bottom of Jaaskelainen's net. Wheeling away, he pulled off his Arsenal shirt, to reveal the "Just Done It" sign, complete with Nike logo. In fact, he'd only equalled the record, and got confused in the process. Ten minutes later, he tapped in the easiest goal of his Arsenal career to ensure that he had written himself into the history books. Team-mate Remi Garde recalls: 'Ian always loved celebrating goals, which proved just what they meant to him. Obviously, afterwards he went ballistic, as did the crowd. The fact that Lee Dixon and David Seaman ran over to congratulate him showed just how delighted they were for him, and what the record meant to them too. Ian lapped up all the celebrations, and went on to get his hat-trick. And the team won 4–1. It was a wonderful afternoon.' Backstage at *Friday Night's Alwright,* Wright confessed: 'The Arsenal fans were fabulous for me that day. For the goal that broke the record, they were practically sucking the ball over the line. It was a fantastic moment for me, and I thank Arsenal fans from the bottom of my heart for making the day so special.'

Arsenal fan Matthew Allgood recalls the match, and its aftermath: 'Avenell Road, five o'clock. Ian Wright is performing his version of the Full Monty, removing his kit and throwing it out of the dressing-room window, down to the delirious throng of Gooners below. Someone, somewhere has a pair of his underpants for a trophy, although the "Just Done It" shirt was torn apart by the throng. It was a hilarious end to a record-breaking day. There's an old saying: "Side before self every time." I think that's right in ninety-nine per cent of cases. But Wright was an exception, a one off. I think any milestone like that is worthy of recognition – there's got to be room for *individual* achievement in football. And it's important to remember that Wright got a hat-trick that day, so it was crucial for the team.'

In the post-match interviews, Arsène Wenger claimed he sub-stituted Wright in order to allow him to revel in the occasion. But there was also a strong message. Wright was replaced that day by Nicolas Anelka, whom Wenger believed would replace Wright over the next few years. Wenger added that he fully expected Wright to march on and reach the 200 goal mark for the Gunners, but it never happened, and his form promptly fell apart. Within two months, Ian Wright reappeared at the dressing-room windows, this time remon-strating with Arsenal fans who'd jeered the team off after a 3–1 home defeat against Blackburn. One of his former team-mates, who on this occasion remains anonymous, reveals: 'The tornado burnt itself out very fast. He'd got the record, and it was as if the hunger and desire quickly ebbed away. It wasn't quite as simple as that, and he had various niggling injuries, as age began to catch up with him. Arsène Wenger was quite lucky in that respect, because he was never placed in a position where he had to tell Ian, "You're dropped." He just sort of faded away. There remained a feeling among some of the newer players that Arsenal had been too much about Ian Wright, and, great player though he was, if we were going to become a successful side, that attitude had to change.'

Bigger things were in store for Wenger's team.

○ TAMING THE MANCS ○

BY THE MID-NINETIES, Arsenal's Highbury clashes with Manchester United were taking on a distinctive flavour. For a period, publicity surrounding the game tended to revolve around Eric Cantona, whether he happened to be on the field or not. In 1992–93, as the two teams battled out a 0–0 draw, the media seemed far more intrigued by the sight of United's recently acquired Frenchman brooding under his eyebrows in the East Stand. During the following season's match, as the two sides fought out a 2–2 draw, Cantona was sent off for a foul on Tony Adams – his second dismissal in a week.

The first clear indication that relations between the two clubs were turning frosty occurred in the February 1997 Highbury clash when Ian Wright – who'd never scored against United – and Peter Schmeichel locked horns. In the fifth minute, both went in feet first for a fifty-fifty ball, only to puncture it. Late on in the game, with Arsenal 2–1 down, and the referee having already blown his whistle to indicate offside, Wright launched a two-footed lunge on the Danish keeper which sent him spinning round in pain. Wright could so easily have been red-carded. Instead, the referee waved the yellow in Wright's direction, and the Arsenal striker became embroiled in an ugly altercation with United skipper Roy Keane. Arsenal lost the match, extinguishing any lingering hopes they had of landing the title in Wenger's first season.

With Sky television now hyping the match, and concluding that Arsenal were a potential threat to United's crown in years to come, the personality clash between Wenger and Ferguson grew. 'He (Wenger) should spend more time trying to control Ian Wright's temper than talking about United,' claimed Ferguson after Wenger suggested that the fixture list could be tinkered with to suit Ferguson's team. Steve Morrow recalls: 'The clash between Wright and Schmeichel was the sequel to that between Winterburn and McClair. Both had really competitive streaks, with Schmeichel taking it as a personal affront if a striker scored against him, and Wright irritated that he couldn't get one over on him.'

As the Gunners prepared to take on United in November 1997, Ferguson's side was still struggling to come to terms with the loss of Cantona, who'd retired during the close season. The striker signed to fill the void was Teddy Sheringham, who was about to become a figure of hate at Highbury. Arsenal fan Ian Jessop says: 'Of all United's players over the years whom we've given stick to, it's Sheringham we hated the most. Why? Well, for a start the guy used to play for Tottenham, so straightaway, he'll always get the "Tottenham reject" thing. Second, he went public and told as many people as cared to listen that, "I hate the Arsenal." He actually said that! I know you want honesty, but after that, he was always going to get grief at Highbury. And third, the bastard always used to score against us: Spurs, United, Pompey . . . he was always bloody well there, a bit like Robbie Fowler used to be for Liverpool. And finally – I suppose you'll have to print this – he's not a bad player, is he? You don't give grief to really crap players, apart from Danny Mills, of course!'

As Arsenal took the field, they trailed United by four points. The media was in general agreement that United would win, and therefore open up a substantial lead in the Premiership race. With Petit and Bergkamp suspended, and Ian Wright's form spluttering, the omens didn't look good for Arsenal. Christopher Wreh, who later came on as a substitute, recalls: 'We'd slipped a bit recently, and we knew the United match was the big one. It's when you need your top players to perform. Despite all the new foreign players, there was still the English defence, who'd seen and done it all. You need that kind of experience going into a game like that. We had to be at our best. What dumbfounded me was the atmosphere in the ground. I'd been led to believe that Arsenal–Spurs clashes were *the* matches, but games against United were something else entirely.

The United players ran towards the Clock End and prepared to warm up. Even Paul Dermott, a Clock End regular for thirty years, was amazed by the vitriolic abuse handed out to United players: 'It was the most ferocious I'd ever heard Highbury. Schmeichel led the United players over, and everyone in the Clock End, it seemed, booed him and made the "wanker sign" at him. Most of us were chanting, "Peter Schmeichel is a wanker, is a wanker." Then, from over my shoulder, something was launched. It hit his shoulder and burst all over him. I later found out it was a bag of chips. Then, when the teams were announced, Sheringham's name was mentioned. Right on cue, the entire ground was chanting "Oh, Teddy, Teddy. You went to Man United and you're still a cunt". It must have gone on for about five minutes. The big screens also played their part, closing in on Fergie. Whoever was in charge knew what they were doing, because now he got the bird off the crowd. "Fuck off Fergie, fuck off Fergie . . . " He quickly glanced at the screen, knew he'd been "had" and looked dead straight ahead of him, tight-lipped. I wouldn't say it was big, or clever, for that matter, but it was an unforgettable atmosphere.'

The Gunners tore into a sluggish United from the first minute. Two pile drivers from Patrick Vieira ('The ball came to me and I thumped it as hard as I could. These shots usually end up in the crowd; but I knew it would go in from the moment I struck it. The crowd went bananas and so did I. I slid to my knees and tore ligaments in the process. Not clever!') and Nicolas Anelka (his first Arsenal goal) put Arsenal into a 2–0 lead. 'We started off like a tornado, and United didn't know what had hit them,' recalls Christopher Wreh. 'A lot of the foreign boys were looking at each other thinking, Welcome to English football, because the crowd, at that point was in total uproar. But you always know that a side like United will hit back at some point, and by half-time they were level.' Somehow, inevitably, it was Teddy Sheringham whose brace of goals made it 2–2. After his second goal, he kissed his shirt, and ran towards the North Bank laughing. Four fans made complaints to stewards, and one supporter reported the matter to the police. North Banker, Tom Lewis recalls: 'Much as I disliked Sheringham, I can't understand people who do that sort of thing. If you're gonna call a guy "a cunt" all match, he's going to na-na in your face when he exacts revenge. I don't know if it's symptomatic of how things are going with the country's blame culture, but fans who report players for making gestures should think a bit more carefully about what they have done to warrant a player reacting like that. I know that he got some verbal abuse from Arsenal fans in the streets because of the Spurs and United connection. I can't understand the mentality of people who do that to players in the street. For the ninety minutes they're on the pitch though, anything goes!'

The match reached its fulminating climax when David Platt headed in from a late corner. As the ex-England captain wheeled away, he motioned for his team-mates to follow, and they proceeded to pile on top of him in celebration. Platt, released by United as a youngster, was hardly a crowd favourite at Highbury due to his poor form, but on this occasion, he was the undisputed hero. There was still time for United to pour forward in search of a late equaliser, and for Christopher Wreh to miss, in his words, ' . . . an absolute sitter. The ball came in late to me, and I knew I had a good chance to beat Schmeichel, and to make a real name for myself. But I flapped at the ball, and somehow dragged it wide when it looked easier to score. The crowd wasn't too happy with me, but luckily the final whistle went soon afterwards anyway. If we'd lost, we'd have been seven points behind United. As it was we only trailed them by a point. The confidence sides take from beating teams like United cannot be overestimated, although ironically, we didn't really play consistently well until the New Year. But the win against United made all the difference at the end of the season. Games against them were turning into the proverbial six pointers.'

As the teams trooped off, Paul Dermott noticed that the screens once again zoomed in on Alex Ferguson. 'The crowd started to give him grief again. He put a consoling arm around Ryan Giggs' shoulders, before doing what he always does after he's lost. He spat his chewing gum out in disgust on to our pitch – our beautiful croquet lawn. I hope they bloody made him pick it up. Then, with a cursory glance back at the jubilant fans, he muttered something, snarled and stormed off. Although there was no physical confrontation, the match showed that we had the team and the stomach to match United that season.'

Patrick Vieira comments: 'That game proved that Arsenal v United was becoming *the* game in the Premiership. It was explosive in every way.'

∘ A BEAUTIFUL DAY ∘

FOOTBALL WRITER David Winner warned me of the perils of false memory syndrome when I was in the process of writing this book. It's the trap into which many fans inevitably fall when scribing the history of their team's stadium; that their side always played well there, that the sun always shone, that it was always a happy home full of cheer . . .

Arsenal's history has often been turbulent, but all Gunners fans who were present at Highbury on 3 May 1998 agree that events that afternoon came pretty close to perfection. At a conservative estimate, you'd have to have been around fifty-eight years of age to recall the last time that Arsenal secured the league title in front of their own supporters at Highbury, when the Gunners beat Burnley to win the old First Division trophy in 1953. Arsenal's 4–0 win against Everton was, in Christopher Wreh's opinion: 'A beautiful match, a beautiful team performance, on a beautiful day, with the growing realisation that Arsenal were becoming a beautiful team.'

The Gunners realised that a win against Howard Kendall's relegation haunted 'Toffees' would secure their first Premiership title. Arsenal had slipped effortlessly into scintillating form when spring came along, with newcomers Anelka and Petit developing into polished Premiership performers. A victory at Old Trafford (the club's first since the 1990–91 season when they won the title) with a goal scored by Marc Overmars instilled the belief that the title could be wrenched away from Old Trafford. Emmanuel Petit recalled: 'When I joined the club, I thought it might take a while for the team to gel. There were so many new faces. And for a while it took some time for myself, Patrick and Marc Overmars to get up to speed. But by March, we were motoring along really well. Some Arsenal fans, after a fantastic win at home to Newcastle United in March, came up to me and said, "Manu, we can now come to Highbury and watch beautiful football. We've never been able to say that before, but we're better to watch than Manchester United." The other boys had the same thing happen to them, but that was no good without trophies to go with those compliments. In that match against Newcastle, Patrick Vieira scored this thunderous thirty-yarder, and Nico (Anelka) scored an excellent double. It was at this point that I thought, We can do something special here. We then followed that up with an excellent 5–0 win over Wimbledon, where I finally got my first goal for the club. The fans were great to me after that. It was lovely for me. But more importantly, it pushed us very close to the title. What really convinced me that we could do it was the look in Tony Adams' eyes. The hunger was there. It had been there from the minute those Manchester bookmakers paid out on United winning the title. There's nothing

Arsenal players relished more than proving doubters wrong. The English boys knew it was ours for the taking.'

Even with the odds stacked so heavily in Arsenal's favour, many Arsenal fans took nothing for granted. George Tyson recalls: 'I belong to what, I suppose, is a dying breed of Arsenal fan. I started going to games in the sixties when your expectations of the team were very low. Then, as you went into the seventies and eighties, we had long periods with little success, and even if we did get some, we still had the "boring" label attached. With, say Anfield 1989, I'd always been used to Arsenal getting success the hard way, under dramatic circumstances, and away from Highbury too. White Hart Lane 1971, Wembley 1979 . . . Arsenal did things the hard way. So many of the supporters who went to the games at the end of the 1997–98 season were brought up on that culture. Always in the back of your mind: Arsenal don't do things the easy way. So things seemed far too good to be true at the end of that season. There were some similarities with the 1988–89 season. I thought back to when everyone had been virtually handing us the title before a game against Derby that year, and I bought a cheap badge off a trader outside the ground that day, which said: Arsenal Champions '89, and we bloody well went and lost to Derby. I looked like a right twat, and was convinced I'd cursed the boys. And the match before the Everton game in 1998? Derby at home. I was absolutely shitting bricks, convinced we'd blow it again. It was a niggly, horrible match, but then Petit whacked in the winner, and I've never celebrated a goal so hard in my life. Those 1–0 scrapes really add up at the end of the season. So when we played Everton on the Sunday, we needed three points from the remaining three games. I was *so* hoping that we could do it at Highbury for a change, rather than at Anfield or Villa Park, the venues for our last two matches.'

Former Arsenal striker Christopher Wreh, who'd been drafted into the side, and contributed some vital goals, recalls events that day very clearly: 'In the dressing room before the match, Arsène Wenger talked about the fact that we were on the threshold of a great achievement, and how wonderful it would be if we could win the title at Highbury. He was extremely calm, as ever, and urged us to go out and play our natural game; to relax. I looked around the room, and saw what this could mean to the others. The English lads have gone on record as saying that Wenger's influence added another five years to their careers, and now they had a chance to win another pot, something which they probably thought could never happen. Tony Adams summed up the Arsenal spirit – fists clenched, calmly urging us on. I think it's called the "caged tiger" approach. An inspirational figure in every way. The French guys – Patrick and Manu – were very close, and slapped hands before we ran out. Overmars – quiet and brooding – collecting his thoughts. Ray Parlour, always the life and soul of the dressing room was cracking his jokes to lift the mood. And then me – just a young guy who'd forced his way into the side, played quite well, and who was grateful to have this chance to win a title. It had come around so fast. Then it was time to go. It's when the studs rattle on the floor that the adrenaline really starts to pump. More hand slaps – "Come on boys, let's go." Everyone fidgeting, and ready to get on to the pitch. We walked out, the crowd roared, it's a beautiful sunny day. All the fans seem to be waving flags. It's like a carnival. There's no way that we can let this lot down.'

As the game got under way, it was clear that Arsenal weren't about to freeze on the big occasion. Within ten minutes, Wreh lobbed in a great cross which Ray Parlour got his head to, only for Everton keeper Myhre to scramble it away. But by half-time, Arsenal were cruising, with Slaven Bilic heading into his own net, and Marc Overmars' shot squirming under Myhre to put the Gunners 2–0 up. Wenger remained cool. Wreh recalls that, 'As usual, we trooped in at half-time, and reflected on our performance for a few minutes. A few points were made by Wenger and Tony Adams, and the message was that we should carry on in a similar manner after the break. Two-nil is often the ideal half-time score, because you can relax a little, but there is no room for complacency. The second half was fabulous. I remember it in snapshots. Marc Overmars marauding through and sliding in a third. Ian Wright coming on as a sub, and the crowd going mental. The Tony Adams goal, where he was put through by Steve Bould. Two English boys linked up to produce a very continental goal. It was fantastic. And the crowd, when the score was 4–0, chanting "We shall not be moved." When the referee blew his whistle, there was a fantastic release. Wrighty was going mad, Adams, Dixon, Bould and Winterburn cackling insanely, and the rest of us delighted that our first season in

England had gone so well. I remember Tony lifting the trophy, as the sun reflected off it, and the crowd saluting us. It was an awesome experience.'

George Tyson recalls Arsenal's fourth goal and the latter stages of the match: 'I've never heard Highbury reverberate like it did when Ian Wright came on as sub. I think we all knew that this was the last time we'd see him in an Arsenal shirt at Highbury, and I'd like to think we gave him a reception he'll never forget. If someone had told me that Tony Adams would crack home a half-volley from a Steve Bould pass, to put us 4–0 up on the day Arsenal would win the title, I'd think they were nuts. When he galloped through, most people were laughing in disbelief, thinking, I know it's time to showboat, but this is ridiculous. One fella stood near me, astonished that Adams was now actually bearing down on the box, shouted to me, "What the fuck is Adams doing *there*?' Then, wallop. His goal was the fulfilment of all my football fantasies, and more. He'd been the archetypal English piss head in the days of George Graham, when he'd probably have been shot for venturing so far forward. When I watched the highlights of the game later, Martin Tyler said, "That sums it all up." It showed just what sort of a side we'd become under Wenger. The beautiful team. Adams' celebration, when he walked towards us with his arms outstretched, still makes the hairs on my neck stand up when I think about it now. It was almost religious in the way it happened. And the power of the experience was unbelievable. Thanks Tone.'

Patrick Vieira describes the aftermath of the game as his favourite Arsenal memory. He recalls: 'All of us were just walking around the pitch, and lapping up the experience. Wrighty, in particular, was going mad and him and Lee Dixon were laughing because "We Are The Champions" was playing and the blokes in the crowd couldn't hit the high note of "fighting" and "we" in the song. I was very pleased for Tony Adams, because he represented all that was great about the club, and delighted for myself because I'd proved myself. Winning the title for the first time is always the most precious experience.'

A week after securing their first Premiership title, Arsenal won the FA Cup final at Wembley to clinch the Double. Over the next few years, Gunners fans were treated to more stellar moments at Highbury, but the Everton match was clearly the most significant. Expectations rose virtually game after game, as did the demand for tickets. Ironically, the team's success proved to be Highbury's undoing.

○ ANNOYING THE NEIGHBOURS (3) ○

IN THE EARLY months of 1997, rumours filtered through to the press that the Arsenal board was seeking to expand Highbury's capacity to a minimum of 45,000. By March, the board had gone public, and formally announced that it aimed to redevelop the Clock End (ten years after it was last structurally altered), and build a brand new West Stand, which would mean issuing compulsory purchase orders on the houses running up Highbury Hill. 'It was around the time of Wenger's first Double,' recalls Alex Fynn, 'that the club began to address the Highbury question seriously. It sort of sneaked up on them, when they realised that the capacity was stymied at around the 45,000 mark. The biggest issue for the board at that time was that Manchester United, with their financial clout, were always able to pull the rabbit out of the hat. Arsenal weren't strong enough to do that, and as such were left with the realisation that dominating English football, as United had done, would be difficult, if not impossible.' As if to back up Fynn's point, the Gunners were linked with a £6 million move for Dutch striker Patrick Kluivert, who seemed set to replace the departing Ian Wright, during the 1997–98 close season. The Gunners pulled out of the deal, and persevered with the inexperienced Chris Wreh and Nicolas Anelka forward line. The Gunners, who struggled to score goals in the early stages of the following season, missed out on regaining the title by a single point.

The issue of redeveloping Highbury was the key topic of conversation at the September 1997 AGM, and Peter Hill-Wood confirmed that staying put was the board's 'favoured option'. Yet ominous signs were present. The Arsenal chairman confirmed that raising the capacity to 45,000 was 'barely sufficient', and to make the rede-velopment of Highbury viable, the new capacity needed to be 50,000. So, effectively, it was a case of building a new West Stand, or bust. Opposition from the vocal Arsenal Stadium Advisory Group (ASAG), formed by local residents in Highbury Hill, was fierce. I managed to obtain a copy of a previously unseen document, in which the ASAG highlighted two main issues regarding the West Stand. They urged that ' . . . the street scene importance of the Victorian terraces of Highbury Hill, which predate the arrival of Arsenal in 1913, should be recognised.' Claude Ferrier's West Stand, which had stood since the early thirties, is arguably the most discreet in the country. A brand new West Stand would most certainly not be tucked away. The ASAG also argued that, 'Houses in Highbury Hill should only be demolished for safety reasons, not to enable the capacity of the stadium to be expanded.' Crucially, the council listed a number of 'design and townscape objectives' and issued a directive that 'any new stands should not seek to fill in corner sites   new West and South stands should not be higher than the ridge of the existing East Stand.' The previously unthinkable – that Arsenal would be forced to leave Highbury – was already becoming an uncomfortable reality. The board's plans for a 50,000 stadium were already remote.

Former *Gooner* editor Mike Francis, along with *One Nil Down*'s Tony Willis and *Highbury High*'s Tony Madden, drafted a letter to David Dein and Ken Friar, informing them of their decision to form the Arsenal Fans *For* Consultation group, 'to ensure', in Francis' words, 'that Arsenal fans weren't kept in the dark about the stadium issue'. All three representatives were invited to attend a meeting on 8 April 1998, with Friar and Clare Tomlinson, the Arsenal press officer. Francis recalls there was a distinct 'we haven't ruled anything out' flavour to the meeting: 'Ken Friar was personable enough, and answered as many questions as he could. He was pretty vague about certain points, but then matters remained unclear for quite a while afterwards, anyway. The gist was that the board still aimed to remain at Highbury, although I got the distinct impression that they were starting to realise that that could be difficult. They aimed to continue pressing ahead with their "Planning Brief" – to expand Highbury to a 50,000 capacity, and before turning that into a planning application, also undertook an "environmental impact analysis". At one point, Friar mentioned that the board would settle for a 45,000 capacity if that meant staying at Highbury. That shows just how quickly events moved.

'It was pretty clear that the club was investigating other options. They'd bid £120 million for Wembley, and only pulled out because Wembley plc hadn't made a decision within the right time-frame. The club, of course, would play its Champion League games at Wembley during the 1998–99 season, and the year after. The club filled Wembley, but it didn't convince too many of us that we'd like to move there, and it didn't improve our results especially! There was also a lot of talk about the club building a new stadium on the King's Cross site, which would have combined the advantages of the space available at Wembley, with being in London. It would also avoid any potential problems associated with hijacking the national stadium, something which probably wouldn't have gone down too well. There were also difficulties at that time similar with those at Highbury. The club would have had to overcome the issues surrounding listed buildings, and brownfield sites. The option of staying at Highbury was more preferable than *any* of the others, and certainly more palatable than upping sticks and moving to that dreaded "M25" location, which lots of people talked about back in the late nineties. The thought of moving to some soulless concrete bowl in the Home Counties filled us all with dread, I think.'

Arsenal fan Tim Howland recalls: 'It's ironic that at a time of such huge success on the pitch for Arsenal, the nineties proved to be the most difficult era for many fans. We'd won the title in 1991, and had the bond scheme thrust on us, and now we'd won the Double, only to discover that we might be leaving our spiritual home. I think that most people are resistant to change, and I'll admit that I never thought I'd accept that it was time to leave Highbury. It's our spiritual home, and it's known throughout the world for being classy and beautiful. But pretty quickly, I think we woke up to ourselves, and realised that United, financially, were miles ahead of us, and that something needed to be done. I also sometimes sit in the West Lower, and the view, to be frank, is awful. The stadium's strength – the fact that it's surrounded by Victorian houses – is also its downfall.

'What worried us was that there didn't seem to be any real compromise. No one, I knew, wanted to go to Wembley. It is a horrible area, and to get to it, you have to traipse across London, and go more or less straight into the ground, because there is nothing to do in the vicinity. Going to Hertfordshire, or wherever, would have killed the club. I'm convinced of that. Going to football isn't just about going to the game. It's about all the rituals you build up over the years, the familiarity of it. But by the late nineties, I was convinced that we were going to have to move from the area, and lose all connections with the pubs, and the burger guys, and everyone else who makes matchday feel special.

'The "compromise deal" would be to have a stadium close enough to Highbury, so fans didn't lose touch with their roots and matchday habits, but big and classy enough in order that the club could move forward. But I never thought that would happen, because, by the late nineties, football was already about cold, hard cash, and not tradition. I honestly thought we'd all be off to Hertfordshire, and that my club would have its heart torn out as a result. How many of us were aware of Ashburton Grove's existence at that time?'

○ WEIRD SCIENCE ○

HIGHBURY REGULARS have seen some bizarre sights, and experienced a raft of truly surreal moments down the years. In 1953, there was the strange case of the phantom own goal. Clock Ender Ian Tatchell recalls: 'We were beating league leaders Blackpool 4–0, and, in the last minute, some joker in the crowd blew a whistle. Dennis Evans had the ball inside his own area, and thinking the whistle had gone, blasted the ball into his own net. The goalkeeper, Con Sullivan, was picking up his cap, because he also believed the match was over. What made it hilarious was that as Evans whacked it in the net, he gave us a little wink, as if to thank us for the support we'd given him during the match. When he glanced behind him and saw that the ref was pointing to the centre circle, and his team-mates were preparing for the restart, he realised he'd made a bit of a booboo. He looked at us, and we looked at him, as if to say, "Oh Gawd". So Arsenal kicked off, and the ref then blew the final whistle. No harm done really, but I know that some of the crowd went looking for the whistle-blower soon after the match.'

There was also the famous FA Cup fourth-round replay at Highbury against Derby in 1972, which was played on a midweek afternoon due to the ongoing fuel shortages which meant that floodlit matches couldn't be staged. Sam Bennett recalls: 'I bunked school that afternoon – I never needed much encouragement to do so – and I honestly thought that when I got to Highbury, there'd be one man and his dog watching the game. I was staggered to see people queuing around the block to get into the North Bank. The crowd, I learned later, was over 63,000. What was funny was that everyone in the crowd was so self-righteous about the whole thing. Older blokes were saying, "Doesn't anyone go to work any more?" and then they looked at me as if to ask, "Why aren't you at school, you lazy little bastard?" When the school contacted home a day later to ask why I had disappeared after lunch, I had to come clean and tell my mum and dad where I'd gone. Dad gave me a good clip around the ear'ole, and went on about how I'd amount to nothing if I carried on like that. Later that afternoon, his boss rang to ask him something about work. But Mum answered, and Dad's boss enquired whether Dad's health was better, as he'd had to go to the doctor's the previous afternoon. Mum eventually got the truth out of Dad, and it turned out that he'd sneaked off to Highbury as well. Mum didn't speak to either of us for a couple of days, and Dad went around blaming Charlie George all week.'

As for the strangest own goal, nothing can surpass Lee Dixon's faux pas against Coventry in August 1991 – recently voted the best ever own goal by Radio Five Live listeners. 'I put up my hand to receive the pass from Lee,' explains Anders Limpar, 'and I was sure that he had looked me in the eye to indicate that he was about to knock it across. The next thing I knew, he'd spun around, and lobbed the ball back to David Seaman, who'd strayed a bit forward off his line. It was an inch-perfect lob, which if Lee had done it at the other end, you'd have been talking about it for months. Lee had his head in his hands, and received a bit of a bollocking from George Graham at half-time. We lost 2–1 that day, and gave Lee massive amounts of stick about it for weeks afterwards.'

The 1998–99 season saw two bizarre Highbury episodes. Midway through the second half of Arsenal's FA Cup clash with Sheffield United, Blades player David Holdsworth knocked the ball out of play so that a Gunners player could receive treatment. Instead of throwing the ball back to a United defender (which was the sporting thing to do), Kanu broke forward, and squared the ball for Marc Overmars to tap in. Pandemonium reigned, as Nelson Vivas recalls: 'I had tuned in to some satellite channel when I was in England, and saw a gurning competition. It's where grown men pull the ugliest faces possible. It always reminds me of Sheffield United's reaction. All the players, including their manager Steve Bruce, surrounded Kanu and Overmars and screamed blue murder at them. Kanu was very upset. Marc didn't seem too bothered. I recall at one point that Steve Bruce tried to motion all of his players off the pitch, because he was so annoyed. There was a bit of a discussion going on between the Arsenal players. Some of the boys reckoned we should deliberately score an own goal, to level things up. But Tony Adams and Steve Bould were having none of that. So we pressed on, and won the game 2–1. Afterwards, Bruce was still going mad, but Arsène Wenger quickly diffused the situation by suggesting a replay, which Arsenal won by the same scoreline 2–1. It was all rather odd.'

Yet, it was the home game with Aston Villa on the final day of the 1998–99 season which was arguably the oddest experience of all. From February onwards, the Gunners had put together an excellent string of results to close the gap on Manchester United. A 5–1 win at home to Wimbledon was, in Nelson Vivas's words, ' . . . an awesome display of attacking football. It was the opinion of many of the players that this side was in many ways a superior outfit to the one which had lifted the Double a year before, especially when Nicolas Anelka began scoring goals towards the end of the season. It was a shame that he never really settled in London. We hit six goals up at Middlesbrough, and then beat Spurs 3–1 at White Hart Lane. The problem was that United were always a small step ahead, and there was no room for error. Unfortunately, I made one up at Elland Road, and let in Hasselbaink to score Leeds' winner. So we went into our last game of the season at home to Villa, knowing that we had to win, and that United had to lose at home to Spurs. It's very difficult in that situation. All we could do was to concentrate on doing our job, and forget about what might happen at Old Trafford. I'll always remember that about twenty minutes into the game, the crowd went bananas. News had filtered through that Les Ferdinand had put Spurs ahead. I distinctly remember hearing Arsenal fans singing "Come on you Spurs" and making a real din. Tony Adams turned around to me and muttered something about weird science going on inside Highbury that afternoon.'

Arsenal fan Dave Carpenter recalls: 'I couldn't bring myself to cheer on Tottenham, although most people around me were doing just that. The problem was, I knew in my heart of hearts that Spurs would never hold on. By that time, George Graham was their boss, and it was just never going to happen that George Graham's Spurs would help Arsenal win the title. Things don't work like that. I reckon there were a lot of Spurs fans that afternoon who wanted Spurs to lose. It sums Spurs up at that time, that whatever they did, they were in a no win situation. Of course, United eventually fought back, and won 2–1, which was the first part of their Treble. It struck me that that afternoon was Spurs all over. They'd tease you a for a bit – like they tease their own fans into believing good things are around the corner – before ultimately letting you down. And that's what happened. Bastards.'

Although Kanu struck late in the game to give Arsenal the win they needed, it didn't matter. Arsenal, in keeping with every Gunners title winning side since the 1930s, had failed to retain their title. Nelson Vivas recalls: 'We were all very disappointed, and my mind went back to a home game with Spurs earlier that season, where only Sol Campbell's heroics kept the score to 0–0. If we'd won that match, and the future Arsenal defender hadn't played out of his skin, we'd have been champions again. It's a very strange world.'

As the players trudged around the pitch to applaud the Arsenal fans, life finally returned to normal at Highbury. Dave Carpenter recalls: 'In order to purge themselves of their sinful pro-Tottenham chants earlier, everyone was singing "Tottenham are shit" and "We hate Tottenham" at full volume. Although the players looked pretty downcast, I saw Adams and Bould laughing to themselves listening to our singing.'

○ REMEMBERING ROCKY ○

IN APRIL 2001, the Arsenal and Spurs teams ran on to the Highbury pitch, and were immediately engulfed by the usual pressure cooker atmosphere. With the Gunners comfortably ahead of Spurs in the Premiership, the game was effectively a dress rehearsal for the forthcoming FA Cup semi-final at Old Trafford, which was scheduled to take place a week later. After Spurs, and Sol Campbell in particular, had kept the Gunners at bay in the first half, Arsenal coasted to a 2–0 win, with excellent strikes by Thierry Henry, and the rapidly improving Robert Pires. After the match, there was a great deal of publicity about Pires' strike, and he admitted to 'being very pleased to have scored today, especially as I had the Number 10 on my back'. For once, many Arsenal fans streaming away from the ground weren't thinking solely about the fact that Spurs had once again been sent packing, but by the passing of another famous Arsenal Number 10.

Geoff White takes up the story: 'I'd arranged to get to the Auld Triangle pub really early that day, because there is always a good sing-song before matches, and North London derbies in particular. The numbers started to grow around half-past one, and before long, the place was rocking to "We Hate Tottenham", and other songs. Then, suddenly, the table who usually led the singing had stopped, and they were all looking at each other strangely. One of the blokes stood up and said, "We've just heard that David Rocastle has died." The whole pub went silent for a minute, before the table led a rousing rendition of the "Rocky, Rocky, Rocky Rocastle" song. There was really nothing else you could do, except shake your head and wonder why someone so young had died. We'd all heard that he was suffering from cancer, but just recently, the newspapers suggested that he was improving, and there was even talk of him getting a coaching job at Arsenal. It was just really, really sad news, especially when you consider that he was only thirty-three, the same age as I was in 2001.

'I bloody loved Rocky, I really did. He was part of that generation which was pretty much my age, and he represented the Arsenal spirit, and commitment which got the club back to the top in the late

eighties. Of that generation – Adams, Thomas, Quinn – Rocky was my
favourite; I loved his buccaneering style. He knew how to have a laugh
and a joke with the fans, but he was also happy to square up to Brian
McClair and defend his team-mates. I loved the fact that the press
would always try and use his name in their headlines. When he was
sent off for kicking Norman Whiteside, it was THE ROCKY HORROR
SHOW. When he played well in one match, and Arsenal won 4–0, it was
ROCKY IV. My best memory of him is when he and Mickey Thomas took
Everton apart in the semi-final of the Littlewoods Cup at Highbury.
They both scored fantastic goals after making swashbuckling runs, and
we all thought they'd run the Arsenal and England midfields for years
to come.

'We bumped into him once in a London wine bar, in the days when
footballers and fans actually drank in the same places. He was fantastic
company, as was Perry Groves, and you could just tell that he loved the
club. We talked to him just after the players' brawl at Old Trafford back
in 1990, and what struck me was that he called his team-mates "my
blood brothers". Now *that* is what I call the Arsenal spirit. What I also
talked with him about, was that he embodied my dreams for the team
when I was about eighteen. We'd had years of underachievement at
Arsenal, but it was Rocky and his generation who brought the success
back to Highbury. When I heard that George Graham had sold Rocky to
Leeds back in 1993, and that Rocky had dissolved in tears in George's
arms, my attitude to Arsenal changed a bit. It hit me then that football
was really just a business; because ideally, you'd want eleven Rockys –
keen and home-grown – in your team. But things don't always work
out like that.'

These are numerous references in this book about Arsenal's famed
team spirit. But that doesn't always mean that players are automatically best buddies away from the pitch. One former Arsenal star
told me: 'I had a long career at Highbury, and in the majority of cases,
players get on well. Occasionally, there are personality clashes, as in
any line of work, and in many cases, although you do get on fine, you
wouldn't choose to socialise with such and such a player. Age is often a
factor. Young, single blokes might not really have too much in
common with married blokes in their thirties.' Several players have
confirmed that relationships within the dressing room can occa-

sionally be strained, because, as the former Arsenal star confirms: 'Football is essentially a dog-eat-dog world. If someone is threatening to take your place in the side, it's hard to be best mates with them.' But, all of David Rocastle's former colleagues speak in glowing terms about him.

Ironically, the most poignant recollection comes from ex-Arsenal midfielder Steve Williams, one of the players whom Rocastle started to replace in the side. He recalls: 'David was a top man, who got on equally well with players from his own age group, like Quinny, and Mickey Thomas, or myself and David O'Leary. I'll always remember a happy, streetwise kid, who was confident from the moment he came into the side. He made his debut in a bloody awful goalless draw with Newcastle at Highbury back in 1985 – we used to have a lot of those back then – and the game was famous because a radio reporter had absolutely nothing to say in his match report, because absolutely nothing had happened. But in my opinion, Rocky deserved a mention, because basically, you could see that the boy could play, right from the off. He was strong, determined, and very impressive going forward. What was strange was that at different times, Stewart Robson, Rocky, and Mickey Thomas were all labelled by the media as future England captains. All of them had left Arsenal by the time they were twenty-four, and had effectively burnt themselves out. That's either a hell of a coincidence, or it's down to the fact that George Graham expected all his midfielders to attack and defend like their lives depended on it. That sort of game wasn't really for me, and my biggest regret when I left Highbury was that I didn't have the opportunity to play alongside him any more. I missed his infectious enthusiasm for all things Arsenal, and that massive grin of his. He was a top man, was Rocky.'

Before the Spurs game in 2001, the Arsenal players – including former team-mates Adams, Seaman, and Dixon – were informed of Rocastle's passing. Silvinho recalls: 'People seem to think that foreign players know little of the history of a club before they arrive. What they forget is that we see as much English football on satellite channels as the natives! David Rocastle's name was synonymous for me with Arsenal's great title winning sides of the late eighties and early nineties. We all knew he was a Highbury legend, and you could see how saddened his former team-mates were. They knew that he wouldn't survive, but for someone so young to die it is very, very sad. The minute's silence for him before the Tottenham match was immaculately observed. I'm not sure you could have a show of such respect in Brazil, as rivalries can often lead to bad behaviour. But you could hear a pin drop inside Highbury, which proves that Rocky was respected by all fans. Afterwards, the English boys were delighted that Robert Pires had scored and worn the number 7 shirt. Tony Adams was grinning: "Rocky would approve of you scoring against Tottenham wearing his shirt, Robert. It was a fitting tribute."'

THE
NOUGHTIES N.5

○ VA VA VOOM (1) ○

'BELIEVE IT OR NOT,' explains former Arsenal full back Silvinho, 'there were some doubters who reckoned that when Thierry Henry first arrived at Arsenal he would have trouble hitting the target even if the goal was twice as wide. He was a winger, and in his early days at the club, it took him a while to adapt to playing up front. Apparently, Thierry was amazed when Arsène Wenger told him he would be playing as a striker. Thierry was arguing: "No, no, I'm a winger," but Arsène persevered anyway. It says a great deal for the manager's vision that he did so. When Thierry played his first Arsenal match in the summer of 1999, he missed two gilt-edged chances against Leicester. The crowd was frustrated, although not necessarily only with him. He was only a little bit off beam with his shooting! By the winter of that season, he was starting to slot into his new role, and sweep forward and score a few goals. You could detect the buzz from the crowd every time he received a pass. His skills and pace were electrifying. Thierry had the kind of presence and approach to the game that you don't really see in English players. So many converted wingers fail miserably to make it as a striker, but Henry did succeed. I just wish I'd been around at Arsenal a bit longer to see him at his very best.'

Two years after joining Arsenal, Henry's form – by his own admission – began to hit the heights he craved. As the clocks went back, his spectacular goalscoring exploits blasted him to world prominence. First of all, there was his double strike against Manchester United, described by Arsenal fan George Butler as 'the most hilarious Highbury experience of recent times'. The season before, Henry had looped an unbelievable shot over United goalkeeper – and France team-mate – Fabien Barthez. Henry claimed afterwards: 'I didn't really think too much about it. It's part of my game to try and do the unexpected.' A degree of one-upmanship was developing between the pair, as Barthez had a reputation for being a showman, and for dropping the odd clanger.

George Butler recalls: 'When Arsenal played United at Highbury in the 2001–02 season, it was at a time when we weren't playing all that well in the league, and there was a feeling that we really had to win the match if we had any chance of lifting the title. Scholes put them ahead, and it looked as if we'd had it, to be honest. Ljungberg pulled us level just after half-time, and then the fun began. Henry took both his goals really well, but I can't remember the last time a player was humiliated so badly at Highbury as Barthez was that day. You could see there might be some fun, because he was venturing out of his box with the ball, and the surface was greasy. I don't know what he was thinking when he miskicked the ball straight into Henry's path for the first – because I'd never seen us gifted anything by United since the days of Paddy Roche! It was everything: the sliced clearance; the fact that Henry tucked it away so well; Barthez's reaction as if he was a stroppy schoolkid; and Fergie's look of utter contempt on the big screen. And, of course, everyone going nuts around us. We couldn't believe it when Barthez cocked it up again, and lost the ball at Henry's feet. A win against United is always vitally important for Arsenal's season, but it was the aftermath of Henry's second, which put us 3–1 up, which will stick with me. Barthez hitched up his shorts, and basically showed the North Bank his arse when we started to give him grief. It seemed like that for about half an hour, everyone in the ground was shouting: "Give it to Barthez" and, "Barthez is a Gooner". He was seething, and flicking his Vs at us behind his back. At one point, he even stuck out his tongue. The guy just lost the plot, and there was Fergie, with his hands in his pockets, looking furious, ready, no doubt, to give Barthez a real earful in the dressing room. Henry's reaction was fairly restrained. It was as if he didn't want to irritate his fellow countryman any more than he already had, so the Arsenal fans did it for him.'

Two weeks later, Henry was goal poaching to devastating effect once again. After going 2–0 down at home to Aston Villa, and away fans chanting 'two-nil in the library' for much of the second half, Sylvain Wiltord pulled a goal back, before Henry scored two late goals to give the Gunners an unlikely 3–2 win, and send Highbury into bedlam. Gilles Grimandi recalls the reaction of Arsenal fans at that time: 'We'd sometimes get Arsenal fans coming up to us, and telling us it was the best football they'd ever seen. The balance was developing in the side at the time, with a gritty defence, a mixture of muscle and skill in midfield, Robert Pires showing excellent form out on the right, and the likes of Bergkamp and Henry really playing well up front. You could tell very early that season that we could be on to something big.'

It would be an exaggeration to say that all Arsenal fans were totally satisfied with the increasing Gallic influence on the side. A month before the Highbury clash against Manchester United, Arsenal were beaten 4-2 at home by Charlton. Gunners fan Martin Gilbert takes up the story: 'Fans' real prejudices rise to the surface when the team is losing. That's when you know what people are really thinking deep down. At one point, we were 4-1 down to Charlton. Some people actually walked out, with most of the second half left, and some sat in silence. A few started whinging about the French. The problem is, that if you've only started supporting Arsenal in the last few years, experiencing defeat in the league is a rare thing, so people tend to lash out, and some retreat into a xenophobic way of thinking. When Henry gets annoyed, his whole body language changes. The shoulders go, the hands are thrown up in the air, and some people latch on to the fact that his reaction is quintessentially French.

'You still occasionally hear comments like: "Get stuck in, you French poof," and at that time, many would say: "We need more English players to get stuck in." It seemed to me that the crowd wanted it both ways, and still does. They expect a much higher skill level, but when things don't come off, it's easy to retreat into an anti-Gallic bunker, and bemoan the lack of English grit and "trench spirit", as espoused by the likes of Adams and Dixon. Part of the problem – especially back in 2001 – was the way Anelka had walked away from Highbury, and in the process reinforced the French stereotype of arrogance and aloofness. And there had been the whole saga of Vieira being linked with a move to Manchester United in the summer, so there was still a lingering suspicion of whether skilful French players really had their hearts at Arsenal.'

Henry's frustration came to the fore after a 3-1 home defeat against Newcastle in December. The Geordies, who'd not won in the capital on their last thirty-seven visits, blitzed Arsenal in the final half an hour, with goals by Shearer and Robert. Henry, incensed by referee Graham Poll's decision to dismiss Ray Parlour for a mistimed tackle, pushed

Martin Keown and physio Gary Lewin aside in order to make his point to Poll. 'Thierry went absolutely nuts,' confirms Gilles Grimandi. 'He thought it was Poll who'd failed to award the penalty we should have had in the FA Cup final against Liverpool earlier in the year. It wasn't the same ref! Thierry had simply got it wrong. But there was the view that the team was dominated by slightly stroppy, overly emotional Frenchmen. In some ways, that's an understandable reaction, as there had been a massive cultural change at Arsenal over the past four years. But all the French players were equally as passionate about the club as English players. There was still, in late 2001, the feeling that although we were a great side, we could blow up at any moment, in every way – emotionally and playing-wise. Critics pointed to the fact that we'd lost the FA Cup final when we should have won it, and that we hadn't won a trophy for more than three years. It took a while for us to convince people that we also had a winning mentality. But you could see that when Thierry blew up at Poll, after the Newcastle defeat, critics were thinking, It's happening again. The French can't handle it. It took a while for us to prove to them that that wasn't the case, and that we were winners.'

○ SIGNED, SEALED, AND DELIVERED ○

BEFORE ARSENAL'S Champions League clash with Juventus in December 2001, there was growing disquiet about the future of manager Arsène Wenger. Despite promises that he'd pledge his future to the club 'very shortly', he'd yet to formally sign an extension to his contract, leading to speculation that he'd replace the (supposedly) outgoing Alex Ferguson, who'd announced that he'd be retiring as United boss at the end of the season. There were also ongoing concerns over Arsenal's spluttering form. Edu recalls: 'At the start of the season, we made a fairly slow start – by Arsenal standards anyway. There was also a great deal of discussion about the future of Arsène Wenger. The feeling was that Arsenal needed to perform well in the Champions League, otherwise there would be a repeat of the previous summer where Patrick Vieira was linked with a move away from Highbury. Performing well in the Champions League was becoming increasingly important in order to keep players happy. And Arsenal's Champions League form hadn't been sufficiently good enough to convince most people that we could beat Juventus.'

Getting to the crux of why the Gunners have so frequently under-achieved in European competition isn't easy. In interviews, Arsène Wenger remains guarded, and is reluctant to discuss the psychological impact of so many failed campaigns under his tutelage, much less admit that Arsenal's playing style isn't always a recipe for success against top drawer opposition. Former Arsenal star Joe Baker, who played for the Gunners in the early days of the Fairs Cup, had one view on Arsenal's underachievement: 'If you look at England's "big two" in European competition – Liverpool and Manchester United – you can see that they enjoyed success in the very early stages. United knew they could compete with the very best, and probably would have won the tournament in the late 1950s and early sixties, if it hadn't been for the Munich air crash. With Liverpool, they won the UEFA Cup in the sixties and knew they could also live with the best. Both teams have that inbuilt confidence when it comes to playing in Europe, that dates back a long way. Arsenal didn't win the Fairs Cup until 1970, and then waited another twenty-four years to lift the Cup-Winners' Cup. I hate to admit it, but even Spurs had the confidence to play well in Europe, because of their success in the sixties. Arsenal haven't had enough of a track record to think, We can do this, when they walk on to the pitch. And in football, confidence is everything.'

Daily Telegraph journalist Henry Winter takes a slightly different slant, especially on Arsenal's lack of Champions League success under Wenger: 'He is the prime exponent of cavalier football. In the years when Arsenal have dominated domestic football, that style worked fan-tastically in the Premiership. Yet, when it comes to the Champions League, against – say German or Spanish opposition – they tend to treat football matches as a game of chess. In order to succeed at that level, you really need a watertight defence. A cursory glance at

Arsenal's backline shows that Cole and Lauren are almost wingers, rather than steady full backs. I'm not sure that Wenger could play a more defensive game, because I'm not sure that approach is really enshrined in his soul. There is a peacock element to the manner in which his sides play football; he insists that they attack incessantly. But when Arsenal come up against obdurate brick-wall defences, they show signs of frustration, and lack the flexibility to be patient, and probe for a way through.'

When the 'Old Lady' of Italian football turned up at Highbury, it seemed to be Arsenal's worst nightmare. Not only did Juve have Buffon – then Europe's most expensive goalkeeper – between the sticks, they also had the formidable backline of Birindelli, Pessotto, Tacchinardi, and Montero. All five of the defensive quintet had made a joint statement in *La Gazzetta dello Sport* vowing: 'We will shut out the Gunners.' Gilles Grimandi, who would come on as a substitute in the game, admits: 'As well as a formidable backline, Juve also had Del Piero, Trezeguet, and Nedved. These players had a style which you tended not to see in the Premiership. They have a secondary instinct, especially in Nedved's case, to create that extra yard of space, spin turn you, and – whoosh – be gone. I remember we played a Champions League game against Auxerre at Highbury and, on paper, Arsenal should have won the game comfortably, but they (especially Cisse) were spinning Arsenal defenders all night. But against Juve, I felt the team approached the match in entirely the correct manner, and our marking was generally very effective.'

Arsenal's record against Italian clubs in Europe is excellent. Parma, Sampdoria, Inter Milan, and Roma have all been put to the sword in the last fifteen years, although the blips against Inter Milan at Highbury, and Fiorentina at Wembley were, in Wenger's words, ' . . . very hard to take'. The Champions League tie with Juve also rekindled memories of the famous Cup-Winners' Cup clash in 1980, where Vaessen's winner settled the tie in Turin. For the first few minutes of the Champions League clash, Trezeguet and Nedved seemed poised to pulverise Arsenal's backline, and Stuart Taylor, deputising for the injured David Seaman, made excellent saves to deny both strikers. It was a Buffon error which led to Arsenal taking the lead midway through the first half. Patrick Vieira thumped a shot directly at him, and Freddie Ljungberg snaffled up the rebound. A few moments later, Thierry Henry revealed his growing penchant for spectacular free kicks by curling home a fantastic twenty-yard drive past Buffon. The Gunners, with Matthew Upson excelling at the back, appeared watertight, although Juve pulled a goal back six minutes after the break when Sol Campbell's attempted clearance cannoned into the Arsenal net off the unlucky Stuart Taylor's back. Gilles Grimandi recalls: 'It was a time for cool heads. We'd all been in that position before, where we'd blown a seemingly impregnable lead. I remember a year earlier, we were 2–0 up and cruising against Bayern Munich, but ended up drawing 2–2. We had to weather the storm against Juve.'

At the death, with Juve seemingly destined to grab an equaliser, Dennis Bergkamp came to the fore. Henry Winter waxes lyrical about the Dutchman: 'He is as great an influence as Cantona was for United. Bergkamp is a magnificent talent, and also ego free. He remains a model professional, with an ability to see openings which other players can't. His magnificent cameo at the end against Juventus to set up Ljungberg's goal was simply breathtaking.' Gilles Grimandi recalls: 'Thierry and Dennis had their spells in Italy, and evidently they didn't enjoy their time in Serie A. The pair of them appeared to raise their game that night, as if to make a statement to Italian football. We were really struggling to contain Juve in the final stages, and we needed an outlet. Dennis got the ball on the edge of their box, did a shuffle, dummied Birindelli, and dinked a pass into the path of Freddie Ljungberg, who lobbed Buffon beautifully. The Highbury turf smelt beautiful that night. It was a really invigorating evening, and the crowd went home delighted with the result. It's a great memory for me.'

Patrick Vieira recalls: 'It was one of the nights that proved what Arsenal *could* do in Europe, but don't do often enough. We defended tight and hit Juve on the break – that's the way to play in Europe. We felt enormous satisfaction at having done the job.'

No one inside Highbury was as happy as Arsène Wenger. During the following lunchtime, he confirmed that he'd extended his contract at Highbury for a further three years. Vice-chairman David Dein was thrilled, describing Wenger as a 'miracle worker'.

His team would perform a few more before the end of the season.

○ ANNOYING THE NEIGHBOURS (4) ○

ALTHOUGH ARSENAL had recently overcome Manchester United, Juventus, and Aston Villa on the pitch, and Arsène Wenger had signed a new contract, the unlikely venue of Islington's Union Chapel was the battleground for the Gunners' most monumental victory of the season. Indeed, Wenger later described it as the 'biggest decision in Arsenal's history since the board opted to bring Herbert Chapman to the club in 1925'. On Monday 10 December, Islington Council held a special meeting to decide whether to ratify the club's proposed move to Ashburton Grove. The plan to move just 150 metres from Highbury was originally conceived by Anthony Spencer, a lawyer based in London's Manchester Square, back in late 1999. While poring over aerial maps of the capital, Spencer was quickly alerted to the triangular industrial site, which was virtually on the club's doorstep.

The plans to keep Arsenal at Highbury had failed. It had proved impossible to find a way around the East and West Stand's listed building's status, meaning that the club was forced into relocating. Although there was much wailing and gnashing of teeth at the prospect of Arsenal leaving what had become known as their 'spiritual home', moving to Ashburton Grove would, in the words of Charlie George, mean that 'at least we'll still be in Islington, and fans, who are creatures of habit, can go about their normal match day rituals'. The process of uprooting from Highbury proved a long and divisive journey – especially for local residents. The first significant milestone in the club's move had been passed in August 2000, at an Islington Council planning meeting.

Arsenal Independent Supporters' Association (AISA) chairman Steven Powell – who attended the meeting – explained that from the start, opposition to the move was strong: 'It was pretty clear that they were extremely well organised, and very articulate. A group of local residents had formed the Islington Stadium Communities Alliance (ISCA) and they had strong links with the Green Party. They were a powerful lobby group. It became clear to me that unless the AISA campaigned hard, the move to Ashburton Grove was by no means a foregone conclusion. As it was, the Islington Planning Committee approved the move by six votes to one, so the first step had been taken. But ISCA fought all the way from then on.'

Local resident, Arsenal season-ticket holder, and ISCA member Tom Lamb opposed the move, and explains why: 'The majority of Arsenal fans and AISA members look at the move in terms of what happens on matchdays, and what the club will gain from the move. Little or no thought was given to the residents who are in Islington every day. My prime concern was an environmental one. I didn't like the thought of hundreds of lorries thundering along Holloway Road, and gridlocking the place, belching out exhaust fumes which my kids would then inhale. That is a consequence which most Arsenal fans would never see, because they are in Islington only for about thirty days a year. The lazy argument is that if you live next door to a football stadium, you should expect development work to take place. That's nonsense. If you live on a road, you don't suddenly expect it to be converted into a motorway, do you? Some of my friends also pointed out that although match days might be good news for chippies and newsagents, it certainly isn't for other shops, which suffer greatly because shoppers don't want the hassle of fighting through crowds of football fans. And the impact of an extra 22,000 fans cramming into Islington would worsen the effect. My feeling at the time was that Arsenal had outgrown the borough, and should relocate entirely, or put up and shut up at Highbury.'

Despite vocal ISCA protests against the move, Steven Powell points out: 'ISCA struggled due to a lack of numbers. One morning – I live near the ground – I looked out of my window, and saw a bustle of activity which was worthy of General Election day. ISCA was about to march, and members were distributing pamphlets. It was their last big gathering before the council made their big decision in December 2001. With all the publicity, and the talk about the move, they could only muster a group of about three hundred to go on their protest march. A gathering of around two hundred Arsenal fans, including me, shouted, "Is that all you take away?" and, "Are you Tottenham in disguise?" at them. Our slogan was a simple one: "Keep Arsenal in Islington." We'd meet old ladies on the street and ask them to sign a petition, and they'd say things like, "Well, of course you've got to have the Arsenal in Islington." ISCA never really appreciated the groundswell of support in our favour. Another common misconception was that all the businesses based in Ashburton Grove (total: 1100 workers) were anti the move. A representative for the businesses in that area – I believe he spoke on behalf of approximately a thousand of the total – accepted that the move would actually benefit many of the businesses, and that some of ISCA's comments were "unintelligent and hysterical". So their campaign wasn't exactly watertight.'

Deadline day finally arrived, and the council prepared to vote on whether to ratify the move to Ashburton Grove. John Simons attended the Union Chapel meeting: 'The atmosphere inside was tense, and you could sense the enormity of the meeting. It really could make or break Arsenal's future. The Islington Mayor – a Councillor Trotter – was wearing a gold chain on top of a turquoise jumper. To me, he looked a bit of a Del Boy, but in fairness, he did a decent job of keeping the meeting in order. At the start, it was made clear that no one would be permitted to speak for longer than three minutes, which wasn't a bad idea, because people do tend to waffle on those occasions. ISCA representatives raised many points, and although they were an articulate bunch, they came up with some bizarre notions. One guy claimed that Arsenal only had around a thousand fans in Islington. I presume he meant season-ticket holders, but it was a pretty big factual error. One guy from the Harvist Estate, where the club is building the flats next to Ashburton Grove, claimed it would be turned into a public latrine, with the influx of football fans, and that the club, indirectly, was creating the same kind of estate in which Damilola Taylor was murdered.

'It got quite House Of Commons-esque, and both sides spent a good deal of time heckling one another. When the votes were finally cast, the councillors had to shout "yes" or "no" in favour of the proposal. In the end, the motion to allow Arsenal to move to Ashburton Grove was passed by thirty-four votes to seven, with one abstention. Pretty unanimous, although I noticed Alison Carmichael – one of ISCA's leading lights – frantically writing down the names of those who voted against. ISCA wasn't entirely finished, although from now on, their battle became a losing one. The guy from the Harvist Estate claimed he'd take the issue to the European Court of Human Rights. But he was drowned out by the cheering from the Arsenal fans inside the Union Chapel. The council then approved the bill to convert Highbury into a residential area, and relocate the rubbish tip to Lough Road. All elements of the move were now in place. It was a fantastic night. After all the fuss, we could actually go ahead with the project.'

One of the councillors who voted in favour of the move claimed: 'These ideas will shape the future of the borough for the next hundred years.' AISA chairman Steven Powell explains how he believes that, despite the opposition, the new development will benefit one of London's poorest boroughs: 'ISCA was terrified that Caledonian and Holloway Road would be paralysed by lorries, but local residents have confirmed that this hasn't been the case. Nor has the expected noise pollution, which many were worried about. Basically, the move has a lot of benefits for the local area. Over the next decade, nine thousand new homes are needed in the borough, and with the flats being built alongside Ashburton Grove, and the conversion of Highbury, eighteen hundred of them will appear in one fell swoop. On a micro level, a halo effect will appear. Light industrial units will be needed, and dozens of new shops and restaurants will also appear as a result of the stadium being built. It will give the area a focal point, and the boost in morale which comes from a scheme like this is huge. The fact is that we're also right next door to Hackney, which is London's poorest borough. There will also be a knock-on effect there job-wise. In addition to that, an estimated eighty per cent of fans will leave the ground on foot, and then catch public transport. So it's a viable project in that sense, too. If some of the opposition groups had had their way, we'd have been driving to somewhere just off the M25, which would hardly be very economically friendly, would it?'

ISCA's final act of defiance was to summon help from the EarthRights group, a legal firm which specialises in dealing with local concerns. Although ultimately unable to block the move, EarthRights's campaign threatened to seriously delay the whole project, and raised some uncomfortable facts about the scheme.

○ CONFESSIONS ○

THE LAWYER

'EarthRights was set up in the early 1990s in order to give legal advice to environmental organisations and local community groups with concerns about developmental damage in their local areas. I lived in Islington during the early 1990s and, although I wasn't an Arsenal fan, it was my local team and I developed a certain fondness for the club. The Islington Stadium Community Alliance (ISCA) called me out of the blue in early 2002, as they felt that throughout the planning stages of Arsenal moving to Ashburton Grove there hadn't been sufficient direct consultation with local residents over what was happening, and that the proposals wouldn't deliver what was being promised. The club had looked at a variety of sites, including Wembley and King's Cross, but now that it had opted to stay in Islington, the council was in a relatively strong bargaining position to get out of Arsenal what they could. ISCA was an umbrella group, comprising people ranging from those who lived in £1 million residences on Highbury Hill, to those residing in less affluent estates. Some members of the group were also fervent Arsenal fans, so it wasn't a case of the group being middle-class NIMBYs, or an anti-Arsenal group. The football club was perceived as a large private company that was showing signs of riding roughshod over local community interests and, as I said, neglecting to consult them over key issues.

'One of ISCA's major bug bears was, after planning permission had been granted, the manner in which the issue of Compulsory Purchase Orders (CPOs) on the Ashburton Grove businesses was handled. The club (via the transport waste recycling centre) dressed up the scheme as a regeneration programme in the borough in order to push the CPOs through. They argued that it was in the public interest to move those businesses out, but ISCA and the local businesses believed they wished to push through the CPOs as quickly as possible, with minimal consultation. The test for the confirmation (viability) of a CPO is whether or not it is seen to be overwhelmingly in the public interest. After all, here was an example of a private company taking away someone else's private land. The question needed to be asked, how was this development of benefit to the public? CPOs have to be scrutinised by an independent inspector, and he sided firmly with ISCA, agreeing that Arsenal's move to Ashburton Grove did not – as the club had suggested –

represent a significant local regeneration opportunity. The club and the council continued to argue vehemently that the provision of the waste recycling centre and the new stadium would provide local employment, social housing, and improvements to the transport infrastructure. The CPO inspector, who reported to Deputy Prime Minister John Prescott's department, said there was insufficient benefit to the public and that CPOs should not be granted. Prescott ignored his own inspector's recommendation and confirmed the CPOs. There is a suspicion that – as in the recent case of Brighton's proposed new stadium in Falmer – he did this due to political reasons, rather than purely for planning reasons.

'After Prescott made his decision, the businesses decided to take the Deputy Prime Minister to Court in December 2004. Their attempt to overturn the decision was unsuccessful. High Courts have a tendency not to interfere too much in the decisions of government ministers, and in January 2005, the court refused to overturn Prescott's ruling. Government ministers have very wide powers of discretion so that unless a lawyer can somehow convince a High Court judge that a Secretary of State is, in polite terms, bonkers, there is no chance of blocking such a scheme. So, by early 2005, ISCA and the businesses were forced to give up the fight, despite having won the only independent inquiry into the whole project.

'An issue which remains shrouded in mystery is the financial viability of Arsenal's move to the new ground. Only a select few members of Islington Council were privy to the precise details, but the bridging loan the club has taken on is believed to be in the region of around £270 million. When you consider that interest rates – which have risen over the last year – and property prices are fluid, it's unclear what the club's financial state will be over the next few years. Another aspect which is open to debate is Arsenal's pledge that swathes of Islington residents will be able to attend Arsenal matches, and have first refusal on up to 10,000 season tickets. It was another part of their claim that the entire scheme will be of benefit to the local area. But Islington is one of London's poorest boroughs, and the question remains: how many locals will be able to afford to go to the new ground on a regular basis? Our evidence proved that only 5% of Arsenal's current 38,000 fans live in the borough, and that over 50% who attend live outside the M25 ring. There are still likely to be serious transport problems due to the new development, particularly for midweek games. The proposed improvements to Holloway Road tube, as well as the suggested overground improvements, have not been forthcoming. Much of the planning took place before Roman Abramovich arrived at Chelsea and, of course, his impact has shifted the goalposts completely. The move to the new ground was designed to

push Arsenal ahead of their closest rivals, but with Abramovich's billions, this
may well prove not to be the case. I still argue that there are key aspects of the
move to Ashburton Grove – especially the huge financial ramifications for the
club – which are yet to come to light. I'm sure that they will in the fullness of
time.'

Charlie Hopkins – EarthRights Lawyer

THE TOUT

Author's note – I felt that any story of Arsenal at Highbury would be
incomplete without an interview with a self-styled 'attendance
facilitator': aka ticket tout. I first came into contact with 'Catweazle'
while writing a piece on ticket touting for *FourFourTwo* magazine in
2004. It was hardly a pleasant experience. Named after the scruffy
children's TV character of the 1970s, Catweazle had lank, greasy hair, a
straggly beard, and a pasty complexion. His nose ran permanently, and
his eyes were watery. Despite being warned about his volcanic temper,
he seemed affable enough. After telling me that he'd ' . . . answer all
your questions as long as you buy me a fry up', Catweazle turned
decidedly nasty when I dared to ask him if he'd just sold forged tickets
to a group of fans who had travelled over from Holland to watch their
hero Dennis Bergkamp in action. Inside one of the numerous greasy
spoons opposite Finsbury Park tube station, he stood up and bawled:
'Who the fucking hell do you think you are, asking me questions like
that.' Despite claiming that the fry up was his ' . . . first decent meal of
the week,' he'd just spent the last few seconds spitting half chewed
shards of egg, bacon and fried bread into my face. Having first
threatened to shove my dictaphone up my arse, he satisfied himself
with hurling it across the room – narrowly missing a table full of
diners – and stormed out.

Eighteen months on, he's in a contrite mood, and talks openly,
without demanding a fry up in advance . . .

'If you're a tout looking for business, then Highbury is the only place to be. The
streets are a tout's paradise. All the pubs, cafes, and chippies are perfect places to
do business. The main reason Highbury is the place to be, is that the team is so
fucking good, and the ground so fucking small. You can make a fortune. It's easy

to flog a £50 ticket on for a ton (£100) – or more for a really big match. Touts around Highbury have got bolder over the years. You'll find a string of at least 20 of us from Finsbury Park tube, down St Thomas's road, past William Hill bookmakers, and on past the Auld Triangle. The police here do virtually nothing to stop us. We're part of the culture of English football, like pubs and chanting at games, it's always gone on. I believe that I provide a service. The other day, some fan walked past me and called me a "thieving wanker". I'm just a businessman. An attendance facilitator. If you want to watch Arsenal badly enough, I'm the man who brings some happiness into your life.

'Most fans don't have a clue where their money ends up. If they did, I bet half of them wouldn't go to touts. Most of the lads are either in debt due to gambling, or drink, or drugs. Half of my wage from today will end up in the casino. All wasted, just like that. Many of the lads have been doing the circuit at Highbury for years, but they've also been in and out of the nick during that time. It's the type of people we are. Some of the lads are up to all sorts behind the scenes. I bet half of the people who read this book won't know that, but they should do. Football chat rooms are a paradise for touts. You put a message on the site, pretend to be a loyal fan who's desperate for a ticket, bullshit a bit about how you've not missed a game for years, and more often than not, someone will email you and send you a ticket at face value. There's one Arsenal tout who gets most of his tickets online these days. It's amazing. Mobile phones are also a massive help, because you can hunt in packs, and help some of the other lads out. All this modern technology is great for business.

'The club is quite proactive in dealing with touts. They've got a hotline where anyone who has bought off a tout can phone in and give details of the name and seat number. Over the years, they've cancelled quite a few ticket registration scheme memberships. What they don't like to admit is that they opened up the market to touts in the early '90s when they launched the Ticket Registration Scheme. Anyone could apply, and lots of the lads seized their chance. Some of them opened 10 or more registration scheme accounts using false names and different addresses of friends around the country. So on match day, some of the lads arrive with a fistful of tickets. It's just business.

'I have no sympathy with fans whose memberships have been stopped because they've sold a ticket before the game in good faith, only for it to fall into the hands of touts. People should be a bit more streetwise.

'In my time, I've had a few police warnings and been told to move on, but after a while you learn to walk alongside the crowd, and not stand still for too long. I've never had a bunch of tickets confiscated, and nor have many of the other lads. Having said all this, my time is probably running out as a tout. Because of the size of Highbury there's always been a high demand for tickets, especially since Arsène Wenger has taken over. But every time I walk along Gillespie Road and I see the new ground going up and the cranes and the flats and all that, my heart sinks. Twenty thousand extra fans inside Ashburton Grove means that there just won't be the demand for extra tickets. No one will probably need any spares. I'm trying to make as much money as I can at Highbury while it's still here. I don't know what I'll do then. I might start working near Stamford Bridge.'

'Catweazle'

THE GROUNDSMAN

'Before I was appointed head groundsman at Highbury, I'd occupied a similar role at the Royal Veterinary College at Brookmans Park. I got the job at Arsenal in a fairly unusual manner. At the college, they had an awards evening where they presented trophies to the kids' team which played there, and they gave me a little prize as a thank you for looking after their turf. The manager of the team, Dennis Morris, was a friend of George Graham, and asked him to present the prizes. I was stunned, because I'm a big Arsenal fan. I asked him on the off-chance whether or not there were any vacancies at Highbury. He took me back a bit when he said there was a position, because the previous groundsman had left. I gave him my mum's telephone number, as I lived in digs which didn't have a phone. Some time passed, and I had moved on, and, one day, I went back to Mum's with some washing, and she casually announced that "someone called George Graham rang, and he wants you to call him back". I got right back to him, and as usual, he came straight to the point.

'"We're interviewing for the groundsman's job," he said, "can you make it over to Highbury for an interview this afternoon." I explained that could be tricky, as I'd got work that afternoon. "Well, can you make it or not?" was his response. So, after telling my boss that I'd got a doctor's appointment, I went to Highbury, completely and utterly unprepared for an interview. Ken Friar and George Graham interviewed me, and I really didn't think the interview had gone well at all. When Ken Friar asked me at the end if I had any questions, I seem to remember asking him if David Rocastle would be fit for the new season. I did get to see the pitch, though, which wasn't in the best condition. I presumed that when

I went for the interview, it was for assistant to the head groundsman, and that I'd gradually work my way up the pecking order. I was pleasantly surprised when I was given the job of head groundsman. It was a daunting prospect.

The big problem with the Highbury pitch at that time was that the club had installed an undersoil heating system, and the pipes weren't laid far enough beneath the surface of the pitch. It made effective drainage virtually impossible. There were several occasions where I was spiking the pitch, and I clouted one of the pipes with the spiker. It was obvious something was seriously wrong. During the 1988–89 season, when Arsenal won the title, the pitch fell apart completely. There was a home match with Sheffield Wednesday where I felt we were lucky that the game went ahead at all. We had to dump sand over it, and around that time, the pitch was known as the "Highbury mudflats". After the Wednesday match, I remember that Brian Marwood – a bit of a joker – was asked about the pitch in a radio interview, and said something along the lines: "Our groundsman will be picking up his P45 shortly." It was meant as a joke, but it was blatantly obvious that something radical needed to be done. Michael Hart, of the Evening Standard, came up with a very accurate description of the pitch when he likened it to "a winkle picker's paradise at low tide".

'In the close season, the pitch was completely reconstructed, and the pipes were buried deeper underneath. I'd done a lot of research by going to see a large number of pitches, including those at Coventry and Sheffield Wednesday, two clubs renowned for having a good turf. A Leicester-based firm relaid our turf, although we used our existing soil throughout the whole process. One of the things I discovered in the process of the pitch being reconstructed was a clinker raft, which dated back to the Chapman era, and was an early form of drainage facility. The fact that the Highbury pitch isn't completely flat also dates back to Chapman's time. The view then was that you needed a slightly sloping pitch in order to drain off surplus water. I was able to persuade the club to invest in better equipment – improved spiking facilities for instance – and from 1989 onwards, we were always regarded as a club with a good pitch.

'In order to maintain the standard of the turf, you need to be aware of the seasonal dip. Pitches decline in quality from when the clocks go back in October, to when they go forward again in late March. The conditions become wetter and darker, and consequently the grass doesn't grow. The club uses the Dutch technique in artificial lighting to grow the pitch in winter, pretty much the same technique the Dutch use in rose growing. Together, with improved education and machinery, pitches are generally of a better quality in the modern era. It was a

great honour to win the Groundsman of the Year awards, but it was also a little embarrassing. You can only work with the conditions and restraints which you have at your club, and the weather down south certainly lends itself to better pitches.

'With the way Arsène Wenger's team plays football these days, he needs a fast, good quality surface, so there is an immense pressure on the staff to keep the turf in pristine condition. It's an enormous job. When I was head groundsman at Highbury, I could work for anything up to sixteen hours a day at the busiest times. I'm obsessive about turf, and I'm also a perfectionist. You have to be in this business. Because of the enormous demands of maintaining the pitches at the club's St Albans training ground, I'm there pretty much all of the time and Paul Burgess has taken over my old role at Highbury. Paul is delighted when he hears the pitch described as the "Highbury croquet lawn". And I'm always pleased when people complement the pitches at St Albans. It's a bit different to the situation we were in back in 1989!'

Steve Braddock – Arsenal Head Groundsman

THE COMMISSIONAIRE

'As Highbury commissionaire, my main responsibility is to direct supporters to the ticket office, show people around, and on matchdays, show players and visitors in and out of the East Stand entrance. What's struck me – and I've been in this job for over thirty years – is how much footballers' fashions have changed over the years. George Best was the first to really embrace fashion in football. He'd turn up on matchday when United played here, and he always seemed to be wearing the most beautifully cut suits, straight off the peg. I'd get the loveliest looking ladies coming up to me and asking if I could "take a note to Georgie", and I always felt very harsh when I had to reply, "Actually no, I can't." Ironically, it was Leicester City whom I recall as the most fashionably dressed side. You'd get the likes of Birchenall and Worthington swanning into Highbury, smelling of expensive aftershave, and wearing really expensive clothes.

'Although Don Revie was always very polite to me, I'd usually laugh at the Leeds martinets, because they'd arrive identically dressed, walk in like they were on a route march, and be gone really quickly after the match.

'Of all the opposition players who came here, the one who struck me most was Johann Cruyff. He was with Ajax who visited a couple of times in the early 1970s, and he seemed impressed by the sheer majesty of the East Stand. He always asked *how I was, and on the second visit, asked if my family were still keeping well. And, he also remembered my name, which was very thoughtful of him.*

The modern Arsenal players don't really come to Highbury unless they have a home match, so I don't see too much of them. Back in the seventies, I used to get on really well with Geordie Armstrong and Frank McLintock, who always had time for a natter. I've not heard of another club in the world which has a commissionaire, and I like to think it adds some extra style to the club. At least that was the idea in the thirties. It was known as the "peacock approach" back then – where you'd show the world how classy you were! Whether or not people think that the idea of a commissionaire is outdated these days, I don't really know. But I love doing my job, helping people out, and working in fantastic surroundings. I enjoy my work as much now, as I did when I started all that time ago. I still see a lot of tourists coming up to me and asking questions about the history of the place. It shows that the East and West Stands have become iconic structures in world football.'

Commissionaire 'Nobby' – speaking in 1999

○ SMELLING SILVER POLISH ○

BY MARCH 2002, Arsenal had embarked on the excellent run of domestic victories which swept them towards the club's third Double. As the days got longer, and the weather warmer, the Gunners' performances hit levels which eclipsed those of the previous Double season back in 1998. It was a time when the team's various components interlocked perfectly. The defence – marshalled by Sol Campbell and Tony Adams – tightened up considerably. Patrick Vieira rediscovered his impressive consistency of the previous season, and protected the back four, and Bergkamp's form was sensational. As is the case with all successful Arsenal sides, two players' form in particular shone. Arsenal fan James Verrier recalls: 'You have to have a player or two who steps forward and plays out of their skins – because

you know that some of the others might tire, or lose form, or get
injured, or whatever. In the 1971 Double season, Charlie George came
back from injury, and it was like having a new player around the place.
He dragged us towards winning the trophies. In 1998, Overmars and
Petit emerged from the pack, and late on, turned in great displays. In
2002, Pires and Ljungberg suddenly began to play out of their skins
when spring time came around.'

Silvinho recalls: 'When Robert (Pires) first arrived at Highbury, it
was evident that he was a great player. Everyone knew he'd played in
the French side which had won Euro 2000. It took him a while to adapt
to the demands, the pace, and the sheer intensity of English football.
He didn't really set the place alight when he first arrived, although he
did score a couple against Tottenham, which always endears you to
Arsenal fans. A year later, he'd grown his hair, got some trendy
whiskers, and looked like a marauding cavalier on the wing. He
summed up Arsenal at their free-flowing, brilliant best, during the
latter half of that season.' Edu concurs: 'It wasn't like one day Arsenal
fans woke up and realised what a great player Robert was. They'd
always known he was good, but it took a while for them to realise that
he was absolutely top class. During the end of that season, Thierry's
goals dropped away a bit, but fortunately, others came along and
chipped in with goals themselves.'

After arriving from Swedish club Halmstads in 1999, and scoring a
goal against Manchester United on his debut, Ljungberg had initially
struggled to adapt to his new environs. Ironically, his stock began to
rise after he was sent off against Tottenham, and flicked his Vs at the
Tottenham fans. Ljungberg has since admitted: 'At first, Arsenal fans
weren't all that sure about me.' During the 2001–02 season, the Swede
gained a reputation for getting on the end of sweeping Arsenal moves.
Team-mates noticed that Ljungberg often played better when fellow
strikers were either injured, or simply having an off day. 'Freddie can
play either as an orthodox winger, or up front,' comments Silvinho.
'But at the end of his greatest season, he was playing in the gap
between Henry and Bergkamp, and those two, sensing that he was
running into a sensational run of form, created many chances for
Freddie. The beauty of the 2002 side was that all the players could
score goals, but they were also sufficiently ego-free to act as providers.

If you had a collection of players up front who were rather more greedy, there could easily have been a traffic jam, but their awareness of space and creativity is awesome. Things all came together for him during that period. He dyed his hair with the red streak at a time when the grunge look was really in, and then Andy Williams re-released "Can't Take My Eyes Off You", and the Arsenal fans adopted it as their anthem when they sang, "We Love You Freddie, because you've got red hair," and all the rest!'

For Arsenal fan Zak Reed, the style of Arsenal's play was the fulfilment of his football dreams: 'By the end of the season, Arsenal's style of play was unbelievably different from the style they had under George Graham, or Don Howe, or Terry Neill. We could never have dreamed, say, twenty years ago, that we'd have players like Bergkamp, Henry, Vieira and Pires at Highbury – guys who'd walk into pretty much any side in the world. Virtually to a man, they'd completely eclipse any Arsenal team from the past, in skill levels and poise. A lot of people, as they know that we're coming to the end of our Highbury time, look back with nostalgia and say, "Oh, things used to be more fun." But to me, the best time to be an Arsenal fan has been over the last few years, because the quality of Arsenal's displays are unbelievable. I can't remember who it was, but someone said at the time of the 1998 Double: "When you watch Arsenal now, you might just be watching the best football of your life." They were spot on.'

The fluency of Arsenal's football was curtailed somewhat at the end of the season, as several teams came to Highbury with the express intention of leaving Arsenal with a draw, as opposed to actually winning the game. Gilles Grimandi explains: 'Football often gets like that at the end of the season. Teams get tense, as they're either fighting relegation, or going for Europe, or whatever. The more there is at stake, the more tense things get. You have to be patient, and break down sides like that.' When Newcastle travelled to Highbury for an FA Cup replay in April, they fielded an uncharacteristically defensive side, but were quickly ripped apart by Pires and Bergkamp strikes. After a seemingly innocuous tangle with the Toon's Dabizas, Pires jumped clear, landed awkwardly, and ruptured knee ligaments in the process. 'It was terrible luck on Robert,' recalls Grimandi, 'and a similar thing happened to Dennis Bergkamp in 1998, where one of the main architects of our success was ruled out because of a freak injury. It could have derailed our challenge, but by then, the momentum was with us. And we had Freddie.'

Zak Reed recalls: 'I had this horrible feeling that either West Ham or Ipswich would come to Highbury and bugger up our challenge. The longer games went on, the more I could sense United or Liverpool preparing to sneak up on us. Against West Ham, everyone was really edgy because we couldn't break through, and my stomach was knotted, because there were only ten minutes to go. Then Bergkamp got the ball, slipped Ljungberg in and Freddie tucked it away. Absolute fucking pandemonium. I'd say that the West Ham match was one of the great Highbury nights, and it makes you realise how much the club means to you, and how much you ache for them to win, at times. The same against Ipswich. Nothing until late in the second half, then Freddie pops up and does the business. Unbelievable. Then against Spurs, when it was really getting to brown pants time, it was Lauren who came to the fore. Let's face it. I'm not too sure that everyone was confident that Lauren would tuck it away, but he was the coolest person inside Highbury. If you're going to win the title, you have to get those tight 1–0 wins. It's part and parcel of the race. And some unlikely heroes – like Lauren – will always emerge from the pack.'

Gilles Grimandi recalls the tension of those final home matches: 'When Freddie squeezed in that shot against West Ham, it was as if the ball took an age to crawl across the line. It reflected just how tight some of those final matches really were. It's all about controlling your nerves. Imagine how difficult it must have been for Freddie, with all that tension surrounding him, to time his run into space perfectly, and slot it past David James. Incredible. You have to have a degree of adrenaline pumping through you during matches, but I think if you ever actually sat there, and considered just how important winning football matches is to the fans, you'd end up as a nervous wreck! But when the boys beat Manchester United at Old Trafford to win the title, and Chelsea to win the FA Cup, we could finally relax. We were able to lift our game against two sides who were prepared to come and attack us. It's only then that you realise the mental exhaustion of it all, and how much you've gone through over the previous months.'

Having secured the Double, the final match of the season against Everton was played in a carnival atmosphere. The Gunners won 4–3, with Henry rediscovering his goal-getting instincts. The celebrations which followed the final whistle will live long in Zak Reed's memory: 'It was a beautiful May afternoon, rather like it had been against Everton back in 1998, when we won the title. The boys showboated a bit, but won anyway. The part I loved were the celebrations, when Pires, who'd been voted Player of the Year, hobbled on to the pitch in his Arsenal top and jeans. The crowd gave him a rapturous reception, and all his team-mates indulged in a spot of "mock genuflecting" at his feet. But he deserved it, because he'd been the bit of class which made the difference so often during that season. Lee Dixon had already announced his retirement, and most of us knew that Tony Adams would probably quit as well, so it was a sad as well as a wonderful day. You always know that a few will fly the nest at the end of a season, but the club will roll onwards. That day at Highbury is my favourite memory of all, and it sums up all the reasons why I love the club.'

○ VA VA VOOM (2) ○

IN THE EARLY 1960s, Arsenal v Spurs was easily the most eagerly awaited game at Highbury each season. Arsenal fan Brian Dawes recalls: 'I was brought up in Haringay, and everything – even down to who were the cowboys and the Indians – boiled down to who supported Arsenal or Spurs. I remember going to the match in 1963 and arrived at Highbury with, I thought, plenty of time to spare. But there were queues right round the block. There was a different buzz surrounding Arsenal v Spurs matches, entirely unlike any other game. At that time, our outlook wasn't as far-reaching as it is now. Arsenal weren't coming into contact with teams like Real Madrid or Barça, and in the days before cheap European travel, they were on what seemed to be another planet, to be honest. The first question, which you always asked when the fixture list came out, was, "When are we playing Spurs?"'

Joe Baker, who played in several derby games during the early sixties, recalls: 'We knew exactly what the match meant to our fans. You'd have fellas coming up to you, pleading with you not to lose the match, because their lives would be made a misery for the rest of the year. I was sorry that we disappointed at that time, because that was the era when you had a dominant Spurs side which had won the Double. At that time, Spurs – rightfully – were acknowledged as the artistes; and Arsenal were seen as a grim, spluttering machine. The view on Arsenal was a bit harsh, I felt. But we were clearly second best at that time.'

In recent times, Spurs had endured years of coming to Highbury, and either suffering defeat, or clinging on for dear life and escaping with a draw. There was an added dimension with Sol Campbell leaving White Hart Lane for Arsenal during the previous summer. But players' attitudes to the North London derby had changed slightly. Edu recalls: 'When a player signs for Arsenal, you are made aware that every game is a big match, and that all opponents will fight tooth and nail to beat you, because you are Arsenal. But there are such things as mega matches. I would say that in recent years, games against United and Chelsea, and big European nights, are such occasions. Spurs matches are big though. Because English football is all about the history behind local rivalry – and the passion. And Highbury is always very noisy when Spurs come to town. In recent years though, Spurs haven't really made a big challenge for the title or anything like that, but, under Martin Jol, they could pose more of a threat; so there might be an edge creeping back in. A couple of years back, it wasn't happening at all for Spurs, so the keen rivalry lessened, because Arsenal were clearly the superior force.'

Arsenal fan Dave Silver comments: 'Arsenal v Spurs matches are tribal. They're neighbourhood scraps. Although Arsenal have clearly been a better side than Spurs over the past fifteen years, the games still matter massively. If you live down south, there's a fair chance that you'll work with Spurs fans, and so to have a good week, you can't go losing to them. It dates back from when Woolwich Arsenal came to London. Spurs supporters always had the feeling that they were the pure ones – right down to the white shirts. We were labelled "ugly" in terms of football and footballers. Henry Norris had cheated Spurs in 1918, so they always felt we could pull a fast one on them. That nagging sense of inferiority has really come to the fore in the last few years, because our style of play is on a different planet to Spurs'. It's become even more accentuated in recent times, with Sol Campbell leaving them to come here. Their only real pleasure has been seeing us occasionally lose out on cups and championships, because they really have so little to cheer about. As we've moved on to greater things, you can sense their fury and frustration. They had George Graham as boss, which put paid to their lingering belief that they were the enter-tainers. Then Glenn Hoddle arrived as boss, and before long, their fans were chanting: "We've got our Tottenham back." They actually believed they were on the verge of something big under him, and so they arrived at Highbury in October 2002 in high spirits!'

The atmosphere at the game, restored to its 3 p.m. Saturday slot, was crackling. Most of the chants revolved around Sol Campbell. While Spurs fans contented themselves by shouting 'Judas' at him, Gunners fans reminded the visitors of the fact that: 'We got Campbell from the Lane,' and that, 'the scum from the Lane have won fuck all again, and Sol Campbell has won the Double.' From the minute the game kicked off, Arsenal tore into Spurs. With ten minutes gone, Sylvain Wiltord volleyed in, but was adjudged to be offside. Ten minutes later, Thierry Henry ran from just inside his own half, outpaced the entire Spurs midfield, sidestepped Matthew Etherington, and slammed the ball past Kasey Keller. Henry celebrated by running virtually the whole length of the pitch, screaming like a madman at anyone who cared to look at him, and slid to his knees in front of the Spurs fans, who responded, in Edu's words ' . . . by indicating that they thought he should go and fuck himself'. After Henry had calmed down, he explained his celebrations: 'The goal itself was a good goal, but when you add all the other factors in, like the fact that the whole crowd was going mad, and that it was a North London derby, it became something more than that. I wanted to carry on celebrating all day, but you have to get your concentration back quickly, because if Spurs had ended up equalising, we'd all have looked a bit stupid.'

With Spurs midfielder Simon Davies sent off after a foul on Patrick Vieira, Arsenal went on the hunt for more goals. Wiltord and Ljungberg finished from close range, after excellent approach work by Henry. The final score was 3–0, with Arsenal fans taunting Spurs counterparts with the chant: 'You've got your Tottenham back.' Dave Silver was delighted with the score, especially as it increased the likelihood of St Totteringham's day being brought forward into March again. He explains: 'It's a moveable feast is St Totteringham's day, but it's the day upon which Spurs can't mathematically finish above Arsenal in the league. In recent years, it's fallen earlier and earlier in the season. The record at the moment (speaking in December 2005) is March thirteenth. We knew that mathematically we'd finished above them, with ten games left over. I'm a little bit worried that the day will be put back a bit over the next few years, or even worse, scrapped completely. St Totteringham's day hasn't had to be cancelled since the 1994–95 season.'

Henry's wonder goal against Spurs sent shock waves around Europe. 'I think I read that over a hundred million had seen that match on satellite television around the world,' explains Edu. 'I believe that although most people are aware that Henry is a special talent, his goal against Tottenham was the one which catapulted him to *super* stardom. Shortly afterwards, he began appearing in the Renault Clio ads, and became linked with the "Va Va Voom" catchphrase. After that match, it seems amazing that we couldn't defend our title, but overall, we let too many sides back into matches when we really should have killed them off. But the core of the team was still there for a really good go at the Premiership during the following season.'

The Arsenal fans who celebrated on their way out of Highbury that afternoon composed an entirely new ditty: 'We've got the best player in the world.'

○ POWER SHIFT ○

DESPITE CONCEDING the Premiership title to Manchester United in May 2003, the feeling within the Arsenal camp remained that the Gunners should have won the title. 'Credit to United that they overhauled us,' recalls Oleg Luzhny, 'but we saw it as their windfall title. They won it because we blew it. You could put our failure down to several things, including injuries and a loss of form. Some claimed we were overconfident after Arsène Wenger was misquoted in the press. The newspapers said that he claimed we'd go through the season unbeaten, whereas he'd actually said that it was a *possibility* that we could do it. The game in which we finally blew it was at home to Leeds United, when we lost 3–2. We played quite well, but they needed to win in order to avoid relegation, and on the day Kewell and Viduka were too good for us. We were crushed afterwards, but we retained the belief that with the players we had, we'd be back with a vengeance. With Vieira, Pires and Henry, I still believed that the power would shift to Highbury within the next couple of years. But things were about to change.'

Arsenal fan Fred Wright recalls his reaction as the much predicted 'power shift' from Old Trafford to Highbury failed to materialise: 'I knew that we'd blow it against Leeds when we all started shouting, "You're just a fat Aussie wanker" at Viduka. He came over when Leeds had a corner early in the game and grinned at us. All it did was inspire him to play his first decent game for Leeds for ages. He had this air of laziness, but he totally ran rings around us all game. Late on, when it became clear that Leeds would get at least a point, I ended up just watching him, and saw his reaction when he curled in the winner past Seaman. It was United's title, and Leeds stayed up. We were pissed off. We had United on the ropes. We should have finished them off, and shown that the balance of force really had shifted south. We'd let them off the hook, but I still reckoned at that time that it was like a boxing match, and we'd taken away United's utter dominance of English football. Then Abramovich hove into view at Chelsea, and we had to re-evaluate those feelings.'

In an ill-informed and pompous sounding *Gooner* article, one Jon Spurling wrote a piece which suggested: 'Arsenal fans have nothing to worry about, as you can't buy team spirit,' and predicted that, 'Gunners fans will be laughing at their Chelsea counterparts for years to come.' This was despite editor Kevin Whitcher's prediction that, 'Chelsea's power is like an impending tidal wave. You know that it's going to hit you hard at some point soon.' Edu sums up the players' mood when they heard the news that Abramovich's billions were being placed at Chelsea's disposal: 'It's in the back of your mind that the new wealth could have a huge impact on English football. But as a player, you simply have to get on with it. Most onlookers – rightly, as it turned out – predicted that it would take a couple of years for the full impact to become clear. At first, it spurred us on to step up our efforts. But it clearly meant that the United–Arsenal "oligopoly" was under threat. Personal views on the morality of bringing in such huge wealth is open to personal opinion, but we certainly coped with the new threat extremely well during the 2003–04 season, domestically at least.'

The Gunners first clash with the newly gold-plated Chelsea took place at Highbury in October 2003. Edu put Arsenal 1–0 up with a deflected free kick, but Hernan Crespo curled home an exquisite equaliser, and for a while, it seemed that Chelsea were poised to gain their first league victory at Highbury for thirteen years. But a second-half error by Carlo Cudicini allowed Thierry Henry to knock home Arsenal's winner – 2–1 to the table-topping, unbeaten Gunners. Point proved, at least for now. Yet away from events on the pitch, Abramovich's arrival was already making waves.

Arsenal fan Paul Collins recalls his feelings as Chelsea emerged as a genuine Premiership force: 'When Abramovich took over, I hoped that he'd pay off some of their debt, and buy in a few flashy, over-the-hill stars, in customary Chelsea fashion. When they started signing guys like Wayne Bridge and Damien Duff – players that Arsenal might have snapped up if Chelsea's new money hadn't been washing around – I had a sinking feeling that this would be bad news for Arsenal, especially at a time when the new stadium development seemed to be diverting money away from Wenger's transfer kitty. It was pretty clear that even if they didn't get it quite right now, or the season after, they would have to eventually. When we played them in October, it was pretty clear that although they'd improved hugely, they still weren't the finished article.

'That didn't stop their fans "largeing it" though. They sang songs at us like, "Shall we buy a ground for you?" and "We've got all the cash". It was all very nouveau riche. Our responses: "You won the league in black and white", "Chelsea ain't got no history", and, "Where were you when you were shit?" – together with the fact that we won the game – silenced them. At that stage, they had no answers to us on the pitch. It was pretty much the same when we played them in the FA Cup. Mutu put them ahead, before Reyes turned things around totally, and we won 2–1. His first goal was absolutely brilliant, and again, we'd just about proved that we were the daddies. And the fact that "skint" Arsenal had paid so much for him shut up the Chelsea fans. Brilliant though it was, I still had this feeling that they were nudging closer to us. When we drew them again in the Champions League, and got a 1–1 draw at Stamford Bridge, critics reckoned we'd beat them again. But I had serious doubts. I thought it might be third time lucky (at Highbury) for them.'

When the two sides met in the quarter final clash in April, it was their fifth clash of the season. Arsenal's seemingly relentless charge towards Premiership glory saw them win 2–1 at Stamford Bridge, with goals from Edu and Patrick Vieira. The Brazilian midfielder recalls the season's final joust with Chelsea: 'This was the time for Arsenal to win the Champions League, with the crop of players they had at the time. You can sense when the time is right, and it seemed that with the away goal advantage, the balance lay in our hands. But Claudio Ranieri had his team really fired up, and in a sense, Chelsea had none of the baggage that Arsenal have when it comes to the Champions League. They could just come and prove themselves. Chelsea had some great players, and it was always the case that on a one-off occasion, they could do us some damage. We took the lead just before half-time, when Jose Antonio scored. But we were playing at a thunderous pace, and hadn't killed off the game. Chelsea knew that they only needed a goal to pull it back, and probably felt that they had more in the tank than us. Remember, we'd played Manchester United in the FA Cup semi-final just a few days before, and lost. At half-time, Arsène urged us to be cautious, but to also kill off the game. But Arsenal like to attack, and Chelsea adopted an incredibly patient second-half approach. The second half was so disappointing.'

As Arsenal laboured to create – much less actually score – a crucial second-half goal, Chelsea's Claude Makelele hammered a speculative thirty-yard drive at Jens Lehmann, who spilled the ball at Frank Lampard's feet. Lampard tapped home the rebound. The fatigued Gunners failed to rally, and with three minutes remaining, Wayne Bridge and Eidur Gudjohnsen played a one-two, to put Bridge clean through on Lehmann. 'It was one of those moments in football when a million thoughts flashed through your mind. From my angle in the East Stand, I could see that as soon as Bridge got the ball, he'd score. And I knew it would change everything. Because there was no way back for Arsenal from being 2–1 down on the night. When he did slot the ball home, their travelling fans at the Clock End all surged down the terrace and went mental. They hadn't beaten us at Highbury for so long, and now, not only had they delivered a painful Champions League lesson to us, they'd also got that monkey off their backs. Ranieri went nuts on the touchline, their fans taunted us with, "You're just a small town in Tottenham", and for all our "Sibneft FC", and "You can stick your Russian money up your arse" chants, you couldn't disguise the significance of that night.'

Patrick Vieira recalls: 'It was almost as if we played too well in the first half, and we had nothing left to give later on. I still believe that over two legs we were better than Chelsea. At times in football, the difference between winning and losing can be down to a tiny piece of luck.'

For the crestfallen Arsenal players, it was time, yet again, to sift through the wreckage of another failed European campaign, and although the Gunners still topped the Premiership, Edu refers to the 'crushing sense of disappointment we all felt'. Critics suggested that Arsenal's season was poised to blow up in their faces, allowing Chelsea or Manchester United to sneak in. The forthcoming Premiership Good Friday clash with Liverpool was about to take on huge significance.

○ THE INVINCIBLES? ○

TO SAY THAT the mood was tense prior to Arsenal's Good Friday meeting with Liverpool would be a massive understatement. Outside the various pubs near Highbury, the talk was still of the Gunners' capitulation against Chelsea in the Champions League. Outside the Auld Triangle, the atmosphere was especially uptight. 'At about midday,' recalls Arsenal fan Marin Winner, 'two mouthy Liverpool fans walked over to us, and asked – in a tone which said that they planned to tell us anyway – if we'd like to hear a good joke. "Why don't Arsenal dartboards sell very well?" one asked the other. "Because they haven't got any doubles or trebles on them," came the reply. Very fucking Stan Boardman. I swear that if a mounted policeman hadn't been nearby, there would have been two less Scousers in the world today. But they'd hit a sore point. Unless we won the game against Liverpool, we would be in serious trouble. We had to get our season back on track.'

During the first half of the match, Arsenal's performance was poor. Goals by Michael Owen and Sami Hyypia put Liverpool 2–1 up at the interval, Arsenal's reply coming courtesy of a supposedly half-fit Thierry Henry. Edu recalls the mood at half-time: 'We had a problem on our hands, no doubt about it. But it was never a case of some players feeling mentally drained. Tired perhaps, but not totally spent. And we re-emerged from the dressing room a different side.' One of Edu's team-mates, who prefers to remain anonymous, recalls: 'Wenger's team talk was very focused. He reminded us that despite our recent setbacks, we still had the chance to win the Premiership title. But in order to do so, we had to sort out the next forty-five minutes. He reinstated our self-belief. We came out convinced that we were the best team in the land. And Thierry Henry emerged in buoyant mood.' The Gunners destroyed Liverpool with a dazzling second-half display, and the Frenchman's second goal – a slaloming run from just inside the opposition half which made the score 2–2 – drew admiring gasps from those watching. Henry later admitted to *Financial Times* journalist Jonathan Wilson that he regarded it as his most important Arsenal goal: 'You could feel that everyone – I could hear people – asking themselves what was going on. You could feel the whole stadium wondering if we were going to blow it right at the end. Then we were back in it . . . ' Manager Arsène Wenger commented: 'That shows just how priceless Thierry is to us. I think that we can go on from here and win the Premiership.' Edu confirms: 'Beating Liverpool 4–2 meant a huge millstone lifted from our necks. All the tension and stress virtually disappeared. We'd rediscovered our focus, and were free to return to the flowing, attacking football which we loved to display.'

Seven days later, Leeds United, whose win twelve months earlier at Highbury had prevented Arsenal from winning the title, were crushed 5–0. Thierry Henry's four-goal haul had team-mates drooling. Edu comments: 'Words are simply not enough to describe Thierry when he is in full flow. He combines all the qualities you'd expect from a highly trained athlete, who also appreciates the aesthetic importance of skilful football. At times during the Leeds match, even his team-mates stopped and watched him with total awe. His last goal, where he tripped, but still managed to score and make it look beautiful, was one of the most amazing sights I've ever seen in football. When Leeds trooped off, I think that a lot of their players made a beeline for Thierry, because even though they were on the brink of relegation, they knew that they'd seen a virtuoso display which almost defied description. It was at that point that Wenger described Thierry as the best player in the world. I find it hard to disagree. And we were still unbeaten.'

On 15 May, after twenty-five Premiership victories and twelve draws, Arsenal took on relegated Leicester City at Highbury knowing that by avoiding defeat, they could rightfully become known as the 'Invincibles', a title first bestowed on Preston North End's title-winning side in 1888–89. No other club in the modern era had achieved such a feat. An anonymous Arsenal player recalls: 'We didn't feel pressure going into the game, but we did feel a huge responsibility. This was our chance to do something which can only ever be equalled, and never beaten. Arsène Wenger is acutely aware of the traditions of the club, and he reminded us that this would be our chance to become – in a footballing sense – immortal. In the first half, we laboured a bit. I think that over the previous few weeks, some of the urgency had gone from our play, and it took time to rediscover that. Paul Dickov shocked us by putting Leicester ahead. That wasn't in the script, but it certainly rattled our cage. At one stage, Dickov could actually have made it 2–0 to Leicester, but then Thierry scored from the spot, and Patrick rolled in our winner with twenty minutes to go. It was a move which befitted the way we'd being playing that season. Dennis Bergkamp found space, somehow, and threaded through a beautiful ball. The last twenty minutes were fantastic, because we finally settled, and I think it dawned on us that we were poised to do something very special indeed. I know that Preston had done it all those years ago, but you can't really compare football in the nineteenth century, with football now. When the whistle went, it was a fantastic feeling. Ours was a record which will be remembered and talked about throughout the world for years to come.'

Amidst the red-and-white ticker-tape celebrations, one knotty issue remained. Would Arsenal players rather have swapped the unbeaten Premiership record for success against Chelsea in the Champions League quarter-final? Press leaks suggested that was indeed the case. Edu explains: 'We're talking hypothetically. What we did in the Premiership in 2003–04 was astonishing. Arsenal players still glow with pride just thinking about the whole Premiership campaign. It is also a fact that in the modern era, players feel the urge to prove themselves on a European stage. Put it this way, if we're talking about emotional reactions, I was as crushed by losing to Chelsea that night as I was elated by remaining undefeated all season. I think people who automatically assume that if we'd have beaten Chelsea, we'd have won the Champions League, are being a bit disrespectful. Who's to say that Porto, who eventually won it and surprised everybody by doing so, wouldn't have beaten us, or Monaco. I can only speak for myself, though. For players who'd won the Premiership title for the first time, they may feel prouder that we remained undefeated in the league, because, as the English say, that is the real bread and butter. It does call into question the whole issue of levels of expectation. In order to ensure that the following season wasn't an anticlimax, we'd have to go through unbeaten again, and target winning the Champions League. Immediately you achieve something in football, the temptation is always to look ahead, and think: How can we improve next year? Sometimes, you should be allowed to bask in what you have achieved.'

Patrick Vieira explains: 'I agree with Edu. It's not a question of *which* achievement we'd have preferred – the unbeaten run or defeating Chelsea – we wanted both. Arsenal is that kind of club. We expect to win every game. It disappointed us to lose the Chelsea match, but for me it can't overshadow the memory of lifting the Premiership trophy in the sun at Highbury. I could feel the enormity of that. And to be captain of an unbeaten team fills me with pride. It always will.'

Arsenal fan Sam Frazer also lapped up the celebrations in the wake of the Leicester City match: 'I loved that afternoon at Highbury after the match. And we'd been so lucky in recent years to see the Premiership trophy paraded around three times. I could wax lyrical about the whole afternoon all day, but instead, I'll give the opposite view. I sensed that behind the smiles, there was a sense of frustration, that although we'd yet again proved ourselves as the best in England, the club hadn't moved on quite as much as the modern breed of Arsenal player would have liked. Highbury – beautiful though it was – was beginning to seem very small, and it was mirrored in what was happening on the pitch. We just couldn't take the step upwards to become a genuine force in Europe. We'd been so spoiled – by the fantastic football and the success – but we still craved more. And at Highbury we clearly weren't getting that. It's embarrassing to talk about whinging when you've stayed unbeaten . . . but in football you have to move on to the next step, which is an indication of how far Wenger has taken us over the last decade. I don't imagine that I'm the only one to think in that way. The players have virtually said it themselves. Tonking Leeds and Leicester is all very well, but when are we going to do the same against European opposition?'

○ CULT HEROES ○

RAY PARLOUR

For much of the 1990s, it was difficult to see Ray Parlour doing much else other than going by the wayside – like several other youth team products of his era. Back in 1992, Mark Flatts, Neil Heaney, Paul Dickov, and Parlour were dubbed by the *Islington Gazette* as the 'next crop of Arsenal starlets who will take the club forward'. Although Dickov has shrugged off his Highbury departure, and gone on to enjoy a good league career, Flatts and Heaney fell off the football map long ago. Ray Parlour's fluctuating form under George Graham led to rumours that he too was doomed to Highbury rejection. Anders Limpar recalls: 'It was clear that Ray was a talented boy, but I think we did wonder whether he could get the consistency in his game to make him a Highbury regular. He could be fantastic in one match, and anonymous in the next. And, of course, he was involved in the drinking scene with Tony Adams, so if he was really going to make a name for himself, he'd need to change his lifestyle dramatically.'

Parlour seemed to be in the newspapers for all the wrong reasons. There was the incident in Hornchurch Pizza Hut, where he and Tony Adams sprayed fellow diners with fire extinguishers; and the fight at Butlins in Bognor Regis, after which Parlour required stitches in his face. Shortly after Bruce Rioch became Arsenal boss, the midfielder was also involved in 'prawn-cracker-gate' where an irate Hong Kong cabbie chased Parlour with a wooden club, after he had thrown a bag of prawn crackers into the bonnet of Lai Pak Yan's taxi. A permanent fixture in *Loaded*'s Platinum Rogues Gallery, his approach to life was in marked contrast with Dennis Bergkamp's monastic lifestyle.

Arsenal fan Paul Miles recalls: 'Ray Parlour's nickname was the "Romford Pele" which is quite clearly a bit of a pisstake. In his early days at Highbury, he was probably the most skilful player we had in midfield, and yet he'd be dropped in favour of guys like Hillier and Jensen, who were steady, I suppose, but not spectacular. Parlour seemed lightweight, to be honest, and not especially committed. He had this really untidy mop of curly blond hair, and visiting fans used to wolf-whistle him every time he received the ball. In his early TV interviews, he used to say "obviously" and "you know" in every sentence. And most of the crowd would have agreed that he went through phases when he didn't seem to be able to pass, tackle or shoot, which is a bit of a drawback if you're a midfielder. I remember the crowd would grumble when he did something wrong. He was lucky, because if he'd been bought for a fee, we'd have thought he was a waste of money, rather than just a waste of space! When Wenger arrived, I honestly don't think anyone believed that Parlour would last longer than a few months at Highbury. Then something amazing happened . . .'

During the 1996–97 close season, Parlour admitted to being a worried man. 'I was convinced that I'd be sold,' he recalls. 'I thought I'd be on my way out, and Paul Merson would take my place. When I heard that Merse had been sold to Middlesbrough, I knew then that I'd been given a second chance. I took a long, hard look at my record, and realised that I hadn't been dedicating myself to the game. It was time to try and follow the example of model players like Dennis Bergkamp and Patrick Vieira. I woke up to the fact that I could be part of something very special at Arsenal.' Throughout the following season, Paul Miles saw a dramatic improvement in Parlour's all-round game. 'I saw him play in those early months, and he looked fitter and leaner. He was making tackles too, which he's never been too good at before. Adams and Dixon said they reckoned Wenger added another five years to their careers, and I wonder where Parlour would have ended up if it hadn't been for Wenger. He even started scoring a few goals. If you compiled a DVD of his goals, it wouldn't be a bad watch, although it might be a bit brief! What I also liked about Parlour was that although he'd improved massively, he was still quintessentially English, at a time when Wenger made it clear that he'd always rather buy more technically gifted continental players. Basically, he was still a little bit crap in certain ways. Like, if you look at Bergkamp's repertoire of skills, and compare them with Parlour's assets, it's a bit embarrassing. As we went into the new century, and more and more of the English players faded from the scene, Parlour came to represent the last bastion of Englishness at Highbury. I found that oddly reassuring, and I noticed that while the crowd had always been a bit nonplussed with him, the reception when his name was called became warmer over the years. We were actually pleased to see him.'

Parlour also gained a reputation off the pitch as a prankster, who was extremely hospitable to the new foreign players. Christopher Wreh recalls: 'On TV, Ray talks quite slowly for the cameras, but otherwise he speaks very fast. He used to enjoy teaching us cockney rhyming slang. He nearly died laughing when, after one game, I came in moaning about my "plates of meat", and a lot of us went around saying that we'd kick so and so up the "bottle and glass". His influence had rubbed off. There was also one time when there was a security alert, and we had to file out of the dressing room. Arsène Wenger had gone to the toilet, and when he came back, he asked us what was going on. Ray piped up: "It's because there is a buurmb" – imitating Inspector Clouseau – and then he fell about laughing, because some of the players referred to Wenger by that name. It dawned on Arsène that Parlour was laughing at him. "I believe you are joking with me, Raymond," came the response. Ray collapsed with laughter.'

Edu recalls how Parlour ' . . . was very friendly and helpful when I joined, and he was keen to take us under his wing to make the transformation easier into English football. You had to be careful with his advice on the English language, though. If you weren't careful you'd end up swearing at important people!' Edu wouldn't confirm whether or not he really told former Manchester United chairman Martin Edwards to 'fuck off you dirty old bastard', or whether it is simply a tabloid myth. Parlour was also referred to in two Irvine Welsh novels – *Filth* and *Glue* – and famously informed Glenn Hoddle's spiritual healer, Eileen Drury, that he'd like a 'short back and sides' when she placed her hands on his head. Edu comments: 'Every side needed a joker in their side, and Ray's sense of humour was excellent to raise spirits. But it's easy to forget what an improved player he was over the years.'

As with many Highbury cult figures, it would be an exaggeration to claim that Parlour won everyone over in his later years at the club. John Booker remained unconvinced: 'I never hated him, and part of my scepticism was that my son John thought the sun shone out of Ray's backside. So it was part of the father-son rivalry thing. But to me, watching Parlour was like going back ten years. Although he got better, his crossing remained poor, and he relied on square passes most of the time. He never had the talent to actually go past players, either, and he was wasteful with the ball. Being brutally frank, if he'd been at Ajax as a youngster, he'd never have made the grade. I also used to have a problem with his goalscoring – his shooting, for the most part, was abysmal. I was never entirely sure what his role was, and if you think about players like Pires, Ljungberg and Reyes, they have an abundance of skills in comparison to Parlour. I'm not even sure if most of the crowd were won over by him. He was the type of player they loved in one way, but loved to hate in another.'

In May 2004, Parlour made an unwelcome return to the front pages of the tabloids, when his former wife, Karen, won an historic landmark case against him in the High Court, and was awarded half of his future earnings as part of their divorce settlement. It coincided with the time when Parlour's midfield position was under threat from the emerging Cesc Fabregas. He moved to Middlesbrough in a £4m deal. Paul Miles explains how the entire episode fits in with his view of Parlour: 'There will always be the suspicion that he moved because he needed the cash to pay his ex-missus. When Middlesbrough came to Highbury at the start of the 2004–05 season, he got a great round of applause, but we also took the piss a bit by shouting: "Does your ex-missus know you're here?" at him. He turned round and gave us a slightly rueful grin. So even though he's not with us any more, there's a kind of old-fashioned, pisstaking relationship between us which is hard to replicate in today's game, when so many players live the life of monks. Ray was probably the last of a dying breed.'

○ FOREIGN LEGION ○

ON 14 FEBRUARY 2005, Arsenal fans were treated to a fantastic display of coruscating attacking football, as the Gunners thrashed

Crystal Palace 5–1. The goals were breathtaking – Bergkamp's slide rule finish from Reyes' pass brought the first goal, before the Spaniard himself blasted home a second. Thierry Henry's sleight of foot helped him bend home a fourth, shortly after his thunderbolt from the edge of the box had increased Palace's misery. As if to sum up the sheer style of the Gunners' display, Patrick Vieira walked in the fifth and final goal, and gave the North Bank an almost embarrassed smile in the process. Edu describes the performance that night as being 'of the highest quality. It was a night when all our attacking instincts paid off, and sent the crowd home in a very good mood'.

The victory closed the gap on second place Manchester United (who'd inflicted upon Arsenal their first home Premiership defeat in eighteen months, a few weeks earlier) to two points – Chelsea were roaring ahead with an eleven-point lead – and restored some much needed confidence. Arsenal's defensive collapse against United during the 4–2 defeat was a far cry from the historic events at the start of the season at Highbury. A dramatic 5–3 win over Middlesbrough saw Wenger's side equal Brian Clough's Forest side in going forty-two league games without defeat, and victory over Blackburn a few days later set a new unbeaten league record. 'It's something which I hope won't be beaten, and will be talked about in years to come,' says Edu. 'To go eighteen months without defeat in what is seen as the toughest domestic league in the world is staggering.' Yet, ever since the Gunners' defeat at Old Trafford in October, their performances had been inconsistent, and allowed Chelsea to surge ahead. Victory over Crystal Palace announced Arsenal's return to form.

Newspapers throughout Europe dedicated more column space to the game than seemed appropriate. Journalists weren't exactly eulogising about the quality of Arsenal's play, either. In *Le Monde*, Arsène Wenger was described as '*une honte*' and in *Die Welt* as '*eine Schande*'. Loosely translated, the Arsenal boss appeared to be 'a disgrace' in every European language. His crime? He'd just selected the first all-continental squad in Premiership history, as Sol Campbell and Ashley Cole were injured. The headlines in France and Germany stemmed from ex-Gunner Paul Merson's comments, which first appeared in the *Daily Mail*, and were quickly taken out of context by an assortment of newspapers around the continent. *Le Monde* excelled itself, suggesting that Merson had also labelled his former manager *'une brome'* ('a joke'). In fact, Merson had described the absence of any British players in Arsenal's squad to face Crystal Palace as 'a joke', rather than directly name-calling Wenger. Edu recalls: 'I can say, in all honesty, that none of us were even aware of the squad containing no British players. The tabloid criticism was ridiculous. Surely football is enough of a global game these days to ensure that people aren't so inward-looking in their thinking?' Patrick Vieira adds: 'Arsène is not interested in people's passports – only their ability. It's a pity that more can't judge others on account purely of what they can do rather than on superficial things.'

Nonetheless, by selecting an all-foreign squad, the Frenchman left himself open to a raft of criticism. Jose Mourinho claimed that 'the backbone of my Chelsea team will always be English', ignoring the fact that only three of his regular starting eleven (Terry, Lampard and Cole) were English, and that a spate of injuries could easily have left him in the same boat as Wenger. Mourinho added: 'He (Wenger) is forgetting the influence which English players have had on Arsenal.' The opposite is true. Wenger is totally *au fait* with the legacy left by English players at Highbury, perhaps overly so.

When he took over as manager eight years ago, Wenger's impressive counselling skills were needed to cajole Tony Adams into extending his playing career, to turn the fitful Ray Parlour into a consistent performer, and to consign tales of Butlins bust-ups and fire extinguisher japes to the past. Despite the defensive heroics of Dixon, Winterburn and Bould, evidence suggests that Wenger fundamentally mistrusts English players – both in terms of attitude and skill levels. The recent signing of Southampton's teenage star Theo Walcott is very much an exception to the rule. Over the last few years, the normally ultra-cautious Frenchman unexpectedly sung the praises of two of his young English talents. He probably regrets it now. Francis Jeffers' arrival was designed – in Wenger's words – to provide 'a perfect complement to Thierry Henry's skills'. The £7m 'fox in the box' proved an enormous let-down. Admittedly, injuries hampered him, but Arsenal's continental stars were none too impressed with Jeffers' often laid back approach. Wenger was furious when he received news that Jeffers had celebrated his move to Highbury by getting paralytic in a nightclub.

And what of Jermaine Pennant – once described by Wenger as 'the boy wonder'? Pennant's drink-driving conviction last year brought a premature end to a once promising Highbury career, which was punctuated by rumours of his suspect attitude. Since his move to Birmingham City, Pennant has hardly proved that Wenger was wrong to let him leave. Neither has Blues' central defender Matthew Upson, whose transfer to the Midlands triggered criticism of Wenger in 2003.

It is ironic that the *Mail's* story revolved around Merson's comments. Wenger's exasperated predecessor Bruce Rioch referred to the 'baggage' carried by Merson as he underwent rehabilitation for gambling and drug addictions in the mid-nineties. In the first major decision of his managerial career at Highbury, Wenger symbolically opted to select the abstemious Dennis Bergkamp ahead of the Englishman who had spent the majority of his Highbury career squandering his talent. This is not to say that continental stars haven't caused him headaches – Nicolas Anelka springs to mind – but as Wenger once said: 'Foreign players seem to have good lifestyle habits inborn. English players have to be taught. I don't really know why.' While the *Mail's* back pages were full of stories flagging up fears about the numbers of foreigners in the Premiership, the front page headline read: OUR NHS, NOT THE WORLD HEALTH SERVICE! lending the *Mail's* support to Michael Howard's pledge to reclaim the NHS from 'health tourists'. The similarity between the two lead stories was, of course, purely coincidental.

A host of former Arsenal stars read the *Daily Mail* story with interest. Anders Limpar comments: 'When Arsenal won the league in 1991, they did so with ten Englishmen in the side on a regular basis, and one Swede, who happened to be me. I recall that the *Sun* labelled the side "Best of British", or something like that. In an age when EU citizens are free to work in other EU states, and travel opportunities are so much more widely available in the world, I find it incredible that these stories have any kind of mileage in them. I don't know whether it goes back to the old "island race" mentality, or whether it's down to genuine fears that English players are being stifled at the youth team level. Some have suggested that continental players don't have the same "Arsenal mentality" as English players. I don't agree. Continental players bring different qualities to the game. Arsenal have done well

over the last few years due to the guile of Bergkamp, and the elegance
of the French players. They have contributed in their own unique ways.
When I first arrived at the club in 1990, it still very much revolved
around the "caged tiger" approach of Tony Adams. Andy Linighan used
to do a Winston Churchill-type impression when he said of opposition
attackers: "They shall never, ever, pass the Arse." The legendary defence
had all the qualities which you'd expect from English players – grit,
determination, and a never-say-die spirit.

'To suggest that foreign players don't care about the club is hugely
disrespectful. Did Patrick Vieira not care about Arsenal? Just ask Roy
Keane. Does Thierry Henry not care? Arsenal fans who've supported
the club way beyond the last ten years will be aware that for long
periods in the eighties, the Arsenal side was full of British players who
did not achieve as much as they could have done for the club. It was
the same in the mid-nineties. It doesn't matter whether or not you are
English or Cameroonian. If you play for Arsenal, the Arsenal spirit lives
and breathes within you. I think that Arsenal fans are aware that continental players like Bergkamp have raised the level of professionalism
at the club to a new level. If the current side drank like some of the
team I played alongside, then they would struggle to finish outside the
relegation zone. Times have changed. I think that fans are more savvy
than many tabloid writers are. It is *they* who have not moved with the
times.'

Arsenal fan Rob Knight explains: 'At some clubs, it might have
mattered that the squad for the Palace game was "all foreign". Arsenal
are bigger than that. We've moved beyond all that kind of shit, and it's
why we're so successful. Arsenal players, fans, and directors are there
to win things, not to act like petty little Englanders. When I started
going to Arsenal, I loved players like Rocastle, Adams and Thomas. But
I didn't love them because they were English. I loved them because
they were great players. Nowadays, I love Henry and Bergkamp equally,
because they're performing miracles for my team. And the fact is that
English players, in general, aren't skilful enough for the Arsenal side
that we watch these days. And because there are so few quality English
players on the scene, the price for them is astronomical. It's like when
we were quoted eighteen million quid to buy Jermaine Jenas from
Newcastle. Ridiculous money. Of course, there might be some latent

whinging from older fans who are perhaps more set in their ways, but Arsenal has always been a cosmopolitan club, and, hopefully, always will be. We can leave the *Daily Mail* type ranting to others.'

○ WAKING UP THE LIBRARY ○

ASIDE FROM 'Champions League – you're having a laugh!' the most cutting chant to be aired at Highbury in recent seasons has been the 'Shall we sing a song for you'? ditty, delivered with unerring accuracy by swathes of visiting supporters. Even more unpalatable has been the prolonged 'Shhhhhh,' which more vocal North Bankers utter, in an attempt to embarrass their fellow Arsenal fans into singing up. Since the advent of all-seater stadiums, most matchdays have been noticeably quieter. The crowd is vocal during high-profile games against Tottenham and Manchester United, and recently, Arsenal fans have proved that their sense of humour has not deserted them. Ever since Thierry Henry was dubbed the 'best player in the world' by Gunners supporters, the error-prone Cygan has also been granted the, 'We've got the worst player in the world, Cygan' chant. Oleg Luzhny, who later became accepted by Arsenal fans after a decidedly shaky start, had the, 'We've got Luzhny, from Ukraine' song, a deliberate aping of the, 'We got Campbell from the Lane' chant.

'It's evidence that there are vocal supporters inside Highbury,' explains Arsenal fan Damien Hatton. 'The piss-taking of defenders like Luzhny and Cygan is a healthy throwback to my favourite chant of the eighties: "When Gus goes up, to lift the World Cup, we'll be there", and it proves that we haven't all completely disappeared up our own arses during the last few years. But not for nothing is Highbury known as "The Library". The worst thing that you see at the ground these days is when guys on the North Bank stand up, wave their arms in disgust and frustration at the fans around them for being so quiet, and implore them to sing up. And then when nobody joins in, they get even more hot under the collar. I hate the silences at Highbury. Football is about being loud and unpleasant. It was never meant to be a genteel weekend pastime. But that is how it's going. And too few people can be arsed to do anything about it.'

The reasons for Highbury's relative quietness are not necessarily unique to Arsenal. Football in general has seen ticket prices rocket skywards in recent years, which has resulted in the loss of the original local and often working-class fans going to matches. The all-seater era has attracted a new breed of fan, one which expects creature comforts, and is, therefore, less likely to sing. Arsenal fan Brian Dawes, who's been going to games since the 1950s, also claims that historically: ' . . . Arsenal fans have never been the most vocal. They can raise themselves on the big occasion, but if you compare the noise on North London derby day with the racket at a Sunderland v Newcastle match we are a very poor second. I don't know whether it's a class issue, or a London "attitude", but Arsenal fans, by and large, are a restrained lot. What we've seen since Highbury went all-seater is that many Arsenal fans go to the stadium with an attitude similar to that of theatregoers. Instead of contributing to the atmosphere themselves, they sit passively, waiting to be entertained. Football matches should be an interactive event.'

Damien Hatton – frustrated at the consequences of the all-seater era – explains: 'Not everything has disappeared song-wise at games. The crowd still sing the players' names, and they in turn usually respond with a clap back. But I feel that with players' earnings skyrocketing, a gap has developed into a "them and us" situation. When I started going in the late eighties, the players and fans would interact far more. We used to ask each player to "do the twist", starting with John Lukic. You'd shout, "Johnny, Johnny do the twist," and immediately Lukic would wiggle his bum. Then you'd move on to Lee Dixon, and so on. Or if you were winning, you'd shout "Lukic, Lukic, what's the score?" and he'd put his fingers up behind his back and tell you. These days, that has stopped, although if we're showboating a bit, we can still ask so and so to "give us a wave". But to some extent, the individuality has gone. And I don't see it coming back.

'Another gripe I have is with the family-orientated pre-match entertainment: Gunnersaurus; kids parading around the pitch; crappy requests on the PA system. Music blaring out so loud that you couldn't even hear yourself chant if you wanted to. It seems to be catering for the day trippers, and families who come to Highbury only occasionally. I'm sure that when I have kids of my own I'll mellow slightly, but I almost feel that single blokes like myself who want a good drink and a good shout-up at games are an optional extra, and it wouldn't bother the club if we were priced out entirely from the ground.

'I sometimes sit there and look around at the crowd, and I'm often reminded of being in a branch of IKEA. There's an assortment of families, who don't particularly look like they're thrilled to be at Highbury, and a few blokes dotted around, who seem uneasy swearing and singing in the company of women and children. It doesn't exactly make for a rocking atmosphere. Someone has suggested that it's another example of how men are unsure of their position in society these days. If you can't go to football and swear and be offensive, just where can you behave badly these days? I sometimes call the new breed of football fan the Hornby generation. *Fever Pitch* – that's the film and the book – suddenly made football seem accessible to a middle-class clientele at a time when all-seater stadiums were being built. It's amazing how much the social make-up of Highbury has changed. Yet, I also know that football grounds had to be made safer, and this is a natural consequence of that process.'

In 2003, REDaction was formed in an attempt to liven up 'The Library'. A representative of the group explains: 'A statistic which isn't much talked about is that the average age of an Arsenal fan is increasing by one year, every year. This is due to increased demand for tickets, and the low amount in supply. The club can then drive up prices, meaning that many young fans, who may be more inclined to sing, don't go to matches. The other issue is that since terracing was phased out, there's been far more fragmentation of fans. Basically, it's impossible to sit with any more than a few of your friends, and this leads to a flat, dull atmosphere. We formed REDaction with the intention of bringing more fun and action to matchdays, with an added touch of eccentricity to enliven Highbury. Far too many self-conscious chappies and chappesses go to games these days. We've made several moves to improve the atmosphere on matchdays. After hassling the club for a while, we pieced together a seven-minute video montage of clips from Arsenal's most famous games, and this is played before home matches. We also managed to set up hand-held red and white card displays before home games, and against Manchester United in February 2005 it was a fabulous sight. And we're also planning several ideas for a Dennis Bergkamp day later in the season.'

Arguably the most important REDaction contribution has been the creation of the REDsection for Carling Cup matches. Ian Palmer explains: 'REDaction deserve huge credit for the singing areas. Many of the "new breed" of Arsenal fans deem Carling Cup games unworthy of their attention, so you get younger fans in, who can't ordinarily attend the Fort Knox that is Highbury. The atmosphere is much better, and it also helps having the Clock End full of away fans. You need a good, noisy away following. It helps to crank up the atmosphere. It's no surprise that in recent years, the FA Cup matches against Chelsea and Stoke were really noisy, because you also had six thousand away fans prepared to sing their hearts out. We're hopefully moving back towards a model of being able to sit next to like-minded people. If the club extend the REDsection into the new stadium, singers can sit next to other singers, and not feel embarrassed about using language that could offend families. It's frustrating for the vocal fans, because you know that you're watching the best football ever played here, and we should be lapping up every last minute, especially as our time at Highbury is nearly up. At times, you feel a bit like King Canute. It's impossible to hold back this tide of indifference displayed by those around you, but you have to keep trying.'

○ WITHOUT PREJUDICE? (2) ○

IN NOVEMBER 2005, Alan Sefton – 'Arsenal in the community' overseer – announced that the club would be setting up five soccer schools across Israel. The soccer school scheme will tie in with those already established in Soweto and the Ukraine. Sefton explained: 'We feel we can do a lot of good using that opportunity in these places, by bringing people together. We hope to do likewise in the Arab-Jewish world.' Arsenal are already involved in working with a number of primary schools in mixed Jewish-Muslim areas, and children are encouraged to co-present religious festivals before playing football together. Sefton later confirmed his, and the club's, belief that ' . . . football unites people of different classes, social groups, races and nationalities . . . we don't want it to focus on divisions and tribalism.'

Sefton played down the claim that Arsenal had launched the initiative because both he, and several Arsenal directors including David Dein and Daniel Fiszman are Jewish. Instead, he argued that it was due to Arsenal's wish that 'different races and cultures should mix together freely'. With Thierry Henry a charismatic front man for the 'Let's Kick Racism Out Of Football' movement, the Gunners are arguably the most forward thinking of all clubs in the battle to fight racial intolerance. Collins Campbell, whom I interviewed in a previous chapter, explains: 'It's staggering to think that when Brendan Batson became the first black player to make his debut for Arsenal, there were reports that some Arsenal fans had walked out in disgust. Fans and players know full well that if they use racist language nowadays, there will be serious repercussions. I've not heard any fans around me at Highbury use racist language since . . . it must be the early eighties.'

Yet despite the club's programme in Israel, and the explicit warnings in and around Highbury that 'racist and foul language will not be tolerated', vast numbers of Arsenal fans continue to use the word 'yid' freely in chants during games. These range from 'yiddo', in connection with anything to do with Tottenham, to the oft-heard ditty which contains the line about 'running round Tottenham with our willies hanging out'. Brendan Batson comments: 'The "Y" word is commonly used among London football fans. That's not to say that it's right, though. Derogatory words used in connection with the colour of someone's skin are considered more inflammatory than words to do with someone's nationality or religion. For instance, if Luis Aragones had described Thierry Henry as a "French shit" rather than a "black shit" last year, there wouldn't have been the type of outcry there was. It's just the way it is.'

Dave Carmen recalls an incident outside the Gaslight pub, near Finsbury Park station, which occurred late in 2005: 'I was standing with three of my mates, one of whom happens to be black. He was rabbiting on about Thierry Henry at the time, and was explaining to us how he was a great example to black people in sport. Suddenly, he spotted a Jewish man walking along the other side of the road, and started shouting "Yiddo, Yiddo" at him. What shocked me was that so many others were willing to join in, including more black guys. I had a right go at him. I told him that using the word "Yiddo" is no better than someone using the word "nigger". He laughed in my face, and told me to "chill out". Using a word which refers to someone's religion, he reckoned, was nowhere near the same deal as derogatory terms which describe someone's skin colour. I asked him if he planned to shout anything at a Muslim guy who'd just walked by. "Not if he's got a backpack on," came the response, "he might explode." When he saw that I didn't find that comment especially funny, he explained that he used the word "Yiddo" because all Spurs fans are Jewish – due to the club's proximity to Stamford Hill. I left the conversation there, but it revealed to me that double standards are rife. I've been in an Arsenal pub, when fans – several of whom were black – have been chanting: "I'd rather be a Paki than a Turk." "It's just a bit of fun mate," they claim. Perhaps some Arsenal fans still aren't quite as enlightened as they'd like to think.'

Arsenal fan Max Hyndes explains the origins of the word 'yid' in London football: 'I've been going to watch Arsenal since the 1950s, and Arsenal fans – in huge numbers – have always used the word "yid". Make no mistake, it started out as an insult to the large contingent of Jewish fans who supposedly went to watch Tottenham. It was also part of a reaction to the large numbers of Jews who came to this country after the Second World War. I've always laughed inwardly at this ridiculous belief Arsenal fans have that Spurs are "the Jewish club". There are thousands of Arsenal fans who happen to be Jewish, me being one of them. I don't care what anyone says. The word "yid" is a derogatory term. You're deliberately drawing attention to the fact that someone either looks different, behaves differently, or follows a different religious orientation to yourself. That, to my knowledge, is a form of prejudice. The chanting at Highbury used to be far more unpleasant than it is now. Up until the late seventies, you'd get songs about "gassing the yids", "Spurs are on their way to Auschwitz", and a hissing noise from thousands of fans to imitate the effect of gas being slowly released. Is laughing about "gassing the yids" as offensive as calling someone a "nigger"? Well, no one's ever insulted me on account of the colour of my skin, but as a Jewish man, I certainly find the word "yid" offensive. And most Saturdays at Highbury, I'd say that over half the North Bank are happy to chant the word "yiddo" in unison.

'It's almost acceptable behaviour in many ways. In the seventies and eighties, Spurs fans began to adopt the word "yid" en masse as a code of honour, and – so the explanation goes – to defend their Jewish fans from Arsenal fans' chanting. When Arsenal played Spurs last season at Highbury, I heard Tottenham fans in the Clock End shouting: "One yid and his baseball cap went to war with Arsenal." It's used in everyday parlance. Another thing that astonished me was that when I went on the Internet the other day to do some research, Wikipedia states that the use of the word "yid" is inoffensive when used by Tottenham fans. I don't know where they get that view from. I've actually pulled a couple of young lads on their use of it at Highbury. They claimed it was just their word to describe Tottenham fans, and that they'd never been taught about the origins of the word. I fail to see how that can be true. All children learn about the Holocaust in history lessons at school. Surely their history teachers tell them that the word "yid" is an offensive term. Ashkenazi Jews use the phrase "yidn" as a way of saying mate or buddy to a fellow Jew. But if outsiders use the term, it's frankly a piss-take. It's not right. Some of my mates have spoken to stewards about it, and been told that "yid" is not a racist word, therefore it isn't offensive. "Everyone says it," argued one steward, "so how can it be offensive?" Well I used to go in the sixties when words like "nigger" and "coon" were bandied about freely, but we've moved on since then, so maybe we need to do a little more to educate Arsenal fans on this subject. People who read this bit of the book will probably be thinking I'm a politically correct bore, but I don't think that's the case. If we live in a multicultural society, then this issue needs to be addressed.'

The club's official stance on the use of the word by its own supporters is unclear. Two letters directed to the club went unanswered, although a telephone operator claimed that the widespread use of the word 'yid' by supporters was the 'last bastion of cultural ignorance among Arsenal fans'.

○ MIXED EMOTIONS ○

AS THE COUNTDOWN to Arsenal's final game at Highbury intensifies, it's become impossible to avoid the feeling that fans and players are regarding the 2005–06 season as a transition year. 'If you've only really followed Arsenal since Arsène Wenger took over,' explains Brian Dawes, 'this is the worst season of your entire Arsenal supporting life. However if, like me, you've followed Arsenal for nearly fifty years, this is actually a reasonable season. We've just been very spoilt over the last decade. It's a shame that we've had a bit of a reality check in our final season at Highbury, but that's sometimes the way in which things work out.'

Before the season began, Arsène Wenger spoke optimistically about his belief that Arsenal could challenge for the title. However, the sale of Patrick Vieira to Juventus, and the failure to replace him left a gaping hole in Arsenal's midfield. Chelsea's phenomenal spending power meant that Wenger failed to strengthen the squad significantly during the summer. These two factors have combined to destroy Wenger's dream of lifting the Premiership crown in this historic season. The crunch Highbury games of the last few years have temporarily lost their sting. After a good start against Chelsea, with Van Persie's goal ruled out, and Henry hitting the post, the Blues won 2–0. Despite not playing particularly impressively, Chelsea easily held

Arsenal at bay in the second half, and the Gunners' fans defiant 'You can stick your Russian money up your arse' chants, took on a mournful quality by the end of the match. The annual 'fight club' with United – such a combustible contest in recent times – also fizzled out in a tame 0–0 draw. Patrick Vieira comments: 'The games have tended to revolve around personality. Maybe without Roy Keane and myself at our respective clubs, things will settle down.'

There have been bright spots. Arsenal's 7–0 trouncing of Middlesbrough in January 2006, equalled the club's Premiership record set nine months earlier against Everton. The scorelines apart, there were notable similarities between the games. As the crowd sang 'One more year' at Dennis Bergkamp during the destruction of the Toffees, there were also similar pleas made to Thierry Henry during the 'Boro match. A current member of Arsenal's squad, who played in both games reveals: 'The crowd was very emotional during the Everton game, because there were lots of rumours that it would be Bergkamp's last match for the club, and he played the best game I'd seen from any player in a long time. He had a hand in five of the goals, and scored one himself, of course. It was the same against Middlesbrough. Understandably, the crowd has been very anxious that Thierry should stay, and in that match, he put on a dazzling show. Everyone at the club will be delighted if he stays in the long term. Our performances at Highbury during the 2005–06 season have generally been very good. But the edge has been taken off because we're not in a position to challenge Chelsea.'

Gunners players, often asked to air their opinions on Arsenal leaving Highbury, appear slightly distracted, with their minds very much on the new home. The player quoted above reveals: 'There have been difficult moments during this season, because we haven't really done ourselves justice in the league, and the Arsenal fans wanted so badly to finish at Highbury on a positive note. Then, in the back of your mind, is the thought of playing at this wonderful new stadium, and the hope that the club will enjoy great times there. It's been an odd season.'

During a recent conversation with *Financial Times* journalist Jonathan Wilson, Thierry Henry said: 'It's difficult to describe why you like it (Highbury). It's the whole thing, from when you arrive with the coach and see all the people before the game waiting for us. Or, when I arrive in the morning, meeting the team to see the pitch when there's nobody there. I don't know, the whole feeling, leading up to the kick-off. Maybe it's because I've played six years at Arsenal: there's something special. I feel the same at Anfield – when you go there you feel the history. I know Man Utd have a bigger stadium, but sometimes it's not a matter of seats. I'm sure Southampton fans still wish they were at the Dell, even though more people can go to watch them at St Mary's. It's a feeling you can't describe. There is something about Highbury . . . for me it's not even a comparison. I've played at Stade de France, but for me it will always be Highbury. A story is going to end right here. People are always going to talk about Highbury and maybe wish they were still here. The history of Highbury spanned ninety-three years. Therefore you're going to miss the ground.' Patrick Vieira agrees: 'The unique characteristics of Highbury, the history and tradition you feel . . . I used to enjoy the aura of Highbury as much in my later years at Arsenal as I did when I arrived from Milan. It will be a terribly sad day.'

If players are occasionally struggling to keep their thoughts in check, many Gunners fans are going through the same experience. Arsenal supporter Ian Robshaw explains: 'I think that because Arsenal haven't been playing as well as they should be, it's actually acted as a bit of a reality test for us. If we'd done really well this year, there would have been a voice in the back of my mind saying, "Well, we don't actually have to move after all. We're doing fine where we are." But it's fairly clear that for the long-term future of the club, we have to go, because things have slipped a bit this year. And whether we like it or not, money talks in the modern game. We have to generate more revenue. For me, the season didn't feel right from the beginning. The boys shouldn't be playing in blackcurrant. Red and white is our colour. We can't even call out "Come on you reds" this season! I've tried to make the most of the last few months, and lap up every tasty moment. I've tried to soak up what Highbury looks like in the beautiful sunshine, what it's like for night games, and what it's like on those autumnal days when the light starts to change. You can also see trees and nearby flats from inside the ground, and you start to appreciate that really, Highbury is quaint, compact, and unique. But from where I sit in the North Bank, I can also see the cranes, and the enticing prospect of what's across the road. It concerns me that we'll lose some aspects of what makes us Arsenal. The sheer compactness of the stadium, the pitch, the fact that it isn't a sprawling bowl. Are Arsenal all about multi-million-pound sponsorship deals, and state-of-the-art stadiums? I worry that we'll lose our soul. But then, Highbury hasn't always been home to Arsenal, and it's the future of the club which must thrive.'

Patrick Vieira adds: 'For the club, it is important the soul and heart doesn't stay at Highbury. It has to go to the new ground because the club must survive. In terms of capacity, the Emriates Stadium will be a bigger stage for Arsenal – but only in the sense that it has a bigger capacity. I hope that the club doesn't lose the extra something by moving from Highbury. People love the old, unusual things about Highbury. Is it possible to love something which is brand, sparkling new? Only time will tell.'

Questions remain over whether the move will pay dividends, and how it's already affecting the size of Arsène Wenger's transfer 'war chest'. Football consultant Alex Fynn explains: 'Football clubs' revenue is derived from three streams. First, there's the money which comes in from matchday. This includes gate money, season tickets, corporate hospitality, programmes, and catering. Second, there is the commercial side of things, which includes advertising, merchandising and sponsorship. Third, there's media money, especially from television. In essence, Arsenal are spending huge sums of money in order to increase – primarily – just one of those revenue streams. Less than a third of their revenue comes from matchday income. As I've mentioned before, a more far-sighted redevelopment of the Clock End back in the eighties, or the possible addition of another deck to the North Bank Stand would have resulted in more revenue coming into the club over the last few years. That would have meant that the club wouldn't have had to have taken such a quantum leap with the new stadium. The fact remains that throughout Arsenal's protracted move to Ashburton Grove, Arsène Wenger's freedom to move in the transfer market has been adversely affected, which has reflected on how the team performs.'

Ian Robshaw adds: 'When Arsenal planned the move to Ashburton

Grove, it seemed that by doing so, we'd be ahead of the rest of the pack, and in terms of financial muscle, get ahead of Manchester United. But with Abramovich's arrival at Chelsea, and United again extending Old Trafford to seventy-two thousand, we seem to be just about keeping up with the Jones' to be honest. Even with extra revenue coming in, we're still not really in a position to outbid Chelsea for anyone, and no one really knows whether the mortgage on the new stadium will still hinder Arsenal in the transfer market, or for how long. What we have on our side is history and tradition. We've always been a big club, but, although I want Arsenal to become a European giant, I hope that by moving from Highbury doesn't mean that we lose everything we hold dear.'

◦ EMBRACING EUROPE ◦

WITH ARSENAL'S LEAGUE form spluttering, and the prospect of no Champions League football beckoning for the first time in almost a decade, the team's European games began to assume added significance, as it appeared that only by winning the trophy would the Gunners actually compete in the 2006–07 tournament. The likelihood of any degree of success appeared a long way off when Arsenal were drawn against Real Madrid in the last sixteen. The *galacticos* may have been a little jaded, but the Gunners, mired in sixth place in the Premiership, were hardly in a healthy position either.

Shortly before he left, Patrick Vieira recalled a conversation between – as he put it – 'senior members of the team' to discuss Arsenal's consistent failure to make strides in the Champions League. 'A number of us talked about the reasons why we hadn't really done it in Europe. I never thought it was a case of the team simply panicking or not being good enough. I believed the issues were more subtle than that. In the Premiership, teams play at a quick pace, and even if a side is packed with foreign players, they play in the English way – fast, up tempo, with little time for thought, the emphasis on attack. Arsenal had some very intelligent players, but it was always very hard for us to snap out of 'Premiership mode' and adapt our style to the more possession-based Champions League. We just couldn't do it. There was also the issue of luck. You have to enjoy a degree of this to succeed in Europe. The players were very aware that this was the last season at Highbury, and we took responsibility for the fact that we'd never given the fans a European run they'd always look back on. The players were determined that before leaving Highbury, they would do something in Europe to be proud of.'

Arsenal cruised through their qualifying group, and led by a single goal after the first leg of the knockout-stage match against Real Madrid. But, even despite Thierry Henry's winner in the Bernabeu, critics still believed that the Spanish giants would make a strong comeback in the return leg. Robert Pires recalled: 'It was an extra motivation – the fact that many football writers continued to doubt us. It showed the extent to which we'd underachieved in the Champions League over the years. In many ways, it was an ideal time to play Real. Their playing style meant that we would be able to attack them on the counter, and the fact that they were 1–0 down meant that they had to come at us. They were not as powerful as they'd once been, but they still had some formidable players. We were able to play a much more passing-based game, and when we could, we launched counterattacks against them. As Patrick said, you need some luck in Europe, and we got ours at Highbury when Jens Lehmann saved from Raul, and then Raul hit the post with the goal at his mercy. It was a hugely important result for us, the 0–0 draw at Highbury, because we showed that we could hang on against one of Europe's best sides. From the celebrations at the final whistle, you could tell that we were in a place where few of us had been before in European competition. We'd beaten Juventus in 2001, but never done this to a giant over two legs. And we'd achieved it at Highbury too. We were delighted, of course. But we didn't get carried away. After all, we were only through to the quarter finals.'

Arsenal had reached the stage from which no Gunners side had ever progressed before, and drawing Juventus meant the return of Patrick Vieira. He recollects: 'In many ways, it was very pleasing to be going back to Highbury and seeing my old team-mates and the fans again. There was obviously an awful lot written about that in the media. I tried to ignore the hype. You have to put aside sentiment on these occasions, but I knew the type of stuff that was being written – that Arsenal were wrong to let me go, that they hadn't replaced me, that players who leave Arsenal rarely do well elsewhere, and that Arsène made his biggest error when he released me. As a footballer approaching thirty, I knew that at some point I'd be sold, and I rarely look back. As for the rest, I leave it for others to judge. The result suggests that in the football world, things simply move on!'

The tabloid hype naturally focussed on Vieira's return, and Arsenal fans looked forward to another epic clash with an Italian giant, in the tradition of past encounters with Juve, Sampdoria, and Lazio. Arsenal wore down Juve by playing their fast tempo passing game. It was one of *the* great Highbury occasions. Robert Pires recalls: 'Juventus were an excellent side. Several of their players were unfairly described as being lumbering by the media, and obviously, the match-fixing scandal took the shine off the fact that they eased their way to the Serie A title. But on that night, we never allowed them a second on the ball. We were able to impose an English style of play on them, and it's almost unheard of for anyone to do that to Juventus. I felt that we were in control throughout, Cesc Fabregas's goal reflected his growing ability, and Thierry's simply reflected his stature in Europe. It was a wonderful night, and we thoroughly deserved to win 2–0.'

Neither player opted to comment on Pires's early tackle on Vieira, which set up Cesc Fabregas's strike, but the symbolism was clear; it simply wasn't to be Vieira's or Juve's night. Arsenal fan John Lowry recalls: 'It was lovely to sit behind the North Bank goal, and just enjoy the fact that Arsenal were demolishing Juventus. The match was largely about Vieira, let's be honest about that. I felt we'd made a huge mistake by letting him go, and when we went to places like Blackburn and Bolton, and got out-muscled in the middle of the pitch, it was clear that he'd not been replaced. I knew all the stuff about how players who left us didn't do so well after they went – like Petit and Overmars – but this felt a bit different. Pires's tackle on Vieira made me feel better, because Pires never bloody tackled anyone, and when he caught Vieira like that, Vieira started to look slow and a bit cumbersome. And then you realised why we'd let him go in the first place. I felt the fans moved on that night, which is important. No player is bigger than the club, but when your big stars go, it occasionally feels like it. The songs then started up at the end: "He played for Arsenal, he's gonna win fuck all", and all that stuff. Very cruel perhaps, but a sign that we'd finally come to terms with it. Mind you, I still reckon we'd be better with him in our side!'

It was ironic that the final European game at Highbury was the one which saw Arsenal take one giant step towards the Champions League Final. Ironic, because the principal reason for leaving Highbury was to ensure that such occasions became a regular event. Having clung on for a 0–0 draw in Turin, Arsenal's semi-final clash with Spanish club Villareal was a tense affair, and in keeping with the rest of the season, the players' attentions were divided. An Arsenal star who played in the home leg recalls: 'Obviously, we needed to focus on the task of reaching the Final. But we all knew that in terms of European football at Highbury – we'd almost reached the end. The crowd was frenetic, but at times, strangely subdued. We never underestimated Villareal, and Kolo's goal meant we won 1–0. It would have been nice to have signed off with a little more style, because it was a very hard game in which to play, so it couldn't have been easy on the eye. Arsenal fans have told me that that's been the way of things though. The hard graft is done at home, and then the real glory nights tend to be away from home.'

○ THE TICKING CLOCK ○

THE CLOCK, in every sense it seemed, had almost completely wound down. With just two games left at Highbury – one of which was against Spurs – Arsenal were running out of time to close the gap on their North London rivals. The media seemed convinced that Thierry Henry was Barca bound, and those unfortunate enough not to receive tickets for the final Highbury clashes frantically scrabbled around in hope.

Arsenal fan Ian Mitchell recalls: 'In those final few weeks of last season, I had to examine pretty closely what it meant to be an Arsenal fan. I was lucky enough to receive a ticket for the Champions League Final through a contact, but then, having missed just one home game all season, I didn't receive tickets for the Spurs or Wigan matches. I looked at all the dodgy ticket-tout websites, and was quoted prices of £600 at the very least. The prices seemed to rise by £100 each day. And even if you pay your money, those type of people operate on what they expect to receive. There's no guarantee that you'll get one in the end. So I opted for the ultimate trade-off. I decided that, having been going to Highbury for twenty years, I couldn't miss out. So I put my Champions League ticket up for sale, in return for Spurs and Wigan tickets, plus I'd pay a bit extra into the bargain. It was the last throw of the dice. But to my surprise, two or three people got back to me right away. The fella I swapped with eventually told me that he'd only been going to Highbury for a couple of seasons, and that the move didn't mean as much to him as it did for me, which I can understand. I gambled on the fact that Arsenal might eventually get to a Champions League final again. There was no way I could miss out on the last matches at Highbury.'

With the team bracing itself for the final Highbury North London derby, touts like Catweazle prepared for their last big paydays. Having decided that migrating to Stamford Bridge would be more profitable and straightforward in the ticketless era of Arsenal playing at the larger Emirates Stadium, Catweazle was in a sombre, and (thankfully) calmer mood when I met him for the final time. Nonetheless, he also looked forward to one final Highbury payoff: 'On the one hand, there aren't many tickets available,' he told me. 'But those that are floating around are like golddust. Fans are paying about £600 a ticket for the Spurs game, and around double that for the Wigan match. Touts are making a fortune, but we know the game's nearly up at Highbury. Believe it or not, we'll miss the camaraderie of it all. Some of the other lads will move on, or just retire. I'll be working outside Chelsea's ground from now on, but it won't be the same as being at Highbury. I'll miss the buzz of it all.'

Supporters viewed the Spurs game with a sense of trepidation not felt for several years: 'To tell the truth,' recalls Arsenal fan Paul Hanley, 'I was absolutely shitting myself on the way to that match. Everyone had read the newspapers that morning which said that Henry was leaving. It felt like the wheels were coming off a bit. With Cole likely to go to Chelsea, Pires and Bergkamp going too, and now our best player liable to go, it was all a bit depressing really. There was the feeling that if Spurs got out of Highbury unbeaten then we'd had it, in terms of getting into the Champions League. We'd picked up the pace against Charlton and Villa. The European run had clearly given us our confidence back. We were looking like our old selves and we were running into some good form, but Spurs matched everything we did. For me, us leaving Highbury was getting in the way of business. The club did loads for the countdown, and I thought quite a lot of it was gimmicky and a waste of time. Things like the old wooden scoreboards and the parades of old players got a bit monotonous, really – although I admired REDaction for setting up the Dennis Bergkamp day against West Brom, which was fully deserved by the great man. But it felt like we were moving home, we'd packed the boxes, and we were now just hanging around. I never really wanted to leave Highbury at all, but now I was actually ready to move on. I felt that the whole season – I guess inevitably – was going down the tubes because of the move which was hanging over us. And being honest, it wasn't going to be much of a send-off if we couldn't finish above Spurs, was it?'

Robert Pires remembers: 'We wanted to win for every conceivable reason, but we were very tense that day, and so was the crowd. Spurs were a good side, and they harried us, just as we harried Juventus a few weeks before. Michael Carrick missed a great opportunity, and Robbie Keane's goal seemed to have won it for them. We were delighted when Thierry came off the bench and scored a fantastic equaliser, but all the players heard the Spurs fans singing about getting into the Champions League at the end of the game. 1–1 wasn't good enough for us. From their faces, you could tell their players also felt they were nearly there, too. None of us felt too good afterwards, and it was shame, because we wouldn't be playing Spurs here again.'

Ian Mitchell, having finally received his ticket for the Spurs game, was disappointed with the result. 'I don't think that too many Arsenal fans left Highbury thinking that St Totteringham's day wouldn't be cancelled that year,' he says. 'I thought we'd blown it. What was particularly galling was the Spurs fans songs. "We only speak English" was one amusing little one, then there were the chants of "England, England". You thought: "Is that all they can muster?" but I had to accept that they deserved their point, and maybe even should have won. After the game, I went to the pub with my Spurs-supporting mate, and I sort of ended up having to look at the historical perspective of it all. He told me that as we'd arrived at Highbury having pissed off Spurs and their fans, it was karmic payback that we leave with our tails between our legs. The "interlopers", as he called us, would always have to live with the memory that Spurs would make our last game at Highbury memorable for the wrong reasons, and that Henry would be leaving shortly afterwards too. The ghosts of those long since deceased Spurs fans were rising to have a last laugh at our expense. Although I thought he was a bit of a tosser for saying that, I could see his point of view. Arsenal fans know that most things don't always have happy endings, and it seemed like we were about to run out of luck. We'd got a genuine rivalry back with Spurs at precisely the wrong time. Or so it seemed!'

○ THE END ○

THE HIGHBURY BUZZ began early on 7 May 2006, with many fans gathering in the greasy spoons from 7.30 a.m. onwards. After 93 years, the end was finally nigh. Despite heavy showers the previous day, the rain thankfully held off for the Gunners' final game at Highbury. Alan Edwards arrived at 8.30 a.m., and was amazed to find the surrounding streets already buzzing with people: 'You wouldn't expect to see many people outside a ground at that time, but already the place was heaving. There were hundreds of people snapping away with their cameras, and Sky, the BBC and plenty of radio crews were around to get fans' thoughts. The police were setting up cordons to prevent non-ticket-holders getting too close later on, but for now, everyone seemed to be descending on Highbury. Programme sellers were already flogging them by the arm load. There was an enormous sense of occasion in the air. We were finally leaving. This really was the end.'

The players' focus was rather different. Robert Pires recalls: 'We had a job to do, and our fate wasn't even in our hands. Of course, our primary aim was to win the game against Wigan. But none of us was stupid enough to say, in the days leading up to the match, "It's just another game." That would have been incredibly unconvincing, and you couldn't help but be affected by the sense of occasion. My mind flashed back to the first time I arrived at Highbury – the marble halls, Herbert Chapman's bust, and the sense of history. When we arrived for the Wigan match, the players' entrance was heaving with fans, and the crowds in Avenell Road stretched back as far as the eye could see. My main feeling as I went in was "We can't let these fans down today."'

After sauntering around for a couple of hours, and having had a leisurely cooked breakfast, Alan Edwards headed for the Auld Triangle at around midday to meet up with some friends. Like all the local pubs, the entire place was crammed with fans – some of whom would be staying inside to catch the game on Sky as they'd been unfortunate enough to miss out on a ticket. Then the story of the day began to unravel:

'The atmosphere inside the Triangle was unforgettable that day. It was like a carnival, and it seemed that everyone simply wanted to make it a day to remember. Then the strange messages began to flash across the TV screen, and text messages started to filter through. We heard that a couple of Spurs players had gone down with what was apparently a stomach bug. By two-ish, half the Tottenham team seemed to have got the bug. It was bizarre. Most of us were steaming by then, and we didn't know whether the Spurs v West Ham game would even take place or not. Already, the conspiracy theories were doing the rounds. Apparently, an Arsenal chef had poisoned them at their hotel. But just as we were ready to go to Highbury for one last time, we heard the Spurs game was on. It was all very well us joking that the squirrel who invaded the pitch against Villareal had been in the Champions League longer than Spurs, but we all knew the joke could easily backfire. There must have been an extra 30,000 fans hovering around the cordons, and I felt for those who couldn't get in. But that was why we were leaving, wasn't it? So fans didn't have to miss out on the big occasions. As I queued up to get into the North Bank one last time, I was really choked up. It was quite overwhelming, actually.'

Several of the former players who were invited to the game also had lumps in their throats. 'I'd not been back to Highbury for several years,' recalls Willie Young, 'but the old place still had the same feel about it. I felt quite sad. I know that moving is progress, but I always loved the quirks of Highbury; the fact that you could see the trees when you were playing, and the way in which you had to get used to where the sun was because the stands were at different heights. The Victorian streets around it added to the feel too, because you barely knew you'd even reached the ground before the East Stand was on top of you. It blended into its surrounding perfectly. It was beautiful, with all those strange nooks and crannies. Modern grounds tend to be completely bowl-like, and cut off from their locality. They feel a bit airtight. Highbury was never like that – it was strongly connected to the surrounding streets. But the die was cast. I do wonder whether the end of Highbury means we're getting rid of the aspects of the match-day experience which make going to football interesting. I was saying to some of the other lads that I was worried new grounds feel too much like airport departures lounges.'

At 4 p.m., the last match ever to be played at Highbury kicked off. Roared on by fans clad in red and white T-shirts, Arsenal started the match strongly. 'Wigan are a good side, who'd had a good first season in the Premiership,' recalls Robert Pires. 'Their fans joined in with the spirit of the day, and wore the blue shirts the club laid on for them. I wonder if Spurs or Chelsea fans would have been so obliging? I was able to put us ahead, and it's one of my greatest career memories that I got a goal on Highbury's last day. There was a lot of confusion about what was going on at West Ham. We'd heard things before the game about Spurs players being ill, but when they took the lead, and we went 2–1 down, it could all have gone horribly wrong anyway.'

Thierry Henry's divine intervention was comparable to Ian Wright's hat-trick on the final day of the 1991–92 season, when the old North Bank shut down. The difference was that the Frenchman's goals were symbolic as well as priceless in a literal sense: 'Whatever else Henry has done for us,' comments Alan Edwards, 'I'll always love him most for that game against Wigan. On the one hand, he stopped it being a miserable day for us, but it was also the fact that he kept looking at the crowd and the Arsenal bench to see what was going on with Spurs. I liked that about the end of Highbury. It was a purely local grudge event between us and Tottenham, just like it was when we arrived all those years before. When he scored the penalty and kissed the turf, I don't think there was anyone inside the ground who didn't think he was kissing us goodbye. I wonder what was really going on inside his head when he did that. He's since said that he was just kissing the perfect pitch farewell, and I'm prepared to give him the benefit of the doubt, and treat it as a perfect moment. Those last few minutes, when we knew that we'd done enough to get into the Champions League, were exactly what you go to football for. It was a perfect ending for Highbury, and St Totteringham's day, at last, was back on. You couldn't have scripted it better.'

As the official celebrations for the end of Highbury began, some fans slipped away, either because of an aversion to the nostalgia which had lingered all season, or simply to reflect on the day in their favourite Highbury local. In the Gunners' pub, attention quickly turned to composing anti-Tottenham songs, based around a lasagne theme. With the players conducting their final lap of honour, and thousands of flash bulbs going off, a degree of reality set in for Arsenal fan Adam Norgrove: 'I knew this was the last time I'd see Bergkamp, Pires and most likely Cole, Campbell, and, it seemed, Henry. You couldn't help but feel that not only was this the end of Highbury, it was also the end of the core of that unbeaten team formed a couple of years earlier. It was very sad for me. But what I quite like about Arsenal fans is that even on the most nostalgic day in our history, we remain realists. When Ashley Cole passed by us with Henry and Pires, no one chanted his name. In his book, he said this was the final dagger through him, that a home-grown player, on the last day at Highbury, should be treated in such a way. But bollocks to him. It was too late for all of that, wasn't it? He'd betrayed us. Everyone knew it. And where was Tony Adams? You wonder why a player who played so many matches for us appears to have shunned Arsenal in recent years. He should have been there, surely. That parade of ex-players was odd, because you had the likes of Carter and McGoldrick alongside Wrighty and McLintock, and those guys frankly should never have been on the same pitch as real Arsenal legends.' Along with Henry and Cole, Robert Pires sat on the Highbury pitch to soak up the atmosphere one final time: 'All three of us had our own thoughts, for obvious reasons. I was remembering some of the goals we'd scored as a team, and the fantastic moves we'd created as a team. It was an intense moment for me – both joyous and sad.'

It was plain odd for Willie Young, who had the misfortune to be directly behind Ian Wright in the parade. He recalls: 'I know that lots of fans wouldn't even remember me, but those who did probably weren't even aware of my presence because Wrighty was in front of me. He was the one who everyone really wanted to see, and you could say that he stole my thunder. But it was still an incredibly powerful event, and I'm so pleased that I was there.' Afterwards Roger Daltrey sang his 'Highbury Highs' creation to fans, and struggled to get supporters singing along to 'My Generation'. ('I felt sorry for Roger Daltrey,' recalls Adam Norgrove, 'because Arsenal fans aren't generally the karaoke-loving type, and when I heard he was bringing a band with him, we all thought he meant Pete Townshend, not a brass band. He tried hard to get us to join in, but it was vaguely cringe-making.') Compère Tom Watt, at precisely 6.29 and 50 seconds, invited Arsène Wenger to lead the countdown of the last ten seconds of Highbury. As the clocks hit zero, Highbury officially closed for business. Showers of red and white streamers rained down on the pitch, and fireworks were fired into the evening sky. Only time will tell whether or not the sky is the limit for Arsenal at Ashburton Grove.

ACKNOWLEDGEMENTS
N.5

THIS BOOK wouldn't have been possible without the cooperation and assistance of many people over the last fifteen years.

The following players and ex-managers gave of their time freely and generously. Many thanks to George Male, Ted Drake, Reg Lewis, Laurie Scott, Peter Goring, Don Roper, Doug Lishman, Gerry Ward, Joe Baker, George Armstrong, Paul Vaessen (I hope I've accurately recorded their conversations with me. Sadly, they are no longer around to thank personally), Jon Sammels, George Eastham, Frank McLintock, Bob Wilson, Bobby Gould, Terry Mancini, Brendan Batson, Malcolm MacDonald, Willie Young, Terry Neill, Alan Hudson, Pat Jennings, Liam Brady, Brian McDermott, Stewart Robson, Paul Davis, Perry Groves, Alan Smith, Brian Marwood, Glenn Helder, Christopher Wreh, Charlie Nicholas, Steve Morrow, Bruce Rioch, Oleg Luzhny, Steve Williams, Anders Limpar, Gilles Grimandi, Stefan Schwarz, Silvinho, Edu, Robert Pires and Patrick Vieira.

Although unable to grant me a formal interview, Emmanuel Petit and Nelson Vivas were both happy to allow me to use extracts from conversations I had with them back in the late 1990s. Thanks also to Ian Wright's agent Jerome Anderson for allowing me to use an extract from a conversation which Wrighty conducted backstage with a group of his gaggling fans (me included) at his chat show in 1999. Charlie George was happy to allow me to ask him a series of questions at a Sportspages event in 2003, and has allowed me to use extracts from his responses here. Thanks also to the current member of the Arsenal squad who, for reasons best known to others (and not either of us) contributed to the book, but was forced to stay anonymous. It's good to live in a democracy.

Huge thanks to the vast numbers of Arsenal fans to whom I spoke. There seem to be an inordinate number of Gunners supporters called Dave and Steve. I've done my best to track you all down, and thank you personally, but I wasn't successful in all cases. Many of the early interviewees responded to adverts placed in the *Islington Gazette* and *The Gooner* during the early 1990s. A number of the supporters listed below have passed away since our conversations. I trust that the memories and accounts which appear in the book reflect the passion you displayed for Arsenal: Leslie Anderson, Pat Standen, David Yates, Philip Jones, Brian Kilbride, Tommy Williams, Clive Williams, Richard Maud, George Stephens, George Frey, George Ridley, Larry Harris, Tommy Jezzard, Paul Drury, Arthur Whatley, Clive Rice, Harry Stone, Stan Chorley, David Baines, David Jones, David Spencer, Celia Raparsadia, Jim Baines, Harry Wright, David White, Bruce Smithers, Steve Hart, Billy Hayes, Rory Hinds, Clive Barnett, John Stubbs, Darren Jarvis, Terry Moore, Dave Squires, Steve Ashford, Frank Standen, Miles James, Alex Soles, Chris Terry, Steve Chambers, Terry Clarke, Jim Fisher, Jim Knight, Collins Campbell, Lloyd Packer, Trevor Barlow, Lee Chilvers, Andy Nicholls, Jim Knowles, Michael Flynn, Steve Brennan, Dave Chambers, Simon Delaney, David Gerrard, Colin Philpott, Kev Wright, Steve Duffy, Steve Edwards, Stewart Marney, Alan Esparza, Sarah George, Frank Saunders, Nick James, Dave Cameron, Mike Francis, Colin White, Guy Havord, George Talbot, Andy Daniels, Sam Frazer, Colin Wingrove, Ian McPherson, George Butler, Martin Gilbert, Dave Silver, Ben Dimech, Ian Tatchall, Sam Bennett, Dave Carpenter, Dave Carmen, Max Hyndes, Tim Kenworthy, Steven Lowry, Tim Howland, Chris James, George Tyson, Dave Carson, Larry Parker, Paul Sheehan, Clive Baker, Robert Hume, Greg Hinds, Tim Yates, Paul Miles, John Booker, Kev Blake, Ian Jessop, Geoff White, Jo Selby, Mickey James, Rob Knight, Nick Saunders, Matt Allgood, Brian Dawes, Ian Robshaw, Fred Wright, Paul Collins, Harry Jones, Leonard Green, James Verrier, Zak Reed, Paul Dermott, Tom Lewis, and Steve Powell.

I'd also like to extend a huge thank you to the extremely helpful staff at the Hammersmith and Fulham Records Office, to former BBC researcher Tony Watts, retired PC Robert Cooper, and to former band member Clive Spencer. Thanks to Daniel Quy and Steve Braddock at Arsenal, and to the late commissionaire 'Nobby' whom I spoke to in 2000. I'm also grateful to Charlie Hopkins at EarthRights, and to 'Catweazle'. Thanks to Alex Fynn for his perceptive analysis of the business side of Arsenal over the last twenty years or so, and for putting me in touch with David Luxton. I owe you lunch several times over, Alex! Thanks also to Henry Winter for his thoughts on Arsenal in Europe. I'm extremely grateful to Jamie Jarvis for arranging the interview with Patrick Vieira, and to Matthew Fisher at First Artist for putting me in touch with Guy Havord. Massive thanks also to Jonathan Wilson for sharing his Thierry Henry interview with me, and to David Winner, who urged me to avoid lapsing into 'false memory syndrome'. I'm not sure I was always successful!

Brian Dawes and Chris Parry at Arsenal World, Dave and Kev on the fanzine and memorabilia stall, *Highbury High* editor Ian Trevett, Adam and Liam at the sorely missed Sportspages, and Paolo Hewitt have always been extremely helpful and encouraging over the years. Thank you all. Also to Andy Lyons at *When Saturday Comes,* Hugh Sleight and Nick Harper at *FourFourTwo* and Anthony Teasdale at *ICE* for allowing me to pen articles for their respective mags over the last few years.

Big thanks, as ever, to my mates, who've long since given up on the hope that one day I might stop wittering on about Arsenal, and talk about something else: Barry, Phil and Tatiana, Seb and Marnie, Jo and Gareth, Louise B, Adam and Nicky, Brummie and Ruth, Ian and Anita, Tim and Lucy, Steve and Lucy, Si and Sandra, Si Barrick, Charlie and Natalie, Louise C, Sam and Simon, and Paul and Vicky. And to my extremely patient boss Catherine, for putting up with my frequently pedantic behaviour.

I owe a huge debt of gratitude to my agent David Luxton, who made the project possible. Also to editor Ian Preece, for his faith in the book, his helpful contribution throughout, and his patience with me as I failed to meet deadlines with alarming regularity. Thank you both. Also thanks to David Mitchell for his excellent copy-editing and to Lorraine Baxter at Orion and to Alison Sieff.

I'm always grateful for the support provided by my family ("Couldn't you write an interesting novel instead?"). Thanks to Mum and Dad, Helen, Murray and Stuart. Also to my wife Helen, for her unswerving support. The book is finally finished!

And to lovely Phoebe, who really is the 'shining one'.